FHG

Self-Catering Holidays in Britain 2004

Including Caravan & Camping

England, Scotland, Wales, Ireland and The Channel Islands

For **Contents** see Page 3

For **Index** of towns/counties see back of book

 FHG Publications
Paisley

 Part of IPC Country and Leisure Media

Other FHG Publications

Recommended Country Hotels of Britain
Recommended Country Inns & Pubs of Britain
Recommended Short Break Holidays in Britain
Pets Welcome!
The Golf Guide: Where to Play/Where to Stay
Farm Holiday Guide to Coast & Country Holidays
in England/Scotland/Wales/Ireland
Britain's Best Holidays
Guide to Caravan and Camping Holidays
Bed and Breakfast Stops
Children Welcome! Family Holiday and Days Out Guide

ISBN 185055 355 6
© IPC Media Ltd 2004

Cover photograph:
Lynmouth, Devon, supplied by Photobank

Cover design: Focus Network

Maps: ©MAPS IN MINUTES™ 2003. ©Crown Copyright, Ordnance Survey
Northern Ireland 2003 Permit No.NI 1675

Typeset by FHG Publications Ltd. Paisley.

Printed and bound in Great Britain by William Clowes Ltd. Beccles, Suffolk

Distribution. Book Trade: Plymbridge House, Estover Road, Plymouth PL6 7PY
Tel: 01752 202300; Fax: 01752 202333
News Trade: Market Force (UK) Ltd, 5th Floor Low Rise, King's Reach Tower,
Stamford Street, London SE1 9LS
Tel: 0207 633 3450; Fax: 0207 633 3572

Published by FHG Publications Ltd., Abbey Mill Business Centre,
Seedhill, Paisley PA1 ITJ (Tel: 0141-887 0428 Fax: 0141-889 7204).
e-mail: fhg@ipcmedia.com

Self Catering Holidays in Britain is an FHG publication, published by
IPC Country & Leisure Media Ltd, part of IPC Media Group of Companies.

CONTENTS

Colour Section........................pages 1-48

Tourist Board Gradings ....page 50

Readers' Offer Vouchers ....pages 53-80

SELF-CATERING HOLIDAYS in Britain 2004

ENGLAND

Buckinghamshire......................81	Norfolk 148
Cambridgeshire 81	Northumberland 151
Cornwall 82	Oxfordshire 156
Cumbria..................................98	Shropshire 157
Derbyshire 111	Somerset..................................159
Devon.....................................113	Staffordshire 164
Dorset....................................127	Suffolk 165
Durham 132	Surrey.....................................167
Gloucestershire 134	East Sussex 168
Hampshire 137	West Sussex 170
Herefordshire 139	Warwickshire 170
Hertfordshire..........................142	Wiltshire.................................171
Isle of Wight...........................142	Worcestershire 172
Kent 143	East Yorkshire 174
Lancashire 146	North Yorkshire........................175
Lincolnshire 147	West Yorkshire 180

SCOTLAND

Aberdeen, Banff & Moray......................184	Fife 198
Argyll & Bute...........................186	Highlands (North) 200
Ayrshire & Arran 191	Highlands (Mid) 201
Borders...................................192	Highlands (South)......................203
Dumfries & Galloway 194	Lanarkshire 207
Dunbartonshire 196	Perth & Kinross 208
Dundee & Angus......................197	

WALES

Anglesey & Gwynedd 212	Ceredigion 220
North Wales.............................216	Pembrokeshire...........................222
Carmarthenshire 219	Powys 225

REPUBLIC OF IRELAND 228   **CARAVANS & CAMPING** 229

Website Directory..252

Index of Towns/Counties 281

ENGLAND and WALES Counties

NORTH WALES
1. Denbighshire
2. Flintshire
3. Wrexham

SOUTH WALES
4. Swansea
5. Neath and Port Talbot
6. Bridgend
7. Rhondda Cynon Taff
8. Merthyr Tydfil
9. Vale of Glamorgan
10. Cardiff
11. Caerphilly
12. Blaenau Gwent
13. Torfaen
14. Newport
15. Monmouthshire

NORTHUMBERLAND

TYNE & WEAR

DURHAM

CUMBRIA

ISLE OF MAN

ISLE OF MAN

NORTH YORKSHIRE

LANCASHIRE

EAST RIDING OF YORKSHIRE

WEST YORKSHIRE

GREATER MANCHESTER

MERSEYSIDE

SOUTH YORKSHIRE

ISLE OF ANGLESEY

CONWY

CHESHIRE

DERBYSHIRE

LINCOLNSHIRE

NOTTINGHAM-SHIRE

GWYNEDD

STAFFORDSHIRE

SHROPSHIRE

LEICESTERSHIRE

RUTLAND

NORFOLK

WEST MIDLANDS

POWYS

CAMBRIDGESHIRE

NORTHAMPTONSHIRE

CEREDIGION

WARWICKSHIRE

WORCESTERSHIRE

SUFFOLK

HEREFORDSHIRE

BEDFORDSHIRE

PEMBROKESHIRE

CARMARTHENSHIRE

GLOUCESTERSHIRE

BUCKINGHAM-SHIRE

HERTFORDSHIRE

ESSEX

OXFORDSHIRE

BRISTOL

BERKSHIRE

GREATER LONDON

WILTSHIRE

SURREY

KENT

SOMERSET

HAMPSHIRE

WEST SUSSEX

E. SUSSEX

DEVON

DORSET

ISLE OF WIGHT

CORNWALL

SCILLY ISLES

Please mention Self-Catering Holidays in Britain when enquiring

Penrose Burden Holiday Cottages

St Breward, Bodmin, Cornwall PL30 4LZ
Tel: 01208 850277 / 850617; Fax: 01208 850915
www.penroseburden.co.uk

Situated within easy reach of both coasts and Bodmin Moor on a large farm overlooking a wooded valley with own salmon and trout fishing. These stone cottages with exposed beams and quarry tiled floors have been featured on TV and are award-winners. Home-made meals can be delivered daily. All are suitable for wheelchair users and dogs are welcomed. Our cottages sleep from two to seven and are open all year.

Please write or telephone for a colour brochure.   Nancy Hall

Close to The Eden Project

Viscar Farm
HOLIDAY COTTAGES
NEAR FALMOUTH

Set in 22 acres, the three cottages are full of character - open-beamed ceilings, stone walls, inglenook fireplace, slate floors, double-glazed, attractive wall lighting, pine furniture, well-equipped. There is a wealth of wildlife to be seen, an ideal location for beaches and touring. Sleep 2-4 + cot. Available all year, short winter breaks. Linen and towels provided; welcome tray.

For brochure tel: 01326 340897

e-mail: BiscarHols@amserve.net
www.viscarfarm-cottages.co.uk

Fiona and Ian welcome you to Hilton Farm

Where coast meets countryside, in an Area of Outstanding Natural Beauty. The ideal place to make the most of Devon & Cornwall. Superb setting in 25 acres of ground.
Self-catering cottages open all year.

★ 16th century Farmhouse, sleeps 10 ★ 3 new luxury cottages
★ 6 fully equipped converted barn cottages ★ Superb heated outdoor swimming pool & Jacuzzi
All-weather tennis court ★ Activity area/play area/BBQ and picnic area
★ Laundry facilities ★ Just 2 miles from sandy beaches
★ World-famous Eden Project 45 minutes' drive.

Whether you want a quiet, relaxing holiday, or a fun-packed leisure and sporting activity holiday, Hilton Farm House & Holiday Cottages are the ideal spot to make the most of your holiday in the West Country.

Hilton Farm & Cottages, Marhamchurch, Bude EX23 0HE • Tel/Fax: 01288 361521
www.hiltonfarmhouse.co.uk • ian@hiltonfarmhouse.freeserve.co.uk

Greenhowe Caravan Park
Great Langdale, English Lakeland.

VERY GOOD

Greenhowe is a permanent Caravan Park with Self Contained Holiday Accommodation. Subject to availability Holiday Homes may be rented for short or long periods from 1st March until mid-November. The Park is situated in the heart of the Lake District some half a mile from Dungeon Ghyll at the foot of the Langdale Pikes. It is an ideal centre for Climbing, Fell Walking, Riding, Swimming, Water Skiing or just a lazy holiday. **Please ask about Short Breaks.**

Greenhowe Caravan Park
Great Langdale, Ambleside
Cumbria LA22 9JU

For free colour brochure
Telephone: (015394) 37231
Fax: (015394) 37464
Freephone: 0800 0717231

Chestnuts, Beeches & The Granary
High Wray, Ambleside

Two charming cottages and one delightful bungalow converted from a former 18th century coach house and cornstore/ tack room. Set in idyllic surroundings overlooking Lake Windermere, making this an ideal base for walking and touring. All three properties have large lounges with Sky TV and video. The Granary (sleeps four) has a separate kitchen/diner. Chestnuts and Beeches (each sleeps six) have balconies overlooking Lake Windermere and dining areas in the large lounges. All properties have bathrooms with bath, shower, fitted kitchens with electric cooker, microwave, washing machine, fridge, freezer and tumble dryer. Included in the cost of the holiday is the oil central heating in The Granary and night storage heaters in Chestnuts and Beeches. Lighting and bed linen included in all three.

Contact Mrs J.R. Benson, High Sett, Sunhill Lane, Troutbeck Bridge, Windermere LA23 1HJ (015394 42731)

'Brookfield'

Torver, Near Coniston, Cumbria LA21 8AY. Tel: 015394 41328.

'Brookfield' is a large attractive modern bungalow property in a rural setting with lovely outlook and extensive views of the **Coniston Mountains**. *Divided into two completely separate self-contained, semi-detached units, the bungalow stands in its own half acre of level garden and grounds. The accommodation consists of a large sitting/dining room, kitchen, utility room, two good bedrooms (one twin and one double), bathroom. Good parking. Well-equipped. Bed Linen included in Price. Sleeps 2 to 4. Lovely walking terrain. Two village inns with restaurant facilities approximately 300 yards. Terms from* **£180** *to* **£280** *weekly, special rates for two persons. Further details on request with SAE please.*

THE EYRIE
Lake Road, Ambleside

A really delightful, characterful flat nestling under the eaves of a converted school with lovely views of the fells, high above the village. Large airy living/diningroom with colour TV. Comfortably furnished as the owners' second home. Well equipped kitchen with spacious airing cupboard; three bedrooms sleeping six; attractive bathroom (bath/WC/shower) and lots of space for boots and walking gear. Colour TV, fitted carpets, gas central heating, use of separate laundry room. Terrace garden with fine views. Sorry, but no pets. Available all year. Weekly rates £200 to £370. Also short breaks. Children welcome. Free parking permit provided for one car. Many recommendations. Brochure available.

Telephone Mrs Clark on:
01844 208208
e-mail: dot.clark@btopenworld.com

HODYOAD COTTAGES

Hodyoad stands in its own private grounds, with extensive views of the surrounding fells in peaceful rural countryside. Mid-way between the beautiful Lakes of Loweswater and Ennerdale, six miles from Cockermouth and 17 from Keswick. Fell walking, boating, pony trekking and trout fishing can all be enjoyed within a three-and-a-half mile radius.

Each cottage is fully centrally heated and has two bedrooms to sleep five plus cot. All linen provided. Lounge with colour TV. Kitchen with fitted units, cooker and fridge. Bathroom with shower, washbasin, toilet, shaver point. Laundry room with washing machine and tumble dryer. Car essential, ample parking. Sea eight miles. Open all year. From £200 to £360 per week. For further details please contact:

Mrs J. A. Cook, Hodyoad House, Lamplugh, Cumbria CA14 4TT • Tel: 01946 861338

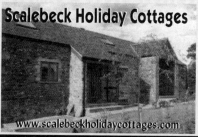

FHG

Publisher's Note

While every effort is made to ensure accuracy, we regret that FHG Publications cannot accept responsibility for errors, omissions or misrepresentations in our entries or any consequences thereof. Prices in particular should be checked because we go to press early. We will follow up complaints but cannot act as arbiters or agents for either party.

The Family Park where the FUN! always shines!

Pets Welcome

Fun-packed Jolly Roger Club

Super 4 pool heated water leisure complex

Cruisers Club - Stylish Bar and Show Lounge

Close to sandy award-winning beach at Dawlish Warren

Discover the best in family holidays right on the glorious South Devon coast.

Why not visit our fun-filled website and see for yourself why so many of our guests come back year after year!

www.welcomefamily.co.uk

...Everything we *do* is for you!

Exeter
Dawlish Warren

FAMILY HOLIDAY PARK

Dawlish Warren
Sunny South Devon • EX7 0PH

www.welcomefamily.co.uk
request a free colour brochure:
Tel: 01626 862070
Email: fun@welcomefamily.co.uk

ROSE AWARD

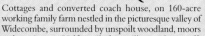
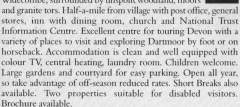
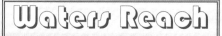

OAKCLIFF
Holiday Park

**AWARD-WINNING SELF-CATERING HOLIDAYS ON
THE GLORIOUS SOUTH DEVON COAST**

- Lodges, Chalets, Caravans & Apartments
- Heated outdoor pool with slide
- Club with live family entertainment
- David Bellamy Conservation Gold Award

Please contact us for colour brochure and information
**OAKCLIFF HOLIDAY PARK
DAWLISH WARREN SOUTH DEVON EX7 0ND
01626 863347 • www.oakcliff.co.uk**

WOOLSBRIDGE MANOR

FARM CARAVAN PARK AA▶▶▶ ETC ★★★

Situated approximately three-and-a-half-miles from the New Forest market town of Ringwood – easy access to the south coast. Seven acres level, semi-sheltered, well-drained spacious pitches. Quiet country location on a working farm, ideal and safe for families. Showers, mother/baby area, laundry room, washing up area, chemical disposal, payphone, electric hook-ups, battery charging. Children's play area on site. Site shop. Dogs welcome on leads. Fishing adjacent. Moors Valley Country Park golf course one mile. Pub and restaurant 10 minutes' walk.

Three Legged Cross, Wimborne, Dorset BH21 6RA   Telephone: 01202 826369

From a honeymoon couple... **...to a "tribe" of a couple of dozen**

Self catering allows you...

TIME TO CHOOSE
the location, the places & the food

FREEDOM
to really enjoy... our golden sands, warm, clean seas and glorious attractions

TO JOIN THE LOCALS...
become a local resident for your stay... no hotel hassles

Call today and find out why people say:
'IT'S ALWAYS BETTER WITH BOURNECOAST'

01202 428 717 / 417 757 www.bournecoast.co.uk

Bournecoast

Est. 1960
K.W. Simmons MBE

"Dormer Cottage", Woodlands, Hyde, Near Wareham

This secluded cottage, cosy and modern, is a converted old barn of Woodlands House. Standing in its own grounds, it is fronted by a small wood with a walled paddock at the back. Pleasant walks in wooded forests nearby. In the midst of "Hardy Country" and ideal for a family holiday and for those who value seclusion. All linen included, beds ready made on guests' arrival and basic shopping arranged on request. Amusements at Bournemouth, Poole and Dorchester within easy reach. Five people and a baby can be accommodated in two double and one single bedrooms; cot and high chair available. Bathroom, two toilets; lounge and diningroom, colour TV. Kitchen with cooker, fridge, washing machine, small deep freeze, etc. Pets welcome. Open all year. Golf course half-mile; pony trekking, riding nearby. SAE, please, for terms.

Mrs M.J.M. Constantinides, "Woodlands", Hyde, Near Wareham BH20 7NT (01929 471239)

These traditional farm cottages, **Jasmine** and **Plumtree**, and recently converted barns, **The Lodge** and **The Stable**, are within easy reach of Dorset's coastline, superb scenery and many other attractions. Private lake with coarse fishing and 17 acres of woodland to explore. The tranquil position nestled under Bulbarrow Hill (second highest point in Dorset) offers a safe haven for children; well-behaved pets are very welcome. The Lodge has large doorways and has been designed for easy access for the partially disabled.

• Open all year round and personally supervised to a high standard • Cots and high chairs supplied • Linen available • Prices from £180-£620 low/high season • Short Breaks from £45 per night.

Contact: Mrs Penny Cooper, Woolland, Blandford Forum, Dorset DT11 0EY•Tel: 01258 817501 • Fax: 01258 818060

Dairy House Farm

e-mail: penny.cooper@farming.me.uk • www.self-cateringholidays4u.co.uk

---

Orchard End
Hooke, Beaminster.

Hooke is a quiet village nine miles from the coast. Good walking country and near Hooke Working Woodland with lovely woodland walks. Trout fishing nearby.

Bungalow is stone built with electric central heating and double glazing. It is on a working dairy farm and is clean and comfortable. Sleeps 6. Three bedrooms, all beds with duvets.

Contact **Mrs P.M. Wallbridge, Watermeadow House, Bridge Farm, Hooke, Beaminster, Dorset DT8 3PD**
Tel: 01308 862619

Cot available. Large lounge/diningroom with colour TV. Well equipped kitchen with electric cooker, microwave, fridge freezer and automatic washing machine. Bathroom and separate toilet. Carpeted. Payphone. Large garden, garage. Terms £210 to £420 per week inclusive of electricity, bed linen and VAT.
ETC ★★★★

Court Farm Cottages
Askerswell, Dorchester DT2 9EJ
Tel: 01308 485668

A Grade II Listed barn has been converted into delightful holiday cottages, fully equipped with all modern conveniences to make your holiday as relaxing as possible. Wheatsheaf and Haywain sleep four and feature king-sized four-poster beds. Threshers has three bedrooms and sleeps five. South Barn has four bedrooms and two bathrooms and sleeps seven. A games room and large garden are provided for guests. Askerswell is an idyllic village in an Area of Outstanding Natural Beauty just four miles from the coast. Perfect for walking and touring holidays. Open all year. Low season short breaks available. From £210 to £690 per week.

e-mail: courtfarmcottages@eclipse.co.uk • www.eclipse.co.uk/CourtFarmCottages/WEBPG2

...an island that will capture your imagination

★ outdoor heated pool
★ direct beach access
★ clubrooms with great sea views
★ multi sports court
★ Dylan's kids club
★ takeaway & shop

Great Value Breaks

Mersea Island, Nr Colchester

Tel:0870 442 9288 ★ www.gbholidayparks.co.uk

...the ultimate in holiday venues

★ golden beaches nearby
★ outdoor pool complex
★ eateries & take away
★ bars & entertainment venues
★ multi sports court
★ Dylan's kids club & play areas
★ mini market

Great Value Breaks

Nr Clacton-on-Sea, Essex

Tel:0870 442 9287 ★ www.gbholidayparks.co.uk

...just beside the sea - with Clacton on your doorstep

★ outdoor swimming pool
★ sandy beach
★ Phoenix Lounge Bar
★ café & take away
★ Dylan's kid's club
★ convenience store
★ kids play area

Great Value Breaks

Clacton-on-Sea, Essex

Tel:0870 442 9290 ★ www.gbholidayparks.co.uk

...total relaxation in a countryside setting

★ outdoor heated pool
★ well-stocked fishing lake
★ adventure playground
★ licensed bar & restaurant
★ multi sports court
★ charming countryside location
★ golf course nearby

Great Value Breaks

Nr Clacton-on-Sea, Essex

Tel:0870 442 9295 ★ www.gbholidayparks.co.uk

Self-catering in the Heart of the Cotswolds

ETC ★★★   Open all year

3 stone cottages, each with its own garden, set in a peaceful hamlet on a hill between two unspoilt valleys. Relax in the garden, explore the Cotswolds, Severn Vale and beyond by car, or walk the many footpaths that radiate from Sudgrove. A warm welcome awaits all year.

Prices: 2 bedroom cottages (sleep 4) £200-£300 per week
3 bedroom cottage (sleeps 6) £225-£410 per week

Sudgrove Cottages

Contact: Carol Ractliffe, Sudgrove, Miserden, Glos. GL6 7JD • Tel/Fax: 01285 821322
e-mail: enquiries@sudgrovecottages.co.uk • website: www.sudgrovecottages.co.uk

Woodkeepers

Barton-on-the-Heath, Moreton-in-Marsh GL56 0PL

Outstanding barn converted into two cottages, quietly set in a rural location. Fabulous views of surrounding farmland and quintessential village of Barton-on-the-Heath. Finished and equipped to a high standard. An enclosed courtyard garden with a private terrace for each cottage, and an old cart shed which provides an idyllic covered seating area. Well placed for the many attractions the Cotswolds has to offer: theatre, music, horse racing, antique collectors' heaven. Places of interest to suit the whole family – stately homes and gardens, castles, farm parks, many traditional market towns.

www.woodkeepers.co.uk
Edward and Wendy Hicks • 01608 684232

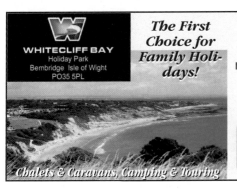

WHITECLIFF BAY
Holiday Park
Bembridge Isle of Wight
PO35 5PL

The First Choice for Family Holidays!

GREAT VALUE FAMILY HOLIDAYS IN A SUPERB LOCATION ON THE ISLE OF WIGHT

Indoor heated pool, nightly live entertainment and cabaret, restaurant, shop, takeaway, coffee shop, fitness centre, crazy golf, children's play area, children's club etc.

PHONE FOR OUR FREE COLOUR BROCHURE
24-HR. TEL: 01983 872671
or visit our website at
www.whitecliff-bay.com

Chalets & Caravans, Camping & Touring

Garden of England
Cottages in Kent & Sussex

Tel: 01732 369168
Fax: 01732 358817
The Mews Office
189A High Street
Tonbridge
Kent TN9 1BX

holidays@gardenofenglandcottages.co.uk
www.gardenofenglandcottages.co.uk

Accommodation for all seasons

Set in part of England's most beautiful countryside, our ETC quality graded cottages offer you a homely atmosphere and ideal locations for your perfect holiday. Visit pretty villages, explore historic castles and famous gardens, and enjoy day trips to London or France. Available all year. Ideal for re-locating, visiting friends, expatriates, and any short let that requires quality furnished accommodation. Prices include linen, towels, fuel and pets. Visit our website or contact us for a free brochure.

WARDEN SPRINGS

...total relaxation in the garden of England

Great Value Breaks

★ heated outdoor pool
★ fine beaches & watersports
★ friendly clubhouse
★ bar meals/takeaway
★ mini market
★ adventure play area
★ stunning coastal walks

GREAT BRITISH Holiday Parks

Isle of Sheppey, Kent

Tel:0870 442 9281 ★ www.gbholidayparks.co.uk

ROMNEY SANDS

...a park designed for families

Great Value Breaks

★ large indoor pool complex
★ access to sandy beach
★ quality live entertainment
★ Dylan's kids club
★ tennis courts & bowling green
★ bar & family diner
★ miniature steam railway

GREAT BRITISH Holiday Parks

New Romney, Kent

Tel:0870 442 9285 ★ www.gbholidayparks.co.uk

Take a Blue Riband Holiday in beautiful Norfolk and take a

pet free*

*One pet stays free when you book through this advert. Extra pet £6

Inexpensive Self Catering Holidays at ●Caister ●Hemsby ●Scratby ●California and ●Great Yarmouth *All year round*

Detached Bungalows at Parklands
Hemsby Village, Children's Playground, Satellite TV, Miniature Railway.

Seafront Bungalows
Caister-on-Sea, with enclosed rear gardens leading to the beach.

Quality, Value and Service from a family business, since 1955

Seafront Caravans
Caister-on-Sea, FREE entertainment, gas and electricity. Swimming pool.

Detached Chalets on Sea-Dell Park
Quiet location, Beach Road, Hemsby.

Belle Aire Park, Beach Rd, Hemsby
Super Chalets, Free electricity and Clubhouse. Safe children's playground. Pets are allowed on local beaches.

All equipped to very high standard
★ Free car parking at all locations
Open Christmas & New Year

● **Popular low season breaks, bungalows from only £75**

● **Bargain Spring & Autumn breaks, excellent value chalets from £60**

Blue Riband *Holidays*

Simply the Best

☎ Direct Line for Bookings & Brochures
01493 730445 – Call 8am to 9pm 7 days a week
Debit / Credit Cards Accepted

Or browse our full brochure on our Website at: www.BlueRibandHolidays.co.uk
For your free colour brochure phone the above number or write to:
Don Witheridge, Blue Riband House, Parklands, North Road, Hemsby, Great Yarmouth, Norfolk NR29 4HA

Parlours, Norwich. Comfortable, recently modernised Victorian house in Norwich city centre, sleeping six. Walk to shops, restaurants, places of interest and recreation, ancient and modern. Accommodation comprises front parlour with TV and telephone, dining room, kitchen, utility room, shower room and wc. Upstairs there are two double and one twin bedroom and bath/shower/wc. Linen, heating and electricity included. Paved garden. Street parking. Sorry, no pets. Terms £420 to £560 per week.

Bookings to: **Susan & Derek Wright, 147 Earlham Road, Norwich NR2 3RG • Tel & Fax: 01603 454169 e-mail: earlhamgh@hotmail.com**

Also available **Earlham Guest House B & B from £25 to £80 • www.earlhamguesthouse.co.uk**

LOWE CARAVAN PARK
SMALL FRIENDLY COUNTRY PARK

Primarily a touring park, we now have four luxury holiday homes for hire in peaceful surroundings ideal for touring East Anglia or for a quiet relaxing break. More suited to over 50s, but children are welcome.

Tel: 01953 881051

May Lowe, Ashdale, Hills Road, Saham Hills (Near Watton), Thetford, Norfolk IP25 7EZ

Holly Farm Cottages

High Common, Cranworth, Norfolk IP25 7SX

Two comfortable, single-storey cottages each sleeping 1-4. Fully equipped, including TV/video, dishwasher, washing machine, central heating. Enclosed garden. Ample car parking. Uninterrupted views of beautiful countryside, peaceful lanes for walking/cycling. Local golf and fishing. Convenient for Norwich, North Norfolk Coast and Broads.

Tel: 01362 821468 • e-mail: jennie.mclaren@btopenworld.com

Holiday Cottages - near Hadrian's Wall, Northumberland
Ald White Craig

•Wren's Nest sleeps 1/2 •Smithy Cottage sleeps 2/3 •Cobblestones Cottage sleeps 4 •Coach House sleeps 5 •Shepherd's Heft sleeps 6. ETC up to ★★★★

On the edge of Northumberland National Park, a superb base for exploring Hadrian's Wall and Roman museums. Lake District, Scottish Borders and Northumberland coast all approx. one hour's drive. B&B also available.

For further information contact: **C. Zard, Ald White Craig Farm, Shield Hill, Near Hadrian's Wall, Haltwhistle NE49 9NW** Tel: 01434 320565 • Fax: 01434 321236

e-mail: whitecraigfarm@yahoo.co.uk • www.hadrianswallholidays.com

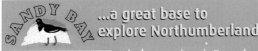

Wake up to the sun rising over the woods on the hill and plan a day of exploration...

Traditional stone courtyard high quality self-catering for 2-4 guests. Situated between Alnwick and Rothbury, the perfect base for exploring Northumberland. Newcastle-upon-Tyne 30 miles.
- **Briar Cottage** • sleeps 2 (four-poster) • pets not allowed
- **Rose Cottage** • sleeps 2 (four-poster) • 2 well-behaved pets welcome
- **Clematis Cottage** • sleeps 4 (one double, one twin) • 2 well-behaved pets welcome.

All have central heating, log-burning stove (all fuel incl.), payphone, colour TV; fully equipped kitchen with electric cooker, microwave, freezer, dishwasher etc. Bed linen and towels incl. Private water supply. Woodland gardens. **NON-SMOKERS ONLY PLEASE**

Helen & Graeme Wyld, New Moor House, Edlingham, Alnwick NE66 2BT • 01665 574638
e-mail: stay@newmoorhouse.co.uk • www.newmoorhouse.co.uk

Isaac's Cottage

Situated in the hills between Northumberland and Durham, Isaac's Cottage overlooks the River Allen. Surrounded by open fields and with the benefit of fishing in the little river only a field away, this cottage is a paradise for families wanting a 'get away from it all' holiday in lovely countryside. The cottage consists of three bedrooms – one double and one twin, family bathroom. Facilities include electric cooker, microwave, fridge, kettle, toaster, coffee maker, slow cooker. Automatic washing machine. Colour TV. Oil-fired central heating, logs for the open fire, electricity included in the rent. Bed-linen and a selection of hand towels. Cot and high chair. Ample parking. Prices from £180 - £350 per week.

Mrs Heather Robson, Allenheads Farm, Allenheads, Hexham NE47 9HJ • 01434 685312

Anita's Holiday Cottages
Banbury, Oxfordshire

'The Shippon' • 'The Byre' • 'The Stables'
Top quality barn conversions sleep 2 to 8. Superbly finished to a high standard. Fitted kitchen, microwave, cooker, washing machine, dishwasher; fully heated; linen included. Suits couples or larger groups. Central for Cotswolds, Oxford, Stratford or just enjoying the surrounding countryside. Walk to village pub. Non-smoking. Sorry no pets. Ample parking. Close to M40 Junction 12. Short breaks available during low season.

★★★ and ★★★★ rating

Contact Anita Jeffries, The Yews, Mollington, Banbury OX17 1AZ
Telephone: 01295 750731 or 07966 171959

Cottages and apartments in Victorian country house surrounded by 12 acres of beautiful gardens and grounds. Prime walking from the doorstep. Caring owners offer: Self-catering (£124 – £432) or Bed & Breakfast. Licensed. Open all year. Short breaks available.

Hesterworth Holidays

Hesterworth, Hopesay, Craven Arms, Shropshire SY7 8EX
Tel: 01588 660487 • Fax: 01588 660153
e-mail: info@hesterworth.co.uk   website: www.hesterworth.co.uk

Gothic House is a Victorian former farmhouse with two self-contained units available. Well-equipped kitchens with washing machine, microwave, cooker, fridge. Free central heating. Comfortably furnished sitting rooms with colour TV. Bed linen and bathroom towels provided. It is situated on the edge of the Somerset Levels in the unspoilt village of Muchelney. Within the village are the ruins of a medieval Abbey and also the medieval priest house belonging to the National Trust.

Gothic House can be found two-and-a-half miles south of Langport and is next door to well-known potter John Leach. Ideal for touring, cycling, fishing, walking and birdwatching.
Terms from £160 to £295 per week.

Mrs J. Thorne,
Gothic House,
Muchelney,
Langport, Somerset
TA10 0DW

01458 250626 • e-mail: joy-thorne@totalserve.co.uk

CHEDDAR - SUNGATE HOLIDAY APARTMENTS
Church Street, Cheddar, Somerset BS27 3RA

Delightful apartments in Cheddar village, each fully equipped. Sleep two/four. Laundry facilities. Private parking. Family, disabled, and pet friendly. Contact: Mrs. M. M. Fieldhouse for brochure

Tel: 01934 842273/742264
Fax: 01934 844994

Little Oaks
Farley Way, Fairlight

Luxury bungalow on one level, situated in quiet coastal village with clifftop parklands, close to ancient towns of Rye, Battle and Hastings. Furnished to a very high standard, the spacious accommodation comprises double bedroom with en suite shower and sauna, twin bedroom, lounge with TV, dining room, fully equipped kitchen/diner, bathroom, conservatory and balcony overlooking beautiful secluded garden, garage. No smoking in bungalow. Pets welcome. Rates from £295 per week to include central heating, electricity and linen.

Janet & Ray Adams, Fairlight Cottage, Warren Road, Fairlight TN35 4AG
Tel & Fax: 01424 812545 • e-mail: fairlightcottage@supanet.com

★★★★
SELF CATERING

CROWHURST PARK
Telham Lane, Battle, East Sussex TN33 0SL
Telephone 01424 773344

Award winning holiday park featuring luxury log cabin accommodation. Magnificent heated pool complex with children's paddling area, Jacuzzi, steam room, sauna, gym with cardiovascular and resistance training equipment, solarium, beauty therapies, aquafit classes, tennis court, children's adventure play area, restaurant, bars and clubhouse.

All this plus beautiful, historic 1066 Country on your doorstep and the Sussex coast just five miles away. Call for a brochure today.

virtual tour: www.crowhurstpark.co.uk

Two Self-Catering Holiday Cottages • West Sussex • Steyning, Near Worthing

Five Star rating by an independent holiday cottage agency

PEPPERSCOMBE FARM, NEWHAM LANE, STEYNING, WEST SUSSEX BN44 3LR • Tel: 01903 813868
e-mail: johncamilleri@btopenworld.com
Each cottage is designed to sleep 2 adults only.

LOCATION is peaceful and quiet, nestling in a combe beneath the South Downs Way, just a few minutes from the old historic market town of Steyning. We offer a direct link to the Downs and the foot and bridle path network, and are close to many places of interest. Previously a dairy farm, part of which is now converted to spacious, comfortable cottages with oak beams, and, for winter lets, have a very efficient underfloor heating system, making them both a warm and cosy place to stay.
Prices from £350 varying to £475 for 7 nights. Pets are welcome at £15 each per week. No smoking.
Please phone for further information and details.

...premier park in a prime location

WHITLEY BAY

★ indoor swimming pool
★ family & adult bar
★ evening entertainment
★ Dylan's children's club
★ fantastic local attractions
★ Cafè & take away
★ multi-sports court

Great Value Breaks

GREAT BRITISH Holiday Parks

Whitley Bay, Tyne and Wear

Tel: 0870 442 9282 ★ www.gbholidayparks.co.uk

St Margarets Holiday Flats

◆ **Fantastic sea views** ◆ **Great family accommodation** ◆ **25 yards to beach**

Centrally situated overlooking the Royal Princess Parade and sea, near harbour entertainments and new shopping complex. All flats have sea views – catering for 2 to 8 persons – all are fully self contained with up to 3 bedrooms with colour TV, cooker, fridge, fire and are fully equipped with cutlery, crockery, glasses, pans etc. From £80 - £450. Two minutes away from Gala Bingo. Flates are meter-operated.

6 MARLBOROUGH TERRACE, BRIDLINGTON YO15 2PA
• **TEL/FAX: 01262 673698** •

ETC ★★ – ★★★

Panoramic views, waterfalls, wild birds and tranquillity

Stone farmhouse with panoramic views, high in the Yorkshire Dales National Park (Herriot family's house in 'All Creatures Great and Small' on TV). Three bedrooms (sleeps 6-8), sitting and dining rooms with wood-burning stoves, kitchen, bathroom, WC. House has electric storage heating, cooker, microwave, fridge, washing machine, colour TV, telephone. Garden, large barn, stables. Access from lane, private parking, no through traffic. Excellent walking from front door, near Wensleydale, Pets welcome. Self-catering from £400 per week.

Westclose House (Allaker),
West Scrafton, Coverdale, Leyburn, North Yorks DL8 4RM
For bookings telephone 020 8567 4862
e-mail: ac@adriancave.com • www.adriancave.com/yorks

Badger Cottage

Comfortable self-catering on small, remote, moorland farm. Seven miles from Pickering on edge of Cropton Forest. Wonderful area for touring, walking, cycling or riding. Accommodation available for guests' horses. Cottage is converted from original stone milking parlours, so all on ground floor. Open plan well-equipped kitchen, dining and sitting room with sofa bed and cosy woodburning stove. Spacious bedroom with double and single beds, en suite shower room, central heating. Parking space and a garden to sit in. Linen and power included. Terms £140 to £200 per week.

Mrs Sue Cavill, Badger Cottage, Stape, Pickering YO18 8HR • 01751 476108

Hill House Farm Cottages

Julie & Jim Griffith
Hill House Farm
Little Langton, Northallerton DL7 0PZ
Tel: 01609 770643 Fax: 01609 760438
e-mail: info@Hillhousefarmcottages.com

These former farm buildings sleeping 2/6 have been converted into 4 well-equipped cottages, retaining original beams. Cosily heated for year-round appeal. Peaceful setting with magnificent views. Centrally located between Dales and Moors with York, Whitby and Scarborough all within easy driving distance. Pets welcome. Exercise Field. Weekly rates from £150 incl. all linen, towels, heating and electricity. Short Breaks available.

• Pub food 1 mile • Golf 2 miles • Shops 3 miles

For a free colour brochure please call 01609 770643

Self-Catering Holidays in Britain 2004

37

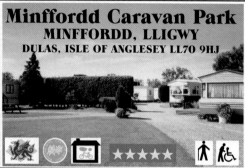

Manorbier Country Park

Tent, Tourers and Static Vans

Enjoy the unspoilt coast and countryside from our secluded Park which offers its guests:

- ▼ Restaurant
- ▼ Adventure & Toddlers Play Park
- ▼ Health suite and Gymnasium
- ▼ A shop selling food, gifts, sweets and newspapers
- ▼ Family amusements and games
- ▼ A convenient launderette
- ▼ Indoor heated swimming pool
- ▼ Hard court tennis
- ▼ Bar with Family Entertainment
- ▼ Internet Facilities

Set in some ten acres of parkland dotted with trees, you could be miles from anywhere, yet the village of Manorbier with its Castle and sandy beach is just a mile and a half away, with Tenby only 5 miles down the road.

Station Road, Manorbier, Tenby, Pembrokeshire SA70 7SN

Tel: 01834 871952
Fax: 01834 871203

BWRDD CROESO CYMRU
WALES TOURIST BOARD
PARC GWYLIAU
★★★★
HOLIDAY PARK
★★★★
TOURING PARK

'The little park with the big heart'

Open March to November 1 ● Total no. of pitches 151 ● Rates per night (tourers) Min: £16 - Max £21.50 ● Rates per week (statics): Min £150 - Max£660

Inistrynich
Dalmally, Argyll PA33 1BQ

Two cottages overlooking Loch Awe
surrounded by beautiful scenery,
the perfect retreat for a peaceful holiday

Garden Cottage (sleeps 8) • Millside Cottage (sleeps 4)

Dalmally 5 miles, Inveraray 11 miles, Oban 28 miles.
Both have garden area, convector heaters in all rooms, open fire
in living rooms, electric cooker, fridge, immersion heater,
electric kettle, iron, vacuum cleaner, washing machine, colour
TV. Cot and high chair by request. Dogs allowed by
arrangement. Car essential, ample parking. Ideal for touring
mainland and Inner Hebrides. Good restaurants, hill walking,
forest walks, fishing, boat hire, pony trekking, National Trust
gardens and golf within easy reach. Open Easter to November.

Colour brochure available, contact: Mrs E. Fellowes

Tel: 01838 200256 • Fax: 01838 200253
E-mail: dlfellowes@supanet.com
Web: www.loch-awe.com/inistrynich

Bridge of Orchy

Two semi-detached self-catering cottages, sleeping 6
and 8, provide an excellent base for a holiday in the
country. Situated on a farming estate, they are superbly
equipped for that 'home from home' feeling, and are set amid
spectacular scenery. We are a friendly, family-run business
and take great care in ensuring that all of our visitors enjoy
their stay. All linen and towels provided. Full central heating (coin meter) and free logs for woodburner. Private
parking and garden. Pets welcome. Open all year. Please contact for brochure and further details.

**Auch Estate, c/o Brynkinalt Estate Office, Brynkinalt, Chirk, Wrexham LL14 5NS
Tel: 01691 774159 • Fax: 01691 778567 • e-mail: brynkinalt@enterprise.net**

**...great Scottish hospitality
on the Ayrshire Coast**

Great Value Breaks

★ indoor swimming pool
★ evening entertainment
★ access to sandy beach
★ family & adult club
★ children's play area
★ mini-market
★ adjacent golf course

Saltcoats, Ayrshire Coast

GREAT BRITISH Holiday Parks

Tel: 0870 442 9312 ★ www.gbholidayparks.co.uk

Millport • Isle of Cumbrae
I Guildford Street
STB 2, 3 and 4 Stars Self-catering
OPEN ALL YEAR

Five flats and one house to cater for 2-10 persons. Two large luxury
Four-Star flats to suit extended family. Superb sea views. Heating included
in rates. Small garden. Sorry, no pets. Close to shops, pubs, restaurants.

*Only a 5-minute ferry crossing from Largs, the Isle of Cumbrae is a small, friendly,
unspoilt island, with cycling, golf, walking, bowling, sailing and birdwatching.*

www.cottageguide.co.uk/millport • **e-mail: b@l-guildford-st.co.uk**
**For further details please contact Mrs Barbara McLuckie, Muirhall Farm,
Larbert, Stirlingshire FK5 4EW • 01324 551570 • Fax: 01324 551223**

Conchra Farm Cottages
Open all year
STB ★★ Self-catering

Comfortable, fully modernised traditional farm cottages adjacent to working farm. Tranquil lochside setting, convenient for exploring Skye and the Highlands. Fully equipped; central heating, electricity and bed linen incl. Excellent value for money and ideal for families, walking and activity holidays.

Gardener's Cottage • 2 single, one double, one twin **£215-£425 per week**
Shepherd's Cottage • one family, one twin
Farmer's Cottage • one double, one single, one family. For details contact:

Conchra Farm Cottages, Tigh-na-Coille, Ardelve, Ross-shire IV40 8DZ
Tel & Fax: 01520 722 344 • www.conchracottages.co.uk
e-mail: enquiries@conchra.co.uk

GLEN AFFRIC CHALET PARK
Great value summer holidays and autumn-winter/spring breaks

Set beside the River Glass and surrounded by spectacular mountain scenery, 15 minutes from Loch Ness, our accommodation provides three-bedroom bungalow chalets, fully equipped and comfortably furnished with central heating and bed linen. An ideal base for walking, climbing, cycling, fishing and stalking, or a central base for touring and viewing the scenery. We have a laundry, games room, children's play area and barbecue area on site; shop, pub and hotel within five minutes' walk. Please contact:
Mr & Mrs G.G. MacDonald, Glen Affric Chalet Park, Cannich, Beauly, Inverness-shire IV4 7LT
Tel: 01456 415369 • Fax: 01456 415429
e-mail: info@glenaffricchaletpark.com • website: www.glenaffricchaletpark.com

Alba Ben View

Enjoy your holiday in a beautiful cottage overlooking Ben Nevis and Aonoch Mor ski resort. The cottage is fully equipped, with two en suite bedrooms, one double and one twin. It is set within a quiet rural area just 10 miles from Fort William, with ample off-road parking. Well-behaved dogs are welcome. The cottage is ideally situated for walking, fishing, cycling, hill walking, skiing in the winter, and touring in the Great Glen and surrounding area.

**Mr & Mrs E. Watson, High View,
Spean Bridge PH34 4EG**
Tel: 01397 712209 • e-mail: jo_eric_watson@tesco.net • www.albabenview.co.uk

Uninterrupted.... Culcrieff Cottages@Crieff Hydro

Uninterrupted is the only description for the views of glorious Perthshire countryside from these newly built cottages. Set in 900 acres the restored steading is in a traditional style with all en suite bedrooms. Woodland off-lead walks directly from the door. Free use of Crieff Hydro's extensive leisure facilities including swimming pool, gym, sauna, steam room, children's club, activity and sports programme for all the family; all included in your rate. *Holidays and short breaks*
For more information or to book call 01764 651 670 or visit www.crieffhydro.com

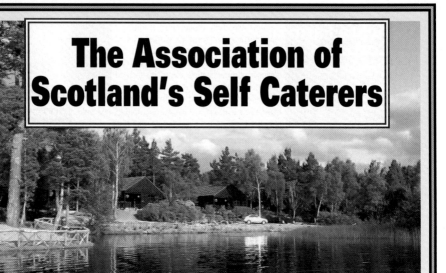

The Association of Scotland's Self Caterers

Selected Self-Catering Holidays in Scotland

Members of the ASSC are committed to high and consistant standards in self catering. Contact your choice direct and be assured of an excellent holiday.

Brochures: 0990 168 571 • Web site: www.assc.co.uk

Owner-Operators ready to match our standards and interested in joining are requested to contact our Secretary for information – 0990 168 571

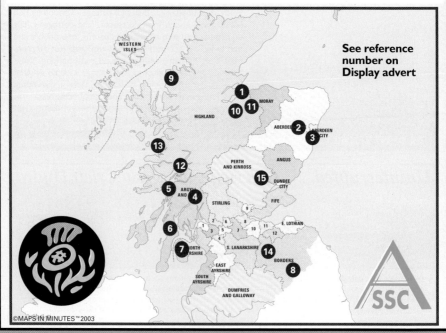

See reference number on Display advert

©MAPS IN MINUTES™ 2003

Please mention Self-Catering Holidays in Britain when enquiring

Tulloch Lodges • *Peace, Relaxation and Comfort in Beautiful Natural Surroundings*

One of the loveliest self-catering sites in Scotland. Modern, spacious, attractive and beautifully equipped Scandinavian lodges for up to 6 in glorious woodland/water setting. Perfect for the Highlands and Historic Grampian, especially the Golden Moray Coast and the Golf, Castle and Malt Whisky Trails. £240-£675 per week. Brochure:

Tulloch Lodges, Rafford, Forres, Moray IV36 2RU
Tel: 01309 673311 • Fax: 01309 671515   STB ★★★/★★★★ *Self-Catering*
E-mail: enquiries@tullochlodges.com • web: www.tullochlodges.com

---

THE GREENKNOWE

A comfortable, detached, renovated cottage in a quiet location at the southern edge of the village of Kintore. Ideally situated for touring castles and pre-historic sites or for walking, fishing and golfing. The cottage is on one level with large sittingroom facing south and the garden. Sleeps four plus cot.

• Walkers Welcome Scheme •

Terms £275–£475 per week including electricity and linen.

Mr & Mrs P. A. Lumsden, Kingsfield House, Kingsfield Road, Kintore, Aberdeenshire AB51 0UD
Tel: 01467 632366 • Fax 01467 632399 • e-mail: kfield@clara.net

---

The Robert Gordon University in the heart of Aberdeen offers a variety of accommodation in the city centre to visitors from June through to August. Aberdeen is ideal for visiting Royal Deeside, castles and historic buildings, playing golf or touring the Malt Whisky Trail. The city itself is a place to discover, and Aberdonians are friendly and welcoming people. We offer Two Star self-catering accommodation for individuals or groups at superb rates, in either en suite or shared facility flats. Each party has exclusive use of their own flat during their stay. The flats are self-contained, centrally heated, fully furnished and suitable for children and disabled guests. All flats have colour TV, microwave, bed linen, towels, all cooking utensils, and a complimentary 'welcome pack' of basic groceries. There are laundry and telephone facilities on site as well as ample car parking spaces.

Contact: The Robert Gordon University, Business & Vacation Accommodation, Schoolhill, Aberdeen AB10 1FR • Tel: 01224 262134 • Fax: 01224 262144
e-mail: p.macinnes@rgu.ac.uk • website: www.scotland2000.com/rgu

---

Mr & Mrs E. Crawford

Blarghour Farm

Loch Awe-side, by Dalmally, Argyll PA33 1BW
Tel: 01866 833246 • Fax: 01866 833338
e-mail: blarghour@btconnect.com
www.self-catering-argyll.co.uk

At Blarghour Farm one may choose from four centrally heated and double glazed holiday homes sleeping from two to six people, all enjoying splendid views of lovely Loch Awe. Kitchens are well appointed, lounges tastefully decorated and furnished with payphone, TV and gas fire, beds are made up and towels supplied while the two larger houses have shower rooms in addition to bathrooms, all with shaver point. The two larger houses are suitable for children and have cots and high chairs. No pets are allowed. Open all year. Centrally situated for touring. Illustrated brochure on request.

When making postal enquiries, remember that a stamped, addressed envelope is always appreciated

---

BLACKPARK FARM Westhill, Inverness IV2 5BP

This newly built holiday home is located one mile from Culloden Battlefield with panoramic views over Inverness and beyond. Fully equipped with many extras to make your holiday special, including oil fired central heating to ensure warmth on the coldest of winter days. Ideally based for touring the Highlands including Loch Ness, Skye etc. Extensive information is available on our website. A Highland welcome awaits you.

Tel: 01463 790620 • Fax: 01463 794262 • e-mail: i.alexander@blackpark.co.uk • website: www.blackpark.co.uk

Cuilcheanna Cottages
Onich, Fort William
Inverness-shire PH33 6SD

A small peaceful site for self catering with three cottages and eight caravans (6 x 2003 models). Situated in the village of Onich, 400 yards off the main road. An excellent centre for touring and hill walking in the West Highlands.

For further details please phone
01855 821526 or 01855 821310
e-mail: onichholidays@mail.com

Arisaig House Cottages – *luxurious secluded accommodation in mature woodland*

- ACHNAHANAT in the grounds of Arisaig House, sleeps up to 8
- THE BOTHY set at the end of the walled gardens, sleeps up to 8
- THE COURTYARD self-contained apartment on first floor, sleeps 2
- FAGUS LODGE set in mature gardens, sleeps up to 6
- GARDENER'S COTTAGE set in gardens off small courtyard, sleeps up to 3
- ROSHVEN overlooks walled gardens of Arisaig House, sleeps up to 4

Set in an area of breathtaking coastal and hill scenery, and wonderful sandy beaches. Mountain bike hire, and fishing on Loch Morar can be arranged. Golf 7 miles, swimming pool 13 miles. Hard tennis court. Day trips to the Small Isles and to Skye. ON-LINE BOOKING.

Details from: **Andrew Smither, Arisaig House, Beasdale, Arisaig, Inverness-shire PH39 4NR**
Tel/Fax: 01687 462 686
e-mail: enquiries@arisaighouse-cottages.co.uk • www.arisaighouse-cottages.co.uk

CARMICHAEL COUNTRY COTTAGES

Westmains, Carmichael, Biggar ML12 6PG • Tel: 01899 308336 • Fax: 01899 308481

200 year old stone cottages in this 700 year old family estate. We guarantee comfort, warmth and a friendly welcome in an accessible, unique, rural and historic time capsule. We farm deer, cattle and sheep and sell meats and tartan - Carmichael of course. Open all year. Terms from £190 to £535. 15 cottages with a total of 32 bedrooms. Private tennis court and fishing loch, cafe, farm shop and visitor centre

e-mail: chiefcarm@aol.com • website: www.carmichael.co.uk/cottages

LAIGHWOOD HOLIDAYS
NEAR DUNKELD
For your comfort and enjoyment

We can provide properties from a large de luxe house for eight to well-equipped cottages and apartments for two to six, some open all year. All are accessible by tarmac farm roads. Laighwood is centrally located for sightseeing and for all country pursuits, including golf, fishing and squash. Sorry, no pets. Brochure on request from:

Laighwood Holidays, Laighwood, Dunkeld PH8 0HB.

Telephone: 01350 724241 • Fax: 01350 724212
e-mail: holidays@laighwood.co.uk • website: www.laighwood.co.uk

FHG PUBLICATIONS 2004

Your guides to
Good Holidays

Recommended COUNTRY HOTELS
a quality selection of Britain's best Country Houses and Hotels

Recommended COUNTRY INNS & PUBS
accommodation, food and traditional good cheer

CARAVAN & CAMPING HOLIDAYS
covers every type of caravan and camping facility

BED & BREAKFAST STOPS
ever more popular independent guide with over 1000 entries

THE GOLF GUIDE Where to Play / Where to Stay
a detailed list covering virtually every club and course in the
UK with hotels and other accommodation nearby,
– recommended by golfers, to golfers.

CHILDREN WELCOME!
Family Holiday and Days Out guide

PETS WELCOME!
the pet world's version of the ultimate hotel guide,
over 1000 properties where pets
and their owners are made welcome

Recommended SHORT BREAK HOLIDAYS
approved accommodation all year round for short breaks

BRITAIN'S BEST HOLIDAYS
user-friendly guide to all kinds of holiday opportunities

COAST & COUNTRY HOLIDAYS
holidays for all the family, from traditional farm houses
to inns, guesthouses and small hotels

SELF CATERING HOLIDAYS
one of the best and perhaps the widest selection
of self-catering accommodation

*Available from bookshops
or larger newsagents*

FHG PUBLICATIONS LTD
Abbey Mill Business Centre,
Seedhill, Paisley PAI ITJ
www.holidayguides.com

The best-selling series
of UK Holiday Guides

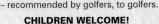

Self-Catering Holidays

in Britain 2004

Farms, Cottages, Houses, Chalets, Flats and Caravans throughout Britain

FHG Publications, part of IPC Country & Leisure Media Ltd

Ratings You Can Trust

ENGLAND

The English Tourism Council (formerly the English Tourist Board) has joined with the **AA** and **RAC** to create a new, easily understood quality rating for serviced accommodation, giving a clear guide of what to expect.

HOTELS are given a rating from One to Five **Stars** – the more Stars, the higher the quality and the greater the range of facilities and level of services provided.

GUEST ACCOMMODATION, which includes guest houses, bed and breakfasts, inns and farmhouses, is rated from One to Five **Diamonds**. Progressively higher levels of quality and customer care must be provided for each one of the One to Five Diamond ratings.

HOLIDAY PARKS, TOURING PARKS and CAMPING PARKS are now also assessed using **Stars**. Standards of quality range from a One Star (acceptable) to a Five Star (exceptional) park.

Look out also for the new **SELF-CATERING** Star ratings. The more **Stars** (from One to Five) awarded to an establishment, the higher the levels of quality you can expect. Establishments at higher rating levels also have to meet some additional requirements for facilities.

SCOTLAND

Star Quality Grades will reflect the most important aspects of a visit, such as the warmth of welcome, efficiency and friendliness of service, the quality of the food and the cleanliness and condition of the furnishings, fittings and decor.

THE MORE STARS,
THE HIGHER THE STANDARDS.

The description, such as Hotel, Guest House, Bed and Breakfast, Lodge, Holiday Park, Self-catering etc tells you the type of property and style of operation.

WALES

Places which score highly will have an especially welcoming atmosphere and pleasing ambience, high levels of comfort and guest care, and attractive surroundings enhanced by thoughtful design and attention to detail

STAR QUALITY GUIDE FOR

HOTELS, GUEST HOUSES AND FARMHOUSES

SELF-CATERING ACCOMMODATION
(Cottages, Apartments, Houses)

CARAVAN HOLIDAY HOME PARKS
(Holiday Parks, Touring Parks, Camping Parks)

★★★★★ Exceptional quality
★★★★ Excellent quality
★★★ Very good quality
★★ Good quality
★ Fair to good quality

In England, Scotland and Wales, all graded properties are inspected annually by Tourist Authority trained Assessors.

SELF-CATERING HOLIDAYS IN BRITAIN 2004

The choices available for self-catering holidays continues to grow and readers of SELF-CATERING HOLIDAYS IN BRITAIN can choose from commercial holiday centres, country and seaside properties well restored and fully equipped with all the comforts of home, traditional cottages, holiday apartments and flats to suit all tastes and pockets, and a small selection of caravans.

SELF-CATERING HOLIDAYS IN BRITAIN 2004 will provide you with the widest possible choice and its greatest strength is that you have the refreshing freedom (and economy) of making your own holiday arrangements by telephone, letter or e-mail directly with the owner or his agent.

Whether booking directly with an independent proprietor, or accepting the higher cost of the choice which an agency has to offer, most of us obviously enjoy the independence which comes with a self-catering holiday. The following points should help you make the most of the huge selection in this edition of the guide.

ENQUIRIES AND BOOKINGS. Give full details of dates (with an alternative), numbers and any special requirements. Ask about any points in the holiday description which are not clear and make sure that prices and conditions are clearly explained. You should receive confirmation in writing and a receipt for any deposit or advance payment. If you book your holiday well in advance, especially self-catering, confirm your arrival details nearer the time. Some proprietors, especially for self-catering, request full payment in advance but a reasonable deposit is more normal.

CANCELLATIONS. A holiday booking is a form of contract with obligations on both sides. If you have to cancel, give as much notice as possible. The longer the notice the better the chance that your host can replace your booking and therefore refund any payments. If the proprietor cancels in such away that causes serious, inconvenience, he may have obligations to you which have not been properly honoured. Take advice if necessary from such organisations as the Citizen's Advice Bureau, Consumer's Association, Trading standards Office, Local Tourist Office, etc., or your own solicitor. It is possible to insure against holiday cancellation. Brokers and insurance companies can advise you about this.

COMPLAINTS. It's best if any problems can be sorted out at the start of your holiday. If the problem is not. solved, you can contact the organisations mentioned above. You can also write to us. We will follow up the complaint with the advertiser – but we cannot act as intermediaries or accept responsibility for holiday arrangements.

FHG Publications Ltd. do not inspect accommodation and an entry in our guides does not imply a recommendation. However our advertisers have signed their agreement to work for the holidaymaker's best interests and as their customer, you have the right to expect appropriate attention and service.

THE FHG DIPLOMA. Every year we award a small number of Diplomas to holiday proprietors who have been specially recommended to us by readers. The names of our 2003 Diploma winners are listed in this book and we will be happy to receive your recommendations for 2004.

Please mention *SELF-CATERING HOLIDAYS IN BRITAIN* when you are making enquiries or bookings and don't forget to use our Readers' Offer Voucher/Coupons if you're near any of the attractions which are kindly participating.

Anne Cuthbertson,
Editor

FHG Diploma Winners 2003

Each year we award a small number of diplomas to holiday proprietors whose services have been specially commended by our readers. The following were our FHG Diploma Winners for 2003.

England

DERBYSHIRE

Mr Tatlow
Ashfield Farm, Calwich
Near Ashbourne
Derbyshire DE6 2EB

DEVON

Mrs Tucker
Lower Luxton Farm, Upottery
Near Honiton
Devon EX14 9PB

◆

Royal Oak
Dunsford Near Exeter
Devon EX6 7DA

GLOUCESTERSHIRE

Mrs Keyte
The Limes, Evesham Road
Stow-on-the-Wold
Gloucestershire GL54 1EN

HAMPSHIRE

Mrs Ellis, Efford Cottage,
Everton, Lymington,
Hampshire SO41 0JD

◆

R. Law
Whitley Ridge Hotel
Beauly Road, Brockenhurst
Hampshire SO42 7QL

HEREFORDSHIRE

Mrs Brown
Ye Hostelrie, Goodrich
Near Ross on Wye
Herefordshire HR9 6HX

NORTH YORKSHIRE

Charles & Gill Richardson
The Coppice, 9 Studley Road
Harrogate
North Yorkshire HG1 5JU

◆

Mr & Mrs Hewitt
Harmony Country Lodge
Limestone Road, Burniston,
Scarborough
North Yorkshire YO13 0DG

Wales

POWYS

Linda Williams
The Old Vicarage
Erwood, Builth Wells
Powys LD2 3SZ

Scotland

ABERDEEN, BANFF & MORAY

Mr Ian Ednie
Spey Bay Hotel
Spey Bay
Fochabers
Moray IV32 7PJ

PERTH & KINROSS

Dunalastair Hotel
Kinloch Rannoch
By Pitlochry
Perthshire PH16 5PW

HELP IMPROVE BRITISH TOURISM STANDARDS

As recommendations are submitted from readers of the FULL RANGE of FHG titles the winners shown above may not necessarily appear in this guide.

A 65-minute journey into the lost world of the English narrow gauge light railway. Features historic steam locomotives from many countries.

PETS MUST BE KEPT UNDER CONTROL AND NOT ALLOWED ON TRACKS

Open: Sundays and Bank Holiday weekends 16 March to 29 October. Additional days in summer.

Directions: On A4146 towards Hemel Hempstead, close to roundabout junction with A505.

FHG PUBLICATIONS, ABBEY MILL BUSINESS CENTRE, PAISLEY PA1 1TJ

Be a giant in a magical miniature world of make-believe depicting rural England in the 1930s. "A little piece of history that is forever England."

Open: 10am to 5pm daily mid February to end October.

Directions: Junction 16 M25, Junction 2 M40.

FHG PUBLICATIONS, ABBEY MILL BUSINESS CENTRE, PAISLEY PA1 1TJ

A working steam railway centre. Steam train rides, miniature railway rides, large collection of historic preserved steam locomotives, carriages and wagons.

Open: Sundays and Bank Holidays April to October, plus Wednesdays in June, July and August 10.30am to 5.30pm.
Directions: off A41 Aylesbury to Bicester Road, 6 miles north west of Aylesbury.

FHG PUBLICATIONS, ABBEY MILL BUSINESS CENTRE, PAISLEY PA1 1TJ

Farm animals, 18th century watermill and farmhouse, farm artifacts, caravan and camping, children's play area. Restaurant and gift shop.

Open: all year 9.30am to 5pm.

Directions: signposted off both A47 and A1.

FHG PUBLICATIONS, ABBEY MILL BUSINESS CENTRE, PAISLEY PA1 1TJ

Cornwall's only Donkey Sanctuary set in 14 acres overlooking the beautiful Tamar Valley. Donkey rides, rabbit warren, goat hill, children's playgrounds, cafe and picnic area.

Open: Easter to end of October and February half-term - daily from 10am to 5.30pm. November to March open weekends. Closed January.
Directions: Just off A390 between Callington and Gunnislake at St Ann's Chapel.

FHG PUBLICATIONS, ABBEY MILL BUSINESS CENTRE, PAISLEY PA1 1TJ

A collection of cars from film and TV, including Chitty Chitty Bang Bang, James Bond's Aston Martin, Del Boy's van, Fab1 and many more.

PETS MUST BE KEPT ON LEAD

Open: Daily 10am-5pm. Closed February half term. Weekends only in December.

Directions: In centre of Keswick close to car park.

FHG PUBLICATIONS, ABBEY MILL BUSINESS CENTRE, PAISLEY PA1 1TJ

World's finest steamboat collection and premier all-weather attraction. Swallows and Amazons exhibition, model boat pond, tea shop, souvenir shop. Free guided tours. Model boat exhibition.

Open: 10am to 5pm 3rd weekend in March to last weekend October.

Directions: on A592 half-a-mile north of Bowness-on-Windermere.

FHG PUBLICATIONS, ABBEY MILL BUSINESS CENTRE, PAISLEY PA1 1TJ

Large range of natural water-worn caverns featuring mining equipment, stalactites and stalagmites, and fine deposits of Blue-John stone, Britain's rarest semi-precious stone.

DOGS MUST BE KEPT ON LEAD

Open: 9.30am to 5.30pm.

Directions: Situated 2 miles west of Castleton; follow brown tourist signs.

FHG PUBLICATIONS, ABBEY MILL BUSINESS CENTRE, PAISLEY PA1 1TJ

A superb family day out in the atmosphere of a bygone era. Explore the recreated period street and fascinating exhibitions. Unlimited tram rides are free with entry. Play areas, shops, tea rooms, pub, restaurant and lots more.

Open: daily April to October 10 am to 5.30pm, weekends in winter.

Directions: Eight miles from M1 Junction 28, follow brown and white signs for "Tramway Museum".

FHG PUBLICATIONS, ABBEY MILL BUSINESS CENTRE, PAISLEY PA1 1TJ

An underground wonderland of stalactites, stalagmites, rocks, minerals and fossils. Home of the unique Blue John stone – see the largest single piece ever found. Suitable for all ages.

Open: Opens 10am. Enquire for last tour of day and closed days.

Directions: Half-a-mile west of Castleton on A6187 (old A625)

FHG PUBLICATIONS, ABBEY MILL BUSINESS CENTRE, PAISLEY PA1 1TJ

A picturesque 200-year old woollen mill with machinery that spins yarn and weaves cloth.
Mill machinery, restaurant, exhibition gallery, shop and gardens in a waterside setting.

Open: February to December daily 10.30am to 5pm.

Directions: Two miles from Junction 27 M5; follow signs to Willand (B3181) then brown tourist signs to Working Woollen Mill.

FHG PUBLICATIONS, ABBEY MILL BUSINESS CENTRE, PAISLEY PA1 1TJ

"England for Excellence" award-winning rural attraction combining traditional rural crafts with hilarious novelties such as sheep racing and duck trialling, Indoor adventure zone for adults and children.

Open: daily, 10am to 6pm April - Oct Phone for Winter opening times and details.

Directions: on A39 North Devon link road, two miles west of Bideford Bridge.

FHG PUBLICATIONS, ABBEY MILL BUSINESS CENTRE, PAISLEY PA1 1TJ

Visit 1000+ gnomes and pixies in two acre beech wood. Gnome hats are loaned free of charge - so the gnomes think you are one of them - don't forget your camera! Also 2-acre wild flower garden with 250 labelled species.

Open: Daily 10am to 6pm 21st March to 31st October.

Directions: Between Bideford and Bude; follow brown tourist signs from A39/A388/A386.

FHG PUBLICATIONS, ABBEY MILL BUSINESS CENTRE, PAISLEY PA1 1TJ

Britain's best preserved lead mining site – and a great day out for all the family, with lots to see and do. Underground Experience – Park Level Mine now open.

Open: April 1st to September 30th 10.30am to 5pm daily. Weekends and half term in October

Directions: Alongside A689, midway between Stanhope and Alston in the heart of the North Pennines.

FHG PUBLICATIONS, ABBEY MILL BUSINESS CENTRE, PAISLEY PA1 1TJ

Craft Village with animals, museum, blacksmith, glassblowing, miniature railway (Sundays and August), craft shops, tea room and licensed restaurant.

DOGS MUST BE KEPT ON LEAD

Open: Craft Village open all year. Farm open 1st March to 31st October.

Directions: M25, A127 towards Southend. Take A176 junction off A127, 3rd exit Wash Road, 2nd left Barleylands Road.

FHG PUBLICATIONS, ABBEY MILL BUSINESS CENTRE, PAISLEY PA1 1TJ

On three floors of a Listed Victorian warehouse telling 200 years of inland waterway history. • Historic boats • Boat trips available (Easter to October) • Painted boat gallery • Blacksmith • Archive film • Hands-on displays "A great day out"

Open: every day 10am to 5pm (excluding Christmas Day).

Directions: Junction 11A or 12 off M5 – follow brown signs for Historic Docks. Railway and bus station - 15 minute walk. Free coach parking.

FHG PUBLICATIONS, ABBEY MILL BUSINESS CENTRE, PAISLEY PA1 1TJ

Discover the fascinating history of cider making. There is a programme of temporary exhibitions and events plus free samples of Hereford cider brandy.

Open: April to Oct 10am to 5.30pm (daily) Nov to Dec 11am to 3pm (daily) Jan to Mar 11am to 3pm (Tues to Sun) **Directions:** situated west of Hereford off the A438 Hereford to Brecon road.

FHG PUBLICATIONS, ABBEY MILL BUSINESS CENTRE, PAISLEY PA1 1TJ

The museum of everyday life in Roman Britain. An award-winning museum with re-created Roman rooms, hands-on discovery areas, and some of the best mosaics outside the Mediterranean.

Open: Monday to Saturday 10am-5.30pm Sunday 2pm-5.30pm.

Directions: St Albans.

FHG PUBLICATIONS, ABBEY MILL BUSINESS CENTRE, PAISLEY PA1 1TJ

Kent's award-winning open air museum is home to a collection of historic buildings which house interactive exhibitions on life over the last 150 years.

Open: Seven days a week from March to November. 10am to 5.30pm.

Directions: Junction 6 off M20, follow signs to Aylesford.

FHG PUBLICATIONS, ABBEY MILL BUSINESS CENTRE, PAISLEY PA1 1TJ

We are a working farm, with lots of animals to see and touch. Enjoy a walk round the Nature Trail or refreshments in the tearoom. Lots of activities during school holidays.

Open: Summer: daily 10.30am to 5pm Winter: weekends only 10.30am to 4pm. **Directions:** Junction 35 off M6, take B6254 towards Kirkby Lonsdale, then follow the brown signs.

FHG PUBLICATIONS, ABBEY MILL BUSINESS CENTRE, PAISLEY PA1 1TJ

The world's largest collection of Grand Prix racing cars – over 130 exhibits within five halls, including McLaren Formula One cars.

Open: Daily 10am to 5pm (last admission 4pm). Closed Christmas/New Year.

Directions: 2 miles from M1 (J23a/24) and M42/A42; to north-west via A50.

FHG PUBLICATIONS, ABBEY MILL BUSINESS CENTRE, PAISLEY PA1 1TJ

Located in 100 acres of landscaped grounds, Snibston is a unique mixture, with historic mine buildings, outdoor science play areas, wildlife habitats and an exhibition hall housing five hands-on galleries. Cafe and gift shop. Plus new for 2003 - Toy Box (gallery for under 5s & 8s).

Open: Seven days a week 10am to 5pm.

Directions: Junction 22 from M1, Junction 13 from M42. Follow Brown Heritage signs.

FHG PUBLICATIONS, ABBEY MILL BUSINESS CENTRE, PAISLEY PA1 1TJ

Well known for rescuing and rehabilitating orphaned and injured seal pups found washed ashore on Lincolnshire beaches. Also: penguins, aquarium, pets' corner, reptiles, Floral Palace (tropical birds and butterflies etc).

Open: Daily from 10am. Closed Christmas/Boxing/New Year's Days.

Directions: At the north end of Skegness seafront.

FHG PUBLICATIONS, ABBEY MILL BUSINESS CENTRE, PAISLEY PA1 1TJ

The Museum In Docklands unlocks the history of London's river, port and people in a nineteenth century warehouse, originally used to house imports of exotic spices, rum and cotton. It now holds a wealth of objects from whale bones to WWII gas masks.

Open: open 7 days 10am to 6pm.

Directions: furthest warehouse along quayside from West India Quay DLR over footbridge from Canary Wharf shopping centre.

FHG PUBLICATIONS, ABBEY MILL BUSINESS CENTRE, PAISLEY PA1 1TJ

Over 100 rides and attractions, including the Traumatizer - the UK's tallest, fastest suspended looping coaster and the Lucozade Space Shot. New for 2003 - Abdullah's Dilemma

Open: March to November, times vary.

FHG PUBLICATIONS, ABBEY MILL BUSINESS CENTRE, PAISLEY PA1 1TJ

Lions, snow leopards,
chimpanzees, otters, reptiles,
aquarium and lots more, set
amidst landscaped gardens.
Gift shop, cafe and picnic areas.

Open: all year round from 10am

Directions: on the coast
16 miles north of Liverpool;
follow the brown
and white tourist signs

It's time you came-n-saurus for a
monster day out set in over 100
acres of parkland. Enjoy the
adventure play areas,
dinosaur trail, secret animal garden
and lots more.

Open: Please call for specific
opening times or see our website.

Directions: Nine miles from
Norwich, follow the brown signs to
Weston Park from the A47 or A1067

The collections of local eccentric
Eric St John-Foti (Mr Norfolk Punch
himself!) on view (over 80) and the
Magical Dickens Experience. Two
amazing attractions for the price of
one. Somewhere totally different,
unique and interesting.

Open: 11am to 5pm (last entry 4pm)
Open all year.

Directions: one mile from town
centre on the A1122
Downham/Wisbech Road.

Beautiful walled garden with
famous collections of herbs and
herbaceous plants, including
Roman Garden, National Thyme
and Marjoram Collections.
Nursery and Gift shop.

Open: From Easter to the end of
October 10am to 5pm daily.

Directions: Six miles north of
Hexham off B6318 next to
Chesters Roman Fort.

A collection of 65 aircraft and
cockpit sections from across the
history of aviation. Extensive aero
engine and artefact displays.

Open: Daily from 10am
(closed Christmas period).

Directions: Follow brown and white
signs from A1, A46,
A17 and A1133.

Journey with us through 300 years of Crime and Punishment on this unique atmospheric site. Witness a real trial in the authentic Victorian courtroom. Prisoners and gaolers act as guides as you become part of history.

Open: Tuesday to Sunday 10am to 5pm peak season 10am to 4pm off-peak.

Directions: from Nottingham city centre follow the brown tourist signs.

Travel back in time to the dark and dangerous world of intrigue and adventure of Medieval England's most endearing outlaw - Robin Hood. Story boards, exhibitions and a film show all add interest to the story.

Open: 10am -6pm, last admission 4.30pm.

Directions: Follow the brown and white tourist information signs whilst heading towards the city centre.

A modern working farm with displays indoors and outdoors designed to help visitors listen, feel and learn whilst having fun. Daily baby animal holding sessions plus a large indoor play barn.

Open: Daily 10am to 5pm.

Directions: 12 miles from Nottingham on A614 or follow Robin Hood signs from J27 of M1.

Historic manor house and farm with traditional animals. Work in the Victorian kitchen every afternoon.

Open: April to 2nd December: Tuesday to Friday 10.30am to 5.30pm. Saturday and Sunday 12-5.30pm.

Directions: Just off A40 Oxford to Cheltenham road at Witney.

The Avon Valley Railway offers a whole new experience for some, and a nostalgic memory for others. Steam trains operate every Sunday Easter to October, plus Bank Holidays and Christmas.
PETS MUST BE KEPT ON LEADS AND OFF TRAIN SEATS

Open: Steam trains operate every Sunday Easter to October plus Bank Holidays and Christmas

Directions: On the A431 midway between Bristol and Bath at Bitton

The world's largest helicopter collection - over 70 exhibits, includes two royal helicopters, Russian Gunship and Vietnam veterans plus many award-winning exhibits. Cafe, shop. Flights.

PETS MUST BE KEPT UNDER CONTROL

Open: Wednesday to Sunday 10am to 5.30pm. Daily during school Easter and Summer (open till 6.30pm) holidays and Bank Holiday Mondays. (10am to 4.30pm November to March)

Directions: Junction 21 off M5 then follow the propellor signs.

FHG PUBLICATIONS, ABBEY MILL BUSINESS CENTRE, PAISLEY PA1 1TJ

Lots of baby animals. FREE pony rides, face painting, green trail, 'pat-a-pet', indoor children's soft play area; gift shop, tearoom, pets' paddocks

DOGS MUST BE KEPT ON LEADS

Open: March to October 10.30am to 6pm

Directions: Follow brown tourist signs off A12 and other roads

FHG PUBLICATIONS, ABBEY MILL BUSINESS CENTRE, PAISLEY PA1 1TJ

With over forty rides, shows and attractions set in fifty acres of parkland - you'll have everything you need for a brilliant day out. The mixture of old favourites and exciting new introductions are an unbeatable combination.

Open: From 10am. Closing time varies depending on season.

Directions: Off A12 between Great Yarmouth and Lowestoft.

FHG PUBLICATIONS, ABBEY MILL BUSINESS CENTRE, PAISLEY PA1 1TJ

A plant lover's paradise with outstanding themed gardens and extensive Museum of Natural History. Conservatory gardens contain a large and varied collection of the world's flora. Sussex History Trail. Dinosaur Museum and park. Rides and amusements.

Open: Open daily, except Christmas Day and Boxing Day.

Directions: Signposted off A26 and A259.

FHG PUBLICATIONS, ABBEY MILL BUSINESS CENTRE, PAISLEY PA1 1TJ

The past is brought to life at the top attraction in the South East 2002 (England for Excellence Awards). Step back in time and wonder through over 30 shop and room settings.

PETS NOT ALLOWED IN CHILDREN'S PLAY AREA

Open: 9.30am to 6pm (last admission 4.45pm, one hour earlier in winter).

Directions: Just off A21 in Battle High Street opposite the Abbey.

FHG PUBLICATIONS, ABBEY MILL BUSINESS CENTRE, PAISLEY PA1 1TJ

Wilderness Wood is a unique family-run working woodland in the Sussex High Weald. Explore trails and footpaths, enjoy local cakes and ices, try the adventure playground. Many special events and activities. Parties catered for.

Open: daily 10am to 5.30pm or dusk if earlier.

Directions: On the south side of the A272 in the village of Hadlow Down. Signposted with a brown tourist sign.

FHG PUBLICATIONS, ABBEY MILL BUSINESS CENTRE, PAISLEY PA1 1TJ

Europe's largest indoor family funfair, with exciting rides like the New Rollercoaster, Disco Dodgems and Swashbuckling Pirate Ship. There's something for everyone whatever the weather!

Open: Daily except Christmas Day. Mon - Wed & Fri - Sat 10am to 8pm, Thurs 10am - 9pm, Sun 11am to 6pm. (Open from 12 noon Monday to Friday during term time).

Directions: Signposted from the A1.

FHG PUBLICATIONS, ABBEY MILL BUSINESS CENTRE, PAISLEY PA1 1TJ

100 acres of parkland, home to hundreds of duck, geese, swans and flamingos. Discovery centre, cafe, gift shop; play area.

Open: Every day except Christmas Day

Directions: Signposted from A19, A195, A1231 and A182.

FHG PUBLICATIONS, ABBEY MILL BUSINESS CENTRE, PAISLEY PA1 1TJ

Wander through a lush landscape of exotic foliage where a myriad of multi-coloured butterflies sip nectar from tropical blossoms. Stroll past bubbling streams and splashing waterfalls; view insects and spiders all safely behind glass.

Open: 10am to 6pm summer, 10am to dusk winter.

FHG PUBLICATIONS, ABBEY MILL BUSINESS CENTRE, PAISLEY PA1 1TJ

Lovely rural farm with 50 breeds of rabbit, and several breeds of poultry, pig, sheep, goat, horses and ponies. Iron Age Roundhouse. Cafe, craft shop, events throughout holidays, famous pig races, nature trail, indoor and outdoor play.

Open: 10.30am to 6pm in season, weekends 10am to 4pm in winter.

Directions: Near Stonehenge, just off the A303 at the intersection with A338 Salisbury/Swindon Road.

FHG PUBLICATIONS, ABBEY MILL BUSINESS CENTRE, PAISLEY PA1 1TJ

The Deep is the world's only submarium. Here you can discover the story of the world's oceans on a dramatic journey from the beginning of time and into the future. You can also explore the wonders of the oceans, from the tropical lagoon to the icy waters of Antarctica.

Open: daily 10am to 6pm (last entry at 5pm). Closed Christmas Eve and Christmas Day
Directions: from the North take A1/M, M62/A63. From the South take A1/M, A15/A63 follow signs to Hull city centre, then local signs to The Deep.

Steam trains operate over a 4½ mile line from Bolton Abbey Station to Embsay Station. Many family events including Thomas the Tank Engine take place during major Bank Holidays.

Open: steam trains run every Sunday throughout the year and up to 7 days a week in summer. 10.30am to 4.30pm
Directions: Embsay Station signposted from the A59 Skipton by-pass; Bolton Abbey Station signposted from the A59 at Bolton Abbey.

A fascinating display of railway carriages and a wide range of railway items telling the story of rail travel over the years.

ALL PETS MUST BE KEPT ON LEADS

Open: Daily 11am to 4.30pm
Directions: Approximately one mile from Keighley on A629 Halifax road. Follow brown tourist signs

---

The Colour Museum is unique. Dedicated to the history, development and technology of colour, it is the ONLY museum of its kind in Europe. A truly colourful experience for both kids and adults, it's fun, it's informative and it's well worth a visit.

Open: Tuesday to Saturday 10am to 4pm (last admission 3.30pm).
Directions: just off Westgate on B6144 from the city centre to Haworth.

A fantastic day out for all at the lively and interactive, award-winning Thackray Museum. Experience life as it was in the Victorian slums, discover how medicine has changed our lives and the incredible lotions and potions once offered as cures. Try an empathy belly and explore the interactive bodyworks gallery.

Open: daily 10am till 5pm, closed 24th - 26th and 31st December and 1st January.
Directions: from M621 follow signs for York (A64) then follow brown tourist signs. From the north, take A58 towards city and then follow brown tourist signs.

Visitor centre dedicated to the much-loved Scottish writer Lewis Grassic Gibbon. Exhibition, cafe, gift shop. Outdoor children's play area. Disabled access throughout.

Open: Daily April to October 10am to 4.30pm. Groups by appointment including evenings.

Directions: On the B967, accessible and signposted from both A90 and A92.

Rare breeds of farm animals, pets' corner, conservation groups, tea room, woodland walk in beautiful location

Open: 10am to 6pm mid-March to end October

Directions: two-and-a-half miles from Oban along Glencruitten road

---

Set in the rolling hills of Ayrshire, Europe's best preserved ironworks. Guided tours, audio-visuals, walks with electronic wands. Restaurant/coffee shop.

Open: April to October daily 10am to 5pm.

Directions: A713 Ayr to Castle Douglas road, 12 miles from Ayr, 3 miles from Dalmellington.

The historic home of the Earls of Glasgow. Waterfalls, gardens, famous Glen, unusual trees. Riding school, stockade, play areas, exhibitions, shop, cafe and The Secret Forest.

PETS MUST BE KEPT ON LEAD

Open: daily 10am to 6pm Easter to October.

Directions: On A78 between Largs and Fairlie, 45 mins drive from Glasgow.

Scotland's seafaring heritage is among the world's richest and you can relive the heyday of Scottish shipping at the Maritime Museum.

Open: all year except Christmas and New Year Holidays. 10am - 5pm
Directions: Situated on Irvine harbourside and only a 10 minute walk from Irvine train station.

An innovative museum exploring the history and environment of West Lothian on a 20-acre site packed full of things to see and do, indoors and out.

Open: Daily (except Christmas and New Year) 10am to 5pm.

Directions: 15 miles from Edinburgh, follow "Heritage Centre" signs from A899.

On show is a large collection, from 1899, of cars, bicycles, motor cycles and commercials. There is also a large collection of period advertising, posters and enamel signs.

Open: Daily April to October 11am to 4pm; November to March: Sundays 1pm to 3pm or by special appointment.

Directions: Off A198 near Aberlady. Two miles from A1.

World famous attraction at Loch Ness. Centre includes shopping complex, coffee shop, restaurants, hotel and boat cruises throughout the summer. Don't miss the Highlands most popular tourist attraction.

Open: all year - times vary.

Directions: 14 miles south of Inverness on the A82 main road.

Award-winning attraction with unique 'Heather Story' exhibition, gallery, giftshop, large garden centre selling 300 different heathers, antique shop, children's play area and famous Clootie Dumpling restaurant.

Open: All year except Christmas Day.

Directions: Just off A95 between Aviemore and Grantown-on-Spey.

Highland croft open to visitors for "hands-on" experience with over 30 different breeds of farm animals "stroke the goats and scratch the pigs". Farm information centre and old farm implements. For all ages, cloud or shine!

Open: July and August 10am to 5pm.

Directions: On A835 15 miles north of Ullapool

FHG Landmark Forest Theme Park

READERS' OFFER 2004

Carrbridge, Inverness-shire PH23 3AJ

Tel: 01479 841613 • Freephone 0800 731 3446

e-mail: landmarkcentre@btconnect.com • website: www.landmark-centre.co.uk

10% DISCOUNT for pet owners. Free admission for pets!
Maximum of four persons per voucher

Valid during 2004

FHG New Lanark World Heritage Site

READERS' OFFER 2004

New Lanark Mills, New Lanark, Lanarkshire ML11 9DB

Tel: 01555 661345 • Fax: 01555 665738

e-mail: visit@newlanark.org • website: www.newlanark.org

One FREE child with every full price adult

valid until 31st October 2004

FHG Finlaystone Country Estate

READERS' OFFER 2004

Langbank, Renfrewshire PA14 6TJ

Tel & Fax: 01475 540505

e-mail: info@finlaystone.co.uk • website: www.finlaystone.co.uk

Two for the price of one

valid until April 2004

FHG Llanberis Lake Railway

READERS' OFFER 2004

Gilfach Ddu, Llanberis, Gwynedd LL55 4TY

Tel: 01286 870549 • e-mail: info@lake-railway.co.uk

website: www.lake-railway.co.uk

One pet travels free with each full fare paying adult

Valid Easter to October 2004

FHG MUSEUM OF CHILDHOOD MEMORIES

READERS' OFFER 2004

1 Castle Street, Beaumaris, Anglesey LL58 8AP

Tel: 01248 712498

website: www.aboutbritain.com/museumofchildhoodmemories.htm

One child FREE with two adults

valid during 2004

Great day out for all the family. Wild Water Coaster*, Microworld exhibition, Forest Trails, Viewing Tower, Climbing Wall*, Tree Top Trail, Steam powered Sawmill*, Clydesdale Horse*. Shop, restaurant and snackbar.
(* Easter to October)
DOGS MUST BE KEPT ON LEADS

Open: Daily (except Christmas Day and attractions marked*).

Directions: 23 miles south of Inverness at Carrbridge, just off the A9.

A beautifully restored cotton mill village close to the Falls of Clyde. Explore the fascinating history of the village, try the 'New Millennium Experience', a magical ride which takes you back in time to discover what life used to be like.

Open: 11am to 5pm daily. Closed Christmas Day and New Year's Day.

Colourful gardens, imaginative woodland play areas and tumbling waterfalls. The Estate combines history with adventure in a fun day out for all the family, where your dog can run freely. Step back in time and uncover its secrets.

Open: Daily 10.30am to 5pm

Directions: Off A8 west of Langbank, 20 minutes west of Glasgow Airport.

A 60-minute ride along the shores of beautiful Padarn Lake behind a quaint historic steam engine. Magnificent views of the mountains from lakeside picnic spots.
DOGS MUST BE KEPT ON LEAD AT ALL TIMES ON TRAIN

Open: Most days Easter to October. Free timetable leaflet on request.

Directions: Just off A4086 Caernarfon to Capel Curig road at Llanberis; follow 'Country Park' signs.

Nine rooms in a Georgian house filled with items illustrating the happier times of family life over the past 150 years. Joyful nostalgia unlimited.

Open:
March to end October

Directions:
opposite Beaumaris Castle

FHG

FHG PUBLICATIONS

publish a large range of well-known accommodation
guides. We will be happy to send you details or you
can use the order form at the back of this book.

Walk through the Rabbit Hole to the colourful scenes of Lewis Carroll's classic story set in beautiful life-size displays. Recorded commentaries and transcripts available in several languages.

Open: All year 10am to 5pm but closed Sundays in winter and Christmas/Boxing Day/New Year's Day.

Directions: situated just off the main street, 250 yards from coach and rail stations.

A unique theme attraction presenting the history and culture of the Celts. Audio-visual exhibition, displays of Welsh and Celtic history, soft play area, tea room and gift shop. Events throughout the year.

Open: 10am to 6pm daily (last admission to exhibitions 4.40pm)

Directions: in restored mansion just south of clock tower in town centre; car park just off Aberystwyth road

---

Journey through the lanes of cycle history and see bicycles from Boneshakers and Penny Farthings up to modern Raleigh cycles. Over 250 machines on display

PETS MUST BE KEPT ON LEADS

Open: 1st March to 1st November daily 10am onwards.

Directions: Brown signs to car park. Town centre attraction.

Make a pit stop whatever the weather! Join an ex-miner on a tour of discovery, ride the cage to pit bottom and take a thrilling ride back to the surface. Multi-media presentations, period village street, children's adventure play area, restaurant and gift shop. Disabled access with assistance.

Open: Open daily 10am to 6pm (last tour 4.30pm). Closed Mondays October to Easter, also Dec 25th to 1st Jan inclusive.

Directions: Exit Junction 32 M4, signposted from A470 Pontypridd. Trehafod is located between Pontypridd and Porth.

FHG

Visit the FHG website
www.holidayguides.com
for details of the wide choice of accommodation
featured in the full range of FHG titles

ENGLAND

UNIVERSITY ACCOMMODATION & FACILITIES
Budget accommodation or fully tailored packages (0870 712 5002; Fax: 020 7017 8273). En suite designer halls across the UK. Groups of any age or size. Sports facilities all year. Tell us your needs and we'll find a location and package to suit.
e-mail: enquiries@thesummervillage.com
website: www.thesummervillage.com

BUCKINGHAMSHIRE

BUCKINGHAM

Chris and Fiona Hilsdon, Huntsmill Farm, Shalstone, Buckingham MK18 5ND (Tel & Fax: 01280 704852; mobile: 07973 386756). Situated midway between the market towns of Buckingham and Brackley, close to Stowe Gardens and the Silverstone Circuit; an ideal touring base for Oxford and the Cotswolds. The farm courtyard is a delightfully peaceful spot, overlooking rolling countryside.Three imaginatively converted traditional stone, timber and slate properties offer the very best in holiday accommodation amidst the peace of the English countryside. Huntsmill is a working, mainly arable farm, with many nature trails and walks. ETC ★★★★, MEMBER FARMSTAY UK.
website: www.huntsmill.com

CAMBRIDGESHIRE

17 ST MARY'S STREET, ELY
CAMBRIDGESHIRE CB7 4ER

Cathedral House

The Coach House has been imaginatively converted into a delightful abode full of character and charm, situated close to Ely Cathedral.
Arranged on two floors, the accommodation downstairs comprises a sitting room and country-style kitchen with a cooker, fridge etc. Upstairs there are two charming double rooms (one has a view of the Cathedral), and a cosy single room. All have an en suite bathroom, with a toilet, wash hand basin and a half-size bath with shower taps. Gas central heating. Linen, towels, toilet soap, cleaning materials and some basic provisions are provided. Prices range from £200 - £1000 depending on season and length of stay. B&B From £40 per person per night (Subject to availablity). Sleeps 4/5.

TEL: 01353 662124   farndale@cathedralhouse.co.uk • www.cathedralhouse.co.uk

See also Colour Advertisement

One child FREE with one full paying adult at
Sacrewell Farm & Country Centre
see our READERS' OFFER VOUCHERS for full details

When making enquiries or bookings,
a stamped addressed envelope is always appreciated

CORNWALL

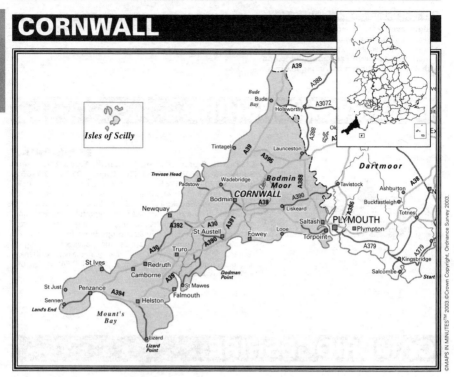

ENGLAND

Penrose Burden
Holiday Cottages
St Breward, Bodmin, Cornwall PL30 4LZ
Tel: 01208 850277 & 850617
Fax: 01208 850915 • www.penroseburden.co.uk

Situated within easy reach of both coasts and Bodmin Moor on a large farm overlooking a beautiful wooded valley with own salmon and trout fishing. These stone cottages with exposed beams and quarry tiled floors have been featured on TV and are award-winners. Home-made meals can be delivered daily. All are suitable for wheelchair users and dogs are welcomed. Our cottages sleep from two to seven and are open all year. Please write or telephone for a colour brochure. Close to The Eden Project.

See also Colour Advertisement

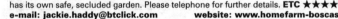
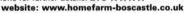

BOSCASTLE

Jackie and Robin Haddy, Home Farm, Minster, Boscastle PL35 0BN (01840 250195). Sleeps 4. Home Farm Cottage is a traditional Cornish Cottage, situated on the National Trust property of Home Farm, a mixed working farm of 145 acres consisting of beef suckler cows, sheep and corn. The farm lies in an Area of Outstanding Natural Beauty, with picturesque views of the Heritage Coast and the historic village of Boscastle with its pretty harbour. The cottage is tastefully furnished to a very high standard, whilst retaining charm and character. It benefits from modern conveniences including dishwasher, washing machine, tumble dryer, colour TV, video, bathroom, separate shower room and equipped utility/laundry room. One double bedroom and one twin room, with optional sofa bed in lounge. The cottage also has its own safe, secluded garden. Please telephone for further details. ETC ★★★★
e-mail: jackie.haddy@btclick.com   website: www.homefarm-boscastle.co.uk

BOSCASTLE

Mrs V.M. Seldon, Tregatherall Farm, Boscastle PL35 0EQ (01840 250277). Two new self-catering cottages on a warm, friendly Cornish farm, midway between Boscastle and Tintagel. Fully equipped en suite bedrooms, luxuriously furnished, sleeping four and six respectively. Oil-fired central heating and own parking. We offer out-of-season, spring and autumn short breaks. Please contact us for special offers and availablility. Brochure on request.
e-mail: tregatherall@ipl.co.uk
website: www.ipl.co.uk/tregatherall/

See also Colour Display Advertisement

BUDE

Fiona & Ian Goodman, Hilton Farm Holiday Cottages, Marhamchurch, Bude EX23 0HE (Tel & Fax: 01288 361521). Where coast meets countryside, in an Area of Outstanding Natural Beauty, the ideal place to make the most of Devon & Cornwall. Superb setting in 25 acres of ground. 16th century Farmhouse, sleeps 10; three new luxury cottages and six fully equipped converted barn cottages. Superb heated outdoor swimming pool and jacuzzi, all-weather tennis court, activity area/play area/BBQ and picnic area; laundry facilities. Just two miles from sandy beaches; world-famous Eden Project 45 minutes' drive. Self-catering cottages open all year. ETC ★★★/★★★★
e-mail: ian@hiltonfarmhouse.freeserve.co.uk
website: www.hiltonfarmhouse.co.uk

When making enquiries please mention FHG Publications

ENGLAND

BUDE (near)

The Priory Holiday Cottages, Thornbury, Holsworthy, Devon EX22 7DA (01409 261495/261546). Nestling in the grounds of a Listed part Tudor Priory, these carefully maintained properties are ideally placed for lovers of tranquillity. Surrounded by mature, landscaped gardens with woodland walks and 17 acres of orchards and meadows, there is ample opportunity to roam, and to enjoy the abundant wildlife. Horse riding available locally, and excellent trout fishing in nearby well-stocked lakes. The local pub is just one mile away. Perfectly placed for touring Datmoor, the north Devon/Cornish coast and the coastal resort of Bude. Please telephone for brochure or further details.
e-mail: priorylight@hotmail.com

CUSGARNE (Near Truro)

Sleeps 2. Dogs welcome. A cosy single-storey, clean, detached dwelling with own garden, within grounds of Saffron Meadow, in quiet hamlet five miles west of Truro. Secluded and surrounded by wooded pastureland. Bedroom (double bed) with twin vanity unit. Fully tiled shower/WC and LB. Comprehensively equipped kitchen/diner. Compact TV room. Storage room. Hot water galore and gas included. Metered electricity. Automatic external safety lighting. Your own ample parking space in drive. Inn a short walk. Central to Truro, Falmouth and North and South coasts. £160 to £230 per week. **Joyce and George Clench, Saffron Meadow, Cusgarne, Truro TR4 8RW (01872 863171).**

FALMOUTH

Mrs Kathleen Terry, 'Shasta', Carwinion Road, Mawnan Smith, Falmouth TR11 5JD (01326 250775). 'Shasta Annex' Sleeps 2. A short walk from Mawnan Smith, with thatched pub, Italian restaurant, shops. Maenporth's sandy beach, the beautiful Helford river, tropical gardens are a short drive away. Ideal for coastal walking, Falmouth approximately four miles. Well equipped comfortable ground floor flat, with patio overlooking lovely mature garden. Cooker, fridge, washing machine, microwave etc. TV and video. Garden furniture, night storage heaters. Towels and linen provided. Electricity included in price. Parking. Welcome pack on arrival. Tourist Board Approved. Terms from £180–£350. Brochure available.
e-mail: katerry@btopenworld.com

PANTILES HOLIDAY APARTMENTS

A warm Cornish welcome awaits you at our family-run self-contained one and two bedroom apartments, sleeping up to six. Situated in a superb location, this unique property has been completely refurbished to an extremely high standard. The apartments are all south-facing, some with balconies, and enjoy sea views from the top and middle floors. Apartments are fully equipped to ensure your every need is catered for, offering home from home comfort. Quiet location yet only two minutes' walk from beautiful beach, coastal walks and ten minutes' walk to harbour and main shopping areas. Off-road parking. Launderette and gardens front and rear for you to relax in. For colour brochure contact:

Colin & Sue Kemp, 6 Stracey Road, Falmouth TR11 4DW • Tel: 01326 211838
Fax: 01326 211668 • www.colinkemp.plus.com. • e-mail: colinkemp@lineone.net

See also Colour Advertisement

CORNISH HOLIDAY COTTAGES

Calamansac, Heathercroft, Rose Cottages, Seagulls
Charming Cottages and Country Houses in Du Maurier country –
Frenchman's Creek, Helford River and Falmouth, including
launching dinghies and moorings. Surrounded by National Trust
gardens and spectacular scenery. A selection of the finest cottages
available, supervised personally by our helpful staff, some with
waterside gardens, some at Port Pendennis, Falmouth.
From £175 to £1,500 per week.
Open all year.

Mrs R. Austen, Cornish Holiday Cottages, Killibrae, West Bay, Maenporth,
Falmouth, Cornwall TR11 5HP • • Telephone/Fax: (01326) 250339
e-mail: postmaster@cornishholidaycottages.net • • website: www.cornishholidaycottages.net

See also Colour Advertisement

See also Colour Display Advertisement

FALMOUTH near

Viscar Farm Holiday Cottages. Sleep 2-4+ cot. Set in 22 acres, the three cottages are full of character – open beamed ceilings, stone walls, inglenook fireplace, slate floors, double glazed, attractive wall lighting, pine furniture, well equipped. There is a wealth of wildlife to be seen, an ideal location for beaches and touring. Available all year, short winter breaks. Linen and towels provided; welcome tray. For brochure tel: **01326 340897**
e-mail: BiscarHols@amserve.net
website: www.viscarfarm-cottages.co.uk

50p OFF per person, up to six persons at
Tamar Valley Donkey Park
see our READERS' OFFER VOUCHERS for full details

*Please mention Self-Catering Holidays in Britain
when writing to enquire about accommodation*

FOWEY

Fowey Harbour Cottages. Sleep 2/6. We are a small Agency offering a selection of cottages and flats situated around the beautiful Fowey Harbour on the South Cornish Coast. Different properties accommodate from two to six persons and vary in their decor and facilities so that hopefully there will be something we can offer to suit anyone. All properties are registered with the English Tourism Council and are personally vetted by us. Short Breaks and weekend bookings accepted subject to availability (mainly out of peak season but sometimes available at "last minute" in season). Brochure and details from **W. J. B. Hill & Son, 3 Fore Street, Fowey PL23 1PH (01726 832211; Fax: 01726 832901).**
e-mail: hillandson@talk21.com

HAYLE TOWANS

Sleeps 6. Detached three-bedroom bungalow with sea views across St Ives Bay. Beach 100 yards, three miles of soft golden sand, backed by rolling sand dunes. Located in an area of Cornwall noted for its scenery and attractions. Local supermarket, or Hayle town shops five minutes by car. Accommodation comprises kitchen, lounge/dining room with colour TV, three bedrooms sleeping six. Bathroom with shower. Storage heating. Off-road parking for two cars. Available all year. **Mrs Langford, 1 Fleetway, Thorpe, Surrey TW20 8UA (Tel & Fax: 01932 560503).**

LAUNCESTON

Mrs Kathryn Broad, Lower Dutson Farm, Launceston PL15 9SP (01566 776456). Working farm. Sleeps 2/6. Play fetch with Fly our sheepdog or watch out for the Kingfisher as you relax or fish down by the lake or riverside. Get up late and enjoy an all day breakfast at Homeleigh Garden Centre, just 400m up the road. Enjoy the suntrap just outside the front door. 17th century, well-equipped cottage with three bedrooms, two bathrooms, TV lounge and kitchen. Situated two miles from historic Launceston with its Norman Castle (even Tescos!). Centrally located for visiting National Trust houses and gardens, Dartmoor, Bodmin Moor and the beaches and harbours of Devon and Cornwall. Pets by arrangement. Terms £180 - £480. **ETC**
★★★

e-mail: francis.broad@btclick.com   **website: www.farm-cottage.co.uk**

LAUNCESTON

Cartmell Bungalow, Trelash, Warbstow, Launceston PL15 8RL. Sleeps 6. Cartmell is a dormer bungalow ideally situated for touring Devon and Cornwall - Crackington Haven five miles, Boscastle six, Tintagel and Camelford seven, Bude and Launceston 12, Plymouth 40 miles. Warbstow with bus services to Launceston and Exeter daily is just two miles away, Marshgate with shop, garage and post office three miles. Golf available at Bude and Launceston, horse riding on coastal paths just four miles away; the Tamar Otter Park, Tamar and Crowdy Lakes are nearby. Accommodation comprises two double and one twin bedroom, bathroom with bath and shower, large lounge/diner with TV and modern kitchen. Electricity included. Linen available for hire. Central heating extra. Ample parking. Sorry no pets, or children under 8. For further information please contact: **Mr & Mrs Dawe (01840 261353).**

Readers are requested to mention this guidebook
when seeking accommodation (and please enclose
a stamped addressed envelope).

LISKEARD

Mrs C.Hutchinson, Caradon Country Cottages, East Taphouse, Near Liskeard PL14 4NH (Tel & Fax: 01579 320355). Luxury cottages located in magnificent countryside between Bodmin Moor and Looe. Ideal location for exploring Cornwall and Devon, coast and countryside, National Trust properties and the Eden Project. Five acre grounds of gardens, lawned play area, sun trap patios and nature trail around the unspoilt hedgerows of our meadow and pony paddock. Children and pets welcome. Central heating and woodburners for Winter Breaks.
website: www.caradoncottages.co.uk

LISKEARD

Lametton Barton, St Keyne, Liskeard PL14 4SQ. Lametton Barton is a working farm set in the very heart of Cornwall, an ideal base from which to visit the Cornish coast. Local attractions include the Lost Gardens of Heligan, the Eden Project and the historic port of Looe. On the first floor there is one double and one twin-bedded room, and a bathroom. There is also a smaller room containing a single bed/optional bunk bed conversion. Cot can be provided. Ground floor comprises sitting room with beamed ceiling, kitchen and dining room. Fully equipped with cooker, fridge, microwave and washing machine etc. Well-behaved dogs are welcome. Prices include electricity, bed linen, duvets and tea towels. Terms from £300 per week. Spring and Autumn weekend rates available. Contact: **Peter & Sharon Clemens (01579 343434).**

LISKEARD

Andy and Jackie Lowman, Cutkive Wood Holiday Lodges, St Ive, Liskeard PL14 3ND (01579 362216). Nestling in the heart of a peaceful and lovely, 41-acre, family-owned private estate, there are just six well equipped and furnished cedarwood lodges. They are set well apart on the edge of bluebell woods, with lovely countryside views, so you can relax and enjoy yourself in a tranquil and informal setting. Ideally situated to enjoy numerous attractions. Children can help to feed the animals, milk the goats, explore the woods and run about in the fields. There is so much to see and do, including the Eden Project, lovely beaches, walks on the moors, theme parks and sporting activities. Dogs are welcome.
e-mail: holidays@cutkivewood.co.uk
website: www.cutkivewood.co.uk

LISKEARD

Alan and Kathleen Hunstone, Rivermead Farm, Twowatersfoot, Liskeard PL14 6HT (01208 821464). Self-catering apartments and farm cottage, set in beautiful wooded Glynn Valley, amidst 30 acres of meadows and water meadows. River and lakeside walks nearby; a mile of sea trout and salmon fishing on the River Fowey. Convenient for both coasts and moors. Pets welcome. Brochure on request.
website: www.zednet.co.uk/rivermead

LISKEARD

Mrs Cotter, Trewalla Farm Cottages, Trewalla Farm, Minions, Liskeard PL14 6ED (Tel & Fax: 01579 342385). Sleeps 3/4 plus cot. Our small, traditionally-run farm on Bodmin Moor has rare breed pigs, sheep, hens and geese, all free-range and very friendly. The three cottages are beautifully furnished and very well equipped. Their moorland setting offers perfect peace, wonderful views, ideal walking country and a good base for exploring both coastlines, or visiting the Eden Project – if you can tear yourself away! Linen and electricity included. Open March to December and New Year. **ETC ★★★★**
e-mail: cotter.trewalla@virgin.net

LOOE

Raven Rock and Spindrift, Looe. Two bungalows adjacent to Plaidy Beach. Spindrift has en suite bedroom, sleeps two; Raven Rock has two bedrooms and sleeps four. Own parking spaces, central heating, wheelchair accessible. Semi-detached bungalows are fully furnished, well equipped and have sea views. Set in peaceful surroundings at Plaidy. Open plan lounge-diner-kitchen. Colour TV. Patio garden. Electricity and gas included in rent. Pets by arrangement. Personally supervised. Looe is a fishing port with a variety of shops and restaurants and is only a few minutes by car or a 15 to 20 minute walk. Weekly terms: Spindrift from £180 to £285; Raven Rock from £210 to £385. Short breaks (three days minimum) before Easter and after middle of October. Apartment in centre of town also available (sleeps 6/8). Contact: **Mrs S. Gill Bodrigy, Plaidy, Looe PL13 1LF (01503 263122).**

See also Colour Display Advertisement

LOOE

Mr & Mrs J Spreckley, Tremaine Green Country Cottages, Pelynt, Near Looe PL13 2LT (01503 220333). "A beautiful private hamlet" of 11 award-winning traditional cosy Cornish craftsmen's cottages between Looe and Polperro. Clean, comfortable and well equipped, with a warm friendly atmosphere, for pets with 2 to 8 people. Set in lovely grounds, only 12 miles from the Eden Project with country and coastal walks nearby. Towels, linen, electricity and central heating included. Dishwashers in larger cottages. Power shower baths. Launderette, games room, tennis court. TV/videos. Cots and highchairs available. Pubs and restaurants in easy walking distance. Pets £16 per week; owners from only £112.
e-mail: stay@tremainegreen.co.uk
website: www.tremainegreen.co.uk

LOOE

Trenant Park Cottages. Secluded country cottages set in idyllic grounds of historic estate in the enchanting Looe Valley. Each has its own charming garden with a further third of an acre of manicured lawn. They are individually furnished with antiques and country furnishings. Although steeped in character, we offer all modern conveniences such as washer dryers, dishwashers, microwaves, linen, colour TV, video, telephone and much more. Open log fires and inclusive heating for warm cosy breaks off season. Guests and dogs are welcome to walk or stroll in the immediate parkland and grounds. Countryside and coastal walking all nearby. Looe one and a half miles with beaches and excellent restaurants. Delicious home-cooked meals service delivered to your door. Contact: **Mrs E.M. Chapman, Trenant Lodge, Sandplace, Looe PL13 1PH (01503 263639/262241).**
e-mail: Liz@holiday-cottage.com   website: www.holiday-cottage.com

ENGLAND

LOOE/POLPERRO

Mrs Pauline Major, Trelawne Cottage, Trelawne, Looe PL13 2NA (01503 272664). Spotlessly clean and comfortable cottage apartments offering quality, relaxing holidays personally supervised by the friendly resident owners. There are two apartments; one on the ground floor and one on the first floor providing a bedroom, shower room, well-equipped kitchen with mircowave and fridge/freezer and a large lounge/diner with TV and video. Although peaceful we are only a few hundred yards away from the A387. Looe and Polperro are two miles away and the picturesque coastline of south east Cornwall is one mile. The Eden Project and other popular gardens are all within a 25 minute drive. Off-road parking. Sorry, no pets. Terms from £125 to £315 weekly. OPEN ALL YEAR.

LOOE VALLEY

Badham Farm, St Keyne, Liskeard PL14 4RW (Tel & Fax: 01579 343572). Sleeps 2-8 plus 2 children. Once part of a Duchy of Cornwall working farm, now farmhouse and farm buildings converted to a high standard to form a six cottage complex around former farmyard. Sleeping from two to ten. All cottages are well furnished and equipped and prices include electricity, bed linen and towels. Most cottages have a garden. Five acre grounds, set in delightful wooded valley, with tennis, putting, children's play area, fishing lake, animal paddock, games room with pool and table tennis. Separate bar. Laundry. Barbecue. Railcar from Liskeard to Looe stops at end of picnic area. Have a 'car free' day out. Children and well behaved dogs welcome (no dogs in high season, please). Prices from £120 per week. **ETC** ★★★, GREEN TOURISM AWARD.
website: www.looedirectory.co.uk/badhamcottages.htm

MARAZION (Near)

Mrs W. Boase, Trebarvah Farm, Trebarvah Lane, Perranuthnoe, Penzance TR20 9NG (01736 710361) Trebarvah Farm Cottages. Three cottages, two sleeping four people, one sleeping six people, with magnificent views across Mount's Bay and St Michael's Mount. Just east of Marazion, Perranuthnoe is easily accessible on foot or by car and has a sandy beach. Accommodation – TUE BROOK: one double and two twin-bedded rooms, one en suite, kitchen/diner, lounge and large conservatory. TAIRUA: one double and one twin-bedded room and a livingroom. KERIKERI COTTAGE: one twin room and a double sofa bed in the livingroom. All properties include duvets, pillows and blankets but no linen or towels. Kitchens are electric and power is through a pre-payment £1 coin meter. Colour TV. Rates from £150 to £465 per week. Short breaks available out of summer season.
e-mail: jaybee@trebarvah.freeserve.co.uk   **website: www.trebarvahfarmcottages.co.uk**

See also Colour Display Advertisement

MAWGAN PORTH

Tredragon Lodge. Five serviced self-catering lodges between Newquay and Padstow at Mawgan Porth. 200 yards from the beach. Fully equipped, including dishwashers; daily maid service; linen provided. Mastercard and Visa accepted. For details contact **J. McLuskie (01637 881610).**
e-mail: tredragonlodge@hotmail.com
website: www.tredragonlodge.co.uk

When making enquiries please mention FHG Publications

NEWQUAY

The Granary and The Bowgie at Trewerry Mill, St Newlyn East. Trewerry Mill nestles in a peaceful valley four miles from the north coast, central for Cornish gardens, coastal walks and The Eden Project (25 minutes). Two newly converted, centrally heated cottages, sleeping two and four, off an enclosed courtyard. Both have large lounge with woodburning stove, dining area and fully-fitted kitchen. The Bowgie has one bedroom with en suite bath/shower; The Granary has a double (king-size) bedroom, with original fireplace, and a second twin-bedded room, sharing a large bathroom/shower. Available Fridays from £250 to £660 per week, electricity, heating and linen included. One well behaved dog welcome. Non-smoking throughout. Colour brochure available. Contact: **Mrs Terri Clark, Trewerry Mill, Trerice, St Newlyn East TR8 5GS (Tel & Fax: 01872 510345).**
e-mail: trewerry.mill@which.net   **website: www.trewerrymill.co.uk**

PADSTOW

Yellow Sands Cottages, Harlyn Bay, Padstow PL28 8SE (01637 881548). Sleeps 1-6. Situated in an Area of Outstanding Natural Beauty, along the magnificent north Cornish coast, Harlyn Bay is a crescent of firm, golden sand - six other spectacular beaches are within close proximity. Surrounded by its own private grounds and gardens, we provide well-appointed cottages to sleep from one to six persons. Each property is furnished and equipped to a high standard. Appliances include cooker/hob, fridge/freezer, microwave, TV/video, CD unit and hairdryer - most have dishwasher. Cleanliness is paramount throughout. Storage heating is provided. Patio, garden and adequate parking adjacent to each property. Cot/highchair available. Linen available, electricity via £1 coin meter. Pets and children welcome. **ETC**
★★★/★★★★★
e-mail: yellowsands@btinternet.com   **website: www.yellowsands.co.uk**

PENZANCE

Mrs James Curnow, Barlowenath, St Hilary, Penzance TR20 9DQ (01736 710409). Working farm. Cottages sleep 4/5. These two cottages are on a farm, in a little hamlet right beside St Hilary Church, with quiet surroundings and a good road approach. A good position for touring Cornish coast and most well-known places. Beaches are two miles away; Marazion two-and-a-half miles; Penzance six miles; St Ives eight; Land's End 16. Both cottages have fitted carpets, lounge/diner with TV/video; modern kitchen (microwave, fridge, electric cooker, toaster, iron); bathroom with shaver point. Electricity by £1 meter, night storage heaters extra. One cottage sleeps five in three bedrooms (one double, twin divans and one single). The second cottage sleeps four in two bedrooms (twin divans in both). Linen not supplied, may be hired by arrangement. Cot by arrangement. Available all year. £95 to £350 weekly, VAT exempt.

PERRANPORTH

"Makhan" and "Kinsi", Liskey Hill Crescent, Perranporth, & Cradock, 7 Wainsway, Liskey Hill, Perranporth. "Makhan' and 'Kinsi' are two adjacent semi-detached houses offering basic accommodation at a budget price. Makhan sleeps 8-12 and Kinsi 6-10. They are simply furnished and suitable for a party of four or five adults with four or five children (N.B. NOT 12 adults!) "Cradock" is a detached bungalow just a stone's throw from the park, shops, pubs and the beach, sleeping 6-8. All three properties have some garden and parking, TV, etc. Perranporth itself has a fine sandy beach with rocky cliffs, caves and pools on one side and excellent surfing. There is also tennis, golf, gliding and a boating lake. Prices from £200 to £550 per house per week. Contact: **D.E. Gill-Carey, Penkerris, 3 Penwinnick Road, St Agnes, Cornwall TR5 0PA (Tel & Fax: 01872 552262).**
e-mail: info@penkerris.co.uk   **website: www.penkerris.co.uk**

PERRANPORTH

St David's Apartments, Tywarnhayle Road, Perranporth TR6 0DX. Sleeps 4-6. Two self-contained three-bedroomed apartments with private patios, overlooking Perranporth. Parking. Two minutes from a good surfing beach and shops. Colour TV, microwave, electric oven, fridge. Duvets and pillows supplied. Washing machine and freezer on property. Golf, riding and Coastal Path nearby. Brochure available from: **Mrs B. Gladwell (01872 571463).**
e-mail: stdavids@aol.com

POLPERRO

Holiday Cottages, Polperro. Sleep 2 to 8. In picturesque Cornish fishing village, spectacularly situated holiday cottages with terraced gardens and fabulous outlook over harbour encompassing 15 mile sea views. Private parking. Two minutes away are shops, beach, quay and National Trust cliff walks. Open all year, children and pets most welcome. All cottages are fully furnished and equipped, including a colour television, microwave, refrigerator, duvets and pillows. Terms from £175 to £450 per cottage per week. For more details please telephone **01579 344080.**

See also Colour Display Advertisement

PORTHLEVEN

Porthleven Holidays, The Harbour Head, Porthleven TR13 9JA (Tel & Fax: 01326 563404). A superb selection of holiday cottages, most with magnificent sea views. Discover why the unspoilt fishing village of Porthleven in West Cornwall is becoming so popular. We offer a wonderful choice of self-catering cottages, ranging from a converted net loft, sleeping two, to a former sea captain's house, sleeping eight, available throughout the year, with sea and harbour views. Some accept dogs, others are for non-smokers only, all are very different from each other. Colour brochure available.
e-mail: enquiries@porthlevenholidays.co.uk
website: www.porthlevenholidays.co.uk

See also Colour Display Advertisement

PORT ISAAC

The Dolphin, Port Isaac. Sleeps up to 10. Port Isaac is a picturesque fishing village surrounded by magnificent coastal scenery. The Dolphin, originally an inn, is a delightful cottage of great character situated just yards from the beach, shops and pub, and within easy access of cliff walks. Five bedrooms, three with washbasins; two bathrooms and WCs; large dining room; cosy sitting room. Spacious and well-equipped kitchen with electric cooker, gas-fired Aga, dishwasher and washing machine. Attractive sun terrace. Nearby attractions include surfing, sailing, fishing, golf, tennis, pony trekking, as well as many interesting places to visit such as Tintagel Castle and the Eden Project. Weekly terms: £500 to £750. Reduced rates offered for shorter stays during off-peak season. Enquiries to **Emily Glentworth, 150 Hammersmith Grove, London W6 7HE (020 8741 2352)**

PORT ISAAC

Ms V. Franklin, "Halcyon", 7 The Terrace, Port Isaac PL29 3SG (01753 862038). Self-catering apartments sleeping 2-6. Port Isaac nestles in a coastal valley unspoilt and little affected by its 600 years' history. Narrow alleys and streets lead down to the harbour where you can watch the local catch being landed and buy fresh crab, lobster and mackerel. Port Isaac and neighbouring Port Gaverne offer bathing and both are a short walk from the accommodation, as are a number of pubs and eating places. Halcyon stands high on the cliff top and all lounges enjoy magnificent views of sea and surrounding coastline. Each has its own front door and is equipped to a high standard. Children and pets welcome. Parking. CTB inspected and registered. Details available. Linen for hire. Weekly terms from £150 to £420; out of season reductions.
website: www.cornwall-online/halcyon

PRAA SANDS

Mrs June Markham, Broom Farm, Packet Lane, Rosudgeon, Penzance TR20 9QD (01736 763738). Sleeps 2. Broom Farm Cottage, a comfortable, detached cottage converted from a granite barn and set on three-acre smallholding. Well furnished, sleeps two, pets welcome. There is a full-size cooker, fridge, colour TV. Covered car space leading to patio overlooking meadow. Shop, post office, village pub, fish and chip shop and bus stop at end of lane. Perfect for summer holidays or an out-of-season break. Two miles Praa or Perran Sands, one mile Prussia Cove. Penzance six miles. Weekly terms from £130 to £270. SAE for illustrated brochure, stating holiday period preferred.

ROCK (near)

Trewillig Cottage, Tredrizzick, Near Rock. Sleeps 9 + sofa bed. Characterful, well-equipped, and cherished Cornish cottage near Rock and the beautiful Camel Estuary. Secluded, sheltered garden with built-in barbecue, well-behaved dogs and children welcome. Within easy distance of three top class golf courses and garden visiting. One mile from surfing and sailing. Most families return. Two bathrooms, three wc's. For more information please telephone: **01653 668638; Fax: 01653 668591.**
e-mail: tetley78@habton.freeserve.co.uk

ST BREWARD

Holiday Cottage. Sleeps 4. Warm and lovely cottage sleeping four in great comfort and utter peace. Log fires, large garden with stream. Glorious walking. Available all year. Terms from £120 to £350 per week, depending on season. Dogs welcome, £6 per week. St Breward is a picturesque village high on Bodmin Moor and within easy reach of both coasts. Situated four miles from the A30. For further details please contact **Mrs Paddy Powell (01208 850186)**
website: www.vacation-cornwall.com

FREE or REDUCED RATE entry to Holiday Visits and Attractions
– see our READERS' OFFER VOUCHERS on pages 53-80

ST COLUMB

Mrs J.V. Thomas, Lower Trenowth Farm, St Columb TR9 6EW (01637 880308). Sleeps 6. This accommodation is part of a large farmhouse, all rooms facing south. Situated in the beautiful Vale of Lanherne, four miles from the sea, eight miles from the holiday resort of Newquay. Golf, horse riding, etc all within easy reach. One double room, one twin-bedded room and one single room with bunk beds, all with washbasins. Bed linen provided. Bathroom. Large lounge with colour TV and video. Fully equipped kitchen/diner. Electricity included in tariff. Large lawn. Ample parking. Dogs accepted if kept under control. SAE for further details please.

ST IVES

The Links Holiday Flats, Lelant, St Ives TR26 3HY (Tel & Fax: 01736 753326). If it's views you want, this is the place for you! Magnificent location alongside and overlooking West Cornwall Golf Course, Hayle Estuary and St Ives Bay. Two well-equipped flats with lovely views. Wonderful spot for walking. Five minutes' from the beach, where dogs are allowed all year round. Open all year.

ST TUDY

Chapel Cottages. Four traditional cottages in quiet farming area and ideal for spectacular north coast, Bodmin Moor and The Eden Project. These two-bedroom cottages have character and charm and are comfortable and well equipped. Garden and private parking. Rental from £130 to £392 per week. Also two smaller cottages at Blisland, suitable for couples, converted from a 17th century barn. These are situated in a peaceful farming hamlet. Rental from £120 to £290 per week. Linen is provided in all cottages. Regretfully no pets. Shop and pub/restaurant within walking distance. Brochure available from **Mr and Mrs C.W. Pestell, Hockadays, Tregenna, Near Blisland PL30 4QJ (Tel & Fax: 01208 850146).**
website: www.hockadaysholidaycottages.co.uk

ST TUDY

Ruth Reeves, Maymear Cottage, St Tudy, Bodmin PL30 3NE (Tel & Fax: 01840 213120). A comfortable, well-equipped end of terrace cottage in the picturesque village of St Tudy which has a pub and post office/stores. Lying between Wadebridge, Bodmin and Camelford it is an excellent base for exploring all Cornwall. The Eden Project and many other places of interest are all within easy reach. The house has a gravelled parking area, enclosed rear garden, kitchen, dining room with woodburner stove, cloakroom/WC, sitting room. Upstairs two twin/double bedrooms and bathroom. Heating by night storage and/or convector heaters. All linen and electricity inclusive. Short breaks. Available all year. Pets welcome.
e-mail: aandr.reeves@virgin.net
website: www.maymear.co.uk

TINTAGEL

Salutations Holiday Cottages, Atlantic Road, Tintagel PL34 0DE. Two comfortable, well-equipped, centrally heated cottages with sea glimpses, each ideal for two people. Off-road parking and small garden area, with seating, for guests' use. Situated close to the village pubs and restaurants we are a short stroll from the Coastal Path and are ideally situated as a base for exploring Cornwall and North Devon. Prices from £110 to £245 per week including linen, towels and electricity. Pets welcome at no extra charge. For further information please visit our website or telephone **01840 770287.**
e-mail: sandyanddave@tinyworld.co.uk
website: www.salutationstintagel.co.uk

TINTAGEL

Cate West, Chilcotts, Bossiney, Tintagel PL34 0AY (Tel & Fax: 01840 770324). Without stepping onto a road, slip through the side gate of your 16th century Listed cottage into a landscape owned by the National Trust and designated as an Area of Outstanding Natural Beauty. Closest cottages to nearby Bossiney beach for rockpools, surfing, safe swimming and caves to explore. Walk the cliffpath north to famous Rocky Valley or onwards to the picturesque Boscastle Harbour. Southwards takes you to the ruins of King Arthur's Castle and onwards to Trebarwith Strand. Notice you have not stepped onto a road yet? Group of three friendly old country cottages, largest ideal for six. Low beamed ceilings and exposed stonework. Double and family bedrooms, all linen supplied. Comfortable lounges, colour TVs. Fully equipped kitchens, night storage heating throughout. Terms £180 to £450. Short winter breaks or Bed and Breakfast (from £20) also available. Directions: Bossiney adjoins Tintagel on B3263 (coast road). "Chilcotts" adjoins large layby with old red phonebox.

TRURO

Garvinack Farm Holidays, Tregavethan, Truro TR4 9EP (01872 560385). Conveniently situated alongside the A30, between Bodmin and Redruth, and yet very secluded and peaceful, the farm is equidistant from St Agnes and Perranporth to the north, and Truro with its excellent shopping facilities, cathedral and other points of interest to the south. Four acre woodland to the rear of the house, with its three-tiered walk amongst camellias, rhododendrons and magnolias. THOMAS BUNGALOW - a compact and comfortable cottage occupying an elevated position with wonderful parkland views. Fully furnished and equipped to a high standard, accommodation comprises one double and one twin bedroom (duvets supplied), sitting room, dining room, modern kitchen with cooker, and bathroom and shower. Small secluded garden. Colour TV. Conservatory. Parking. Pets by arrangement. Contact **Carol MacKenley** for further details

See also Colour Display Advertisement

TRURO near

King Harry Ferry Cottages. Two comfortable well-equipped cottages set in an Area of Outstanding Natural Beauty, each with its own charming garden. Individually furnished with co-ordinating furnishings. Full central heating and double glazed. Microwave, colour TV and video, telephone, washing machine, fridge and all bed linen. We also offer use of our boat during your stay. All these included in the price. Pets are welcome. Beautiful woodland walks for you to stroll through. Perfect for fishing and bird watching. **Tel: 01872 861915**
e-mail: jean@kingharry.f9.co.uk
website: www.kingharry-info.co.uk

See also Colour Display Advertisement

WADEBRIDGE (near)

Polgrain Holiday Cottages, Higher Polgrain, St Wenn PL30 5PR (01637 880637; Fax: 01637 881944). Beautifully converted and well-equipped barn conversions in glorious countryside location, superbly positioned to tour the spectacular north coast, this is a holiday destination which offers the best of both worlds. Polgrain is the most perfect place to relax, unwind and enjoy the peace and tranquillity of the surrounding countryside. Once a flourishing farm and mill, the main farmhouse is now our family home, while the granite barns and mill have been converted into comfortable, well-equipped holiday cottages – each with its own individual character and features. Adjoining the main farmhouse is the HEATED INDOOR POOL. Each cottage has a fully fitted kitchen including washing machine and microwave, and each living area is also equipped with colour TV, video recorder and compact disc hi-fi system. Alarm clock radios can be found in the bedrooms and all linen is provided free of charge. Central heating, power and lighting are all included within the price of the holiday. Each cottage also has its own patio, complete with furniture and brick built barbecue. Car parking. Tariffs and booking details on request. Open March – January. ETC ★★★★.
e-mail: Polgrainholidaycottages@ukgateway.net   website: www.selfcateringcornwall.uk.com

---

When making enquiries please mention FHG Publications

ENGLAND

WADEBRIDGE/BODIEVE

Cornish Cottage. Sleeps 6 plus cot. 300 year old farmhouse, converted in 1990, surrounded by sunny gardens, parking space in front of house in quiet country crescent. Only three miles from the sandy beaches at Rock and Daymer Bay, the surfing beach at Polzeath, close to the ancient fishing harbour of Padstow. Ideal for surfing, safe bathing, walking, fishing, sailing, golf, cycling (cycle hire in Wadebridge). The excellent shops and pubs at Wadebridge are half-a-mile away. Wadebridge Leisure Centre with its indoor swimming pool is only a five minute walk. The house comprises lounge with wood/coal burner in fireplace, colour TV, comfortable sofa bed (double). Large, cosy, well-equipped kitchen/diner with fridge, electric cooker, dishwasher, microwave, double aspect windows; laundry room with automatic washing machine, tumble dryer, fridge/freezer. Three bedrooms - large master bedroom (double aspect windows) with king size bed, one twin bedroom and a bedroom with bunk beds. Linen and towels on request at extra charge. Bathroom, shower, toilet. Night storage heaters. Pets by arrangement. Available all year. High season rates: £290 to £540 per week (including electricity and cleaning). Saturday to Saturday bookings. Ring or write for further details. **Mrs Angela Holder, Roseley, Bodieve, Wadebridge PL27 6EG (01208 813024). From 1st April 2004 contact: Mrs Simpson, 45 Hill Avenue, Victoria Park, Bristol B53 4SR (0117 3738001).**

ISLES OF SCILLY

ST MARY'S

Sallakee Cottage, Sallakee Farm, St Mary's, Isles of Scilly TR21 0NZ (01720 422391). Sallakee Cottage is attached to a farmhouse, parts of which are 250 years old. Situated between Perthellick and the Heliport, it stands in a rural area with access to coastal paths, nature trails, bird hides, etc. Situated at the end of a farm road, it is about 25 minutes' walk from town. One spacious double bedroom, and one bedroom with three single beds. Bathroom with shower, toilet and heated towel rail (towels supplied), Emerson heater for hot water. Kitchen equipped with all essentials. £1 meter for electricity. Lounge with woodburner, wood and coal provided, colour TV. Access to small pleasant garden with furniture.

FHG

PLEASE MENTION THIS GUIDE WHEN YOU WRITE

OR PHONE TO ENQUIRE ABOUT ACCOMMODATION

IF YOU ARE WRITING, A STAMPED, ADDRESSED

ENVELOPE IS ALWAYS APPRECIATED

CUMBRIA

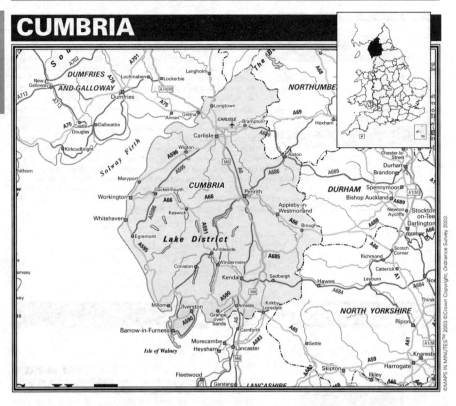

AMBLESIDE

Betty Fold, Hawkshead Hill, Ambleside LA22 0PS (015394 36611). Sleeps 4. Betty Fold is a large country house in its own spacious grounds with magnificent views and set in the heart of the Lake District National Park. The quaint village of Hawkshead and Tarn Hows are nearby and Coniston and Ambleside are within four miles. Betty Fold offers self-catering accommodation in a comfortable ground floor apartment with private entrance and central heating. One double bedroom en suite and one small twin room with bathroom and colour TV. Open-plan kitchen/living room, with electric cooker, fridge and microwave. Pets welcome. Terms inclusive of heat, light, power, bed linen and towels.

website: www.bettyfold.co.uk

See also Colour Display Advertisement

AMBLESIDE

Chestnuts, Beeches & The Granary, High Wray, Ambleside. Sleep 6/4. Two charming cottages and one delightful bungalow converted from a former 18th century coach house and cornstore/tack room. Set in idyllic surroundings overlooking Lake Windermere with magnificent panoramic views of the Langdale Pikes, Coniston Old Man and the Troutbeck Fells, making this an ideal base for walking and touring. All three properties have large lounges with Sky TV and video. The Granary (sleeps four) has a separate kitchen/diner. Chestnuts and Beeches (each sleeps six) have balconies overlooking Lake Windermere and dining areas in the large lounges. All properties have bathrooms with bath, shower, fitted kitchens with electric cooker, microwave, washing machine, fridge, freezer and tumble dryer. Included in the cost of the holiday is the oil central heating in The Granary and night storage heaters in Chestnuts and Beeches. Lighting and bed linen included in all three. **Contact Mrs J.R. Benson, High Sett, Sunhill Lane, Troutbeck Bridge, Windermere LA23 1HJ (015394 42731).**

See also Colour Display Advertisement

AMBLESIDE

"The Eyrie", Lake Road, Ambleside. Sleeps 6. A really delightful, characterful flat nestling under the eaves of a converted school with lovely views of the fells, high above the village. Large airy living/dining room with colour TV. Comfortably furnished as the owners' second home. Well-equipped kitchen with spacious airing cupboard; three bedrooms sleeping six; attractive bathroom (bath/WC/shower) and lots of space for boots and walking gear. Colour TV, fitted carpets, gas central heating, use of separate laundry room. Terrace garden with fine views. Sorry, but no pets. Available all year. Weekly rates £200 to £370. Also short breaks. Free parking permit provided for one car. Many recommendations. Children welcome. Brochure available. Telephone **Mrs Clark (01844 208208).**

e-mail: dot.clark@btopenworld.com

AMBLESIDE

2 Lowfield, Old Lake Road, Ambleside. Sleeps 4/5. Ground floor garden flat situated half a mile from town centre. The accommodation comprises lounge/dining room, kitchen, bathroom/WC, two bedrooms with twin beds. Linen supplied. Children and pets welcome. Parking for one car. Bookings run from Saturday to Saturday. Terms from £130 to £200 per week. Contact: **Mr P.F. Quarmby, 3 Lowfield, Old Lake Road, Ambleside LA22 0DH (Tel & Fax: 015394 32326).**

AMBLESIDE

Mr Evans, Ramsteads Coppice, Outgate, Ambleside LA22 0NH (015394 36583). Six timber lodges of varied size and design set in 15 acres of mixed woodland with wild flowers, birds and native wild animals. There are also 11 acres of rough hill pasture. Three miles south west of Ambleside, it is an ideal centre for walkers, artists, birdwatchers, and country lovers. No pets. Children welcome. Open March to November.

AMBLESIDE

Swiss Villas, Vicarage Road, Ambleside LA22 9AE (015394 32691). Sleeps 2-6 Traditional Victorian terrace house in the centre of Ambleside, off the main road and convenient for shops, cinema, restaurants, walks, parks and a ten minute stroll to Lake Windermere. Newly refurbished with full central heating and an open fire. Private parking. Resident owner. Three double bedrooms, all furnished to a high standard. Terms from £300 to £430 per week
e-mail: sowerbutts@tinyworld.co.uk

See also Colour Display Advertisement

APPLEBY

Scalebeck Holiday Cottages, Great Asby, Appleby CA16 6TF (01768 351006; Fax: 01768 353532). Originally a farmstead, Scalebeck nestles peacefully in the Upper Eden valley, just one mile from the village of Great Asby. It makes an ideal place to relax, unwind and enjoy the numerous walks and wildlife in the area. Converted from the former hay barn, the cottages have been well equipped and tastefully furnished, to provide cosy accommodation. With gas central heating for all-year-round comfort. Electricity, gas, towels and bed linen inclusive. Garden furniture, barbecue/patio area. Games room with table tennis and pool table. One well-behaved pet on lead welcome. No smokers please.
e-mail: mail@scalebeckholidaycottages.com
website: www.scalebeckholidaycottages.com

APPLEBY-IN-WESTMORLAND

Mrs Edith Stockdale, Croft House, Bolton, Appleby-in-Westmorland CA16 6AW (Tel & Fax: 017683 61264). Sleep 2/5 and 10. Three cosy cottages recently converted from an old Westmorland style barn adjoining the owner's house. With an abundance of open stone work and oak beams and many original features. An excellent base for fell and country walking, horse-riding or as a touring base for the Lake District, beautiful Eden Valley, Scottish Borders, Hadrian's Wall and North Yorkshire Dales. Bed linen, towels, electricity and heating included in rent. Facilities include electric cooker, washing machine, fridge-freezer, microwave, colour TV, video, hi-fi and dishwasher. Stabling provided for anyone wishing to bring pony on holiday. Weekly terms from £160. Brochure available.
website: www.crofthouse-cottages.co.uk

ENGLAND

APPLEBY-IN-WESTMORLAND

David & Madeleine Adams, The Station, Milburn Road, Long Marton, Appleby CA16 6BU (0161-775 5669). WHY NOT TRY SOMETHING A LITTLE DIFFERENT? Long Marton Station, on the historic Settle - Carlisle Railway, has been painstakingly restored over the past 10 years. Situated in the unspoilt Eden Valley between the Lakes and the Pennines, the Station occupies a commanding position in half an acre of land just outside the village. There is a large lounge with original marble fireplace, dining room, kitchen, bathroom, large double bedroom with cot, and twin bedroom. Gas central heating, colour TV/video, music centre, electric cooker, microwave, fridge/freezer, washing machine, bath/shower, large lawn. Ample on-site parking. Electricity, gas, firewood, bed linen and towels (on request) included. Welcome pack on arrival. Pets by arrangement.
website: www.LongMartonStation.co.uk

2o u expensive!

BOWNESS-ON-WINDERMERE

Canterbury Flats, Bowness-on-Windermere. Popular apartments in superb location, an ideal base for a Lake District holiday. You will enjoy the peace of Quarry Rigg, a quiet cul-de-sac, yet just a stones throw away from the centre of Bowness - offering numerous restaurants, pubs, interesting shops and visitor attractions. The splendour of Lake Windermere less than five minutes' walk and Parklands Country Club a similar distance away (Parklands membership included in the price). It really would be hard to find a better base for your holiday. **Bowness Lakeland Holidays, 131 Radcliffe New Road, Whitefield, Manchester M45 7RP (0161-796 3896; Fax: 0161-272 1841).
e-mail: info@bownesslakelandholidays.co.uk
website: www.bownesslakelandholidays.co.uk**

BOWNESS-ON-WINDERMERE

45 Quarry Rigg, Lake Road, Bowness-on-Windermere. Sleeps 4. Very well appointed modern flat with lake views situated in a new development. Ideally placed in the centre of the village for shops, restaurants, etc. Parking for tenants. Within easy reach of tennis, boating, fishing, golf. Ideal for touring and walking. Attractive second floor flat comprising lounge/diner with newly fitted kitchenette, two bedrooms (one twin, one double), bathroom with bath and shower. Furnished, decorated and equipped to a very high standard for owner's personal use including colour TV, video, fridge, microwave, duvets. Electric heating including storage heaters. Metered electricity. No pets or children under 10 years. Non-smokers only. Terms from £130 to £250 per week. SAE for further details. **Mrs J. Kay, 11**

Sommerville Close, The Belfry, High Legh, Near Knutsford, Cheshire WA16 6TR (01925 755612).

CARLISLE

Mrs Sarah Hodgson, Grange Cottages, Drumburgh, Wigton, Carlisle CA7 5DW (01228 576551). Relax in this traditional style cottage with open fire and exposed beams - located in this rural hamlet of Drumburgh in an Area of Outstanding Natural Beauty, with views across the Solway Firth. Hadrian's Wall National Trail, Campfield RSPB Reserve and English Nature Reserves are nearby. Bed and Breakfast available. Sleeps two to four people. Non-smoking. Prices from £180 - £280. Please telephone for brochure. **ETC ★★★ – ★★★★
e-mail: messrs.hodgson@tesco.net
website: www.thegrangecottage.co.uk**

A useful Index of Towns/Villages and Counties appears on page 281 – please also refer to Contents Page 3.

CONISTON

Thurston View Cottage, Sleeps 4. An old stone miner's cottage located a few minutes' walk from the centre of Coniston. It commands superb panoramic views over the village and lake. Recently refurbished, it now has gas central heating, double glazing, and a living flame gas fire in the lounge. Fully tiled bathroom with bath and electric shower. A dishwasher, washer/tumble dryer, microwave, fridge/freezer, TVs and video are also provided. The garden has a patio and barbecue area and superb views. There is private parking for one car. Prices from £205 to £375 per week. **ETC ★★★★**. Enquiries to **Mr and Mrs Jefferson, 21 Chalegreen, Harwood, Bolton BL2 3NJ (01204 419261).**
e-mail: alan@jefferson99.freeserve.co.uk
website: www.jefferson99.freeserve.co.uk

CONISTON

Thurston House, Coniston. Flats sleep 2/6. A Lakeland stone house converted into self-contained, spacious, clean, comfortable apartments sleeping two to six. The property is carefully maintained by the owners. Open all year (storage heaters early and late season). Quiet location yet only a short walk to village centre and lake. Private parking. Children and pets welcome. Prices from £90 to £260 per week. **ETC/CTB ★★**. Enquiries to **Mr and Mrs Jefferson, 21 Chalegreen, Harwood, Bolton BL2 3NJ (01204 419261).**
e-mail: alan@jefferson99.freeserve.co.uk
website: www.jefferson99.freeserve.co.uk

`See also Colour Display Advertisement`

CONISTON

Coniston Country Cottages. Sleep 2-6. A range of quality cottages in superb surroundings in and around Coniston. Each cottage is well equipped and individually and tastefully furnished. Central location with easy access to the lakes and mountains. Ideal for walking, mountain biking, climbing and sailing. Nearby in Coniston village are shops, banks, restaurants and pubs. Complimentary leisure club membership. Off-road parking. Electricity included. Private patio or garden area with each cottage. Short breaks available November to March. **Tel & Fax: 015394 41114. ETC ★★★ / ★★★★**
e-mail: enquiry@conistoncottages.co.uk
website: www.conistoncottages.co.uk

`See also Colour Display Advertisement`

CONISTON (near)

Mrs J. Halton, "Brookfield", Torver, Near Coniston LA21 8AY (015394 41328). Sleeps 2/4. "Brookfield" is a large attractive modern bungalow property in a rural setting with lovely outlook and extensive views of the Coniston mountains. The bungalow stands in its own half-acre of level garden and grounds. The inside is divided into two completely separate self-contained units (semi-detached). The holiday bungalow accommodation consists of large sitting/dining room, kitchen, utility room, two good bedrooms (one twin and one double), bathroom. Good parking. Well-equipped. Bed linen included in price. Lovely walking terrain. Two village inns with restaurant facilities approximately 300 yards. Terms from £180 to £280 weekly. Special rates for two persons. Further details on request with SAE please.

expensive!

DENT VILLAGE

Situated in the centre of the attractive old village of Dent with its narrow cobbled streets and surrounded by marvellous scenery. This delightful 17th century cottage is a Grade ll Listed building and has been restored with care. The accommodation is comfortably furnished and is situated opposite Dent Church. This lovely holiday home enjoys an outlook over the surrounding countryside to the hills beyond and makes an ideal base for touring the Dales, or as a walking centre with open fells close at hand.

2 bedrooms - 1 double and 1 twin (with vanity unit), lounge with dining area, kitchen, and bathroom with toilet. Services: Electric fire in lounge, night storage heaters – all electricity included in the rent. Colour TV, shaver point, microwave oven. Large basement garage.

Character cottage for four
www.dentcottages.btinternet.co.uk
E-mail: dentcottages@btinternet.com
Tel: 015396 25294

DERWENTWATER

Derwent House and Brandelhowe, Portinscale, Keswick. Sleeps up to 6. In the picturesque village of Portinscale, Derwent House with Brandelhowe is a traditional stone Lakeland building renovated and converted to four self-contained comfortable well appointed holiday suites, each with parking. BRANDELHOWE COTTAGE SUITE on ground floor has two double bedrooms both with en suite shower/w.c. SHIRE, HUNTER AND COB SUITES have views south over Derwentwater. Central heating included. Colour TV and video. All bed linen provided. Children from age six and pets welcome. Open all year. Prices from £95 to £345 per week. Some reductions for two people. Short breaks available. **ETC ★★★**. Brochure from **Mary and Oliver Bull, Stone Heath, Hilderstone, Staffordshire ST15 8SH (01889 505678; Fax: 01889 505679).**

e-mail: thebulls@globalnet.co.uk

website: www.dhholidays-lakes.com

ELTERWATER

Lane Ends Cottages. The cottages are situated next to "Fellside" on the edge of Elterwater Common. Two cottages accommodate a maximum of four persons: double bedroom, twin bedded room; fully equipped kitchen/diningroom; bathroom. Third cottage sleeps five: as above plus single bedroom and separate diningroom. Electricity by meters. The cottages provide an ideal base for walking/touring holidays with Ambleside, Grasmere, Hawkshead and Coniston within a few miles. Parking for one car per cottage, additional parking opposite. Open all year; out of season long weekends available. Rates from £200 per week. Brochure on request (SAE please). **Mrs M. E. Rice, "Fellside", Elterwater, Ambleside LA22 9HN (015394 37678).**

GRANGE-OVER-SANDS

Cornerways, Field Broughton. Detached bungalow, own private garden with parking. Quiet situation with all round Lakeland views. Three miles from historic village of Cartmel, three miles from Newby Bridge, southern end of Lake Windermere. Ideal base for enjoying Lakeland holiday pursuits and countryside. The bungalow has entrance hall, living/dining room with colour TV, fitted breakfast kitchen, fridge/freezer, microwave and full electric cooker. Bathroom/WC. Double and twin-bedded bedrooms sleeping four. Duvets, linen provided. Well equipped. Electric and oil heating by meter reading. Incoming telephone. No pets or children under four years. Personal supervision. £250 to £350 per week. **ETC ★★★**. Brochure and details from: **Mrs Rigg, Prospect House, Barber Green, Grange-over-Sands LA11 6HU (015395 36329).**

e-mail: peter@lakesweddingmusic.com

GRIZEDALE FOREST

High Dale Park Barn, High Dale Park, Satterthwaite, Ulverston LA12 8LJ. Delightfully situated south-facing barn, newly converted, attached to owners' 17th century farmhouse, with wonderful views down secluded, quiet valley, surrounded by beautiful broadleaf woodland. Oak beams, log fires, full central heating, patio. Grizedale Visitor Centre (three miles) includes award-winning sculpture trails, gallery and unique sculptured playground. Grizedale Forest is one of the Lake District's richest areas of wildlife. Accommodation in two self-contained units, one sleeping six, the other two plus baby, available separately or as one unit at a reduced rate. Hawkshead three miles, Beatrix Potter's home three miles. **ETC ★★★.** Contact: **Mr P. Brown, High Dale Park Farm, High Dale Park, Satterthwaite, Ulverston LA12 8LJ** (01229 860226).
website: www.lakesweddingmusic.com/accomm

HOLMROOK

G. and H.W. Cook, Hall Flatt, Santon, Holmrook, Near Wasdale CA19 1UU (019467 26270). Working farm. Sleeps 7. This comfortably furnished house is set in own grounds with beautiful views. The approach road is a short but good lane off Gosforth/Santon Bridge road. Ideal centre for climbers and walkers. Within easy reach of Muncaster Castle and Narrow Gauge Railway from Ravenglass to Eskdale, about three miles from the sea and Wastwater. Accommodation comprises two double bedrooms, two single and child's bed; bathroom, two toilets; sittingroom, dining room; all electric kitchen with cooker, fridge, kettle, immersion heater, stainless steel sink unit. Fully equipped except for linen. Open Easter to Christmas. Pets by arrangement. Shopping about two miles and car essential. SAE, please, for weekly terms.

KENDAL

The Barns, Field End, Patton, Kendal. Properties sleep 6/8. Two detached barns converted into five spacious architect-designed houses. The Barns are situated on 200 acres of farm, four miles north of Kendal in a quiet country area with River Mint passing through farmland, and lovely views of Cumbrian Hills. Many interesting local walks, with the Dales Way passing close by; central to Lakes and Yorkshire Dales National Parks. Fishing is available on the river. The Barns consists of four houses each with four double bedrooms, and one house with three double bedrooms. Each house has full central heating for early/late holidays, lounge with open fire, diningroom; kitchen with cooker, microwave, fridge and washer; bathroom, downstairs shower room and toilet. Many interesting features include oak beams, pine floors and patio doors. Electricity at cost. Pets and children welcome. Terms from £185 to £450. **ETC ★★★/★★★★.** For brochure apply to **Mr and Mrs E.D. Robinson, 1 Field End, Patton, Kendal LA8 9DU** (01539 824220 or 07778 596863; Fax: 01539 824464).
e-mail: robinson@fieldendholidays.co.uk **website: www.fieldendholidays.co.uk**

KENDAL

Dora's Cottage, Natland, Kendal. Sleeps 2/4. Adjoining farmhouse in a tranquil village south of Kendal, this delightful cottage overlooks the garden amid the Lakeland Fells. Ground floor bedrooms, TV, fridge, ironing facilities, electric cooker, microwave, central heating and linen provided to help make the most of a country holiday with the Lakes and Dales nearby. Golf, riding, inns, restaurants, leisure centre, historic visits within easy distance. Children welcome. Car parking. Terms from £180 to £350 per week. Short Breaks can be arranged. **ETC ★★★.** For further details apply to **Mrs Val Sunter, Higher House Farm, Oxenholme Lane, Natland, Kendal LA9 7QH** (015395 61177; Fax: 015395 61520).

✓ expensive!

e-mail: **cottages@heaves.freeserve.co.uk**

KENDAL

Wain Gap Cottage, Heaves, Near Kendal. Sleeps 5 + cot. Wain Gap Cottage is located in woodland on the Heaves Estate at the end of a lane close to open fields. Kendal four miles, Junction 36 M6 four miles just off the A590. The newly refurbished cottage is equipped with all modern conveniences including washer/dryer, microwave, dishwasher, fridge/freezer. TV/video, stereo, central heating and payphone. The garden has table and chairs and barbecue. Two bedrooms. Linen and gas/electricity included. Ample parking. Family-owned and run along with the country house hotel at the centre of the estate. Regret, no pets. No smoking. Terms from £200 to £400 per week. Contact: **Mrs C. Whitelock, Heaves Hotel, Heaves, Near Kendal LA8 8EF (015395 60396; Fax: 015395 60269).**

website: **www.heaveshotel.co.uk**

KESWICK

Barrowside & Swinside Cottages, 30 & 32 Church Street, Keswick. These converted cottages provide a perfect base for a Lakeland holiday, compact and comfortable and within easy walking distance of the centre of Keswick. The property, renovated and refurbished to a high standard is carpeted throughout and has full double glazing and gas central heating. Lounge with focal fireplace, colour TV, video recorder, radio cassette and dining area. Fully fitted kitchen. Barrowside has a double-bedded room and small twin bedded room (with limited storage). Swinside has a family room with double and single bed (extra single bed if required). All bed linen is provided and the cost of all heating is included in the tariff. For further information please contact: **Mrs Walker, 15 Acorn Street, Keswick CA12 4EA (017687 74165).**

See also Colour Display Advertisement

KESWICK

Keswick Cottages, Kentmere, How Lane, Keswick CA12 5RS (017687 73895). Keswick Cottages offer a superb range of cottages in and around Keswick. There are numerous things to do, fell walking, theatre, boating, canoeing, cinema, two parks with various outdoor activities, indoor climbing wall and several museums. From a one-bedroom cottage to a four-bedroom property, we have something for everyone. All of our properties are well-maintained and finished, warm and cosy, most with views towards the fells, one with private lakeshore access. Prices for two start from £165 for a week or £102.50 for a short break and include all heating, lighting and linen.
e-mail: **info@keswickcottages.co.uk**
website: **www.keswickcottages.co.uk**

KESWICK

Mrs M. Beaty, Birkrigg Farm, Newlands, Keswick CA12 5TS (017687 78278). Sleeps 4. The cottage adjoining the farm guest house is extremely nice with an excellent outlook. Situated very pleasantly and peacefully amongst beautiful mountain scenery in the lovely Newlands Valley in the heart of Cumbria. Five miles from Keswick, between Braithwaite and Buttermere. Perfect base for hill walking, central for touring the Lake District. Clean and comfortable, comprising lounge, TV, kitchen, fridge freezer, cooker, microwave, one double and one twin room, shower/toilet. Linen and towels provided. Oil central heating, electric stove-type fire. Available all year. Ample parking. No dogs. No smoking. Short breaks out of season. £175 – £320 weekly. **ETC ★★★**

For details of Tourist Board Gradings in England, Scotland and Wales see page 50

KESWICK

16 Hewetson Court, Main Street, Keswick. Sleeps 1/4. A modern apartment with balcony, giving spectacular hill views, located in Keswick town centre. Very well equipped with all necessary amenities and central heating. Non-smoking. Children and pets are welcome. Parking is provided. Prices from £280 to £350 per week. All enquiries to **Martyn Dougherty, 23 East Murrayfield, Bannockburn, Stirling FK7 8HS (01786 814955).**
e-mail: martyn_d2@hotmail.com

See also Colour Display Advertisement

KESWICK

Lakeside Studio Apartments, Derwent Water Marina, Portinscale, Keswick. Three self-catering apartments, all with stunning views of the Lake and fells, are fully equipped for two or a couple and small child. They have en suite bath or shower, TV and stereo radio/CD, and make an extremely comfortable base for a family holiday, whether you are a sailing enthusiast, a fell walker or just want a relaxing time away from it all. Children are especially welcome, and a cot and high chair are available. The Marina is an ideal location for water or mountain-based activities, and facilities include changing rooms with showers, and a well-stocked chandlery. RYA sailing and windsurfing training centre; tuition available. Terms on request. Non-smoking. Pets welcome. For details please contact: **Derwent Water Marina, Portinscale, Keswick CA12 5RF (017687 72912) or visit our website: www.derwentwatermarina.co.uk**

See also Colour Display Advertisement

KIRKOSWALD

Crossfield Cottages and Leisure Fishing. Accessible secluded tranquil cottages overlooking two lakes, amidst Lakeland's beautiful Eden Valley countryside, only 30 minutes' drive from Ullswater, Hadrian's Wall, North Pennines and the Scottish Borders. Your beds freshly made for your arrival. Exclusive residents' coarse fishing; fly fishing on River Eden. Tranquillity and freedom to roam. Cottages are guaranteed clean, well-maintained and equipped. Centrally located. Exceptional wildlife and walking area. Relax and escape to your 'Home' in the country. Pets very welcome. **ETC ★★★** 24hr Brochure Line **Tel & Fax: 01768 898711**, bookings/availabilty 6pm to 10pm, or SAE to **Crossfield Cottages, Kirkoswald, Penrith CA10 1EU. Fax available.**

e-mail: info@crossfieldcottages.co.uk   website: www.crossfieldcottages.co.uk

HODYOAD COTTAGES

Hodyoad stands in its own private grounds, with extensive views of the surrounding fells in peaceful rural countryside. Mid-way between the beautiful Lakes of Loweswater and Ennerdale, six miles from Cockermouth and 17 from Keswick. Fell walking, boating, pony trekking and trout fishing can all be enjoyed within a three-and-a-half mile radius.

Each cottage is fully centrally heated and has two bedrooms to sleep five plus cot. All linen provided. Lounge with colour TV. Kitchen with fitted units, cooker and fridge. Bathroom with shower, washbasin, toilet, shaver point. Laundry room with washing machine and tumble dryer. Car essential, ample parking. Sea eight miles. Open all year. From £200 to £360 per week. For further details please contact:

Mrs J. A. Cook, Hodyoad House, Lamplugh, Cumbria CA14 4TT • Tel: 01946 861338

See also Colour Advertisement

LOWESWATER

Jenkinson Place Cottage, Loweswater. Sleeps 4. Jenkinson Place is a 17th century Lakeland farmstead, but no longer a working farm.

The holiday cottage has been carefully and tastefully constructed from a former stable building to provide a maximum of four guests plus infant with comfortable, modernised accommodation while retaining those traditional period features. The proprietors resident in the farmhouse are able to give guests personal help and attention if or when required. Linen not supplied. Sorry, no pets. Spectacular location for a quiet, relaxing holiday away from the crowds yet within easy reach of Crummock Water, Buttermere, Ennerdale, the old market town of Cockermouth, Keswick and the lovely West Cumbrian coast. Available May to September. Weekly terms from £135. Further details on request from **Mrs E.K. Bond, Jenkinson Place, Loweswater, Cockermouth CA13 0SU (01946 861748).** e-mail: alec.bond@virgin.net

MUNGRISDALE

Copy Hill, Mungrisdale, Penrith. An 18th century farm cottage, recently renovated to a high standard featuring oak beams and open fireplace. Situated in the quiet and unspoilt village of Mungrisdale overlooking the fells, eight miles from Keswick and 10 miles from Penrith. An ideal base for touring the Lakes or walking in the hills. Comprises comfortable lounge/dining room, fully equipped kitchen, cloakroom with shower, three bedrooms (two oubles and one twin), bathroom. Price from £230 to £400 per week including electricity, central heating, colour TV and bed linen. Ample parking. Sorry, no pets. Available all year. SAE or telephone for details. **Mrs Wilson, High Beckside, Mungrisdale, Penrith CA11 0XR (017687 79636).**

MUNGRISDALE

Mrs Weightman, Near Howe Hotel Cottages, Mungrisdale, Penrith CA11 0SH (017687 79678; Fax: 017687 79462). Grisdale View Cottage (sleeps four) is a beautifully converted old barn, with views over the fells. Living room with kitchen, dining area, cooker, microwave, fridge/freezer, toaster. Bathroom. Double and twin bedrooms. Garden. Children and pets welcome. Weekly rates from £160 to £280. Saddleback Barn (sleeps seven) is an outstanding property with two floors. It has spectacular views and is close to the North Lakes and Caldbeck Fells. Ground floor double and family bedrooms with private facilities. Boiler/store room ideal for drying clothes. First floor has double en suite bedroom. Large open plan lounge/kitchen area; colour TV, video, music centre, electric hob, microwave, fridge freezer, etc. Bed linen and electricity inclusive. Cot and high-chair available. Weekly rates from £300 to £500. ETC ★★★★ website: www.nearhowe.co.uk

PENRITH

Skirwith Hall Cottages. Escape to Eden! Get away from it all in one of two comfortable well-equipped cottages on dairy farm in the Eden Valley between the Lake District and the Pennine Dales. Set on the edge of the village of Skirwith in the shadow of Crossfell, the highest mountain in the Pennine range, the properties are maintained to the highest standard with every modern convenience. Accommodating two/five and five/eight people both cottages have riverside gardens and open fires. Well behaved children and pets welcome. ETC ★★★/★★★★. Please contact for brochure or see our website. **Mrs L. Wilson, Skirwith Hall, Skirwith, Penrith CA10 1RH (Tel & Fax: 01768 88241)**.
e-mail: idawilson@aol.com
website: www.eden-in-cumbria.co.uk/skirwith

SILLOTH-ON-SOLWAY

See also Colour Display Advertisement

Tanglewood Caravan Park, Causeway Head, Silloth-on-Solway CA7 4PE (016973 31253). Tanglewood is a family-run park on the fringes of the Lake District National Park. It is tree-sheltered and situated one mile inland from the small port of Silloth on the Solway Firth, with a beautiful view of the Galloway Hills. Large modern holiday homes are available from March to October, with car parking beside each home. Fully equipped except for bed linen, with end bedroom, central heating in bedrooms, electric lighting, hot and cold water, toilet, shower, gas fire, fridge and colour TV, all of which are included in the tariff. Touring pitches also available with electric hook-ups and water/drainage facilities, etc. Play area. Licensed lounge with adjoining children's play room. Pets welcome free but must be kept under control at all times. Full colour brochure available. ★★★, AA *THREE PENNANTS*.
e-mail: tanglewoodcaravanpark@hotmail.com   website: www.tanglewoodcaravanpark.co.uk

ULLSWATER

Beckside Cottage, Martindale, Ullswater. Sleeps 2/4. The cottage, which is part of the 17th century farmhouse, is set close to a babbling brook in the tiny hamlet of Sandwick. Situated on a traditional Lakeland farm surrounded by spectacular fells, Lake Ullswater only five minutes' walk away, making it an ideal retreat or base for walking. A cosy two-bedroomed cottage with oak beams and log fire awaits your arrival, with additional modern touches - oil central heating, fully fitted and well-equipped kitchen and shower; with books, videos and games to while away those evenings. A warm and friendly welcome is assured. Terms from £225 to £430 depending on season, short breaks available. Colour brochure available. ETC ★★★★. Please contact: **Andrew and Caroline Ivinson, Beckside Farm, Sandwick, Martindale, Penrith CA10 2NF (Tel & Fax: 017684 86239)**.
e-mail: ivinson_becksidefarm@hotmail.com

ENGLAND

Birthwaite Edge, Windermere

Situated in extensive grounds in one of the most exclusive areas of Windermere, 10 minutes from village and Lake, this is the perfect all year round holiday base. 10 self catering apartments for two to six people. Resident proprietors personally ensure the highest standards of cleanliness and comfort. Swimming pool open May to September. Colour TV. Well equipped kitchens. Hot water included. Coin metered electricity for lighting, cooking and electric fires. Background central heating during winter. Duvets and linen provided. High chairs and cots extra. Ample car parking. Regret, no smoking and no pets. Terms from £180 to £530.

Brochure from: **Bruce and Marsha Dodsworth, Birthwaite Edge, Birthwaite Road, Windermere LA23 1BS • Tel & Fax: 015394 42861 e-mail: fhg@lakedge.com • website: www.lakedge.com.**

See also Colour Advertisement

See also Colour Display Advertisement

ULLSWATER

The Estate Office, Patterdale Hall Estate, Glenridding, Penrith CA11 0PJ (017684 82308; Fax: 017684 82867). Our range includes three very comfortable large Coach Houses, two stone built Cottages with open fires, three three-bedroomed pine Lodges, six two-bedroomed cedar Chalets, a unique detached converted Dairy and two converted Bothies which make ideal, low cost accommodation for two people. All set in a private 300 acre estate between Lake Ullswater and Helvellyn and containing a working hill farm, a Victorian waterfall wood, private lake foreshore for guests to use for boating and fishing and 100 acres of designated ancient woodland for you to explore. Children welcome. Dogs by appointment in some of the accommodation. Colour TV, central heating, launderette, payphone; daytime electricity metered. Linen hire available. Weekly prices from £145 to £465. Please phone for full brochure.
ETC ★★ – ★★★. *NATIONAL ACCESSIBILITY SCHEME CATEGORY 3.* (Four properties.)
e-mail: welcome@patterdalehallestate.com   website: www.patterdalehallestate.com

---

See also Colour Display Advertisement

WINDERMERE

Lakelovers, Belmont House, Lake Road, Bowness-on-Windermere LA23 3BJ (015394 88855; Fax: 015394 88857). Quality holiday homes in England's beautiful Lake District. Over 200 ETC inspected and graded properties throughout the southern and central Lake District. Lakelovers are sure to have a property to meet your needs. **ETC ★★★ - ★★★★★**
e-mail: bookings@lakelovers.co.uk website: www.lakelovers.co.uk

---

PUBLISHER'S NOTE

While every effort is made to ensure accuracy, we regret that FHG Publications cannot accept responsibility for errors, misrepresentations or omissions in our entries or any consequences thereof. Prices in particular should be checked because we go to press early. We will follow up complaints but cannot act as arbiters or agents for either party.

DERBYSHIRE

ASHBOURNE

Derbyshire Cottages, Ashbourne . Derbyshire Cottages are set in the grounds of our 17th century Inn, overlooking the Staffordshire Moorlands. Very close to the Peak District, Dovedale, Alton Towers and the quaint town of Ashbourne. Each cottage is built of stone and has its own patio with tables and chairs overlooking open countryside. Fully fitted kitchen, including fridge and split-level cooker. Colour TV, radio and direct-dial telephone with baby listening. Children and pets welcome. Open Christmas and New Year. Call **Mary (01335 300202),** for further details. **website: www.dogandpartridge.co.uk**

BARLOW

Mill Farm Christian Holiday Cottages, Barlow. Five holiday cottages sleeping two to six, three having four-poster bed. Peacefully situated in 50 acres of conservation area on the edge of the Peak District. Fishing free with cottages, four trout, four coarse lakes and a brook. Snack cabin on site. Ideal base for walking. Shop and pub with meals 200 yards. Cottages equipped with central heating, colour TV, fridge/freezer, microwave, electric/gas cooker and shaver point. Linen provided. Launderette. Dogs welcome. Bus at gate. Open all year. Terms from £131 to £248. Three-day bookings accepted. Contact: **Naomi Ward, Mill Farm, Dronfield, Derbyshire S18 7TJ (0114-289 0543).**

BUXTON (Near)

Mr & Mrs C.J. Lawrenson, Grove House, Elkstones, Near Buxton SK17 0LU (01538 300487). Sleeps 2/3. Leave behind the crowds and traffic and stay in a delightful stone cottage, with original exposed beams, in the quiet Peak District village of Elkstones. Several public footpaths radiate from the village with the famous Dove Valley and Manifold Valley three to five miles away. Central for the market towns of Leek, Buxton and Ashbourne and for following the 'China Trail` in the Staffordshire Potteries, numerous National Trust properties and Alton Towers. Pubs/restaurant nearby. One double bedroom. Bed linen and towels supplied. Furnished and comprehensively equipped. Patio garden with sunny aspect. Parking close to cottage. Dog by arrangement. Short Breaks out of season. Brochure. Terms from £150 to £225. **ETC ★★★**
e-mail: elkstones@talk21.com

HARTINGTON

Hartington Cottages. Spacious picture-postcard cottage sleeping six in three en suite bedrooms, and two further cottages in private courtyard behind sleeping two/three. All three cottages totally up-graded in 2002; fully equipped kitchen with gloss work-tops and real granite sink; fully controllable central heating (included in rental). The larger cottage is over 500 years old and of cruck construction, extensive beams, inglenook fireplace and walls over two feet thick with stone mullion windows. The village, situated in the heart of the White Peak, has tea shops, gift shops and pub; only 300 yards from the River Dove. Two cycle trails under two miles away. **ETC ★★★★/★★★★★**. Contact: **Patrick and Frances Skemp, Cotterill Farm, Liffs Road, Biggin-by-Hartington, Buxton SK17 0DJ (01298 84447).**
e-mail: enquiries@hartingtoncottages.co.uk   website: www.hartingtoncottages.co.uk

---

Please mention Self-Catering Holidays in Britain
when enquiring about accommodation featured in these pages.

MILLDALE

Old Millers Cottage, Milldale, Near Ashbourne. Sleeps 2.
Situated in the beautiful hamlet of Milldale, beside the River Dove, with its famous Packhorse Bridge, the cottage is an ideal starting point for exploring the "Peak National Park". This cosy 18th century miller's cottage has been beautifully renovated to a very high standard, to retain all its charm and character, with exposed beams and featured limestone walls. Accommodation fully furnished and equipped except for linen. Pets welcome. Colour TV, electricity for storage heating and cooking included in the rental of £190 to £210 per week. Open all year. **ETC ★★★**. Details on request from: **Mrs P.M. Hewitt, 45 Portway Drive, Tutbury, Burton-on-Trent, Staffordshire DE13 9HU (01283 815895).**

PEAK DISTRICT

Shatton Hall Farm Cottages, Peak District. Sleep 4-6.
THREE COTTAGES, INCL. £250–£425 PER WEEK. We offer a quiet and peaceful setting on this Elizabethan farmstead, in the centre of a superb walking, climbing and caving area. We have extensive gardens, way-marked field and woodland farm walks, a trout lake and hard tennis court on the farm. Each of our three stone cottages has individual character, beamed livingroom, open gas fire or wood burning stove, well set out new kitchen and bathroom with shower. Ample parking, safe play areas and a visitors laundry. TOWNFIELD BARN is a newly converted facility for Group Activities such as Creative Art, Craft, Nature Study (Programme 2002) and for specialist groups to hire with our cottage accommodation. This beautifully situated barn has a kitchen, toilet, cloakroom and two large rooms with a wood burning stove, opening to superb views. Tariff and course details on application. **ETC ★★★★. Angela Kellie, Shatton Hall Farm, Bamford, Hope Valley S33 0BG (01433 620635; Fax: 01433 620689).**
e-mail: ahk@peakfarmholidays.co.uk   website: www.peakfarmholidays.co.uk

PEAK DISTRICT (Near Buxton)

Sutton, Peak District (Near Buxton). Sleep 4 plus 2.
Cottage conversions on peaceful 32 acre smallholding on the edge of the Peak District, within easy reach of Bakewell, Chatsworth Hall, Tatton Park, Jodrell Bank and the Silk Museum at Macclesfield. Ideal for a relaxing or active holiday, mountain bikes are available for hire and there are lovely walks in the surrounding countryside. Each cottage has double, bunk room and toilet upstairs with sofa bed in sitting/diningroom, TV, shower room. Excellently furnished and equipped throughout, with heating, electricity, bedlinen and towels included in the price. Two pets welcome. Terms from £180 weekly. Short Breaks available. Further details from **Greg and Sue Rowson, Lower Pethills Farm, Higher Sutton, Macclesfield, Cheshire SK11 0NJ (01260 252410).**

TADDINGTON

Judith Hawley, Ash Tree Barn, Taddington, near Buxton SK17 9UB (01298 85453). Ash Tree Barn offers comfortable accommodation in a self-contained wing of a newly converted nineteenth century barn in a quiet, unspoilt village. The village sits midway between the famous spa town of Buxton and the ancient market town of Bakewell. Taddington makes an ideal base for exploring the Peak District by car or cycle and has many wonderful local walks. The accommodation comprises living room with exposed beams and log burning stove; bright kitchen with electric cooker, microwave, fridge and ironing facilities; spacious hallway, double bedroom with en suite bath/shower room; off-road parking. Terms from £175 to £250 per week.
e-mail: jah@ashtreebarn.fsnet.co.uk

DEVON

See also Colour Display Advertisement

UNIVERSITY ACCOMMODATION & FACILITIES

Budget accommodation or fully tailored packages (0870 712 5002; Fax: 020 7017 8273). En suite designer halls across the UK. Groups of any age or size. Sports facilities all year. Tell us your needs and we'll find a location and package to suit.
e-mail: enquiries@thesummervillage.com
website: www.thesummervillage.com

See also Colour Display Advertisement

Holiday Homes & Cottages S.W (01803 663650; Fax: 01803 664037). Large selection of cottages in Devon and Cornwall. Pets welcomed. ETC rated. Coastal and rural locations.
website: www.swcottages.co.uk

See also Colour Display Advertisement

North Devon Holiday Homes, 19 Cross Street, Barnstaple EX31 1BD (01271 376322 (24 hrs); Fax: 01271 346544). Easily the best choice of cottages in Devon and comfortably the best value. Contact us now for a free colour guide and unbiased recommendation service to the 400 best value cottages around Exmoor and Devon's unspoilt National Trust Coast. Bargain breaks from only £35 per person to luxury manor house for 16 from only £995 per week.
e-mail: info@northdevonholidays.co.uk
website: www.northdevonholidays.co.uk

See also Colour Display Advertisement

Devoncoast Holidays. We are a highly experienced holiday letting agency on Devon's sunny south coast. We have numerous properties on our books ranging from one-bedroom flats to large three bedroomed houses, all in sunny South Devon. We have personally inspected all of our properties and all of the accommodation is of a high standard and comes fully equipped with colour TV, microwave, full cooker and car parking. Our properties are available all year round, for mini breaks or for full week lettings. Pets and children are welcome. Many have a flat access. All of our properties are within easy reach of the coast, some have sea views. We accept all credit cards. Please telephone for a free brochure and map - 24 hour operation. **Devoncoast Holidays, P.O. Box 14, Brixham, Devon TQ5 8AB (Tel & Fax: 07050 338889).**
website: www.devoncoast.com

See also Colour Display Advertisement

APPLEDORE

Waters Reach, West Quay, 71 Irsha Street, Appledore. LOCATION! LOCATION! LOCATION! Stunning uninterrupted views across the twin estuaries of the rivers Taw and Torridge. This Georgian, three storey house enjoys a fine location on West Quay. A well-fitted kitchen with breakfast room off, a separate diningroom, comfortable elegant drawing room, two good bedrooms, two good-sized bathrooms. Bedding can be supplied and beds made up. It has ideal sheltered accommodation out of season, as well as during the summer months. Contact: **Viv or Peter Foley (01707 657644).**
e-mail: viv@vfoley.freeserve.co.uk

ENGLAND

ASHBURTON

Mrs Angela Bell, Wooder Manor, Widecombe-in-the-Moor, Near Ashburton TQ13 7TR (Tel & Fax: 01364 621391). Cottages and converted coach house, on 160-acre working family farm nestled in the picturesque valley of Widecombe, surrounded by unspoilt woodland, moors and granite tors. Half-a-mile from village with post office, general stores, inn with dining room, church and National Trust Information Centre. Excellent centre for touring Devon with a variety of places to visit and exploring Dartmoor by foot or on horseback. Accommodation is clean and well equipped with colour TV, central heating, laundry room. Children welcome. Large gardens and courtyard for easy parking. Open all year, so take advantage of off-season reduced rates. Short Breaks also available. Two properties suitable for disabled visitors. Brochure available. **ETC ★★★**

e-mail: angela@woodermanor.com   website: www.woodermanor.com

ASHWATER

Braddon Cottages, Ashwater, Beaworthy EX21 5EP (Tel & Fax: 01409 211350). Six secluded cottages in quiet countryside of meadow and woodland, on 500 acre site. Four barn conversions and two purpose-built houses surrounded by gardens and lawns, with views over lake to Dartmoor. All-weather tennis court; adults' snooker room and children's games room. Very comfortable, with gas central heating, wood fires, dishwashers, washing machines, clothes dryers, microwaves, colour TVs, videos and payphones. Bed linen and towels supplied. Pleasant walks; large summer house with barbecue; free fishing. Licensed shop. Package holidays available for one or two weeks, including transfer to/from West Country stations and airports. Open all year. Credit cards accepted. Brochure available. Resident owners **George and Anne Ridge. ETC ★★★**

e-mail: holidays@braddoncottages.co.uk   website: www.braddoncottages.co.uk

AXMINSTER

Cider Room Cottage, Hasland Farm, Membury, Axminster. Sleeps 4. This delightfully converted thatched cider barn, with exposed beams, adjoins main farmhouse overlooking the outstanding beauty of the orchards, pools and pastureland, and is ideally situated for touring Devon, Dorset and Somerset. Bathing, golf and tennis at Lyme Regis and many places of interest locally, including Wildlife Park, donkey sanctuary and Forde Abbey. Membury Village, with its post office and stores, trout farm, church and swimming pool is one mile away. The accommodation is of the highest standard with the emphasis on comfort. Two double rooms, cot if required; shower room and toilet; sitting/diningroom with colour TV; kitchen with electric cooker, microwave, fridge. Linen supplied if required. Pets by arrangement. Car essential. Open all year. No smoking. Terms from £135 to £270. **ETC ★★★★.** SAE, please, to **Mrs Pat Steele, Hasland Farm, Membury, Axminster EX13 7JF (01404 881558).**

North Hill Cottages, North Devon

Surround yourself in rolling hills at **North Hill Cottages, Barnstaple** where 17th century farm buildings have been sympathetically converted into cottages with exposed beams and wood stoves. Enjoy the peace and tranquillity that North Hill offers with its abundance of wildlife ranging from squirrels and badgers to deer. North Hill is central for many activities, be it shopping, walking, cycling, visiting the local attractions or just relaxing on our vast sandy beaches at Croyde and Woolacombe. Facilities include: Indoor heated swimming pool, toddlers pool, spa, solarium, sauna, all weather tennis court, badminton/volleyball court, fitness room, games room,children's play area and BBQs.

NORTH HILL COTTAGES

For a free colour brochure please telephone Best Leisure on 01271 850 611 or fax: 01271 850 693 or visit our website at www.bestleisure.co.uk or write to us at: Best Leisure, North Hill, Shirwell, Barnstaple,Devon, EX31 4LG.

BARNSTAPLE (Exmoor)

Hillcroft, Natsley Farm, Brayford, Barnstaple. This bungalow is an ideal holiday centre, being near the moors and within easy reach of the coasts. Hillcroft is situated beside a quiet country road in the Exmoor National Park. Lovely walks, touring, pony trekking available locally or just relax and enjoy the glorious views. Lawn at front and back of bungalow. Three double bedrooms and cot available. Sittingroom, dining room; bathroom, toilet; kitchen with electric cooker. Available all year round. Electric heating metered. Everything supplied except linen. Terms from £95 to £250 weekly. Please apply to **Mrs M.E. Williams, Natsley Farm, Brayford, Barnstaple EX32 7QR (01598 710358).**

BIDEFORD

Honeysuckle Cottage, Weare-Giffard, Bideford. Sleeps 4-6. Honeysuckle is a picturesque thatched property, comfortably and tastefully furnished, with many original features including inglenook fireplace, wall lighting, beams etc. Fully centrally heated; two bedrooms (family room and twin-bedded room); enclosed front garden with patio and garden furniture. Free off-road parking. Weare-Giffard lies on the river, off the A386, twixt Bideford and Torrington. Village inn five minutes' walk, golf course one mile and Tarka Trail for cycling easily accessible from the village. Rosemoor (RHS) Gardens three and a half miles, equally not far from the coast and other attractions. Terms £140 to £395 per week excluding gas/electricity. Open all year. Contact: **Mrs Curtis, "Bracken Haven", Weare-Giffard, Bideford EX39 4QR (01237 472918).**

BRADWORTHY

Mrs L Lewin, Lake House Cottages and B&B, Lake Villa, Bradworthy EX22 7SQ (01409 241962; Fax: 01409 241579). Come and stay in one of our four cosy, character cottages in peaceful countryside, half-a-mile from Bradworthy village square in this hidden corner of Devon. Perfectly situated to explore the spectacular coastline of North Devon and Cornwall as well as the West Country moors. There are also several gardens within reach (Rosemoor, Eden Project) and other places of interest. The cottages sleep six, four, three and two and are well-furnished and fitted with everything you will need for a great cottage holiday. There are also two B&B rooms available in our own home. Tennis court and gardens. Pets welcome. **ETC ★★★**
e-mail: info@lakevilla.co.uk   **website: www.lakevilla.co.uk**

FHG

Visit the FHG website
www.holidayguides.com
for details of the wide choice of accommodation
featured in the full range of FHG titles

Devoncourt is a development of 24 self-contained flats, occupying one of the finest positions in Torbay, with unsurpassed views. At night the lights of Torbay are like a fairyland to be enjoyed from your very own balcony.

EACH FLAT HAS:

Marina views	Heating	Sea Views over Torbay
Private balcony	Own front door	Separate bathroom and toilet
Separate bedroom	Bed-settee in lounge	Lounge sea views over Marina
Kitchenette - all electric	Private car park	Opposite beach
Colour television	Overlooks lifeboat	Short walk to town centre
Double glazing	Open all year	Mini Breaks October to April

DEVONCOURT HOLIDAY FLATS, BERRYHEAD ROAD, BRIXHAM, TQ5 9AB. Tel: 01803 853748
Fax: 01803 855775   www.devoncourt.net
Outside business hours telephone: 07050 338889

VISA
MasterCard

BRIXHAM

Brixham Holiday Homes, South Devon. We are an independent agency offering a selection of self-catering fishermen's cottages and town houses around beautiful Brixham harbour. Most of our properties have spectacular sea and harbour views. Brixham offers plenty to do for all the family - a working fishing port, outdoor seawater swimming pool, secluded coves and the Berry Head Country Park. Call **0870 071 3344; Fax: 01803 851773** for our brochure.
e-mail: info@brixhamholidayhomes.co.uk
website: www.brixhamholidayhomes.co.uk

CHUDLEIGH

Finlake Holiday Park, Chudleigh TQ13 0EJ (01626 853833; Fax: 01626 854031). 130 acres to explore. Self-catering accommodation and holiday homes for sale. Amenities include: restaurant and takeaway, licensed bar, family entertainment, indoor and outdoor swimming pools, children's indoor and outdoor activities, coarse fishing, fitness suite, outdoor tennis courts, 9-hole pitch and putt, horse riding.
website: www.haulfryn.co.uk

COLYTON

Church Approach Cottages, Farway, Colyton EX24 6EQ. Sleep 5/6. Situated beside the village church, the cottages have been tastefully renovated to maintain the old style of the barn. With panoramic views over the Coly valley, they provide a quiet holiday and offer many interesting walks. A countryside park, riding stables and ancient monuments are all within walking distance. Honiton Golf Course, swimming pool and bowling green are four miles away. Lyme Regis, Sidmouth and Exmouth plus many other quaint scenic coastal resorts are all within half an hour's drive. Each cottage has a modern kitchen complete with washing machine and microwave as well as a conventional cooker, comfortable lounge with colour TV and video, two bedrooms and bathroom with bath and shower. Central heating. Electricity by £1 meter. Bed linen supplied. Brochure on request. Bed and Breakfast available at our farmhouse. For further details please contact: **Sheila Lee (01404 871383/871202; Fax: 01404 871233). e-mail: lizlee@eclipse.co.uk**

See also Colour Display Advertisement

COMBE MARTIN

Wheel Farm Country Cottages, Berry Down, Combe Martin, Devon EX34 0NT (01271 882100; Fax: 01271 883120). High quality conversion of 18th century watermill and barns into cosy, centrally heated, well-equipped accommodation with great rustic charm, surrounded by 11 acres of tranquil award-winning grounds, views of Exmoor, near North Devon's superb beaches. Indoor heated pool, sauna, fitness room, tennis court, playground, four-posters, log fires, dishwashers, TV and video, bed linen, cots and high chairs, midweek maid service, fresh flowers, laundry room, provision service, babysitting. Nearby: riding, cycling, walking, golf, sea and lake fishing, surfing, family attractions, historic houses and gardens. 8 cottages and 2 apartments (sleep 2 to 6 +cot). Open February to October. Low Season short breaks available. Sorry, no pets. **ETC ★★★★ e-mail: holidays@wheelfarmcottages.co.uk   website: www.wheelfarmcottages.co.uk**

COMBE MARTIN

Yetland Farm Cottages, near Combe Martin. Our six luxury 18th century barn conversions situated around a flower filled courtyard, sleep from 2 to 6 persons plus a cot, and are extremely well equipped. With 18 acres of fields, and nearly one mile of cut paths, there is plenty of room to exercise yourself and your dog, relax and enjoy our stunning views across to South Wales. Between trips to Exmoor and Devon's wonderful sandy surfing beaches, you could relax in our spa bath, play table tennis or pool in one of our games rooms. Our large children's play area and tennis court are always a favourite. **ETC ★★★★.** Contact: **Alison & Alan Balcombe, Yetland Farm, Berry Down, Combe Martin EX34 0NT (01271 883655). e-mail: enquiries@yetlandcottages.co.uk website: www.yetlandcottages.co.uk**

See also Colour Display Advertisement

DARTMOOR NATIONAL PARK

Badger's Holt, Dartmeet, Dartmoor PL20 6SG (01364 631213; Fax: 01364 631475). Luxury self catering holiday accommodation nestling by the River Dart at the foot of Yar Tor adjacent to the famous Badger's Holt tea rooms – a traditional Devonshire cream tea not to be missed! Three purpose-built apartments all fully equipped and maintained to the highest standard. "Bench Tor" has two bedrooms and sleeps four, "Yar Tor" has three bedrooms and two bathrooms and sleeps from six to eight. Accommodation available all year. Pets welcome. Tea rooms open March to October.

ENGLAND

Dawlish Warren
Sunny South
Devon • EX7 0PH

request a free colour brochure:

Tel: 01626 862070
Email: fun@welcomefamily.co.uk

See also Colour Advertisement

Pets Welcome

Discover the best in family holidays right on the glorious South Devon coast.

Why not visit our fun-filled website and see for yourself why so many of our guests come back year after year!

www.welcomefamily.co.uk

DARTMOUTH
Mrs Ridalls, The Old Bakehouse, 7 Broadstone, Dartmouth TQ6 9NR (Tel & Fax: 01803 834585; mobile: 07909 680884). Five character cottages with free parking, one with private parking. Cottages are in the centre of Dartmouth, two minutes' walk from river Dart, Royal Avenue Gardens, Coronation Park, shops and restaurants. The beautiful Blackpool Sands is a 15 minute drive away. The historic town of Dartmouth is a good centre for boating, fishing, sailing and swimming. National Trust, coastal and inland walks. Four cottages with beams and old stone fireplaces, one with four-poster bed. Open all year. Central heating. Specialising in Autumn, Winter and Spring Breaks. Babysitting available. Pets welcome free. Terms from £180 to £695. ETC ★★★

DAWLISH
Mrs F. E. Winston, "Sturwood", 1 Oak Park Villas, Dawlish EX7 0DE (01626 862660). Comfortable, self-contained holiday flats accommodating 2-6. Each flat has own bathroom, 1/2 bedrooms; colour television. Garden. Parking. Full Fire Certificate. Leisure centre and beach close by. Pets welcome.

When making enquiries please mention FHG Publications

DAWLISH WARREN

Oakcliff Holiday Park, Mount Pleasant Road, Dawlish Warren, South Devon EX7 0ND (01626 863347). Award-winning self catering holidays on the glorious South Devon coast. Lodges, chalets, caravans and apartments. Heated outdoor pool with slide. Club with live family entertainment. Please contact us for a colour brochure and information. *ROSE AWARD, DAVID BELLAMY CONSERVATION GOLD AWARD.* ETC ★★★★
website: www.oakcliff.co.uk

EXMOUTH

Raleigh Holiday Homes. Comfortable family flats and house sleeping 2-11 people in quiet road near sea and shops. One home suitable for wheelchair. Dogs by arrangement. Terms reasonable £220 to £650 per week inclusive. Open mid-June to mid-September only. Please write or telephone: **Mrs C. E. Duncan (Dept FHG), 24 Raleigh Road, Exmouth, Devon EX8 2SB (01395 266967).**

HOLSWORTHY

Dairy Cottage

Dairy Cottage and Beech Barn. Situated on our farm in a quiet and peaceful location, yet within easy reach of the North Devon and North Cornwall Coasts. Close to many other attractions including Clovelly, Tintagel, Boscastle, Widemouth Sands, Dartmoor and Bodmin, plus the Eden Project is only an hour's drive away. You are welcome to walk our farmlands or just relax. Both cottages are furnished to a high standard, with two bedrooms (one double and one twin), bathroom with wc and bath/shower. Lounge/kitchen/diner with woodburner, colour TV, video (Beech Barn also has a DVD player), radio/cassette/CD, auto washing machine/dryer, dishwasher, microwave, fridge/freezer. Bed linen (duvets), towels and electricity inclusive, central heating extra. A cot can be provided on request. Contact: **Derek and Annie Griffiths, Bagbeare, Thornbury, Holsworthy, Devon EX22 7DF (Tel & Fax: 01409 261437).**
e-mail: griff.bagbeare@virgin.net

website: www.selfcatering-devon.com

HOPE COVE

Mike and Judy Tromans, Hope Barton Barns, Hope Cove, Near Salcombe TQ7 3HT (01548 561393). Sleep 2/10. Nestling in its own valley, close to the sandy cove, Hope Barton Barns is an exclusive group of 17 stone barns in two courtyards and three luxury apartments in the converted farmhouse. Superbly furnished and fully equipped accommodation ranges from a studio to four bedrooms. Heated indoor pool, sauna, gym, lounge bar, tennis court, trout lake and a children's play barn. We have 35 acres of pastures and streams. Farmhouse meals from our menu. Ample parking. Golf, sailing and coastal walks nearby. Open all year. A perfect setting for family Summer holidays, a week's walking in Spring/Autumn or just a get away from it all break. Free range children and well behaved dogs welcome.
Open all year. For a colour brochure please contact **Mike or Judy.** ★★★★
website: www.hopebarton.co.uk

Unpretentious and comfortable. Dogs welcome with well-behaved owners. Relax in a setting so peaceful, you can actually hear the silence!

Beachdown

Comfortable, fully-equipped, detached cedarwood chalets with parking alongside. Just 150 yards from the beach and the South West Coastal Path. Beachdown is located within the beautiful South Hams area of South Devon. Nestled within a private and level secluded site of over two and a half acres. A stress busting stay is always on the cards.

•••••• *Short Breaks Available* ••••••

Call Nigel/Gareth for a brochure on **01548 810089** *or visit our website.*

CHALLABOROUGH BAY, KINGSBRIDGE, SOUTH DEVON TQ7 4JB
Tel: 01548 810089 • e-mail: enquires@beachdown.co.uk • website: www.beachdown.co.uk

---

Nuckwell Cottage
Churchstow, Near Kingsbridge TQ7 4NZ
Tel: 01548 550368

Picturesque stone-built cottage, sleeps 5, in peaceful and secluded setting, bordered by fields and cider orchards. Recently refurbished and retaining many of the original features, such as stone and timber floors and old beams, but with the benefit of central heating. Fully fitted kitchen with Aga (for the winter months), granite worktops, dishwasher, microwave, etc. Lounge with log burner, TV and video. Bedrooms: one double, one twin, one single. Bedding, electricity, heating and logs all inclusive. Near to beautiful sandy beaches, fantastic pubs and golf courses, etc. Exclusively for non-smokers. Sorry, no pets. Telephone for brochure and prices. *Terms from £295 to £710 per week.*

See also Colour Display Advertisement

INSTOW

Tides Reach Cottage. Seafront cottage – photo shows view from garden of sandy beach and sea. Parking by the cottage. Instow is a quiet seaside village; shops, pubs and restaurants serving meals overlooking the water. Cottage has 3 bedrooms, enclosed garden, many sea views. Colour TV, washing machine, coastal walks. Dogs welcome. Other sea front cottages available. Please send SAE for colour brochure of this and other sea edge cottages to **S.T. Barnes, 140 Bay View Road, Northam, Bideford EX39 1BJ (or phone 01237 473801 for prices and dates).**

KINGSBRIDGE (Near)
Mill Cottage, Marsh Mills, Aveton Gifford, Kingsbridge TQ7 4JW (Tel & Fax: 01548 550549). In the beautiful Avon Valley, four miles from Kingsbridge, eight miles south of Dartmoor, Mill Cottage offers single-storey holiday accommodation for two to three people (children 12 years and over) and well-trained dogs. Bedroom with double and single beds, en suite bathroom with separate WC. Large, well-equipped kitchen with electric cooker, combination microwave, refrigerator and freezer. Lounge/dining room with sofa-bed, colour TV and video. This room, which overlooks the mill race and pond, opens on to a private, south-facing sun terrace. We have large gardens and orchard, which you are welcome to share. Electric storage radiators plus electric fire in lounge. Rates £250/£300 per week all inclusive.
e-mail: **Newsham@Marshmills.co.uk**
website: **www.Marshmills.co.uk**

ENGLAND

MOORLANDS

Woody Bay, Devon EX31 4RA

Where countryside and comfort combine, two self-contained apartments within a family-run guest house sleeping two or three persons. Our ground floor apartment is one bedroom, lounge, kitchen and bathroom and has its own entrance and private patio area. The second apartment is on the first floor, comprising two bedrooms, lounge with screened kitchen and shower room. The house is set in six acres of garden surrounded by Exmoor countryside. Guests are welcome to use all hotel amenities, including the bar, dining room and outdoor swimming pool. Dogs welcome with well-behaved owners.

Telephone: **01598 763224** for brochure

www.moorlandshotel.co.uk

See also Colour Advertisement

NEWTON ABBOT

Mrs M. A. Gale, Twelve Oaks Holiday Cottages, Twelve Oaks Farm, Teigngrace, Newton Abbot TQ12 6QT (Tel & Fax: 01626 352769). Working farm, join in. Sleeps 4. Join us at one of the two carefully converted cottages on our 220 acre beef farm, bordered by the River Teign, on the edge of the village of Teigngrace. Each self-contained cottage has one double and one twin room with bathroom and shower room. Heating, TV, fridge, microwave and laundry facilties. Parking. Children welcome. Non-smoking accommodation available. Find us off the A38 Expressway. Rates from £250 to £450. **ETC ★★★** *HOLIDAY COTTAGES*. Also Twelve Oaks Caravan Park (**ETC ★★★★**) with electric hook-ups, TV hook-ups and awnings available. Hot water, shower, pets and swimming pool free of charge.

OFFWELL (near Honiton)

Offwell Mews, Offwell House, Offwell EX14 9SA (01404 831794). Self-catering units within a converted stable block with access to the grounds of a country house. Easy reach of sea - World Heritage Jurassic Coast - and surrounded by beautiful countryside with interesting walks, cycle ways and a choice of golf courses. Ideal for a relaxing break. Units are fully equipped with cooker, microwave, dishwasher etc. and all bedrooms are en suite. Choice of one or two bedrooms and a level access apartment for guests with mobility problems. Light, heating, hot water and linen are all provided. Good private parking. Dogs welcome by arrangement. Non-smoking. Flexible booking arrangements. Please send for a leaflet. Terms from £225 per week. Open all year. Short breaks available.

OKEHAMPTON

East Hook Cottages. An outstanding location in the heart of Devon, with a beautiful panoramic view of the Dartmoor National Park, on the Tarka Trail and Devon Coast to Coast Cycle Route. Three comfortably furnished country cottages with exposed beams, log fire and full of character. Sleep 2/6. Quiet and peaceful, set in own large grounds with garden furniture. Ample parking. Very accessible, one mile from Okehampton, less than two miles from Dartmoor, three miles from the A30. The most central point for leisure In the West Country. Children and pets welcome. Open all year. Flexible short breaks. Terms £145 to £395 per week. Guests return yearly! **Mrs M.E. Stevens, West Hook Farm, Okehampton EX20 1RL (01837 52305).** e-mail: marystevens@westhookfarm.fsnet.co.uk

---

TWO Adult tickets for the price of one at

Coldharbour Mill Visitor Centre & Museum

see our READERS' OFFER VOUCHER for full details

SEATON

Mrs E.P. Fox, "West Ridge", Harepath Hill, Seaton EX12 2TA (Tel & Fax: 01297 22398).Sleeps 3/4. "West Ridge" bungalow stands on elevated ground above the small coastal town of Seaton. It has one-and-a-half-acres of lawns and gardens and enjoys wide panoramic views of the beautiful Axe Estuary and the sea. Close by are Axmouth, Beer and Branscombe. The Lyme Bay area is an excellent centre for touring, walking, sailing, fishing, golf, etc. This comfortably furnished accommodation is ideally suited for two to four persons. Cot can be provided. Available March to October, £195 to £425 weekly (fuel charges included). Full gas central heating. Colour TV. SAE for brochure. **ETC ★★★.**
e-mail: foxfamily@westridge.fsbusiness.co.uk
website: www.cottageguide.co.uk/westridge

SIDMOUTH

Sweetcombe Cottage Holidays, Rosemary Cottage, Weston, Near Sidmouth EX10 0PH (01395 512130; Fax: 01395 515680). Attractive, carefully selected coastal cottages, farmhouses and flats in Sidmouth and East Devon. Please ask for our colour brochure.
e-mail: enquiries@sweetcombe-ch.co.uk
website: www.sweetcombe-ch.co.uk

SOUTH MOLTON

Mike and Rose Courtney, West Millbrook, Twitchen, South Molton EX36 3LP (01598 740382). Properties sleep 2/8. Adjoining Exmoor. Two fully-equipped bungalows and one farmhouse annexe in lovely surroundings bordering Exmoor National Park. Ideal for touring North Devon and West Somerset including moor and coast with beautiful walks, lovely scenery and many other attractions. North Molton village is only one mile away. All units have electric cooker, fridge/freezer, microwave and colour TV; two bungalows also have washing machines. Children's play area; cots and high chairs available free. Linen hire available. Games room. Car parking. Central heating if required. Electricity metered. Out of season short breaks. Weekly prices from £70 to £375. Colour brochure available. **ETC ★★/★★★**
e-mail: wmbselfcatering@aol.com   website: www.westcountrynow.com

SOUTH MOLTON (near)

Court Green, Bishop's Nympton, Near South Molton. Sleeps 5. A most attractive, well-equipped, south-facing cottage with large garden, on the edge of the village of Bishop's Nympton, three miles from South Molton. Ideal holiday centre, easy reach of Exmoor, the coast, sporting activities and places of interest. Three bedrooms - one double, one twin-bedded with washbasin and one single. Two bathrooms with toilets. Sitting and dining rooms, large kitchen. Central heating, electric wood/coal effect fires, TV. One mile sea trout/trout fishing on River Mole. Well behaved pets welcome. Terms April to October £200 to £240. **Mrs J. Greenwell, Tregeiriog, Near Llangollen, North Wales LL20 7HU (01691 600672).**

Please mention Self-Catering Holidays in Britain
when enquiring about accommodation
featured in these pages.

TORQUAY

Atherton Holiday Flats, 41 Morgan Avenue, Torquay TQ2 5RR (01803 296884). A warm welcome is assured at Atherton. Run by an ex-Yorkshire couple who still give the famous Yorkshire hospitality. We aim for high standards particularly regarding cleanliness. Our self-contained flats are modern and comfortable with own showers and toilets. Very centrally located being 300 yards from town centre. Riviera Centre and beach within walking distance. Flats sleep 2-4 people, have bed linen provided, microwave and colour TV. Car parking. Open all year with out of season short breaks available. Reasonable rates with prices from £80 per week for two people. Full central heating included in price. Brochure from resident proprietors **Beatrice and Terry Kaye.**

TORQUAY

Atlantis Holiday Apartments, Solsbro Road, Chelston, Torquay TQ2 6PF (01803 607929). Close to the seafront, Riviera Centre and Cockington. Dishwasher, washer/dryer, video and CD/stereo in all apartments. Linen and towels included. NO PETS! NO SMOKING! NO WASHING UP! Open all year. ETC ★★★
e-mail: enquiry@atlantistorquay.co.uk
website: www.atlantistorquay.co.uk

See also Colour Display Advertisement

TORQUAY

Sunningdale Apartments, 11 Babbacombe Downs Road, Torquay TQ1 3LF. Spacious one and two bedroom apartments. All self-contained with bathroom with shower. Separate fitted kitchens, many apartments with stunning sea views over Lyme Bay. All are fully equipped with everything necessary for guests to enjoy the highest levels of comfort and convenience. Large private car park. Laundry room. Fully double glazed with central heating. Level walk to shops and restaurant, bars and theatre, and most sporting activities. Close to beaches and moors. Excellent touring centre for south west. Terms from £195 to £595 per week. **ETC ★★★.** For brochure and further details please telephone: **Mrs H. Carr (01803 325786; Fax: 01803 326911).**
website: www.sunningdaleapartments.co.uk

WOOLACOMBE

Mrs B.A. Watts, Resthaven Holiday Flats, The Esplanade, Woolacombe EX34 7DJ (01271 870248). Situated on the sea front opposite the beautiful Combesgate Beach, with uninterrupted views of the coastline. Two self-contained flats – ground floor sleeps five, first floor sleeps nine. Family, double and single bedrooms, all with washbasins. Comfortable lounges with sea views, colour TV and videos. Fully equipped electric kitchens. Bathrooms have bath and shower. Electricity by £1 meter. Payphone. Free lighting, parking, hot water and laundry facility. Terms from £160 to £800 per week. Please write, or phone, for brochure.

When making enquiries or bookings, a stamped addressed envelope is always appreciated

ENGLAND

WOOLACOMBE

Chichester House Holiday Apartments, The Esplanade, Woolacombe EX34 7DJ (Tel: 01271 870761). Quiet, relaxing, fully furnished apartments situated opposite Barricane Shell Beach – central seafront position with outstanding sea and coastal views. Equipment including colour TV, fridge, cooker etc. Watch the sun go down into the sea from your own balcony. Open all year. Free parking. Pets by arrangement. Off-peak reductions. Short Break details on request. SAE to resident proprietor, **Mrs Joyce Bagnall.**

WOOLACOMBE

Cliffside Sea Front Holiday Flats. Sleep 2-6. Self-catering flats providing well-equipped comfortable accommodation. Spectacular views overlooking Baggy Point, Hartland Point and Lundy Island. Surrounded by National Trust with many coastal walks, four minutes' walk to village, two minutes' walk to beach. Pleasant garden and car parking. Reduced rates for early and late season. SAE please to **Peter and Avril Bowen, Cliffside, The Esplanade, Woolacombe EX34 7DJ (01271 870210).** **e-mail: avril.bowen@cliffside.fsworld.co.uk**

•• *Some Useful Guidance for Guests and Hosts* ••

Every year literally thousands of holidays, short breaks and overnight stops are arranged through our guides, the vast majority without any problems at all. In a handful of cases, however, difficulties do arise about bookings, which often could have been prevented from the outset.

It is important to remember that when accommodation has been booked, both parties – guests and hosts – have entered into a form of contract. We hope that the following points will provide helpful guidance.

GUESTS:
- When enquiring about accommodation, be as precise as possible. Give exact dates, numbers in your party and the ages of any children.
- State the number and type of rooms wanted and also what catering you require – bed and breakfast, full board etc. Make sure that the position about evening meals is clear – and about pets, reductions for children or any other special points.
- Read our reviews carefully to ensure that the proprietors you are going to contact can supply what you want. Ask for a letter confirming all arrangements, if possible.
- If you have to cancel, do so as soon as possible. Proprietors do have the right to retain deposits and under certain circumstances to charge for cancelled holidays if adequate notice is not given and they cannot re-let the accommodation.

HOSTS:
- Give details about your facilities and about any special conditions. Explain your deposit system clearly and arrangements for cancellations, charges etc. and whether or not your terms include VAT.
- If for any reason you are unable to fulfil an agreed booking without adequate notice, you may be under an obligation to arrange suitable alternative accommodation or to make some form of compensation.

While every effort is made to ensure accuracy, we regret that FHG Publications cannot accept responsibility for errors, omissions or misrepresentations in our entries or any consequences thereof. Prices in particular should be checked because we go to press early. We will follow up complaints but cannot act as arbiters or agents for either party.

DORSET

ENGLAND

A map of Dorset and surrounding counties (Somerset, Wiltshire) showing major towns including Bridgwater, Taunton, Yeovil, Sherborne, Blandford Forum, Dorchester, Weymouth, Poole, Bournemouth, Swanage, and various road routes (A35, A37, A303, A30, A31, A354).

©MAPS IN MINUTES™ 2003 ©Crown Copyright. Ordnance Survey 2003

DORSET COTTAGE HOLIDAYS

Large selection of graded self catering cottages, bungalows, town houses and apartments, all within 10 miles of the heritage coastline and sandy beaches. Excellent walking in idyllic countryside, pets welcome. All fully modernised retaining many olde features, open fires and exposed beams and enjoying panoramic views of coastline and countryside. Open all year, 1 to 4 bedrooms, sleeping from 2-10 guests. From £135 per week per cottage. Short breaks available.   ETC★★★/★★★★

SOUTHERN TOURIST BOARD

Free brochure: 01929 553443
Email: enq@dhcottages.co.uk   www.dhcottages.co.uk

FHG

FHG PUBLICATIONS

publish a large range of well-known accommodation guides. We will be happy to send you details or you can use the order form at the back of this book.

See also Colour Display Advertisement

Bournecoast (01202 428717/01202 417757). From a
honeymoon couple to a "tribe' of a couple of dozen, self-catering
allows you – the time to choose the location, the places and the
food; freedom to really enjoy our golden sands, warm, clean
seas and glorious attractions; to join the locals, become a local
resident for your stay, with no hotel hassles. Call today and find
out why people say 'It's always better with Bournecoast'. Est.1960,
K.W. Simmons MBE.
website: www.bournecoast.co.uk

See also Colour Display Advertisement

BEAMINSTER

Orchard End, Hooke, Beaminster. Sleeps 6. Hooke is a quiet
village nine miles from the coast. Good walking country and near
Hooke Working Woodland with lovely woodland walks. Trout
fishing nearby. Bungalow is stone built with electric central heating
and double glazing. It is on a working dairy farm and is clean and
comfortable. Three bedrooms, all beds with duvets. Cot available.
Large lounge/diningroom with colour TV. Well equipped kitchen
with electric cooker, microwave, fridge freezer and automatic
washing machine. Bathroom and separate toilet. Carpeted.
Payphone. Large garden, garage. Terms £210 to £420 per week
inclusive of electricity, bed linen and VAT. **ETC ★★★★**. Contact
**Mrs P.M. Wallbridge, Watermeadow House, Bridge Farm,
Hooke, Beaminster DT8 3PD (01308 862619).**

See also Colour Display Advertisement

BLANDFORD FORUM

**Mrs Penny Cooper, Dairy House Farm, Woolland, Blandford
Forum DT11 0EY (01258 817501; Fax: 01258 818060).**
These traditional farm cottages, JASMINE and PLUMTREE, and
recently converted barns, THE LODGE and THE STABLE, are within
easy reach of Dorset's coastline, superb scenery and many other
attractions. Private lake with coarse fishing and 17 acres of
woodland to explore. The tranquil position nestled under Bulbarrow
Hill (second highest point in Dorset) offers a safe haven for children;
well-behaved pets are very welcome. The Lodge has large
doorways and has been designed for easy access for the partially
disabled. Open all year round and personally supervised to a high
standard Cots and high chairs supplied; linen available. Prices
from £180-£620 low/high season; Short Breaks from £45 per night.
ETC ★★★
e-mail: penny.cooper@farming.me.uk
website: www.self-cateringholidays4u.co.uk

HOLIDAY FLATS AND FLATLETS

- • A SHORT WALK TO GOLDEN SANDY BEACHES •
- • MOST WITH PRIVATE BATHROOMS •
- • CLEANLINESS AND COMFORT ASSURED •
- • LAUNDRY ROOM • FREE PRIVATE PARKING •
- • DOGS WELCOME • COLOUR TV IN ALL UNITS •
- • NO VAT CHARGED •

**CONTACT: M. DE KMENT, 4 CECIL ROAD,
BOURNEMOUTH BH5 1DU (07788 952394)**

BLANDFORD FORUM

Murray and Amanda Kayll, Luccombe Country Holidays, Luccombe, Milton Abbas, Blandford Forum DT11 0BE (01258 880558; Fax: 01258 881384). Superior self-catering holiday cottages. Set in the heart of beautiful and unspoilt Dorset countryside with stunning views and a peaceful, traffic-free environment. Luccombe offers quality accommodation for two to seven people in a variety of converted and historic farm buildings, with original timbers and panelling. Well-equipped kitchens. Large shower or bath. Cosy lounge/dining room with colour TV. Bed linen, duvets, towels provided. Laundry room. Children and well behaved pets welcome. Ample parking. Disabled access. Riding, tennis, swimming pool and gymnasium/games room (new for 2003). Clay pigeon shooting and fishing nearby. Post Office and stores in local village. Open throughout the year. Group/family enquiries welcome. Short breaks available. **ETC ★★★★**
website: www.luccombeholidays.co.uk

BRIDPORT (Near)

Court Farm Cottages, Askerswell, Dorchester DT2 9EJ (01308 485668). A Grade II Listed barn has been converted into delightful holiday cottages, fully equipped with all modern conveniences to make your holiday as relaxing as possible. Wheatsheaf and Haywain sleep four and feature king-sized four-poster beds. Threshers has three bedrooms and sleeps five. South Barn has four bedrooms and two bathrooms and sleeps seven. A games room and large garden are provided for guests. Askerswell is an idyllic village in an Area of Outstanding Natural Beauty just four miles from the coast. Perfect for walking and touring holidays. Open all year. Low season short breaks available. From £210 to £690 per week. **ETC ★★★★/★★★★★**
e-mail: courtfarmcottages@eclipse.co.uk
website: www.eclipse.co.uk/CourtFarmCottages/WEBPG2

BRIDPORT/NETTLECOMBE

The Studio, The Old Station, Nettlecombe, Bridport. Sleeps 2. Enjoy a peaceful stay in beautiful countryside. Off-road parking, two-and-a-half acres of garden. The 150-year-old stone building, originally the linesmen's hut at Powerstock Station, was later enlarged, forming a fashion designer's studio. Recently double glazed, it has a bedsit, kitchen, shower room, toilet, for one to two non-smoking adult guests (no children or pets). Two single beds; duvets, bed linen and towels provided. Electricity also included (small winter surcharge). Microwave, fridge, TV, heating. Garden furniture, putting. Badger-watching at the adjacent Old Station. Terms from £140-£160 per week. Low season short stays by arrangement. SAE please: **Mrs D.P. Read, The Old Station, Powerstock, Bridport DT6 3ST (01308 485301).**

LYME REGIS

Mrs M.J. Tedbury, Little Paddocks, Yawl Hill Lane, Lyme Regis DT7 3RW (01297 443085). Sleeps 2. A chalet situated in the garden of a smallholding which overlooks Lyme Bay and surrounding countryside for perfect peace and quiet. Two-and-a-half miles Lyme Regis, three-and-a-half miles Charmouth. Easy driving distance Seaton, Beer, Sidmouth. The chalet is ideal for two people liking plenty of room; it has a double bedroom and is fully equipped except linen. Mains water, hot and cold, flush toilet and shower, electric light, fridge, fire, TV. Parking space for cars. Pets welcome. Terms from £90. Also six berth caravan from £110. SAE, please.

LYME REGIS.

"Moorlands", The Bowling Green, Lyme Regis. Sleeps 4. Fully furnished, well-appointed chalet with balcony and sea views. Situated close to the beach. Parking. Available from 1st March to 6th November. For further details please send an SAE to **Mrs S. Johnson, "Quarry Lodge", Crewkerne Road, Raymonds Hill, Axminster, Devon EX13 5SY (01297 35852).**

MEYRICK PARK

Mr & Mrs B. W. Lonnen, Langlea House, 18 St Anthony's Road, Meyrick Park, Bournemouth BH2 6PD (01202 558426). Langlea House Self Catering Apartments are open all year, delightfully situated, peaceful and central. Few minutes' walk to town, beaches and gardens. Attractive apartments with a high standard of cleanliness. Parking, Sky TV. Linen and hand towels at cost. Guest telephone. Central heating. Pets, children and disabled welcome. Member of Bournemouth Holiday Flats Association. Weekly terms from £95 to £150 per person.

Trill Cottages

SHERBORNE

Mrs J. Warr, Trill Cottage, Trill House, Thornford, Sherborne DT9 6HF (01935 872305). Two cottages situated in the Blackmore Vale only five miles from both Sherborne and Yeovil, and one mile from the villages of Yetminster and Thornford. Ideally placed for exploring the wonderful counties of Dorset and Somerset, where there is so much to see and do. The cottages are comfortably furnished, accommodation in each comprising three bedrooms (one double bed and four singles); lounge with colour TV and dining-room; well-equipped kitchen with fridge and microwave; shower and toilet, and bathroom and toilet. Laundry room. A cot and high chair are available on request. Electricity by £1 slot meter. Storage heating. Quiet, peaceful and safe for children. We regret that we do not allow pets. Terms from £130 to £325. **ETC ★★★**
e-mail: trill.cottages@ic24.net

SHERBORNE

White Horse Farm, Middlemarsh, Sherborne DT9 5QN (01963 210222). Toad Hall sleeps 4; Badger's sleeps 2; Ratty's sleeps 2/4; Moley's sleeps 2. Set in beautiful Hardy countryside, we have four cottages furnished to high standards and surrounded by two acres of paddock and garden with a duck-pond. We lie between the historic towns of Sherborne, Dorchester and Cerne Abbas. Within easy reach of several tourist attractions. Situated next door to an inn serving good food, we welcome children, partially disabled guests and pets. All cottages have central heating, colour TV and video recorder with unlimited free video-film rental. Electricity, bed linen, towels inclusive. Ample parking. Good value at £165 to £390 per week. Discounted two weeks or more. Contact: **David, Hazel, Mary and Gerry Wilding on 01963 210222. ETC ★★★★**
e-mail: **enquiries@whitehorsefarm.co.uk** website: **www.whitehorsefarm.co.uk**

TOLLER PORCORUM

"The Annexe". Sleeps 2-3. Toller Porcorum is situated in picturesque rural Dorset, mid-way between the market towns of Dorchester and Bridport (20 minutes), and only six miles to West Bay and Heritage Coast. The accommodation, a self-contained cottage with front and rear entrance, adjoins Barton Farmhouse at the end of the village High Street. Own driveway with ample parking for two cars and garden to both front and rear. Upstairs accommodation comprises one double and one single bedroom, and a modern bathroom, all fully carpeted.The downstairs is open-plan, with a spacious well-equipped modern kitchen/diner, which includes fridge, electric cooker and washing machine. The lounge is comfortably furnished, fully carpeted, with colour TV. Cloakroom and second toilet on the ground floor. Heating and hot water by electric meter (£1 coins). All linen supplied. Pets by arrangement. Terms: £150 – £200 per week, deposit required. For bookings and enquiries contact: **T.G. Billen, Barton Farmhouse, Toller Porcorum, Dorchester DT2 0DN (01300 320648).**

WAREHAM (near)

"Dormer Cottage", Woodlands, Hyde, Near Wareham. Sleeps 5. This secluded cottage, cosy and modern, is a converted old barn of Woodlands House. Standing in its own grounds, it is fronted by a small wood with a walled paddock at the back. Pleasant walks in wooded forests nearby. In the midst of "Hardy Country" and ideal for a family holiday and for those who value seclusion. All linen included, beds ready made on guests' arrival and basic shopping arranged on request. Amusements at Bournemouth, Poole and Dorchester within easy reach. Five people and a baby can be accommodated in two double and one single bedrooms; cot and high chair available. Bathroom, two toilets; lounge and diningroom, colour TV. Kitchen with cooker, fridge, washing machine, small deep freeze, etc. Pets welcome. Open all year. Golf course half-mile; pony trekking, riding nearby. **SAE, please, for terms. Mrs M.J.M. Constantinides, "Woodlands", Hyde, near Wareham BH20 7NT (01929 471239).**

WEST BAY

Robins, Meadway, West Bay, Bridport. Sleeps 6. This comfortably furnished bungalow, with attractive garden in a quiet cul-de-sac at West Bay, overlooks open field, only three minutes' walk to the harbour and beach. Ideal for family holidays, walking, fishing, visiting many places of interest or just relaxing. Three bedrooms, two double and one twin bedded, sleeping six, cot available if required. Sitting room with colour TV. Well equipped kitchen/dining room. Bathroom and separate toilet. Garden and parking space. Open all year, out of season short breaks available. Personally supervised. **Mrs B. Loosmore, Barlands, Lower Street, West Chinnock, Crewkerne, Somerset TA18 7PT (01935 881790).**

DURHAM

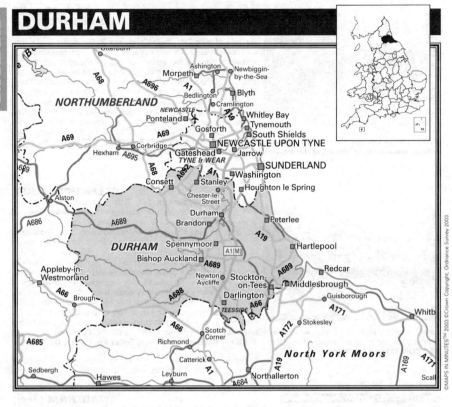

BISHOP AUCKLAND

New Cottage, 'Law One', Hollymoor Farm, Cockfield, Bishop Auckland DL13 5HF (Tel & Fax: 01388 718567/ 718260). New Cottage is a delightful little cottage in a very peaceful location. The accommodation is very cosy and comfortable and all on one level – there are no stairs. The panoramic views from the lounge are a never-ending source of delight – they are stunning, and made even more beautiful in the winter when there is a light dusting of snow. The cottage is also so accessible for country walks and sightseeing, and being able to start walks from the cottage is a real bonus. And the sunsets are something else – truly magnificent. **ETC ★★★** Details from **Mrs Margaret Partridge.**

BISHOP AUCKLAND

Low Lands Farm, Low Lands, Cockfield, Bishop Auckland DL13 5AW. Two award-winning, beautifully renovated, self-catering cottages on a working family farm. If you want peace and quiet in an area full of beautiful unspoilt countryside packed with things to see and do then come and stay with us. Each cottage sleeps up to 4 people plus cot. Beams, log fires, gas BBQ, own gardens and parking. Close to Durham city, the Lake District and Hadrian's Wall. Pets and children most welcome, childminding and equipment available. Terms from £150 - £295, inclusive of linen, towels, electricity and heating. More information available on our website. One cottage has *DISABLED ACCESSIBILTY CATEGORY 3*. Both cottages are **ETC ★★★★** Contact: **Alison and Keith Tallentire on 01388 718251 or 07745 067754** for brochure.
e-mail: info@farmholidaysuk.com   website: www.farmholidaysuk.com

LANCHESTER

Mrs Ann Darlington, Hall Hill Farm, Lanchester, Durham DH7 0TA (01207 521476; Tel & Fax: 01388 730300). Two country cottages. Well-equipped and comfortable. Both cottages have one double and one twin room – sleep up to four people. Downstairs is a livingroom and large kitchen/dining room, upstairs two bedrooms and bathroom. Kitchen contains washing machine/tumble dryer, microwave and fridge/freezer. Linen and towels are provided. Both cottages are heated. The cottages are in an ideal location for Durham City and Beamish Museum. You will have a free pass for the week to visit our own open farm. Prices from £160 per week. Children welcome. Sorry no pets. Please write or telephone for brochure. **ETC ★★★**
e-mail: cottages@hallhillfarm.co.uk
website: www.hallhillfarm.co.uk

MIDDLETON-IN-TEESDALE

Laneside & Honeypot Cottage. Laneside and Honeypot are well-equipped former farmhouses on the Lord Barnard's Upper Teesdale Raby Estate. Surrounded by delightful scenery where tranquillity is assured they combine the best features of traditional Dales life with modern facilities. Ideal bases for walking, cycling, bird watching or simply to relax and enjoy the peace and quiet of the countryside. Superb touring bases for local amenities and places of interest within the Durham and Yorkshire Dales and Durham City. **Raby Estates Holiday Cottages, Upper Teesdale Estate Office, Middleton-in-Teesdale, Barnard Castle DL12 0QH (01833 640209; Fax: 01833 640963).** **ETC ★★-★★★★**
e-mail: teesdaleestate@rabycastle.com
website: www.rabycastle.com

MIDDLETON-IN-TEESDALE

Mrs Scott, Westfield Cottage, Laithkirk, Middleton-in-Teesdale, Barnard Castle DL12 0PN (Tel & Fax: 01833 640942). Sleeps 6. Westfield Cottage is a Grade II Listed building very recently renovated and furnished to a high standard. Situated on a working farm in beautiful Teesdale which is excellent touring, cycling and walking country with the Pennine and Teesdale Ways close by. The Cumbrian border is about six miles away. Ample parking area; free fishing. About half a mile from the local village. Open all year. From £185-£380. **ETC ★★★★**

GLOUCESTERSHIRE

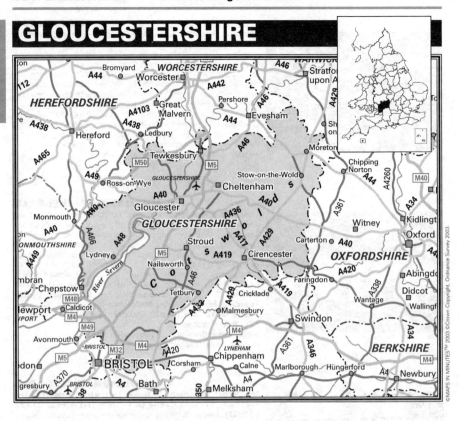

UNIVERSITY ACCOMMODATION & FACILITIES

CHELTENHAM

Mrs D. Murray, Stepping Stone, Great Rissington, Cheltenham GL54 2LL (01451 821385). Sleep 2. Set in a quiet village overlooking the Wind Rush Valley, Stepping Stone is perfectly placed for exploring The Cotswolds. Near to Bourton-on-the-Water, Burford and Stow-on-the-Wold. Accommodation provided in two self-contained units each with double bed, en suite shower and lounge area with dining. The Flat has a newly fitted oak kitchen and balcony to rear garden. The Garden Room has a well-equipped kitchenette and patio. Linen, duvets and towels included. Non-smoking, no pets. Ample parking. Two day breaks from £70, low season weekly rate from £210.

COTSWOLDS

Mrs A. Lane, Hill Barn, Clapton Road, Bourton-on-the-Water GL54 2LF (01451 810472). In the midst of beautiful rolling pastures, yet only five minutes' drive from the picturesque village of Bourton-on-the-Water, this cottage offers the best of both worlds. With sleeping accommodation for up to five persons, it offers all modern facilities with old fashioned charm. With beautiful views which in the summer can be enjoyed from the spacious patio or in the winter from the large windows whilst wallowing in the cosy warmth from the woodburner. Adjoining the main barn, which houses the owners, the cottage has a large parking area and totally private entrance. Sorry, no pets. Prices from £180 to £300 per week. One bedroom cottage also available.

MINSTERWORTH

Mrs Carter, 'Severn Bank', Minsterworth GL2 8JH (01452 750357). Sleeps 6. 'Severn Bank' is a large country house set in riverside gardens, four miles west of Gloucester. Ideally situated for touring nearby Forest of Dean, Severn Vale, Cotswolds and Malverns, and is recommended viewpoint for the Severn Bore tidal wave. The area is rich in history and packed with intriguing places of interest, from caves to castles. The three bedroomed flat has kitchen/dining area, sitting room, TV and separate shower room and toilet. One of the three bedrooms is en suite. It is situated on the second floor. Sorry, but no pets or children under 12 years. No smoking. Terms from £250 low season to £350 high season.

MISERDEN

Sudgrove Cottages, Miserden GL6 7JD. One three-bedroom cottage sleeping six, and two two-bedroom cottages sleeping four on 'no through road' in the heart of the Cotswolds. Each cottage has views across fields, a garden, wood-burning stove, TV, radio/CD/tape player, electric cooker, microwave, fridge/freezer, washer/dryer. Cot/high chair available. Pub serving good food and general store/post office in Miserden (½ mile). Footpaths radiate from Sudgrove or short scenic drives lead to Cirencester, Stroud, Cheltenham or Gloucester. Explore the Cotswolds and beyond. Open all year. Weekly rates £200-£300 (two-bedroom), £225-£410 (three-bedroom). Bed linen/towels included. Electricity extra. Winter short breaks. Non-smoking available. **ETC ★★★**. Contact **Carol Ractliffe (Tel & Fax: 01285 821322).**

e-mail: enquiries@sudgrovecottages.co.uk   website: www.sudgrovecottages.co.uk

MORETON-IN-MARSH

Edward and Wendy Hicks, Woodkeepers, Barton-on-the-Heath, Moreton-in-Marsh GL56 0PL (01608 684232). Outstanding barn converted into two cottages, quietly set in a rural location. Fabulous views of surrounding farmland and quintessential village of Barton-on-the-Heath. Finished and equipped to a high standard. An enclosed courtyard garden with a private terrace for each cottage, and an old cart shed which provides an idyllic covered seating area. Well placed for the many attractions the Cotswolds has to offer: theatre, music, horse racing, antique collectors' heaven. Places of interest to suit the whole family – stately homes and gardens, castles, farm parks, many traditional market towns.
website: www.woodkeepers.co.uk

MORETON-IN-MARSH

The Laurels. A modern cottage bungalow five minutes' walk from the centre of Moreton-in-Marsh. Many well-known picturesque villages just a short drive away and close to Cheltenham, Oxford and Stratford-upon-Avon. Well-presented, in excellent decorative order and furnished to a high standard throughout. Two bedrooms, well-equipped kitchen with electric cooker, microwave, washing machine and fridge, bathroom; lounge/dining room wth TV, radio and CD player, that opens onto an attractive patio and garden. Central heating, electricity, gas linen and towels all included in price. Ample parking. Payphone available in main house. Starter pack on arrival. Prices: Low Season from £224; High Season from £301 to £371. **ETC ★★★.** Contact: **Graham and Sandra Billinger, Blue Cedar House, Stow Road, Moreton-in-Marsh, Gloucestershire GL56 0DW (01608 650299).**
e-mail: gandsib@dialstart.net

NEWLAND

Mrs Anne Edwards, Rookery Farm House, Newland, Near Coleford GL16 8NJ (01594 832432). Converted stables on the edge of the lovely 13th century village of Newland, overlooking a stream with ducks and surrounded by fields and woods. Newland is situated in the beautiful and unspoilt 'Forest of Dean'; ideal walking and fishing country with stables, cycle paths and golf courses nearby. Central heating, electricity, bed linen and towels are all provided. Dogs welcome with prior arrangement. Terms from £165 - £250. Bed and Breakfast accommodation is also available. **ETC ◆◆◆**

Please mention Self-Catering Holidays in Britain
when enquiring about accommodation featured in these pages.

HAMPSHIRE

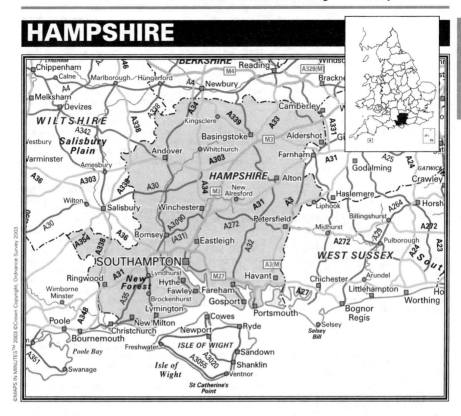

©MAPS IN MINUTES™ 2003. ©Crown Copyright. Ordnance Survey 2003.

ENGLAND

SOUTH COAST & NEW FOREST

Shorefield Holidays Ltd. Two high quality destinations to choose from – OAKDENE FOREST PARK, ST LEONARDS, RINGWOOD BH24 2RZ and SHOREFIELD COUNTRY PARK, SHOREFIELD ROAD, MILFORD-ON-SEA SO41 0LH. Shorefield Holidays offers you the best of both worlds in self-catering locations. Both our parks are set in peaceful, unspoilt parkland in the beautiful New Forest or South Coast areas. There are comprehensive facilities including entertainment and free Leisure Club membership. For full details ask for our brochure or browse on-line. For further details telephone **01590 648331** (Ref SCH).
e-mail: holidays@shorefield.co.uk
website: www.shorefield.co.uk

FHG

FHG PUBLICATIONS

publish a large range of well-known accommodation guides. We will be happy to send you details or you can use the order form at the back of this book.

LYNDHURST

The Penny Farthing Hotel, Romsey Road, Lyndhurst, Hampshire SO43 7AA (023 8028 4422; Fax: 023 8028 4488). We have some neighbouring cottages available as Hotel annexe rooms or on a self-catering basis. These have been totally refitted, much with "Laura Ashley", and offer quieter, more exclusive accommodation. The Penny Farthing is a cheerful small Hotel ideally situated in Lyndhurst village centre, the capital of "The New Forest". The Hotel offers en suite single, double, twin and family rooms with direct dial telephones, tea/coffee tray, colour TV and clock radios. The hotel has a licensed bar, private car park and bicycle store. Lyndhurst has a charming variety of shops, restaurants, pubs, and bistros and "The New Forest Information Centre and Museum". **ETC ★★★★ website: www.pennyfarthinghotel.co.uk**

MILFORD-ON-SEA

Mrs Jean Halliday, Westover House, Westover Road, Milford-on-Sea, Lymington SO41 0PW (01590 642077). Sleeps 6. Westover House is a partly thatched period house 300 yards from the sea and half-a-mile from Milford's village green. Its East Wing, available for letting throughout the year, is self-contained and equipped for six, with modern services yet retaining an air of mature tranquillity reminiscent of a past age. There is a sheltered informal half-acre garden of unusual botanical interest, outstanding for its spring flowers. Milford is near the old-world market town of Lymington and the New Forest, yet is also convenient for Bournemouth and many popular holiday attractions of central Southern England. Terms from £140 per week, full tariff available on request.
e-mail: hallidaymos@tinyworld.co.uk

MILFORD-ON-SEA (New Forest)

Carolyn Plummer, Ha'Penny House, 16 Whitby Road, Milford-on-Sea, Lymington SO41 0ND (01590 641210). 'PENNYPOT' sleeping two, is a nicely furnished apartment adjoining Ha'penny House (a guest house offering luxury bed and breakfast accommodation). Set in a quiet area of the unspoilt village of Milford-on-Sea and just a few minutes' walk from both sea and village, it is ideally situated for touring the New Forest, Bournemouth, Salisbury and the Isle of Wight. The apartment has its own separate entrance, a double bedroom, lounge with TV and video, diningroom, fully equipped kitchen and bathroom, use of a large garden and summer house. Heating, power, linen and towels are included. Private parking. Non-smokers only; sorry no pets. Friday to Friday bookings from £150 to £255 per week. **ETC ★★★★**

e-mail: info@hapennyhouse.co.uk   **website: www.hapennyhouse.co.uk**

HEREFORDSHIRE

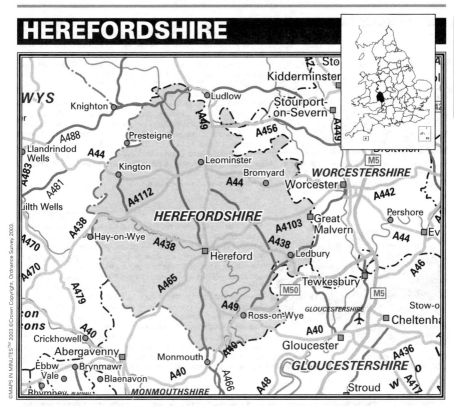

THE LODGE

The Lodge, being the former Verger's cottage, can be found in a tranquil setting just eight miles north of the historic cathedral town of Hereford. Peacefully located next to the Parish Church. Guests can enjoy the pleasure of the gardens of Felton House, the stone-built former Rectory. The Lodge has been completely renovated and restored to its Victorian character but with the convenience of central heating, a modern kitchen, two shower rooms, a dining room and a sitting room with TV and video. There are three bedrooms with accommodation for five people (One double room, one twin, one single), and in addition a cot is available. Linen may be hired. Children, and pets with responsible owners, are most welcome. Private parking, patio and garden. The Lodge is a cosy, restful cottage, spotlessly clean. Short Breaks catered for and weekly terms range from £150 to £275 per week, exclusive of electricity. Brochure available.

Marjorie and Brian Roby, Felton House, Felton, HR1 3PH • Tel/Fax: (01432) 820366
Website: www.SmoothHound.co.uk/hotels/felton.html

See also Colour Advertisement

ENGLAND

GOODRICH

Mainoaks Farm Cottages, Goodrich, Ross-on-Wye. Six units sleeping 2,4,6 & 7. Mainoaks is a 15th century Listed farm which has been converted to form six cottages of different size and individual character. It is set in 80 acres of pasture and woodland beside the River Wye in an Area of Outstanding Natural Beauty and an SSSI where there is an abundance of wildlife. All cottages have exposed beams, pine furniture, heating throughout, fully equipped kitchens with microwaves, washer/dryer etc., colour TV. Private gardens, barbecue area and ample parking. Linen and towels provided. An ideal base for touring the local area with beautiful walks, fishing, canoeing, pony trekking, golf, bird-watching or just relaxing in this beautiful tranquil spot. Open throughout the year. Short breaks available. Pets by arrangement. Brochure on request. **ETC ★★★/★★★★. Mrs P. Unwin, Hill House, Chase End, Bromsberrow, Ledbury, Herefordshire HR8 1SE (01531 650448).**
e-mail: mainoaks@lineone.net   **website: www.mainoaks.co.uk**

HEREFORD

Rose Cottage, Craswall, Hereford. Sleeps 5. Rose Cottage is a modernised stone-built cottage, retaining its original character situated at the foot of Black Mountains, on a quiet country road. Hay-on-Wye, Hereford and Abergavenny are easily accessible and the cottage is the ideal base for walking and touring. Many churches and castles of historic interest; close to River Monnow where trout fishing is available. Pony trekking, hang-gliding nearby. A car is essential and there is ample parking. Rose Cottage is comfortably furnished with full central heating and wood fire (heating and hot water included). Linen provided free of charge, towels available if required. Electricity by meter reading. Two bedrooms, one with double bed, one with three single beds. Cot can be provided. Bathroom, toilet. Kitchen fully equipped with electric cooker, kettle, fridge, etc. Sittingroom; diningroom. TV. Dogs are allowed. Available all year round. Terms from £150 to £160. **ETC ★★★. Mrs M. Howard, The Three Horseshoes, Craswall, Hereford HR2 0PL (01981 510631).**

HEREFORD

Mrs S. Dixon, Swayns Diggins, Harewood End, Hereford HR2 8JU (01989 730358). This highly recommended first floor flat is completely self-contained at one end of the main house. The bedroom, sitting room and private balcony all face south with panoramic views over farmland towards Ross and Symonds Yat. The well-equipped kitchen overlooks the garden with grand views towards Orcop Hill and the Black Mountains. Open all year, rental from £150 to £165 per week includes electricity, linen, heating, colour TV. Ideal base for exploring the beautiful Wye Valley, Herefordshire, Gloucestershire and the historic Welsh Marches. There is much to see and do in the area. Write or phone for further particulars.

KINGTON

The Harbour, Upper Hergest, Kington. Properties sleep 5/9. This bungalow is on a good second-class road facing south with beautiful views from its elevated position, across the Hergest Ridge and Offa's Dyke. The Welsh border is a mile away. Shops are two-and-a-half miles away. Kington Golf Club nearby. Accommodation for five/nine in two double rooms (one with extra single bed) downstairs and two double dormer bedrooms; two cots; bathroom, toilet; sittingroom (TV); diningroom; sun porch for relaxing; kitchen with electric cooker, microwave, fridge, food store and usual equipment. Central heating. No linen. Children and pets welcome. Car essential - parking. Available all year. SAE, please, to **Mrs B.F. Welson, New House Farm, Upper Hergest, Kington, Herefordshire HR5 3EW (01544 230533).**

Please mention Self-Catering Holidays in Britain
when enquiring about accommodation featured in these pages.

LEOMINSTER

Nicholson Farm Holidays. Self-catering properties on a working dairy farm. Beautiful views. Wide choice of restaurants and bar meals in the area. Supermarket 10 minutes. Excellent walking, golf, riding, carp fishing available on the farm, swimming and tennis 10 minutes. Dogs are welcome but must not remain in during the owner's absence. Non- smoking. Contact: **Mrs J. Brooke, Brimstone Cottage, Docklow, Leominster HR6 0SL (01568 760346).**

MALVERN

Kate and Denis Kavanagh, Whitewells Farm Cottages, Ridgeway Cross, Near Malvern WR13 5JR (01886 880607; Fax: 01886 880360). Sleep 2-6. Charmingly converted cottages. Fully equipped with colour TV, microwave, barbecue, fridge, iron, etc. Linen, towels also supplied. One cottage is equipped for the disabled with full wheelchair access. Children and pets welcome. Short breaks and long lets, suitable for relocation. Also see advert under Great Malvern, Worcestershire. **ETC ★★★★**
e-mail: info@whitewellsfarm.co.uk   website: www.whitewellsfarm.co.uk

ROSS-ON-WYE (Near)

Kiln House, Yatton, Near Ross-on-Wye. Sleeps 6. The Kiln House is a converted hop kiln, situated just off the A449 in the peace and quiet of lovely Herefordshire countryside. The historic towns of Ledbury and Ross-on-Wye are nearby, as well as the Wye Valley, Forest of Dean, Malvern Hills and many more places of interest. The accommodation sleeps six in three bedrooms - two with double beds and one with single bed plus guest bed. Cot and high chair available. Large lounge with woodburner and TV; well-equipped kitchen; downstairs toilet. Airing cupboard with immersion heater. Garden and ample parking, car essential. Children welcome. Sorry, no pets. Available all year. SAE for terms and further details to: **Mrs P.A. Ruck, Lower House, Yatton, Near Ross-on-Wye HR9 7RB (01531 660280).**

ROSS-ON-WYE (Near)

A rendered stone cottage tucked away down a country lane in a tiny village on the edge of the Royal Forest of Dean in the Wye Valley, an Area of Outstanding Natural Beauty. Excellent acccommodation for up to 12 people. The cottage is typical of the Herefordshire countryside, but when entered, quality and high standards are very much in evidence. Five bedrooms, one with handmade oak four-poster, king-size bed; one of the bathrooms has a jacuzzi bath; two showers. Two beamed lounges with TV and video, open fires and storage heaters. Oak-fitted kitchen with dishwasher, fridge, freezer etc. Linen and towels for hire. Children and pets welcome. Ample parking. The River Wye is a haven for fishermen, with salmon, trout and coarse fishing. For the adventurous, cycling in Royal Forest of Dean, golf, canoeing, quad biking, hovercraft, clay pigeon shooting, archery and orienteering. Also B&B (**AA/RAC ◆◆◆◆** *SPARKLING DIAMOND AWARD*) . Details from **Mrs H. Smith, The Old Kilns, Howle Hill, Ross-on-Wye HR9 5SP (Tel & Fax: 01989 562051).**

SYMONDS YAT

Mrs J. Rudge, Hilltop, Whitchurch, Near Ross-on-Wye (01600 890279). Chalet bungalow with panoramic views looking over Symonds Yat and surrounding countryside. One mile from the A40 dual carriageway and within easy reach of Forest of Dean, Symonds Yat Rock and the Welsh Borders. The chalet stands in the garden of a seven acre smallholding, next to owners' bungalow, enjoying peace and quiet, yet close to the local shop, post office, public house and the local attractions. Accommodation comprises livingroom, kitchen with fridge /freezer; bathroom, shower; two bedrooms, one with two single beds and one with double bed. Porch with washing machine and tumbledryer. Oil fired central heating. Children welcome. No pets. Accommodation particularly suitable for the elderly. No linen supplied. £1 electric meter. Terms from £175 to £225. SAE, please.

HERTFORDSHIRE

SOUTH MIMMS

Mr W.A.J. Marsterson, The Black Swan, 62/64 Blanche Lane, South Mimms, Potters Bar EN6 3PD (01707 644180; Fax: 01707 642344). Sleep 2/6. The Black Swan, a timber framed building dating from 1600, looks across the village green in South Mimms. Once a village inn, it is now our home. We have two flats and a cottage, convenient for M25 and A1(M), half-an-hour's drive, tube or train from central London. Near Junction 23 on M25. Follow signs to South Mimms village. Stay with us to see London and the South-East or use us as a staging post to or from the Channel Ports. Self-catering from £185 to £295 per week. Children and pets welcome. Non-smoking accommodation available. ETC ★★/★★★

ISLE OF WIGHT

ISLE OF WIGHT

Island Cottage Holidays. Sleep 1/14. Charming individual cottages in lovely rural surroundings and close to the sea. Over 50 cottages situated throughout the Isle of Wight. Beautiful views, attractive gardens, delightful country walks. All equipped to a high standard and graded for quality by the Tourist Board. Open all year. £132 to £1195 per week. Short breaks available in low season from £89 to £395 (three nights). For a brochure please contact: Mrs Honor Vass, The Old Vicarage, Kingston, Wareham, Dorset BH20 5LH (01929 480080; Fax: 01929 481070). ETC ★★★/★★★★★
e-mail: enq@islandcottageholidays.com
website: www.islandcottageholidays.com

BEMBRIDGE

See also Colour Display Advertisement

Whitecliff Bay Holiday Park, Bembridge PO35 5PL. Family-owned and managed, Whitecliff Bay Holiday Park continues to promote great value family holidays on the beautiful Isle of Wight. Open March to October, we can offer self-catering, half board, chalet or caravan, camping and touring caravans, with special theme holidays. Situated in a rural location adjacent to our own secluded, sandy beach, we have an extensive range of facilities for all ages. Brochure request line 01983 872671 or visit our award-winning website.
website: www.whitecliff-bay.com

TOTLAND BAY

3 Seaview Cottages, Broadway, Totland Bay. Sleeps 5. This well-modernised cosy old coastguard cottage holds the Farm Holiday Guide Diploma for the highest standard of accommodation. It is warm and popular throughout the year. Four day winter break - £45; a week in summer £260. Located close to two beaches in beautiful walking country near mainland links. It comprises lounge/dinette/kitchenette; two bedrooms (sleeping five); bathroom/toilet. Well furnished, fully heated, TV, selection of books and other considerations. Another cottage is also available at Cowes, Isle of Wight. Non-smokers only. Mrs C. Pitts, 11 York Avenue, New Milton, Hampshire BH25 6BT (01425 615215).

KENT

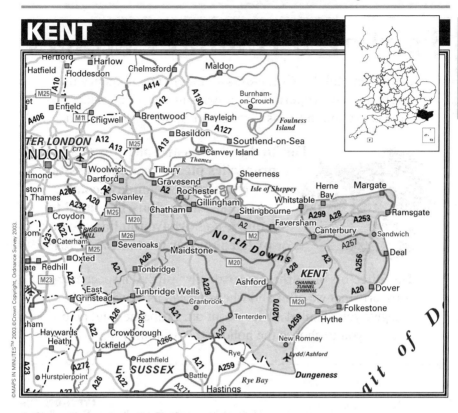

©MAPS IN MINUTES™ 2003 ©Crown Copyright, Ordnance Survey 2003.

UNIVERSITY ACCOMMODATION & FACILITIES

Budget accommodation or fully tailored packages (0870 712 5002; Fax: 020 7017 8273). En suite designer halls across the UK. Groups of any age or size. Sports facilities all year. Tell us your needs and we'll find a location and package to suit.
e-mail: enquiries@thesummervillage.com
website: www.thesummervillage.com

KENT & SUSSEX

Garden of England Cottages, The Mews Office,189A High Street, Tonbridge TN9 1BX (01732 369168; Fax: 01732 358817). Accommodation for all seasons. Set in part of England's most beautiful countryside, our ETC quality graded cottages offer you a homely atmosphere and ideal locations for your perfect holiday. Visit pretty villages, explore historic castles and famous gardens, and enjoy day trips to London or France. Available all year. Ideal for re-locating, visiting friends, expatriates, and any short let that requires quality furnished accommodation. Prices include linen, towels, fuel and pets. Visit our website or contact us for a free brochure.
e-mail: holidays@gardenofenglandcottages.co.uk
website: www.gardenofenglandcottages.co.uk

Two tickets for the price of one (cheapest ticket free) at
Museum of Kent Life
see our READERS' OFFER VOUCHER for details

Fairhaven Holiday Cottages

Fairhaven Holiday Cottages is an independent agency that offers holiday properties of all types in the countryside, on the coast and in towns throughout South East England.

For further details and pictures of all our properties please visit our website www.fairhaven-holidays.co.uk or request a brochure by e-mail to enquiries@fairhaven-holidays.co.uk or by telephone or fax to 01634 570157

The Directors of Fairhaven personally visit and inspect every property that we offer and when you call us we will be able to give you detailed advice about our properties and help you to choose the holiday that will suit you.

LYDD-ON-SEA

98 Coast Drive, Lydd-on-Sea, Romney Marsh. Sleeps 6. Lydd-on-Sea is a small hamlet on the south coast near New Romney/Dungeness. We offer a three bedroomed bungalow situated opposite the sea front with uninterrupted sea views from the sun lounge/diner. There is an inner lounge. Colour TV, linen and duvets provided. Central Heating. A separate bathroom and toilet. New kitchen. Utility area in garage, tiled with worktops, washing machine, drawer unit and freezer. Lawns to front and rear plus expanse of natural garden. Small patio to rear with garden furniture. Easy access to Dover and Folkestone for cross-Channel trips. The ancient towns of Rye and Hastings are a short distance away. Good sea fishing off Dungeness Point. Romney, Hythe and Dymchurch small gauge railway passes rear of the house and buses stop a few yards away. Children welcome. Weekly terms from £185 to £385 plus £20 winter fuel supplement - October to April. No pets. Contact: **Mrs Frances I. Smith, Holts Farm House, Coopers Lane, Fordcombe, Near Tunbridge Wells TN3 0RN (01892 740338).**

FHG PUBLICATIONS

FHG publish a large range of well-known accommodation guides. We will be happy to send you details or you can use the order form at the back of this book.

MAIDSTONE

Brick Kiln Cottage, White House Farm, Chart Sutton, Maidstone ME17 3ES (01622 842490). Our self-catering accommodation has recently undergone a complete renovation from the original farm barn. It can accommodate six guests, or be made into three separate units, one completely self-catering, the other two with bedrooms and showers on a bed and breakfast basis (breakfast available in our farmhouse). All rooms are en suite or private facilities with colour TV. Disabled facilities such as ramps, rails, seat in shower and disabled access shower are built into Brick Kiln Cottage. All bedding, linen, towels, etc are included in the price. Fully equipped with washer/dryer, full sized fridge, cooker and microwave. Full central heating and double glazing. Electric and heating inclusive in terms. No smoking. Please telephone for details. **Mrs Spain**.

e-mail: info@whitehousefarm.co.uk   **website: www.whitehousefarm-kent.co.uk**

ST MARGARET'S BAY

Reach Court Farm Cottages, St Margaret's Bay. Working Farm. Situated in the heart of a family-run farm, surrounded by open countryside, these five luxury self-contained cottages are very special. They are set around the old farm yard in an attractive setting of lawns and shrubs with open views from the front or rear. The cottages sleep from two to six plus cot and the accommodation is of the highest standard giving them a relaxing country feel with the kitchens equipped with ovens, fridges, microwaves, toasters, coffee makers, etc. There is also a washing machine and tumble dryer in an adjoining laundry room. Reach Court Farm is the nearest farm to France and was known as the "Front Line Farm" during World War II. St Margaret's is a rural village with shops and public houses offering a range of eating facilities. Dover, Folkestone, Canterbury and Sandwich are all within easy reach. **ETC ★★★★**. For brochure contact: **Mrs J. Mitchell, Reach Court Farm, St Margaret's-at-Cliff, St Margaret's Bay, Dover CT15 6AQ (01304 852159; Fax: 01304 853902).**

ENGLAND

LANCASHIRE

BLACKPOOL (Norbreck)

Mrs C. Moore, 'Cotswold', 2a Haddon Road, Norbreck, Blackpool FY2 9AH (01253 352227). The flats are situated in a quieter, select area on the edge of town adjoining the promenade with acres of grass and level walking. Our famous trams pass by frequently for the town centre, Cleveleys and Fleetwood. The Fylde is well known by golf and bowls enthusiasts. Our ground floor flat is spacious, fully self-contained and centrally heated. Sleeps up to six persons. We also have a flatlet with private bathroom and central heating sleeping up to two persons. Travel cot and high chair available. Pets welcome by arrangement. Midweek/Weekend Short Breaks can be arranged early season and during the illuminations. Rates from £120 per week. Phone or send SAE for brochure.

MORECAMBE

Mrs G.A. Tamassy, Gizella Holiday Flats, 8 Marine Road, West End, Morecambe LA3 1BS (01524 418249). Sleep 5. Luxury holiday flats and flatlets overlooking the gardens with a beautiful view of Morecambe Bay and Lakeland Hills. All modern facilities including en suite and colour TV. Easy access to Lake District, Lune Valley and Lancaster, and ideal for golf and birdwatching. Open all year. Overnight guests welcome. (Sorry, no children and no pets). Reasonable rates, with reductions for Senior Citizens off season. SAE please for confirmation. Member Morecambe Bay Warmth of Welcome.
**websites: www.morecambeholidayflats.co.uk
www.gizellaholidayflats.co.uk**

PILLING

Self-catering cottage. Sleeps 4. Quiet, rural location with easy access to Blackpool and local Wyre villages. Good area for cycling and walking. Well equipped with cooker, washing machine, microwave, TV, video etc. Ground floor comprises one double bedroom, one twin bedroom, both with en suite facilities; on the first floor a kitchen and dining area, lounge with good views and steps for access to the patio and garden. Brochure and prices on request. Contact: **Beryl and Peter Richardson, Bell Farm, Bradshaw Lane, Scronkey, Pilling, Preston PR3 6RN (01253 790324).**
website: www.bellfarm.co.uk

LINCOLNSHIRE

ALFORD

Mrs Stubbs, Woodthorpe Hall Country Cottages, Near Alford LN13 0DD (01507 450294; Fax: 01507 450885). Very well appointed luxury one and three bedroomed cottages, overlooking the golf course, all with central heating, colour TV, microwave, washer, dryer, dishwasher and fridge freezer. Woodthorpe is situated approximately six miles from the coastal resort of Mablethorpe and offers easy access to the picturesque Lincolnshire Wolds. Adjacent facilities include golf, fishing, garden centre, aquatic centre, snooker, pool and restaurant with bar and family room. ETC ★★★★
e-mail: enquiries@woodthorpehall.com
website: www.woodthorpehall.com

BARNOLDBY-LE-BECK

Grange Farm Cottages and Riding School, Waltham Road, Barnoldby-le-Beck DN37 0AR (for Cottage Reservations Tel: 01472 822216; Fax: 01472 313811; mobile: 07947 627663 or 07984 510192). Three well appointed cottages and riding school situated in the heart of the Lincolnshire Wolds. The tasteful conversion of a spacious, beamed Victorian barn provides stylish and roomy cottages, two sleeping four and one sleeping six in one double and one twin bedroom, plus bed settee in lounge/ dining area. Fully equipped kitchen. Bathroom with bath and shower. The Equestrian Centre offers professional tuition, an all-weather riding surface, stabling for guests' own horses, horses for hire, and an extensive network of bridle paths. ETC ★★★★
website: www.grangefarmcottages.com

MARKET RASEN

Mr R. Cox, Manor Farm Log Cabins, Manor Farm, East Firsby, Market Rasen LN8 2DB (01673 878258). New for 2004 - two log cabins set amongst trees. Each has three bedrooms accommodating up to six people; gas cooking and central heating, with breakfast and evening meal available at Manor Farm. Situated between Lincoln and the Wolds, ideal for exploring both. Terms from £300 to £500 per week, short breaks available. Please telephone for brochure.
e-mail: info@lincolnshire-lanes.com
website: www.lincolnshire-lanes.com

PLEASE NOTE

All the information in this book is given in good faith in the belief that it is correct. However, the publishers cannot guarantee the facts given in these pages, neither are they responsible for changes in policy, ownership or terms that may take place after the date of going to press. Readers should always satisfy themselves that the facilities they require are available and that the terms, if quoted, still apply.

ENGLAND

NORFOLK

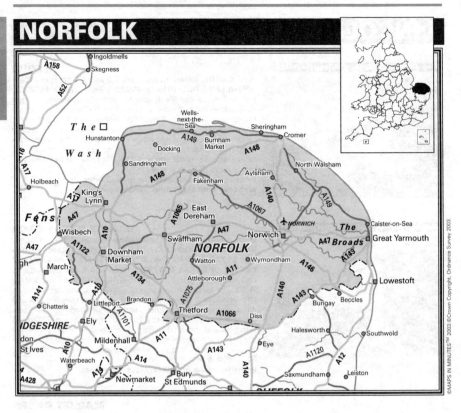

©MAPS IN MINUTES™ 2003 ©Crown Copyright. Ordnance Survey 2003

When making enquiries please mention FHG Publications

Small, family-run coastal site with direct access to sandy beach. Caravans, flats and centrally heated chalets, all with showers, flush toilets, refrigerators and colour television. Some accommodation available with sea view. On site licensed bar. Ideal location for touring the Broads or sightseeing North Norfolk. DOGS VERY WELCOME. Open from March to January.

Red House Chalet and Caravan Park, Paston Road, Bacton-on-Sea, Norfolk NR12 0JB Telephone 01692 650815

BLUE RIBAND HOLIDAYS
Tel: 01493 730445 • www.BlueRibandHolidays.co.uk
Inexpensive self-catering holidays at Caister, Hemsby, Scratby, California and Great Yarmouth.

BELLE AIRE PARK, Hemsby – luxury chalets close to beach and amenities. **SEA-DELL PARK**, Hemsby – detached chalets on spacious park. **CAISTER BEACH** – caravans in unrivalled seafront position. **PARKLANDS**, Hemsby – detached bungalows on private estate. All accommodation is of a very high standard and is only a short drive from Great Yarmouth. Dogs are welcome on local beaches. Open all year including Christmas and New Year. Please phone for colour brochure (seven days). Debit/credit cards accepted.

See also Colour Advertisement

CROMER
Hobby Cottage, Driftway Farm, Felbrigg, Cromer. Sleeps 4/6 plus cot. Completely modernised, comfortable cottage at the end of a quiet farm lane. Two miles from sandy coast and within easy access of North Norfolk bird sanctuaries, stately homes and Norfolk Broads. The cottage sleeps four/six, having a sitting room with TV and bed settee; two double bedrooms (one with double bed, one with twin beds); diningroom, well-equipped kitchen and bathroom. Garden and parking for two cars. Own transport essential. Available March-October. From £130 - £270 per week, including electricity. No linen. Enquiries, with SAE please, to **Mrs E. Raggatt, The Ferns, Berkeley Street, Eynesbury, St Neots, Cambs PE19 2NE (01480 213884).**
website: http://web.onetel.net.uk/~raggatt/

HORNING (Norfolk Broads)
Wake Robin Village Chalet. Sleeps 4. Set in the picturesque village of Horning on the River Bure at the heart of the Norfolk Broads. The Chalet has one double and two single bedrooms. A comfortable lounge with river-view balcony and well-equipped kitchen make a relaxing holiday home in Summer or Winter. Large garage for a car and safe storage of fishing tackle, bicycles, etc. Wake Robin guests have private access to the River Bure a few yards from the door for mooring boats and renowned coarse fishing. Electricity and linen supplied. Pets are welcome. **Contact: Bob Oldershaw, Heroncote, Lower Street, Horning, Norfolk NRl2 8PF (01692 631255).**
e-mail: bob.oldershaw@virgin.net

MUNDESLEY

Holiday Properties (Mundesley) Ltd. Self-catering modern brick built holiday chalets to let on three pretty sites in village of Mundesley on North Norfolk coast. Ideal location for visiting the Norfolk Broads, Cromer, Sheringham and Great Yarmouth. All chalets are close to lovely sandy beach and village amenities. All are heated, with fully equipped kitchens, colour TVs (Royal chalets have videos) and sleep 4-6. Cots available. Senior Citizen discount. Pets welcome. Short Breaks available out of season. For colour brochure: **01263 720719.**
e-mail: holidayproperties@tesco.net
website: www.holidayprops.freeuk.com

See also Colour Display Advertisement

NORWICH

Parlours, Norwich. Comfortable, recently modernised Victorian house in Norwich city centre, sleeping six. Walk to shops, restaurants, places of interest and recreation, ancient and modern. Accommodation comprises front parlour with TV and telephone, dining room, kitchen, utility room, shower room and wc. Upstairs there are two double and one twin bedroom and bath/shower/wc. Linen, heating and electricity included. Paved garden. Street parking. Sorry, no pets. Terms £420 to £560 per week. Bookings to: **Susan & Derek Wright, 147 Earlham Road, Norwich NR2 3RG (Tel & Fax: 01603 454169).**
e-mail: earlhamgh@hotmail.com

STANFIELD

Mr & Mrs Moore, Mangreen Farm, Stanfield, Near Dereham NR20 4HZ (01328 700272). Come and enjoy the relaxing, friendly atmosphere of one of our converted barns, set in 35 acres of unspoilt countryside in the heart of Norfolk. Ideal for exploring the surrounding historic towns, coastal villages and bird sanctuary. Three cottages sleeping up to eight. TV, microwave, washing machine, tumble dryer. Terms from £150 to £600; power and linen included. Open all year, short breaks available. Children and pets welcome.
website: www.mangreen.co.uk

See also Colour Display Advertisement

THETFORD

Holly Farm Cottages, High Common, Cranworth IP25 7SX (01362 821468). Two comfortable, single-storey cottages each sleeping one to four persons. Fully equipped, including TV/video, dishwasher, washing machine, central heating. Enclosed garden. Ample car parking. Uninterrupted views of beautiful countryside, peaceful lanes for walking/cycling. Local golf and fishing. Convenient for Norwich, North Norfolk Coast and Broads.
e-mail: jennie.mclaren@btopenworld.com

WINTERTON-ON-SEA

The Timbers, The Lane, Winterton-on-Sea. Sleeps 5 + cot. Comfortable, well-furnished ground floor flat in timber cottage, situated in quiet seaside village, just eight miles north of Great Yarmouth. Broad sandy beach and sand dunes (Nature Reserve) for pleasant walks. Three miles from Norfolk Broads for boating and fishing. Flat is carpeted throughout and fully equipped for self-catering family holidays. Ideal for children, and pets welcome. Double, twin and single room. Bed linen provided, and maid service twice a week. Attractive beamed sittingroom with colour TV and video. Secluded garden. Car parking. Available May to September. Terms from £200 to £320 per week. For details please contact: **Mrs Elly Field, 80 Hillside Gardens, Barnet, Hertfordshire EN5 2NL (0208 441 3493).**

NORTHUMBERLAND

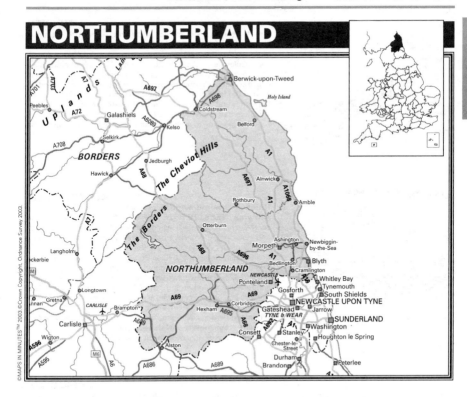

**Town Foot Farm, Shilbottle, Alnwick, Northumberland NE66 2HG Tel/Fax: 01665 575591
E-mail: crissy@villagefarmcottages.co.uk Website: www.villagefarmcottages.co.uk**

VILLAGE FARM *SELF-CATERING*

Choice of cosy cottages, airy chalets or 17th century farmhouse. Sleep between two and twelve. Perfectly situated; three miles from beaches and historic Alnwick. Fantastic facilities include an indoor forty-foot heated swimming pool, health club, sauna/steam room, sunshower, tennis court and a games room. Visit our beauty therapist. Also try fishing and riding.

Terms from £135 – £975.

Free colour brochure.   ETC ★★★ to ★★★★★

PLEASE SEND A STAMPED ADDRESSED ENVELOPE WITH ENQUIRIES

ALNMOUTH

Mrs A. Stanton, Mount Pleasant Farm, Alnmouth, Alnwick NE66 3BY (01665 830215). Mount Pleasant is situated on top of a hill on the outskirts of the seaside village of Alnmouth with spectacular views of surrounding countryside. We offer fresh air, sea breezes, green fields, beautiful beaches, country roads and peace and quiet. There are two golf courses and a river meanders around the farm with all its bird life. Convenient for Holy Island, the Farnes and the Cheviots. The farmhouse has an annexe which is self-contained, and sleeps two adults. Pets welcome. Chalet available sleeping four plus six berth caravan available - prices on application.

See also Colour Display Advertisement

ALNWICK near

Helen & Graeme Wyld, New Moor House, Edlingham, Alnwick NE66 2BT (01665 574638). Traditional stone courtyard high quality self-catering for 2-4. Situated between Alnwick and Rothbury, the perfect base for exploring Northumberland. Newcastle-upon-Tyne 30 miles. Briar Cottage sleeps two (four-poster); pets not allowed. Rose Cottage sleeps two (four-poster); two well-behaved pets welcome. Clematis Cottage sleeps four (one double, one twin); two well-behaved pets welcome. All have central heating, log-burning stove (all fuel incl.), payphone, colour TV; fully equipped kitchen with electric cooker, microwave, freezer, dishwasher etc. Bed linen and towels incl. Private water supply. Woodland gardens. Non-smokers only please. ETC ★★★★
e-mail: stay@newmoorhouse.co.uk
website: www.newmoorhouse.co.uk

BAMBURGH

Point Cottages, Bamburgh. POINT COTTAGES consist of a cluster of cottages in a superb location at the end of the Wynding, next to a beautiful golf course on the edge of Bamburgh, only a short drive away from many other attractive Links courses. Bamburgh is an unspoilt coastal village dominated by a magnificent castle and is an ideal base for visiting other parts of historic Northumbria. The cottages overlook the sea with fine views of the Farne Islands and Lindisfarne. Sandy beaches nearby. They share a large garden with lawns and a total of ten car parking spaces are provided (two per cottage). The cottages are in excellent order, have open fire or woodburning stove and are comfortably furnished. Each cottage has its own special atmosphere but all are warm, cosy and well-equipped. **ETC**
★★★. For further information, availability, prices and booking please contact: **John and Elizabeth Sanderson, 30 The Oval, Benton, Newcastle-upon-Tyne NE12 9PP (0191-266 2800 or 01665 720246 (weekends); Fax: 0191-215 1630).**
e-mail: info@bamburgh-cottages.co.uk   **website: www.bamburgh-cottages.co.uk**

BELFORD (NEAR)

Etive Cottage, Warenford, Near Belford. Tastefully converted from a stable/blacksmith's forge, Etive is a lovely two-bedroomed stone cottage with double glazing and central heating. Situated on the outskirts of the hamlet of Warenford with sweeping views over open countryside to the Bamburgh coast. Accommodation is on one level, the lounge is comfortably furnished including a TV/video and music centre, fully equipped kitchen/dining room, one twin and one double bedroom with wash basin and shaver point, bathroom with bath and shower. All linen, towels and electricity included. Fenced garden with secure courtyard parking. Dogs and children welcome to bring their well-behaved owners. For brochure please contact: **Jan Thompson (Tel & Fax: 01668 213233).**

Bluebell Farm Holiday Cottages

Bluebell Farm enjoys a quiet central location in the village of Belford, a pleasantly quiet and charming village in north Northumberland, with its diverse range of shops and pubs, all within easy walking distance.

Bluebell Farm Holiday Cottages are converted from the original stone-built farm buildings. Situated away from the road, with ample off-street parking, the cottages are in a location which is safe for children and convenient for all the village amenities.

Each cottage is equipped with gas cooker, microwave, fridge/freezer or fridge, coffee machine, kettle, toaster and colour television with DVD player. All have gas-fired central heating. Living/dining/kitchen areas are open plan in all cottages except Cheviot, which has a separate kitchen. Private laundry facility is available at a small additional charge. Fold-out bed by prior arrangement. Weekly bookings and short breaks include all gas and electricity charges, bed linen and towels.

- CHEVIOT COTTAGE: 1 double room – sleeps 1 or 2 plus cot if required. Single storey. Small front patio.
- BLUEBELL COTTAGE: 1 double and 1 children's bedroom - sleeps up to 4. Small front garden.
- CHILLINGHAM COTTAGE: 1 double and 1 bunk bedroom – sleeps up to 4. Front patio area.
- FARNE COTTAGE: 1 double and 1 twin - sleeps up to 4. Front patio area.
- LINDISFARNE COTTAGE: 2 doubles and 1 children's bedroom – sleeps up to 6. Front patio area.
- ST ABBS COTTAGE: 2 doubles and 1 twin - sleeps up to 6. Front and side patio areas.

Mrs Phyl Carruthers, Bluebell Farm, Belford, Northumberland NE70 7QE
Tel: 01668 213362• E-mail: phyl.carruthers@virgin.net

BERWICK-UPON-TWEED

The Boathouse, Norham, Berwick-Upon-Tweed. Sleeps 10. A delightful south-facing, 18th century house offering spacious accommodation with frontage to the River Tweed and spectacular views over the surrounding countryside. The ground floor consists of a sitting room with TV, lounge with open fire and TV, dining room, kitchen with electric cooker, fridge/freezer, microwave, automatic washing machine, tumble dryer and dishwasher; bathroom with bath, shower, basin and WC; en suite bedroom with king-size bed. First floor has three bedrooms, all with washbasins and bathroom with bath/shower, WC and washbasin. Oil central heating, duvets and linen are provided (not towels).Sports centre, golf course, beaches, places of historic interest, salmon fishing and abundant wildlife. Tariffs from £350 to £750 per week. Open all year. **ETC ★★★.** For further information contact **Mrs M Chantler, Great Humphries Farm, Grafty Green, Maidstone, Kent ME17 2AX (Tel & Fax: 01622 859672).** e-mail: chantler@humphreys46.fsnet.co.uk

CHATHILL

Mrs Naomi Barrett, Gardener's Cottage, Tuggal Hall, Chathill NE67 5EW (01665 589229). Gardener's Cottage is detached from the Hall and stands in a yard overlooking a paddock and fields to a view of the sea. Situated near the coast between Embleton and Beadnell, it takes about five minutes by car to reach the nearest beach. Accommodation consists of one bedroom with double bed, large bathroom and lavatory on the first floor. On the ground floor there is one bedroom with twin beds, sitting room with sofa bed, open fire and colour TV. Kitchen with electric cooker, microwave and dining area, fridge and automatic washing machine. Bathroom and separate lavatory. Bed linen can be hired by request. We regret pets cannot be taken without prior arrangement.

HALTWHISTLE

Ald White Craig Cottages. On the edge of Northumberland National Park, a superb base for exploring Hadrian's Wall and Roman museums. Lake District, Scottish Borders and Northumberland coast all approximately one hour's drive. B&B also available in farmhouse. WREN'S NEST sleeps one/two persons; SMITHY COTTAGE sleeps two/three; COBBLESTONES COTTAGE sleeps four; COACH HOUSE sleeps five; SHEPHERD'S HEFT sleeps six. **ETC** up to ★★★★. For further information contact: **C. Zard, Ald White Craig Farm, Shield Hill, Near Hadrian's Wall, Haltwhistle NE49 9NW (01434 320565; Fax: 01434 321236).**
e-mail: whitecraigfarm@yahoo.co.uk
website: www.hadrianswallholidays.com

HALTWHISTLE

Scotchcoulthard, Haltwhistle NE49 9NH (01434 344470; Fax: 01434 344020). Situated within Northumberland National Park, Scotchcoulthard is surrounded by splendid scenery with magnificent views and not another inhabited dwelling in sight. Fully equipped, our five cottages have been professionally designed and furnished with comfort in mind. All bedrooms are en suite, and all cottages have open fires to give that warm welcome after a day out exploring. There is a large indoor heated swimming pool and a games room with full-size table tennis table, pool table, hi-fi system and a variety of toys for younger visitors. Although remote, Scotchcoulthard is not isolated - it is possible to be parked in the Metro Centre or the middle of Newcastle or Carlisle within an hour. Please send for our brochure.

Well behaved pets and horses welcome. **ETC** ★★★★
e-mail: info@scotchcoulthard.co.uk   **website: www.scotchcoulthard.co.uk**

HEXHAM

Isaac's Cottage. Situated in the hills between Northumberland and Durham, Isaac's Cottage overlooks the River Allen. Surrounded by open fields and with the benefit of fishing in the little river only a field away, this cottage is a paradise for families wanting a 'get away from it all' holiday in lovely countryside. The cottage consists of three bedrooms - one double and one twin, family bathroom. Facilities include - electric cooker, microwave, fridge, kettle, toaster, coffee maker, slow cooker. Automatic washing machine. Colour TV. Oil-fired central heating, logs for the open fire, electricity included in the rent. Bed-linen and a selection of hand towels. Ample parking. Prices from £180 - £350 per week. **Mrs Heather Robson, Allenheads Farm, Allenheads, Hexham NE47 9HJ (01434 685312).**

HOLY ISLAND (NEAR)

Janet Dunn, Lickar Lea, Bowsden, Berwick-Upon-Tweed TD15 2TP (01289 388500; Fax: 01289 388507). Situated in the former farm steading of Lickar Lea our one bedroom cottage offers the highest standard of accommodation and comfort. Full oil central heating combined with high insulation values ensure a warm and cosy stay. Accommodation comprises light, airy living room with French doors to patio, fully equipped kitchen, large bathroom with bath, washbasin and separate shower, and large double bedroom. The cottage is only four miles inland from Holy Island and has lovely views over the coast and local Kyloe hills. (ETC award pending) Rates: April - October £260, November - March £210, Christmas and New Year weeks £300. Sorry, no smoking. Pets by arrangement. **ETC** ★★★
e-mail: janet@lickarlea.co.uk   **website: www.lickarlea.co.uk**

ROTHBURY/HARBOTTLE

Mrs J.D. Blakey, Woodhall Farm Holiday Cottage, Woodhall Farm, Harbottle, Morpeth NE65 7AD (Tel & Fax: 01669 650245). Sleep 6 + Cot. Spacious, well-equipped farmhouse, set within the National Park in the Coquet Valley, an ideal location for a relaxing holiday, and a great area for cycling, walking and exploring beautiful Northumberland. Woodhall is easy to find, being situated on the main road seven miles west of Rothbury and between Sharperton and Harbottle. Pets welcome. Terms from £190 to £400 per week. Please contact for further details. **ETC ★★★**
e-mail: Blakey@woodhall65.freeserve.co.uk
website: www.woodhallcottage.co.uk

WOOLER

Coach House Cottages, Ilderton Glebe, near Wooler. Sleeps 4/5. Two cottages converted from a Grade II Listed barn, offering comfortable accommodation. Electricity, fuel and linen included in rent. Ilderton is a hamlet on the edge of the Northumbrian National Park and close to the Cheviot Hills. It is an ideal spot for walking, bird watching, visiting historic houses and castles. There are beautiful beaches 15 miles away and trips to the Farne Islands and Holy Island. Both cottages have garages, ample parking, one has an open fire, night storage heating and fitted carpets throughout. There is a walled garden with garden chairs. Children and dogs welcome. Also Bed and Breakfast available at Ildderton Glebe. Rents: £175–£455 per week. **ETC ★★★.**
Contact: **Mrs Sale, Ilderton Glebe, Ilderton, near Wooler NE66 4YD (01668 217293).**

PLEASE NOTE

All the information in this book is given in good faith in the belief that it is correct. However, the publishers cannot guarantee the facts given in these pages, neither are they responsible for changes in policy, ownership or terms that may take place after the date of going to press. Readers should always satisfy themselves that the facilities they require are available and that the terms, if quoted, still apply.

ENGLAND

OXFORDSHIRE

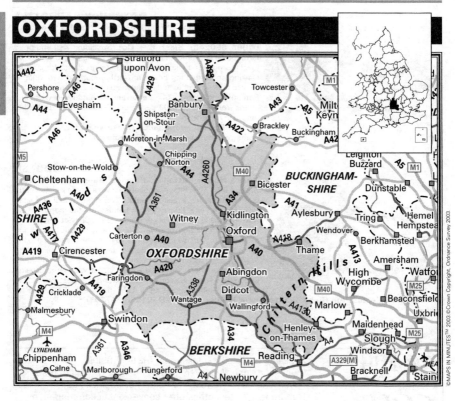

©MAPS IN MINUTES™ 2003 ©Crown Copyright. Ordnance Survey 2003

BANBURY

Anita's Holiday Cottages: The Shippon, The Byre, & The Stables. Sleep 2-8. Top quality barn conversions, superbly finished to a high standard. Fitted kitchens include microwave, cooker, washing machine, dishwasher. Fully heated. Linen included. Suits couples and large parties. Central to the Cotswolds, Oxford and Stratford or just enjoying the surrounding countryside. Walk to village pub. Non-smoking. Sorry no pets. Ample parking. Close to M40 Junction 12. Short breaks available during low season. **ETC ★★★/★★★★**. For further details please telephone **01295 750731 or 07966 171959.**

THAME

The Hollies, Thame. Sleeps 6/7. A beautifully situated luxury bungalow with a pretty, secluded garden only five minutes from the centre of the historic market town of Thame and conveniently situated for Oxford, M40 and trains to London and Birmingham. Three double bedrooms (one en suite shower), and one single bedroom. Bathroom and additional toilet. Modern fully fitted French kitchen and utility room with microwave, dishwasher, self-cleaning cooker, split level gas and electric hob, fridge and deep freeze, washing machine and tumble dryer. Off-street parking for two cars. Terms from £350 to £450 per week. **ETC★★★★**. Barn also available - one large bedroom, bathroom, shower room, lounge, open plan kitchen, sleeps 4, from £300 per week. Contact: **Ms Julia Tanner, Little Acre, Tetsworth, Near Thame, Oxon OX9 7AT (01844 281423; mobile: 077986 25252).**
e-mail: info@theholliesthame.co.uk
website: www.theholliesthame.co.uk

SHROPSHIRE

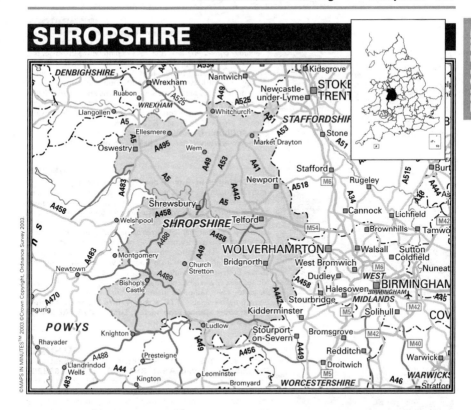

ENGLAND

CRAVEN ARMS

Mrs Davies, Hesterworth Holidays, Hesterworth, Hopesay, Craven Arms SY7 8EX (01588 660487; Fax: 01588 660153). A selection of comfortable country cottages and apartments, surrounded by 12 acres of beautiful gardens and grounds. Large dining room ideal for families or groups, residential licence. Short breaks available. We truly believe that there is no better centre in Britain for the bird watcher, walker, historian, motorist or for people who love the countryside. Groups welcome. Open all year. Half a mile from Aston-on-Clun off B4368. Ludlow 10 miles. Also Bed and Breakfast. Self-catering £124 - £432 per week. **ETC ★★–★★★.**
e-mail: info@hesterworth.co.uk
website: www.hesterworth.co.uk

CRAVEN ARMS

Mrs B. Freeman, Upper House, Clunbury, Craven Arms SY7 0HG (01588 660629). Sleeps 4. Welcome to Horseshoe Cottage which is situated in the beautiful gardens of Upper House (17th century Listed) in Clunbury, a village of archaeological interest in a designated Area of Outstanding Natural Beauty – A.E. Housman countryside. This private self-catering cottage is completely furnished and equipped; being on one level the accommodation is suitable for elderly and disabled persons. Colour TV. Children and pets welcome; cot available. Ample parking. This Welsh Border countryside is rich in medieval history, unspoilt villages and natural beauty. Enjoy walking on the Long Mynd and Offa's Dyke, or explore Ludlow and Ironbridge. £135 to £180 per week. Please write or phone for further details.

ENGLAND

IRONBRIDGE

Virginia Evans, Church Farm, Rowton, Near Wellington, Telford TF6 6QY (Tel & Fax: 01952 770381). Three beautifully converted barn cottages, sleeping between 2-8 people. Decorated and equipped to a high standard, situated in a quiet hamlet yet only 15 minutes from Shrewsbury and the World Heritage site of Ironbridge Gorge Museum. All cottages have some ground floor bedrooms and bathrooms and are wheelchair friendly. They have enclosed patio gardens looking onto the fields beyond making it safe for children and pets. Ample parking. Prices: £170–£550 per week. **ETC ★★★**
e-mail: Churchfarm49@beeb.net
website: www.virtual-shropshire.co.uk/churchfarm

LUDLOW

The Cottages at Ravenscourt Manor are superb, newly renovated units at this magnificent Tudor Manor set in two acres of gardens and just three miles from Ludlow. Near excellent pubs and restaurants, it is a wonderful area for touring, walking and historic Ludlow. One cottage has two bedrooms, one double with extra bed and the other with three single beds; one full bathroom and shower room and wc. Downstairs kitchen/diner and separate sittingroom. The other cottage has a kitchen/diner, large sittingroom and a double bedroom; twin-beds in the gallery above. Both have full central heating, electric cooker, microwave, fridge/freezer, washing machine, dishwasher, TV and video, and cassette player/radio. All inclusive. Terms from £140 to £330. Short breaks available. **ETC ★★★★. Mrs Elizabeth Purnell, Ravenscourt Manor, Woofferton, Ludlow SY8 4AL (01584 711905).**

LUDLOW

Sally and Tim Loft, Goosefoot Barn, Pinstones, Diddlebury, Craven Arms SY7 9LB (01584 861326). Converted in 2000 from stone and timbered barns, the three cottages are individually decorated and equipped to the highest standards. Fresh linen and towels are also provided for your comfort. Each cottage has en suite facilities and private garden or seating area. Situated in a secluded valley with walks from the doorstep through beautiful Corvedale. Ideally located for exploring South Shropshire, only eight miles from Ludlow. Cottages sleep up to six people and pets are welcome. Games room with full-sized snooker table, darts, toys, games, videos and books. Short breaks available. **ETC ★★★★**
website: www.goosefootbarn.co.uk

LUDLOW

Hazel Cottage, Duxmoor, Onibury, Craven Arms. Sleeps 4. Beautifully restored, semi-detached, yet private, period cottage, set in its own extensive cottage-style garden with its own drive and ample parking space. Amidst peaceful surroundings and panoramic views of the countryside, it is situated five miles north of historic Ludlow and one-and-a-half miles from the A49. The cottage retains all its original features and fittings with traditional decoration and is fully furnished, with antiques throughout. It comprises a comfortable living room with a Victorian range for coal and log fire; TV, wireless and telephone; diningroom with bread oven; fully equipped kitchen, hall, Victorian bathroom; two bedrooms (one double and one twin-bedded) with period washbasins. Electric central heating throughout. All linen included. Tourist information. Open all year. Short Breaks available. No pets. Terms from £195 to £410 per week. **ETC ★★★★. Mrs Rachel Sanders, Duxmoor Farm, Onibury, Craven Arms SY7 9BQ (01584 856342).**

Readers are requested to mention this guidebook
when seeking accommodation (and please enclose
a stamped addressed envelope).

SOMERSET

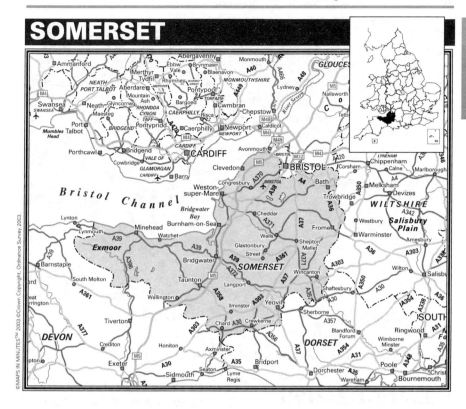

BATH near

David and Jackie Bishop, Toghill House Farm, Wick, Near Bath BS30 5RT (01225 891261; Fax: 01225 892128). Situated just four miles north of Bath and within a few miles of Lacock, Castle Combe, Tetbury and the Cotswolds. The 17th century farm buildings have been converted into luxury self-catering cottages with well-equipped kitchens, TV and video. Separate laundry room and all bed linen, towels etc. included. Ample car parking. Pets welcome. You are welcome to roam amongst our many animals and enjoy the outstanding country views. B&B also available in warm and cosy 17th century farmhouse.

website: www.toghillhousefarm.co.uk

CATCOTT

'Upalong', 5 Weares Lane, Catcott. M5 six miles, midway Wells/Quantocks, edge of Levels; waterfowl, birdwatching (particularly winter/spring), coast 11 miles, coarse fishing two miles; quiet picturesque village. Shop hairdresser, play area, two pubs serving good food. Homely, comfortable three-bedroomed bungalow sleeps five plus; all beds have king-sized duvets, electric blankets, matching curtains. Lounge with open fire (logs free), colour TV, video. Night storage central heating and immersion heater. All electricity by slot meter. Payphone. Bathroom with shower over bath, washbasin and toilet. Kitchen with dishwasher, washing machine, full cooker, microwave, fridge etc. All linen, towels etc supplied. Children welcome, cot available. Pets by arrangement. Large garden, patio set and barbecue. Off-road parking. Terms from £150 to £235. Contact: **Mrs Eileen Chilcott, Silverdale, 5 Langland Lane, Catcott, Bridgwater TA7 9HR (01278 722085**

ENGLAND

WOOLCHAMBER COTTAGES

A choice of four cottages overlooking the River Barle in the heart of Exmoor. The cottages are converted to a very high standard from a 300 year-old Woolchamber. Sleeping between 2 and 6 people, all the cottages are centrally heated and come fully equipped with cooker, microwave, washing machine/ tumble dryer, fridge freezer, Colour TV and telephone. The perfect setting to explore the magnificent Exmoor countryside and coastline. Dogs welcome. Guided walks by arrangement.

Contact for more details:

(01643) 831259

e-mail: cottages@simonsbathhouse.co.uk
website: www.simonsbathhouse.co.uk

Wintershead

EXMOOR

Jane Styles, Wintershead Farm, Simonsbath, Exmoor TA24 7LF (01643 831222). Occupying a unique location with breathtaking views within the National Park, five quality stone cottages converted from original farm buildings, offering peace, tranquillity, privacy and all the comforts of home. A special place to recharge your batteries away from the stresses of everyday life. Stabling, grazing and DIY livery available. Please telephone or write for a colour brochure. **ETC ★★★★**
website: www.wintershead.co.uk

GLASTONBURY

Mrs S. Kavanagh, Middlewick Holiday Cottages, Wick Lane, Glastonbury BA6 8JW. (Tel & Fax: 01458 832351). Eight delightful cottages set in eight acres of gardens and orchards. With far-reaching views over the Somerset Levels to the Mendip hills beyond. Centrally located for many places of interest. The cottages were converted from a 17th century Listed farmhouse and its barns. Retaining a wealth of beamed ceilings and inglenooks, each cottage is different; sleep from two to six. Set in a courtyard and complemented by a heated indoor swimming pool for guests' use only. Cots and highchairs available. Terms from £200 to £650 per cottage per week, depending on size and time of year.
e-mail: info@middlewickholidaycottages.co.uk
website: www.middlewickholidaycottages.co.uk

MINEHEAD

16th century thatched cottages. Sleep 2 - 6. All well equipped and attractively furnished, and situated within ten minutes' walk of shops, sea and moor. Rose-Ash cottage (sleeps 2) is all electric. Little Thatch (sleeps 5) has two double and a single bedroom, and Willow Cottage (sleeps 6) has one double and two twin bedrooms; both have gas central heating and electric fires for chilly days. All have enclosed patio/garden and private parking. Electricity and gas are metered; bed linen can be provided at extra cost. Pets welcome. Please send SAE for details to: **Mr T. Stone, Troytes Farmstead, Tivington, Minehead TA24 8SU (01643 704531).**

MINEHEAD

St Audries Bay Holiday Club, West Quantoxhead, near Minehead TA4 4DY (01984 632515; Fax: 01984 632785). The family holiday centre on the Somerset coast. Facilities include indoor heated pool, family entertainment programme, wide range of sports and leisure facilities, licensed bar and restaurant and an all day snack bar. Situated only 15 miles from the M5, near Exmoor at the foot of the Quantock Hills. Well-maintained level site with sea views. On-site shop. Family owned and managed. Half board holidays available in comfortable chalets, self-catering in luxury caravans. Touring caravans and tents welcome. Luxury holiday homes for sale.
e-mail: mrandle@staudriesbay.demon.co.uk
website: www.staudriesbay.co.uk

MUCHELNEY

Mrs J. Thorne, Gothic House, Muchelney, Langport, Somerset TA10 0DW (01458 250626). Gothic House is a Victorian former farmhouse with two self-contained units available. Well-equipped kitchens with washing machine, microwave, cooker, fridge. Free central heating. Comfortably furnished sitting rooms with colour TV. Bedlinen and bathroom towels provided. It is situated on the edge of the Somerset Levels in the unspoilt village of Muchelney. Within the village are the ruins of a medieval Abbey and also the medieval priest house belonging to the National Trust. Gothic House can be found two-and-a-half miles south of Langport and is next door to well-known potter John Leach. Ideal for touring, cycling, fishing, walking and birdwatching. Terms from £160 to £295 per week. **ETC ★★★**
e-mail: joy-thorne@totalserve.co.uk

PORLOCK

Lucott Farm, Porlock, Minehead. Sleeps 12. Comfortable farmhouse on working Exmoor hill farm, with wood-burning fireplaces and all modern conveniences. It lies at the head of Horner Valley and guests will delight in the wonderful scenery. Excellent base for walking, pony trekking nearby. The house has three double and three twin bedrooms, bathroom with shower over bath, large sitting room, dining room, kitchen with oil-fired Aga, cloakroom and toilet, utility room with shower, and a garden. Shops and pubs three miles. Parking for five cars. All fuel and bed linen included. Terms from £400 to £900. Discount for parties of four or less. **Mrs J. Stapleford, West Lucott Farm Cottage, Ley Hill, Porlock, Minehead TA24 8LU (01643 862669).**
e-mail: fred.stapleford@talk21.com

SHEPTON MALLET

Knowle Farm, West Compton, Shepton Mallet BA4 4PD (01749 890482; Fax: 01749 890405). Working farm. Cottages sleep 2/5/6. Knowle Farm Cottages are converted from the old cowstall and stables, set around the old farmyard now laid out as a pleasant garden. Quiet location at the end of a private drive. Excellent views and plenty of wildlife. All cottages furnished to a high standard - bathroom (bath, shower, toilet, washbasin); fully fitted kitchen (automatic washing machine, fridge/freezer, microwave, full size cooker). Two cottages have kitchen/diner, separate lounge with colour TV, the other two have kitchen, lounge/diner, colour TV. Cot, high chair by prior arrangement. Bed linen supplied, towels by request. Surrounding area full of interesting places to visit. Five miles from Wells and Mendip Golf Clubs; the area also has a wide selection of family attractions, fishing, selection of pubs and restaurants. Around the farm plenty of walks, play area for children. Sorry no pets. Terms from £150 to £450. Car essential, ample parking. Payphone for guests. Open all year. Short breaks available. **ETC ★★★**
e-mail: info@knowle-farm-cottages.co.uk   **website: www.knowle-farm-cottages.co.uk**

SHEPTON MALLET

Pat and Ted Allen, Springfield Cottage Holidays, Springfield House, Maesdown Hill, Stoney Stratton, Evercreech BA4 6EG (01749 830748). Sleep 4/5 +cot. Springfield Cottages have been tastefully converted from the stables in the adjoining yard to Springfield House, a large country house set in eight acres of beautiful Somerset countryside, on the south slopes of the Mendip Hills. Ideal for bird lovers, walkers, cyclists, fishing, golfing or for visiting the many sites of historical and international interest. Historic Wells, Glastonbury and Bath are only a short drive away; many country pubs and restaurants nearby. Both cottages are well-equipped, with wheelchair access throughout the ground floor. Both have lounge/diner with bed settee; downstairs bathroom/showerroom; enclosed gardens with furniture and barbecue. Cot and high chair available. All linen provided, electricity by meter reading, payable on departure. Ample parking. Open all year. Short Breaks available. Well-behaved pets welcome. Non-smoking. Terms from £210 to £480 per week. **ETC ★★★/★★★★**
e-mail: Ted.Allen@btinternet.com

See also Colour Display Advertisement

WATCHET

Croft Holiday Cottages, Anchor Street, Watchet TA23 0BY (01984 631121; Fax: 01984 631134). A courtyard of six cottages/bungalows situated in a quiet backwater of the small harbour town of Watchet. A short, level walk from shops, pubs, restaurants, marina and steam railway station. Use of heated indoor pool. Lawned area. Children's play equipment. Sleep 2-8 persons. Three properties with private gardens. Central heating, bed linen incl. Washing machine, TV, microwave, BBQ. Cots, highchairs on request. Towels for hire. Watchet is an ideal base for touring/walking the beautiful Exmoor, Brendon and Quantock Hills. Travel on the steam railway and visit ancient Dunster with its castle or enjoy the numerous local beaches. Short Break details on request. **ETC ★★★★**
e-mail: croftcottages@talk21.com
website: www.cottagessomerset.com

See also Colour Display Advertisement

WESTON-SUPER-MARE

Gwen Wilson, Seaford Lodge Holiday Flats, 28 Clifton Road, Weston-Super-Mare BS23 1BL (01934 429866/ 628105). Modernised and refurbished to a high standard, all flats are self-contained with their own toilet and shower room. Fully equipped with fridge/freezer, full electric cooker, electric kettle, ironing facilities, toaster, microwave and electric radiators. All flats have fitted carpets, 20" colour television; own keys and meters. Cotton sheets, pillow cases and continental quilts provided, all freshly laundered. Heating with night storage heaters inclusive in early and late season. Towels and tea cloths not supplied. Regret, no pets. Parking. Fully fire protected.

A useful Index of Towns/Villages and Counties appears on
page 281 – please also refer to Contents Page 3.

ENGLAND

STAFFORDSHIRE

LEEK

Wren Cottage at Fairboroughs Farm, Rudyard, Near Leek ST13 8PR (01260 226341). Robert and Elizabeth Lowe extend a warm welcome to their Grade II Listed 16th century holiday cottage, set in the beautiful Staffordshire Moorlands. Situated on a working beef/sheep farm and recently converted from a shippon (cow shed), the original historic features have been left to add to the ambience of the cottage. On one level with one double and one twin-bedded room, cot available, with linen provided. Fitted kitchen; electric cooker; fridge freezer; microwave; bath/shower; TV/video; radio/CD; garden furniture/barbecue; laundry available. Sorry, no smoking or pets. Easy reach of Peak District, Alton Towers, Potteries; Manchester Airport 45 mins. **ETC ★★★★**

PEAK DISTRICT

Field Head Farmhouse Holidays, Calton. Situated midway between Leek and Ashbourne within the Southern Peak District and the Staffordshire Moorlands, Grade II Listed farmhouse with stables, set within its own grounds with open views. Well equipped, with SKY TV. Sleeps 11 plus campbed and cot. Ample space for family caravan. Set in beautiful secluded surroundings close to Dovedale and the Manifold Valley. Ideal country for the walker, horse rider or cyclist. Alton Towers 15-minute drive. All pets and horses welcome. Open all year. Short winter breaks. Late booking discount. Contact **Janet Hudson (01538 308352).** **ETC ★★★★**
website: www.field-head.co.uk

The River Trent, near Great Haywood, Staffordshire

SUFFOLK

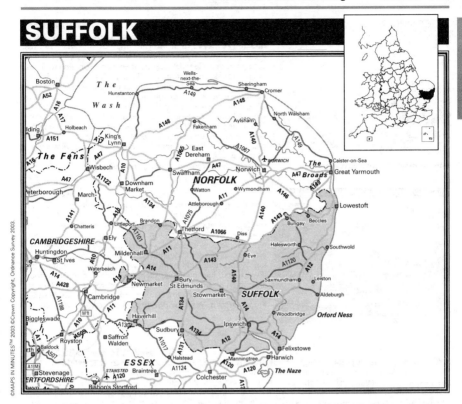

CRATFIELD/HALESWORTH

Cherry Trees at Cratfield. Set deep in the Suffolk countryside, 25 minutes from Southwold and the Heritage Coast, Cherry Trees offers an ideal family holiday or peaceful retreat. Standing alone within a large garden enclosed by trees, it is a suitable holiday home for children and pets. Accommodation comprises sitting room with open fire, kitchen with all modern appliances, bathroom with bath/shower and single bedroom downstairs, twin and double bedrooms upstairs. Garage/playroom. Garden equipped with table and chairs plus barbecue. Outside parking for two cars. Contact: **Chris Knox (01379 586709; Fax: 01379 588033)**
e-mail: J.L.Knox@farming.co.uk

KESSINGLAND

Kessingland Cottages, Rider Haggard Lane, Kessingland. Sleeps 6. An exciting three-bedroomed recently built semi-detached cottage situated on the beach, three miles south of sandy beach at Lowestoft. Fully and attractively furnished with colour TV. Delightful sea and lawn views from floor-to-ceiling windows of lounge. Accommodation for up to six people. Well-equipped kitchen with electric cooker, fridge, hot and cold water; electric immersion heater. Electricity by £1 coin meter. Luxurious bathroom with coloured suite. No linen or towels provided. Only 30 yards to beach and sea fishing. One mile to wildlife country park with mini-train. Buses quarter-of-a-mile and shopping centre half-a-mile. Parking, but car not essential. Children and disabled persons welcome. Available 1st March to 7th January. Weekly terms from £50 in early March and late December to £250 in high season. SAE to **Mr S. Mahmood, 156 Bromley Road, Beckenham, Kent BR3 6PG (Tel & Fax: 020 8650 0539).**
e-mail: jeeptrek@kjti.freeserve.co.uk   website: www.k-cottage.co.uk

LAVENHAM

The Grove Cottages, Priory Green/Edwardstone CO10 5PP (01787 211115 or International: 0044 1787 211115). Enjoy the romantic atmosphere of your own 300-year-old farm cottage, with ancient oak beams, open log fires, period furniture, ducks, roses and a touch of luxury. Set in lovely Suffolk countryside, just 90 minutes from London or 60 minutes from Cambridge, our seven cottages are close to the beautiful medieval villages of Lavenham, Long Melford and Kersey. Bikes and canoes are available to explore 'Constable Country'. Pets are welcome. The cottages sleep from 2-6. Please visit our New Superfast Website where you will find lots of photos, information and prices, plus an Availability Calendar. Short Breaks are always welcome. **ETC ★★★★**

e-mail: mark@grove-cottages.co.uk   website: www.grove-cottages.co.uk

ORFORD

The Gedgrave Broom. A unique chance to truly get away from it all. Situated on a traditional mixed farm in the heart of Suffolk's Heritage Coast, the Gedgrave Broom retains its 18th century character, yet offers comfortable accommodation for up to nine people. The weekly hire charge includes linen, towels and electricity and a small quantity of firewood. Ideal for those who enjoy an active rural holiday. Five bedrooms (including two downstairs); fully equipped kitchen, laundry room, dining room and sitting room; two bathrooms, shower room. Fenced garden with BBQ. Non-smoking. **ETC ★★★★. Mrs Watson, Newton Farm, Orford, Woodbridge IP12 2AG (01394 450488)**

SOUTHWOLD/WALBERSWICK

H.A. Adnams, Estate Agents, 98 High Street, Southwold IP18 6DP (01502 723292; Fax: 01502 724794). Furnished Holiday Cottages, Houses and Flats, available in this charming unspoilt seaside town. Convenient for sandy beaches, with safe bathing, sailing, fishing, golf and tennis. Near to 300 acres of open Common. Attractive country walks and historic churches are to be found in this area, also the fine City of Norwich, the Festival Town of Aldeburgh and the Bird Sanctuary at Minsmere, all within easy driving distance. SAE, please, for brochure with full particulars. **website: www.haadnams.com**

STANSFIELD

Plough Hill Bungalow, Stansfield, Sudbury. Sleeps 4. Plough Hill Bungalow, with attractive garden to front, is situated in a small village with pub, within 15 miles of Sudbury, Gainsborough's birthplace, Newmarket Racecourse and historic Bury St Edmunds, Long Melford and Lavenham. At picturesque Clare, five miles distant, there are shopping facilities. The Bungalow is well equipped to accommodate four people in twin-bedded rooms, sittingroom, kitchen/diner with electric cooker, microwave, fridge, cutlery and crockery. Colour TV. Bathroom, toilet. Car essential, parking. Children and pets welcome; cot available. Electric fires. Linen supplied on request. Open all year round at very reasonable rates. Terms from £61 to £122 per week. For further details send SAE to **Mrs M. Winch, Plough House, Stansfield, Sudbury CO10 8LT (01284 789253).**

SURREY

See also Colour Display Advertisement

KINGSTON-UPON-THAMES (Near)

Sunny House. An attractive alternative to staying in hotels. Designed to suit the discerning business executive or independent traveller away from home, Sunny House has the appeal of a modern upmarket establishment whilst still retaining the charm and characteristics of a well-cared for home. Easy availability of transport to almost anywhere in London, overlooking the quaint surroundings of Royal Bushy Park. All accommodation equipped with en suite facilities, colour TV with satellite, fridge, tea/coffee facilities, direct-dial telephone; use of spacious well-fitted kitchen and dishwasher, washing machine, microwave etc. Also use of beautiful lounge; five-day maid service; full parking facilities. For full details contact: **Chase Lodge Hotel, 10 Park Road, Hampton Wick, Kingston-upon-Thames KT1 4AS (020 8943 1862; Fax: 020 8943 9363).**
e-mail: info@sunnyhouse.uk.com
website: www.sunnyhouse.uk.com

THE FHG DIPLOMA

HELP IMPROVE BRITISH TOURIST STANDARDS

You are choosing holiday accommodation from our very popular FHG Publications.
Whether it be a hotel, guest house, farmhouse or self-catering accommodation, we think you will find it hospitable, comfortable and clean, and your host and hostess friendly and helpful.

Why not write and tell us about it?

As a recognition of the generally well-run and excellent holiday accommodation reviewed in our publications, we at FHG Publications Ltd. present a diploma to proprietors who receive the highest recommendation from their guests who are also readers of our Guides. If you care to write to us praising the holiday you have booked through FHG Publications Ltd. – whether this be board, self-catering accommodation, a sporting or a caravan holiday, what you say will be evaluated and the proprietors who reach our final list will be contacted.

The winning proprietor will receive an attractive framed diploma to display on his premises as recognition of a high standard of comfort, amenity and hospitality. FHG Publications Ltd. offer this diploma as a contribution towards the improvement of standards in tourist accommodation in Britain. Help your excellent host or hostess to win it!

FHG DIPLOMA

We nominate ....

....

Because

Name ....

Address...

....

Telephone No...

SUSSEX

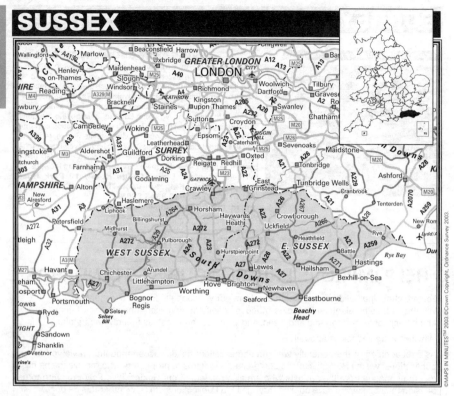

EAST SUSSEX

ALFRISTON

Mr and Mrs G. Burgess, Polhills, Arlington, Polegate BN26 6SB (01323 870004). Idyllically situated on shore of reservoir and edge of Sussex Downs within easy reach of the sea. Fully furnished period cottage (approached by own drive along the water's edge) available for self-catering holidays from April to October (inclusive). Fly fishing for trout can be arranged during season. Accommodation consists of two main bedrooms; tiled bathroom. Lounge with colour TV; large well-fitted kitchen with fridge freezer, electric cooker, microwave, washing machine; dining room with put-u-up settee; sun lounge. Central heating. Linen supplied. Most rooms contain a wealth of oak beams. Children and pets welcome. Car essential. Ample parking. Shops two miles. Golf, hill climbing locally. Sea eight miles. Weekly terms from £220 to £295 (electricity included).

CROWHURST PARK

Telham Lane, Battle, East Sussex TN33 0SL

Telephone 01424 773344

Award winning holiday park featuring luxury log cabin accommodation. Magnificent heated pool complex with children's paddling area, Jacuzzi, steam room, sauna, gym with cardiovascular and resistance training equipment, solarium, beauty therapies, aquafit classes, tennis court, children's adventure play area, restaurant, bars and clubhouse.

All this plus beautiful, historic 1066 Country on your doorstep and the Sussex coast just five miles away. Call for a brochure today.

virtual tour: www.crowhurstpark.co.uk

See also Colour Advertisement

Cadborough Farm

Udimore Road, Rye, East Sussex TN31 6AA
Tel: 01797 225426; Fax: 01797 224097

Five newly converted individual cottages. Each sleeps two, some with own courtyards. Direct access to '1066' country walks and cliff track with sea views to Rye (1 mile). Full GCH & CTV and CD player. Rates from £165 - £395 per week. Double and Twin available. Minimum two day lets from £55/night. Linen, towels, gas and electricity inclusive. Full G.C.H. Sorry no children and no smoking. One small well-behaved pet welcome.

Website: www.cadborough.co.uk   E-mail: info@cadborough.co.uk

---

See also Colour Display Advertisement

FAIRLIGHT

Little Oaks, Farley Way, Fairlight. Luxury bungalow on one level, situated in quiet coastal village with clifftop parklands, close to ancient towns of Rye, Battle and Hastings. Furnished to a very high standard, the spacious accommodation comprises double bedroom with en suite shower and sauna, twin bedroom, lounge with TV, dining room, fully equipped kitchen/diner, bathroom, conservatory and balcony overlooking beautiful secluded garden, garage. No smoking in bungalow. Pets welcome. Rates on application, which include central heating, electricity, bed linen and towels. ETC ★★★★. Contact: **Ray and Janet Adams, Fairlight Cottage, Warren Road, Fairlight, East Sussex TN35 4AG (Tel & Fax: 01424 812545).**
e-mail: fairlightcottage@supanet.com

GLYNDE (near Lewes)

Caburn Cottages, Ranscombe Farm, Glynde, Lewes BN8 6AA (01273 858062). Sleeps 2-8. Caburn Cottages are a group of eight newly built holiday cottages. Situated by the South Downs under Mount Caburn, they are all well-equipped and comprise between one and four bedrooms, with a kitchen/lounge and a bathroom. Each kitchen has an electric cooker, microwave, fridge (with freezer compartment), toaster, kettle and colour TV. Each bathroom has wc and power shower over the bath. Bed linen and towels are included. Laundry room. Table tennis room. Awarded 1st Prize in the Sussex Heritage Awards 2001 for an outstanding development using traditional skills within an Area of Outstanding Natural Beauty. Close to many places of interest and within easy reach of Lewes, Brighton and Eastbourne. Sorry, no smoking. Please send for colour brochure. ETC ★★★★. Contact: **Philip and Rosemary Norris.**
website: www.caburncottages.co.uk

ENGLAND

WEST SUSSEX

HENFIELD

The Holiday Flat and Cottage, New Hall, Small Dole, Henfield. New Hall, the manor house of Henfield, stands in three-and-a-half acres of mature gardens, surrounded by farmland with abundant footpaths. The holiday cottage is the orginal 1600 farmhouse. It has one en suite bedroom, a large livingroom, dining room with two folding beds, and kitchen; a door opens into the walled garden. The holiday flat is the upper part of the dairy wing. Its front door opens from a Georgian courtyard and it has three bedrooms sleeping five, lounge/diner, kitchen and bathroom. Both units are fully equipped and comfortably furnished. Children welcome. Open all year. Terms from £175 to £325 per week. **ETC ★★★**. Send SAE for details and availability to **Mrs M.W. Carreck, New Hall, Small Dole, Henfield BN5 9YJ** or phone **(01273 492546)**.

See also Colour Display Advertisement

STEYNING

Pepperscombe Farm, Newham Lane, Steyning, Near Worthing BN44 3LR (01903 813868). Two self-catering holiday cottages, with a Five Star rating by an independent holiday cottage agency. Each cottage is designed to sleep two adults only. The location is peaceful and quiet, nestling in a combe beneath the South Downs Way, just a few minutes from the old historic market town of Steyning. We offer a direct link to the Downs and the foot and bridle path network, and are close to many places of interest. Previously a dairy farm, part of which is now converted to spacious, comfortable cottages with oak beams, and, for winter lets, have a very efficient underfloor heating system, making them both a warm and cosy place to stay. Prices from £350 varying to £475 for 7 nights. Pets are welcome at £15 each per week. No smoking. Please phone for further information and details.
e-mail: johncamilleri@btopenworld.com

WARWICKSHIRE

WARWICK

Copes Flat, Brook Street, Warwick. Sleeps 3. Warwick town centre, secluded first floor flat dating from the mid 17th century has its own entrance and high level garden, ideal for al fresco meals. The timber framed sitting/dining room is comfortably furnished for eating and relaxing and has a colour TV and telephone. A bathroom, bedroom with twin or double bed and fully fitted kitchen with washing machine and tumble dryer complete this charming accommodation in the interesting, historic town of Warwick. Sorry, no pets. No smoking. We are ideally situated for visiting Stratford-upon-Avon, Oxford, the Cotswolds and the main towns and attractions in the Heart of England. Terms from £200 to £320. **ETC ★★★**. **Mrs Elizabeth Draisey, Forth House, 44 High Street, Warwick CV34 4AX (01926 401512; Fax: 01926 490809).**
e-mail: info@forthhouseuk.co.uk   **website: www.forthhouseuk.co.uk**

A useful Index of Towns/Villages and Counties appears on page 281 – please also refer to Contents Page 3.

WILTSHIRE

CHIPPENHAM

Cedarwood, Grove Farm, Sutton Lane, Langley Burrell, Chippenham SN15 4LW (01249 720413/721500; mobile: 0777 0690530). Grove Farm is a 400 acre mixed livestock/arable farm in the charming village of Langley Burrell, where a small village pub serves excellent meals. The area provides many opportunities for walking and cycling, with the MacMillan Way, Wiltshire Cycle Way and the Ridgeway close by. Cedarwood is a very private and spacious country bungalow set in its own garden with private parking. It comprises comfortable lounge with colour TV, large farmhouse kitchen and dining area, three bedrooms (one double, one twin and one single) with additional bedsettee in lounge. Central heating and electricity inclusive. Towels, bed linen and duvets supplied. Short breaks available. No smoking and no pets. **ETC ★★★★.** Contact: **Helen and Brian Miflin.**
e-mail: **miflin@btinternet.com**

DEVIZES

The Gate House Annexe, Wick Lane, Devizes. Very well equipped, spacious, ground floor annexe accommodation, surrounded by large, peaceful, well-kept gardens. So many people have said; "In all the years we've been taking holidays, we've never stayed in anywhere as nice as this!". **Mrs Laura Stratton, The Gate House, Wick Lane, Devizes SN10 5DW (01380 725283).**
e-mail: **info@visitdevizes.co.uk**
website: **www.visitdevizes.co.uk**

LACOCK (Near Bath)

The Cheese House & The Cyder House. The Cheese House, with exposed elm and oak timbers, sleeps up to five and consists of an open living/dining room with an arch leading to a fitted kitchen. The first floor has one double and one single bedroom and a shower room/toilet. The second floor has one twin-bedded room and a gallery with casual seating area. The Cyder House, with stepped fireplace and wood-burning stove, sleeps up to four persons. The first floor has two single bedrooms and a shower room/toilet. On the second floor there is a gabled double bedroom. The Cyder House also has the attraction of having the original cyder press on the ground floor, separating the fitted kitchen from the sitting room. Each has a garden with seating and barbecue and a separate drive. Locked cycle store/laundry room. Both properties are non-smoking. Short breaks and business stays are welcome. **ETC ★★★★.** *WELCOME HOST, FARM STAY UK MEMBER.* **Sue and Philip King, Wick Farm, Lacock, Chippenham SN15 2LU (01249 730244; Fax: 01249 730072).**
e-mail: **kingsilverlands2@btinternet.com** website: **www.cheeseandcyderhouses.co.uk**

TROWBRIDGE

John and Elizabeth Moody, Gaston Farm, Holt, Trowbridge BA14 6QA (01225 782203). The self-contained accommodation is part of a farmhouse, which dates from the 16th century, on the edge of the village of Holt with views across open farmland. Within 10 miles of Bath, Bradford-on-Avon two miles, Lacock eight miles. Private fishing on River Avon available. The apartment consists of a large lounge/dining room with open fire and sofa which converts into a double bed; two generously proportioned bedrooms upstairs, one twin-bedded, one with a double bed, both with washbasins; a separate toilet (downstairs); a large kitchen in the single storey wing, fitted with light oak finish units, electric cooker, microwave, refrigerator and automatic washing machine; shower room which opens off the kitchen. Off-road parking. Choice of pubs in village. Terms £170 to £195. Brochure and further details available.

ENGLAND

WORCESTERSHIRE

WHITEWELLS FARM COTTAGES
Ridgeway Cross, Near Malvern, Worcestershire WR13 5JR   ETC ★★★★
Tel: 01886 880607 Fax: 01886 880360 E-mail: info@whitewellsfarm.co.uk Web: www.whitewellsfarm.co.uk

Seven well-established cottages converted from old farm buildings and a hop kiln, full of charm and character with original exposed timbering. These award-winning cottages are exceptionally clean and comfortable and equipped to the highest standards. One cottage is suitable for the disabled with full wheelchair access. Idyllically set around a duckpond in 10 acres, with 2 ½ acres of the property being a fully-fenced woodland plantation, ideal for exercising dogs, on or off the lead. Set in unspoilt countryside on the Herefordshire/Worcestershire border, with outstanding views of the Malvern Hills . Children and pets welcome. Short breaks and long lets; suitable for relocation.

Colour brochure available from: Kate and Denis Kavanagh.

MALVERN

Greenbank Garden Flat, Malvern. Greenbank Garden Flat is situated in the Malvern Hills overlooking Herefordshire. It is self-contained and fully equipped with gas cooker, microwave, central heating, fridge, TV, bath and shower, immersion heater. Large conservatory. Sleeping two/four (double bed and studio couch which converts for two); Z-bed also available. Inclusive charge covers bedlinen for the double bed, towels and all fuel etc. Village shop and public house within five minutes' walk of Greenbank. Terms £140 to £205 weekly. Guests have the use of our garden. An excellent base. Dogs welcome by arrangement, £10 charged per pet. **ETC ★★★**. Apply: **Mr D.G. Matthews, Greenbank, 236 West Malvern Road, Malvern WR14 4BG (01684 567328**
e-mail: matthews.greenbank@virgin.net

PLEASE NOTE

All the information in this book is given in good faith in the belief that it is correct. However, the publishers cannot guarantee the facts given in these pages, neither are they responsible for changes in policy, ownership or terms that may take place after the date of going to press. Readers should always satisfy themselves that the facilities they require are available and that the terms, if quoted, still apply.

YORKSHIRE

©MAPS IN MINUTES™ 2003. ©Crown Copyright, Ordnance Survey 2003.

EAST YORKSHIRE

ENGLAND

BARMBY MOOR

Mr & Mrs Thorpe, Parklands, York Road, Barmby Moor, York YO42 4HT (01759 380260). Sleeps 2.
Newly converted stables tastefully finished and self-contained, set in nine acres of private grounds. Easy access to the Wolds, moors, dales and east coast, and only 20 minutes from York city centre. Restaurant, filling station and public house within half a mile. Full central heating. Terms include fuel, power and linen. Under-cover car parking available. Pets welcome free of charge. No smoking. Available all year. Tariff £40 per night, £250 per week.

BRIDLINGTON

Mrs Audrey Marshall, Rialto Holiday Flats, 63/65 Trinity Road, Bridlington YO15 2HF (01262 677653). Sleep 2-8.
Well established and highly recommended fully equipped flats situated close to the North Beach. All flats have their own private facilities and include a colour TV. Car park and public telephone available. Bed linen and cots may be hired. Close to shops, Leisure World and North Beach. Phone for a brochure. Prices from £95 to £255. Fully Fire Certificated. **ETC ★★**
e-mail: enquiries@rialto-bridlington.co.uk
website: www.rialto-bridlington.co.uk

See also Colour Display Advertisement

BRIDLINGTON

St Margarets Holiday Flats, 6 Marlborough Terrace, Bridlington YO15 2PA (Tel & Fax: 01262 673698). Fantastic sea views, great family accommodation, 25 yards to beach. Centrally situated overlooking the Royal Princess Parade and sea, near harbour entertainments and new shopping complex. Flats for one to eight persons, all fully self-contained, with up to three bedrooms. All flats have sea views and are fitted with colour TV, cooker, fridge, fire and are fully-equipped.with cutlery, crockery, glasses, pans, etc. Hot water supplied. Two minutes from Gala Bingo. Prices from £80.00. Flats are meter operated.
ETC ★★/★★★

DRIFFIELD

The Wold Cottage, Driffield. Brand new barn conversion comprising two self-catering cottages and one apartment. "The Granary" has spacious ground floor accommodation, entrance with cloakroom, kitchen, dining area and lounge with sofa bed if needed. First floor has one double and one twin bedroom both with en suite facilities. "The Hayloft" has ground floor double room with shower en suite, first floor twin room with bath en suite. Kitchen, dining area, sitting area with arched window, south-facing with open views of the Wolds. " Bar End" is a four-poster suite with kitchen and sitting area, en suite corner bath with walk-in shower. Prices from £160 - £395 per week, includes VAT, heating, bed linen, towels, electricity and laundry facilities. Non-smoking. No pets. Contact: **Mrs K Gray, The Wold Cottage, Wold Newton, Driffield YO25 3HL (Tel & Fax: 01262 470696).**
website: www.woldcottage.com

Please mention Self-Catering Holidays in Britain
when enquiring about accommodation
featured in these pages.

NORTH YORKSHIRE

COVERDALE

Westclose House (Allaker), West Scrafton, Coverdale, Leyburn DL8 4RM. Stone farmhouse with panoramic views, high in the Yorkshire Dales National Park (Herriot family's house in 'All Creatures Great and Small' on TV). Three bedrooms (sleeps six/eight), sitting and dining rooms with wood-burning stoves, kitchen, bathroom, WC. House has electric storage heating, cooker, microwave, fridge, washing machine, colour TV, telephone. Garden, large barn, stables. Access from lane, private parking, no through traffic. Excellent walking from front door, near Wensleydale. Pets welcome. Self-catering from £400 per week. For bookings telephone: **020 8567 4862**
e-mail: ac@adriancave.com
website: www.adriancave.com/yorks

HARDRAW

Cissy's Cottage, Hardraw, Hawes. Sleeps 4. A delightful 18th century cottage of outstanding character. Situated in the village of Hardraw with its spectacular waterfall and Pennine Way. Market town of Hawes one mile. This traditional stone built cottage retains many original features including beamed ceilings and an open fire. Sleeping four in comfort, it has been furnished and equipped to a high standard using antique pine and Laura Ashley prints. Equipped with dishwasher, microwave and tumble dryer. Outside, a south-facing garden, sun patio with garden furniture, and a large enclosed paddock make it ideal for children. Cot and high chair if required. Open all year. Terms £120-£295 includes coal, electricity, linen and trout fishing. For brochure, contact **Mrs Belinda Metcalfe, Southolme Farm, Little Smeaton, Northallerton DL6 2HJ (01609 881302/881052).**

See also Colour Display Advertisement

HARROGATE

Rudding Holiday Park, Follifoot, Harrogate HG3 1JH (01423 870439; Fax: 01423 870859). These superior holiday cottages and lodges are set in picturesque surroundings just south of Harrogate. The luxury cottages have been completely restored retaining many of their original features (sleep 2-10 persons). The Timber Lodges are situated in beautiful parkland, many overlooking a small lake (sleep 2-6 persons). All are centrally heated and fully equipped. Facilities within the private country estate include; heated swimming pool and paddling pool, children's adventure playground, Deer House, games room, 18 hole Pay and Play golf course plus floodlit driving range. Please send for free illustrated brochure. ETC ★★★★★ Lodges, ★★★ Cottages.
e-mail: holiday-park@ruddingpark.com   **website: www.ruddingpark.com**

HARROGATE

Mrs Janet Hollings, Dougill Hall, Summerbridge, Harrogate HG3 4JR (01423 780277). Working farm. Sleeps 4. Dougill Hall is of Georgian design, built in 1722 by the Dougill family who lived on this farm from 1496 to 1803. It is in Nidderdale, half-a-mile from the village of Summerbridge, just by the River Nidd, where there is fishing available for visitors. There are good facilities for horse riding, tennis, swimming, squash, etc. Well situated for the walking enthusiast and within easy reach of the Dales, the beautiful and ancient city of York, Fountains Abbey, How Stean Gorge and many other places of interest. The Old Cooling House flat sleeps up to four people. Well equipped, with electric cooker and fridge, iron, vacuum cleaner. Linen by arrangement. Car essential, parking. Terms from £135 to £220. SAE please for details.

ENGLAND

HARROGATE

Mrs Hardcastle, Southfield Farm, Darley, Harrogate HG3 2PR (01423 780258). Two well equipped holiday cottages on a farm in an attractive area between Harrogate and Pateley Bridge. An ideal place to explore the whole of the dale with York and Herriot country within easy driving distance. Riverside walks, village shop and post office within quarter-of-a-mile, and local pub one mile away. Each cottage has two bedrooms, one double and one with bunk beds. Games room. Large lawn for ball games, with garden chairs and barbecue. Pets welcome. Ample car parking. Prices from £170 to £200 low season, £200 to £270 high season.

KIRKBYMOORSIDE

Mrs Karen Tinkler, Kirby Mills, Kirkbymoorside, York YO62 6NP (01751 432000; Fax: 01751 432300). Sympathetically restored stable mews cottages in converted two-acre 18th century watermill complex on the River Dove. Tranquil, well-appointed accommodation with linen and towels, TV, video and central heating included as standard. Bed and bath downstairs, living upstairs with "indoor balcony". Garden and barbecue by millrace. Breakfasts and dinners can be provided in the Mill by arrangement. On-site parking. Open all year round.
e-mail: cornmill@kirbymills.demon.co.uk
website: www.kirbymills.demon.co.uk

LEYBURN

Park Grange Farm Cottage. A working farm situated just a mile from the picturesque market town of Leyburn, Wensleydale. Comfortable self-catering cottage. Superb views of beautiful countryside. Ideal for walking, cycling, fishing, horse-riding, playing golf and touring the Dales. The cottage comprises two double rooms, one bunk-bed room and a double bed-settee if required. The kitchen is equipped with cooker, fridge, dishwasher and washer. Children, dogs and horses welcome. Grazing/stabling for your equine friends, and kennels available if you wish to bring working dogs on holiday. We cater for special occasions, and include a Yorkshire welcome pack with each booking. Short breaks available. For brochure and rates, contact: **Pam Sheppard, Low Gill Farm, Agglethorpe, Leyburn DL8 4TN (01969 640258).**
e-mail: pamsheppardlgf@aol.com

LOW BENTHAM

Mrs L.J. Story, Holmes Farm, Low Bentham, Lancaster LA2 7DE (015242 61198). Sleeps 4. Attractively converted and well equipped stone cottage adjoining 17th century farm house. In a secluded position surrounded by 127 acres of beautiful pastureland. Central heating, fridge, TV, washing machine, games room. Ideal base for visiting Dales, Lake District and coast. **ETC ★★★★**

NORTHALLERTON

Julie & Jim Griffith, Hill House Farm, Little Langton, Northallerton DL7 0PZ (01609 770643; Fax: 01609 760438). Sleep 2-6. These former farm buildings have been converted into four well-equipped cottages, retaining original beams. Cosily heated for year round appeal. Peaceful setting with magnificent views. Centrally located between Dales and Moors with York, Whitby and Scarborough all within easy driving distance. Pets welcome. Weekly rates from £150 inclusive of all linen, towels, heating and electricity. Short breaks available. Pub food one mile. Golf two miles, shops three miles. Please telephone for a free brochure. **ETC ★★★★**
e-mail: info@Hillhousefarmcottages.com

PICKERING

Mrs Sue Cavill, Badger Cottage, Stape, Pickering YO18 8HR (01751 476108). Comfortable self-catering on small, remote, moorland farm. Seven miles from Pickering on edge of Cropton Forest. Wonderful area for touring, walking, cycling or riding. Accommodation available for guests' horses. Cottage is converted from original stone milking parlours, so all on ground floor. Open plan well-equipped kitchen, dining and sitting room with sofa bed and cosy woodburning stove. Spacious bedroom with double and single beds, en suite shower room, central heating. Parking space and a garden to sit in. Linen and power included. Terms £140 to £200 per week.

PICKERING (NORTH YORK MOORS)

2 Spring Gardens, Keld Head, Pickering. Situated on the edge of the market town of Pickering, the accommodation comprises kitchen/diner, lounge, double bedroom, twin bedroom and guest beds, bathroom with electric shower over bath. Central heating throughout. TV, video, fridge, washer/dryer, oven, microwave. Pickering is an ideal base for visiting North Yorkshire Moors steam railway, the coast, Castle Howard, Eden Camp and Dalby Forest. Well-behaved dogs welcome. There is a pleasant walk for dogs and owners nearby, passing Keld Head pond and into open countryside. Electricity, linen and heating included in the price. Private parking. No smoking. Terms from £200 to £450 per week. Awaiting ETC inspection. Open all year. Short breaks available. For further information please telephone **Mrs Sandra M. Pickering on 01751 474279.**

ROBIN HOOD'S BAY (Near)

Ken and Nealia Pattinson, South House Farm, Fylingthorpe, Whitby YO22 4UQ (01947 880243). Glorious countryside in North York Moors National Park. Five minutes' walk to beach at Boggle Hole. Super large farmhouse sleeps 10 people. Four spacious cottages sleeping two to six. All inclusive and fully-equipped. Gardens. Parking. Terms from £120 to £1800.
e-mail: kmp@bogglehole.fsnet.co.uk
website: www.southhousefarm.co.uk

ENGLAND

SKIPTON

Mrs Brenda Jones, New Close Farm, Kirkby Malham, Skipton BD23 4DP (01729 830240; Fax: 01729 830179). Sleeps 5. A supa dupa cottage on New Close Farm in the heart of Craven Dales with panoramic views over the Aire Valley. Excellent area for walking, cycling, fishing, golf and touring. Two double and one single bedrooms; bathroom. Colour TV and video. Full central heating and double glazing. Bed linen, towels and all amenities included in the price. Low Season £250, High Season £300; deposit required. Sorry, no young children and no pets. Non-smokers preferred. The weather can't be guaranteed but your comfort can. *FHG DIPLOMA AWARD PAST WINNER.*
e-mail: brendajones@newclosefarmyorkshire.co.uk
website: www.newclosefarmyorkshire.co.uk

STOCKTON-ON-FOREST

Orillia Cottages, Stockton-on-Forest, York. Four converted farm workers' cottages in a courtyard setting at the rear of the 300-year-old farmhouse in Stockton-on-Forest three miles from York. Golf course nearby, pub 200 yards away serving good food; post office, newsagents and general stores within easy reach. Convenient half-hourly bus service to York and the coast. Fully furnished and equipped for two to eight, the cottages comprise lounge with colour TV, etc; kitchen area with microwave, oven, grill and hob; bedrooms have double and twin beds. Gas central heating. Non-smokers preferred. Children and pets welcome. Available Easter to October - Short Breaks may be available. Terms from £195 to £495 weekly includes heating, linen, etc. Please contact **Mr & Mrs G. Hudson, Orillia House, 89 The Village, Stockton-on-Forest, York (01904 400600).**
website: www.orilliacottages.co.uk

SUTTON-ON-FOREST (NEAR YORK)

Stable and Wren Cottages. Working farm. Sleeping 2 and 4 plus cot. Converted from old working stables these single storey cottages while retaining the old roof beams are spacious, comfortable and fully equipped. Storage heating plus electric fire and bed linen are all included in the price - no extras! Cot available. Set on a mainly arable farm one mile from Sutton the cottages are in a very peaceful rural location yet are very handy for trips into the old city of York, with many stores and shops on the outskirts of town. This is a good central touring base for visits to the North Yorkshire Moors, East Coast and Dales. Well insulated and cosy these cottages are also ideal for winter holidays/short breaks too. Plenty of excellent reasonable eating places all round the area. Prices from £140 to £310 per week. **ETC ★★★.** Brochures from **Mrs H. Knowlson, Thrush House, Sutton-on-Forest, York YO61 1ED (Tel & Fax: 01347 810225).**
e-mail: kmkholcottyksuk@aol.com
website: www.holidayskmkholcotts-yks.uk.com

THIRSK

Foxhills Hideaways, Felixkirk, Thirsk YO7 2DS (01845 537575). Quiet and secluded, but easily accessible, these four Scandinavian log cabins are situated between the North York Moors and the Dales National Parks. Convenient for the coast and the city of York, with wonderful walks from the top of Sutton Bank. Pretty garden setting, centrally heated and fully equipped. Pets are welcome. There is a village pub just around the corner and we are open all year. Fully inclusive prices (£180 to £340 per week). Out of season short breaks from £90 inc. Please write or phone for brochure.

Valley View Farm

Old Byland, Helmsley, York, North Yorkshire YO6 5LG
Telephone: 01439 798221   HIGHLY COMMENDED

Four holiday cottages sleeping two, four and six persons respectively.
Each with colour TV, video, washer, dishwasher, microwave.
Peaceful rural surroundings on a working farm
with pigs, sheep and cattle. Winter and Spring Breaks
available. Short Breaks from £90 and High Season weeks up
to £495. Bed and Breakfast also available. Please telephone
for brochure and further details to: Mrs Sally Robinson.

E-mail: sally@valleyviewfarm.com
Website: www.valleyviewfarm.com

WHITBY

Nick Eddleston, Greenhouses Farm Cottages, Greenhouses Farm, Lealholm, Near Whitby YO21 2AD (01947 897486). The three cottages have been converted from the traditional farm buildings. The old world character has been retained with the thick stone walls, exposed beams and red pantile roofs typical of North Yorkshire. Set in the tiny hamlet of Greenhouses and enjoying splendid views over open countryside, the cottages offer a very quiet and peaceful setting for a holiday. All the cottages are equipped with colour TV, electric cooker, fridge/freezer, microwave and automatic washing machine. Linen, fuel and lighting are all included in the price. There are ample safe areas for children to play. Sorry, no pets. Prices from £188 to £509 per week. Winter Breaks from £142.

WHITBY

Swallow Holiday Cottages, The Farm, Stainsacre, Whitby YO22 4NT (01947 603790). Stainsacre is an excellent base for many popular tourist areas. Discover historic Whitby, two miles away, pretty fishing villages, countryside with waymarked walks, etc. Four cottages with panoramic view of the Esk valley each with one or two bedrooms, plus a three bedroom detached house. All are fully furnished, including linen. Private parking. Children and dogs welcome. Non-smoking accommodation available. Resident owners Jill and Brian McNeil look forward to welcoming you. Please phone or write for a brochure. Weekly rates from £120 to £410.

YORK

Baile Hill Cottage, Bishophill, York. Sleeps 4 to 5. This Victorian town cottage is in a peaceful area within the historic city centre and overlooks the ancient city walls with roadside parking outside the front door. It is furnished and equipped to a very high standard including a fully fitted modern kitchen with a microwave. The master bedroom has a four-poster bed, the second has twin single pine beds. The lounge has a cosy coal-effect gas fire and a colour teletext TV. The Victorian style bathroom has gold plated and dark mahogany fittings with an over bath shower. There is a private patio garden area, barbecue and utility room with an automatic washing machine and tumble dryer. **ETC ★★★.** For further information contact: **Mrs Hodgson, Avalon, North Lane, Wheldrake, York YO19 6AY (01904 448670; Fax: 01904 448908).**

e-mail: enquires@holiday-cottage.org.uk   website: www.holiday-cottage.org.uk

ENGLAND

YORK

Coronation Farm Cottage. "The best of Yorkshire – coast, city and countryside." Deceptively spacious luxury cottage in conservation village, on delightful cul-de-sac with thatched roof cottages and charming ivy-clad pub. Ideal Whitby, Scarborough and York. The cottage sleeps two to eight plus cot in four bedrooms. Mediterranean style, south-facing patio area with gas barbecue for lazy summer evenings. Off-street parking. Pets and children very welcome. Non-smoking. Open all year. Other properties available – all ETC 4 Star. **(01653 698251; Fax: 01653 691962).**
e-mail: enquiries@coronationfarmcottage.co.uk
website: www.coronationfarmcottage.co.uk

YORK/SELBY

Cawood Holiday Park, Ryther Road, Cawood, Near Selby YO8 3TT (01757 268450: Mobile: 0777986 7198; Fax: 01757 268537). Twixt York and Selby, a quiet and idyllic rural setting where we have worked hard to create an environment which keeps its natural simplicity, and at the same time provides a trouble-free holiday. Bungalows/Caravan, some suitable for the disabled, and touring pitches sheltered by trees, or with views over our fishing lake. Facilities include a comfortable licensed bar and occasional weekend entertainment. Bar meals may be served in our no smoking area. Excellent amenity building, FREE showers, camp shop and indoor swimming pool. York 10 miles, A1 nine miles, Selby five miles. Adults only (no under 18s, excluding seasonals). **ETC ★★★★★**

e-mail: william.archer13@btopenworld.com   **website: www.ukparks.co.uk/cawood**

WEST YORKSHIRE

HUDDERSFIELD

Ashes Farm Cottages. Surrounded by open country, yet near town, these two 17th century Listed barns, converted and furnished to a high standard, make highly individual cottages. Both have gas central heating, fully equipped kitchens with cooker, microwave, fridge/freezer, washing machine and tumble dryer. Cruck Cottage has one double and two single bedrooms. The Barn House will sleep six/eight in one double, two twin bedrooms (two en suite) and double sofa bed. Another bedroom/bathroom wing is available on request. All linen inclusive, ample parking. For more details our brochure is available on request or visit our website. **ETC ★★★★. Mrs Barbara Lockwood, Ashes Common Farm, Ashes Lane, Almondbury, Huddersfield HD4 6TE (01424 426507).**

e-mail: enquiries@ashescommonfarm.co.uk   **website: www.ashescommonfarm.co.uk**

FHG Diploma Winners 2003

Each year we award a small number of diplomas to holiday proprietors whose services have been specially commended by our readers. The following were our FHG Diploma Winners for 2003.

England

DERBYSHIRE

Mr Tatlow
Ashfield Farm, Calwich
Near Ashbourne
Derbyshire DE6 2EB

DEVON

Mrs Tucker
Lower Luxton Farm, Upottery
Near Honiton
Devon EX14 9PB

◆

Royal Oak
Dunsford Near Exeter
Devon EX6 7DA

GLOUCESTERSHIRE

Mrs Keyte
The Limes, Evesham Road
Stow-on-the-Wold
Gloucestershire GL54 1EN

HAMPSHIRE

Mrs Ellis, Efford Cottage,
Everton, Lymington,
Hampshire SO41 0JD

◆

R. Law
Whitley Ridge Hotel
Beauly Road, Brockenhurst
Hampshire SO42 7QL

HEREFORDSHIRE

Mrs Brown
Ye Hostelrie, Goodrich
Near Ross on Wye
Herefordshire HR9 6HX

NORTH YORKSHIRE

Charles & Gill Richardson
The Coppice, 9 Studley Road
Harrogate
North Yorkshire HG1 5JU

◆

Mr & Mrs Hewitt
Harmony Country Lodge
Limestone Road, Burniston,
Scarborough
North Yorkshire YO13 0DG

Wales

POWYS

Linda Williams
The Old Vicarage
Erwood, Builth Wells
Powys LD2 3SZ

Scotland

ABERDEEN, BANFF & MORAY

Mr Ian Ednie
Spey Bay Hotel
Spey Bay
Fochabers
Moray IV32 7PJ

PERTH & KINROSS

Dunalastair Hotel
Kinloch Rannoch
By Pitlochry
Perthshire PH16 5PW

HELP IMPROVE BRITISH TOURISM STANDARDS

As recommendations are submitted from readers of the FULL RANGE of FHG titles the winners shown above may not necessarily appear in this guide.

THE FHG DIPLOMA

HELP IMPROVE
BRITISH TOURIST STANDARDS

You are choosing holiday accommodation from our very popular FHG Publications.
Whether it be a hotel, guest house, farmhouse or self-catering accommodation, we think you will find it hospitable, comfortable and clean, and your host and hostess friendly and helpful.

Why not write and tell us about it?

As a recognition of the generally well-run and excellent holiday accommodation reviewed in our publications, we at FHG Publications Ltd. present a diploma to proprietors who receive the highest recommendation from their guests who are also readers of our Guides. If you care to write to us praising the holiday you have booked through FHG Publications Ltd. – whether this be board, self-catering accommodation, a sporting or a caravan holiday, what you say will be evaluated and the proprietors who reach our final list will be contacted.

The winning proprietor will receive an attractive framed diploma to display on his premises as recognition of a high standard of comfort, amenity and hospitality. FHG Publications Ltd. offer this diploma as a contribution towards the improvement of standards in tourist accommodation in Britain. Help your excellent host or hostess to win it!

FHG DIPLOMA

We nominate ....

....

Because

Name ....

Address ....

....

Telephone No...

Castle Fraser, Aberdeenshire

SCOTLAND

Scotland
Self-catering Holidays

ABERDEEN, BANFF & MORAY

SCOTLAND

©MAPS IN MINUTES™ 2003. ©Crown Copyright. Ordnance Survey 2003.

ABERDEEN

The Robert Gordon University, Business & Vacation Accommodation, Schoolhill, Aberdeen AB10 1FR (01224 262134; Fax: 01224 262144). The Robert Gordon University in the heart of Aberdeen offers a variety of accommodation in the city centre to visitors from June through to August. Aberdeen is ideal for visiting Royal Deeside, castles and historic buildings, playing golf or touring the Malt Whisky Trail. The city itself is a place to discover and Aberdonians are friendly and welcoming people. We offer 2-Star self-catering accommodation for individuals or groups at superb rates in either en suite or shared facility flats. Each party has exclusive use of their own flat during their stay. The flats are self-contained, centrally heated, fully furnished and suitable for children and disabled guests. All flats have colour TV, microwave, bedlinen, towels, all cooking utensils and a complimentary "welcome pack" of basic groceries. There are laundry and telephone facilities on site as well as ample car parking spaces. *ASSC MEMBER.*

e-mail: p.macinnes@rgu.ac.uk   **website: www.scotland2000.com/rgu**

ABERDEEN

University of Aberdeen, Hospitality Services, Kings College, Aberdeen AB24 3FX (01224 273444; Fax: 01224 276246) Sleep 4/7. Situated on the edge of Seaton Park and Old Aberdeen, the Hillhead Halls Complex of self-catering accommodation is available during Easter and Summer vacations. Sleeping four to seven guests, the flats are centrally heated, fully furnished and suitable for children. Bed linen, telephone and cooking utensils are provided along with a 'Welcome Pack` on arrival to get you started. Other facilities on site include a laundry, shop, TV lounge, bar, leisure facilities and a car park. **STB ★★** *SELF-CATERING.*

e-mail: accommodation@abdn.ac.uk
website: www.abdn.ac.uk/catering

SCOTLAND

BALLINDALLOCH

Cragganmore Lodge, Cragganmore, By Ballindalloch.
Extremely comfortable and well-equipped Scandinavian style lodge set in a peaceful enclave beside the Speyside Way. Sleeps up to eight comfortably in three bedrooms and additional three piece shower room. Ideal base for touring Highlands, Malt Whisky Trail and all the attractions and activities of the Spey Valley. Fridge/freezer, dishwasher, washer/dryer, microwave. Prices from £350 to £550 per week inclusive of all electricity and linen. Weekend deals available during winter season. **STB ★★★★** *SELF-CATERING. ASSC MEMBER.* Enquiries and brochure: **0141 649 9696.**
website: www.cragganmorelodge.co.uk

See also Colour Display Advertisement

FORRES

Tulloch Lodges. Peace, Relaxation and Comfort in beautiful Natural Surroundings. One of the loveliest self-catering sites in Scotland. Modern, spacious, attractive and beautifully equipped Scandinavian lodges for up to six in glorious woodland/water setting. Perfect for the Highlands and Historic Grampian, especially the Golden Moray Coast and the Golf, Castle and Malt Whisky Trails. £240 to £675 per week. **STB ★★★/★★★★** *SELF-CATERING.* For a brochure contact: **Tulloch Lodges, Rafford, Forres, Moray IV36 2RU (01309 673311; Fax: 01309 671515).** *ASSC MEMBER.*
e-mail: enquiries@tullochlodges.com
website: www.tullochlodges.com

GRANTOWN-ON-SPEY

Mr & Mrs J.R. Taylor, Milton of Cromdale, Grantown-on-Spey PH26 3PH (01479 872415). Sleeps 4. Fully modernised cottage available Easter to October. Excellent centre for touring with golf, tennis and trekking within easy reach. Large garden with views of River Spey and Cromdale Hills. Fully equipped except linen. Refrigerator, electric cooker. Two double bedrooms sleeping four. Bathroom with shower. Colour TV. Children and pets welcome. Car desirable. Terms £100 per week.

See also Colour Display Advertisement

INVERURIE

Mr and Mrs P. A. Lumsden, Kingsfield House, Kingsfield Road, Kintore, Inverurie AB51 0UD (01467 632366; Fax: 01467 632399). 'The Greenknowe' is a comfortable detached and renovated cottage in a quiet location at the southern edge of the village of Kintore. It is in an ideal situation for touring castles, historic sites and distilleries, or for walking, fishing and even golf. The cottage is all on one level with a large south-facing sittingroom overlooking the garden. It sleeps four people in one double and one twin room. A cot is available. Parking adjacent. Open from March to November. Prices from £275 to £475 per week, inclusive of electricity (the cottage is all-electric) and linen. Walkers Welcome Scheme. **STB ★★★★** *SELF-CATERING. ASSC MEMBER.*
e-mail: kfield@clara.net

FHG

PLEASE MENTION THIS GUIDE WHEN YOU WRITE

OR PHONE TO ENQUIRE ABOUT ACCOMMODATION

IF YOU ARE WRITING, A STAMPED, ADDRESSED

ENVELOPE IS ALWAYS APPRECIATED

ARGYLL & BUTE

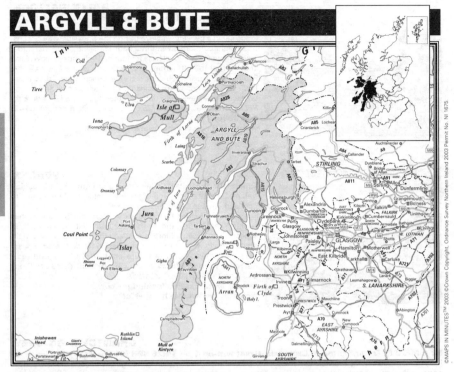

©MAPS IN MINUTES™ 2003 ©Crown Copyright. Ordnance Survey Northern Ireland 2003 Permit No. NI 1675.

APPIN

Ardtur Cottages, Appin. Two adjacent cottages in secluded surroundings on promontory between Port Appin and Castle Stalker, opposite north end of Isle of Lismore. Ideal centre for hill walking, climbing, etc. (Glen Coe and Ben Nevis half-hour drive). Direct access across the field to sea (Loch Linnhe). Tennis court available by arrangement. Boat hire, pony trekking, fly fishing all available locally. Accommodation in first cottage for eight people in four twin bedrooms, large dining/sittingroom/ kitchenette and two bathrooms. Second cottage accommodates six people in three twin bedrooms, dining/sittingroom, kitchenette and bathroom. Everything is provided except linen. Shops one mile; sea 200 yards. Pets allowed. Car essential, parking. Open March/October. Terms from £165 to £375 weekly. SAE, please, for full details to **Mrs J. Pery, Ardtur, Appin PA38 4DD (01631 730223 or 834172).**

BRIDGE OF AWE

Tigh an Daraich Self Catering Lodges, Bridge of Awe, Taynuilt PA35 1HR (01866 822693; Fax: 01866 822339). The four lodges are set in a small exclusive woodland development of five acres enjoying spectacular views across the River Awe to Ben Cruachan (the hollow mountain - inside is a hydroelectric power station). The location provides an ideal base for touring the Western Isles, Oban, Fort William, Glencoe and Inveraray. Our lodges are constructed and finished to a very high standard. Each lodge has oven, hob, fridge, freezer, washing machine, tumble dryer, dishwasher, satellite TV, video, hi-fi and telephone. Strictly no smoking within the lodges. Pets welcome (4 Star only). **STB ★★★★/★★★★★,** *CATEGORY 2 DISABILITY.*

**e-mail: b.awe@dnet.co.uk; bookings@tighandaraich.co.uk; info@tighandaraich.co.uk
website: www.tighandaraich.co.uk**

SCOTLAND

BRIDGE OF ORCHY

Auch Estate. Two semi-detached self-catering cottages, sleeping 6 and 8, provide an excellent base for walking, biking, skiing, (only 15 minutes' drive from Glencoe) or touring holiday. Situated on a farming estate, they are superbly equipped for that 'home from home' feeling, and set amid spectacular scenery. All linen and towels provided. All modern electrical appliances. Payphone. Full central heating (coin meter) and free logs for woodburner. Private parking and garden. Cot and stairgate available. Pets welcome. Range of local amenities only four miles away. Open all year. Short breaks also available. Please contact for further details, brochure and late availability offers. **Auch Estate, c/o Brynkinalt Estate Office, Brynkinalt, Chirk, Wrexham LL14 5NS (01691 774159; Fax: 01691 778567).** **e-mail: brynkinalt@enterprise.net**

CONNEL

West Coast Character Cottages. Sleep 2 to 7. Six interesting and individual privately-owned holiday homes, beautifully located in rural areas within easy driving distance of Oban. Each has a large garden and pleasant outlook, some have stunning views. All are equipped and presented to a high standard and are personally supervised by the local owners. Walking, fishing and many other pursuits to be enjoyed amidst wonderful scenery. Electricity included. Linen available. Call for a brochure. **Tigh Beag, Connel, By Oban PA37 1PJ (01631 710504).** **e-mail: johnandjanet@wccc.sol.co.uk** **website: www.obanholidaycottages.co.uk**

DALMALLY

Mr & Mrs E. Crawford, Blarghour Farm, Lochaweside, By Dalmally PA33 1BW (01866 833246; Fax: 01866 833338). At Blarghour, a working hill farm on the shores of lovely Loch Awe, the holiday guest has a choice of high quality, well appointed, centrally heated, double glazed accommodation of individual character, each enjoying its own splendid view over loch and mountain in this highly scenic area. Barn House sleeps two, Stable House accommodates four, Barr-beithe Lower sleeps five and Barr-beithe Upper sleeps six. All have fitted kitchens with fridge/freezer, washing machine, microwave and electric cooker; telephone and TV. The cottages at Barr-beithe also include a dishwasher, and a cot and highchair are also available. Linen and towels are supplied. Parking beside each house. Barn and Stable Houses are unsuitable for children under five years. No pets allowed. Open all year. The area, centrally situated for touring, offers opportunities for walking, bird-watching, boating and fishing. Golf is available at Dalmally and Inveraray. Colour brochure sent on request.
e-mail: blarghour@btconnect.com   **website: www.self-catering-argyll.co.uk**

e-mail: dlfellowes@supanet.com

DALMALLY

Mrs E. Fellowes, Inistrynich, Dalmally, Argyll PA33 1BQ (01838 200256; Fax: 01838 200253). Two cottages overlooking Loch Awe surrounded by beautiful scenery, making the perfect retreat for a peaceful holiday. Garden Cottage (sleeps 8), Millside Cottage (sleeps 4). Dalmally five miles, Inveraray 11 miles, Oban 28 miles. Both have garden area, convector heaters in all rooms, open fire in living rooms, electric cooker, fridge, immersion heater, electric kettle, iron, vacuum cleaner, washing machine, colour TV. Cot and high chair by request. Dogs allowed by arrangement. Car essential, ample parking. Ideal for touring mainland and Inner Hebrides. Good restaurants, hill walking, forest walks, fishing, boat hire, pony trekking. NT gardens and golf within easy reach. Open Easter to November. Colour brochure available. **STB ★★★** *SELF CATERING*
website: www.loch-awe.com/inistrynich

SCOTLAND

INVERARAY
Minard Castle, Minard PA32 8YB (Tel & Fax: 01546 886272). 19th century Minard Castle beside Loch Fyne is a peaceful location for a quiet break. Stroll in the grounds, walk by the loch, explore the woods, or tour this scenic area with lochs, hills, gardens, castles and historic sites. THE LODGE, a comfortable bungalow with small garden and view through trees to the loch, sleeps four to six. THE MEWS APARTMENTS both sleep four to five. Well equipped; central heating, hot water, linen and towels included. Terms £120 to £370 per week. Open all year. **STB ★★★** *SELF-CATERING.* Also Four Star B&B in Minard Castle; £45pppn, open April to October.
e-mail: reinoldgayre@minardcastle.com
website: www.minardcastle.com

ISLE OF GIGHA
Gigha Hotel, Isle of Gigha PA41 7AA (01583 505254, Fax: 01583 505244). Situated in the Inner Hebrides, the community owned Isle of Gigha (God's Island) is surely one of Scotland's most beautiful and tranquil islands. Explore the white sandy bays and lochs. Easy walking, bike hire, birds, wildlife and wild flowers. Home to the famous Achamore Gardens with rhododendrons, azaleas and semi-exotic plants. Grass Airstrip, 9-hole golf course and regular ferry service (only 20 minutes from the mainland). We are dog-friendly. Holiday cottages also available. **STB ★★★** *SMALL HOTEL.*
website: www.isle-of-gigha.co.uk

LOCH FYNE (East Shore)
A single isolated fisherman's cottage, right by a river mouth accessed by rough farm track. Clean beach, wild hills, sea and river fishing included. Although just two delightful hours' drive from the M8 at Glasgow, Auchalick Bay is a haven of peace. Spacious living room with colour TV, VCR, radio, table tennis etc. Double bedroom, small bunkroom for two, foldaway bed in livingroom. All electric plus open fire, double glazing throughout. Payphone. Please bring bedsheets, towels etc. Open all year. From £220 to £388 per week (normally Friday to Friday), reductions for longer stays, electricity charged at cost. Rowing boat included in the price (April - October). Farm animals about, so dogs must be under control. Eight miles to Kames for shops, golf, sailing school, tennis etc. Descriptive leaflet and bookings:
John and Lynn Rankin, 12 Hamilton Place, Perth PH1 1BB (01738 632580).
e-mail: john@claddie.co.uk   website: www.claddie.co.uk

OBAN
Mrs C. Adams, Westmount, Dalriach Road, Oban PA34 5JE (01631 562884). Sleeps 5. Semi-detached villa in residential area, three minutes' walk from tennis courts, bowling green and swimming pool. Accommodation comprises two bedrooms, living room; kitchen with electric cooker, washing machine, tumble dryer, fridge; bathroom with bath and shower. Electric convector for heating. Garden. Pets accepted by arrangement. Open April to October. Terms from £180 to £300 per week. £1 electricity coin meter. Parking. **STB ★★** *SELF-CATERING.*

SCOTLAND

e-mail: cologin@west-highland-holidays.co.uk

OBAN

Cologin Country Chalets. Set in a tranquil glen less than three miles from Oban, our cosy chalets and atmospheric country pub/restaurant are a winning combination. Enjoy the waymarked forest trails in the hills above our farm, or relax in front of the fire and sample home-cooked local produce in the pub. The attractions of Oban – "Gateway to the Islands" – are minutes away. Pets and children are welcome – we have a playpark, games byre, and 17,000 acres to walk the dog. Disabled access chalets are available. Free fishing on our hill loch; boats and rods provided. Short breaks from £30, weekly lets from £180 to £510. STB ★★★ to ★★★★ *SELF CATERING.* **Mrs Linda Battison, Cologin House, Lerags Glen, By Oban PA34 4SE (01631 564501; Fax: 01631 566925).** *ASSC MEMBER.*

website: www.west-highland-holidays.co.uk

ROTHESAY

"Morningside" Sleep 3/5. Quality holiday flats, Isle of Bute. "MORNINGSIDE" is a charming Victorian villa with magnificent views. Tastefully converted one and two bed-roomed self-contained apartments with spacious sittingroom, fitted kitchen, bath/shower room and central heating. Minutes from the Pier, golf course, indoor pool and town centre. Communal laundry. **STB** ★★★ *SELF-CATERING.* Phone Jacqualine on **01700 505772** **website: www.isleofbuteholidayflats.co.uk**

TARBERT

Mrs Barker, Barfad Farm, Tarbert, Loch Fyne PA29 6YH (Tel: 01880 820549). Three stone cottages set in 80 acres of woodland with beaches and beautiful scenery. THE CHICKEN COOP, sleeps 2 plus cot. Compact open plan kitchen/dining area, double bedroom, shower/wc. THE DAIRY sleeps four plus cot and one extra. Large open plan living/dining room with kitchen area, one family room (one double and one single), one single bedroom, sofa bed for one extra. Shower/wc. THE STABLE sleeps 4 plus one extra. Spacious open plan kitchen/living room, one large bedroom, normally three single beds, four possible. Sofa bed for one extra. Shower, bath, two wcs. All cottages include colour TV, laundry room (shared), parking, electric heating, linen and towels; electricity extra.

TARBERT

Amanda Minshall, Dunmore Court, Kilberry Road, Near Tarbert, Argyll PA29 6XZ (01880 820654). Five cottages in architect design conversion of home farm on the estate of Dunmore House. Spacious accommodation for 2-8 persons. All have stone fireplaces for log fires. Bird-watching, fishing and walking. Easy access to island ferries. Pets welcome. Open all year. Colour brochure. From £175-£490. **STB** ★★. *ASSC MEMBER*
e-mail: dunmorecourtsc@aol.com
website: www.dunmorecourt.com

AYRSHIRE & ARRAN

Millport • Isle of Cumbrae
I Guildford Street
STB 2, 3 and 4 Stars Self-catering
OPEN ALL YEAR

Five flats and one house to cater for 2-10 persons. Two large luxury Four-Star flats to suit extended family. Superb sea views. Heating included in rates. Small garden. Sorry, no pets. Close to shops, pubs, restaurants.

Only a 5-minute ferry crossing from Largs, the Isle of Cumbrae is a small, friendly, unspoilt island, with cycling, golf, walking, bowling, sailing and birdwatching.

www.cottageguide.co.uk/millport • e-mail: b@I-guildford-st.co.uk
For further details please contact Mrs Barbara McLuckie, Muirhall Farm, Larbert, Stirlingshire FK5 4EW • 01324 551570 • Fax: 01324 551223

See also Colour Advertisement

SCOTLAND

See also Colour Display Advertisement

ARRAN

Arran Hideaways, Invercloy House, Brodick, Isle of Arran KA27 8AJ. Choice of properties on the island, available throughout the year. All villages, all dates. Self-catering and bunk house accommodation available. STB Quality Assured. Short breaks available. Major credit cards accepted. Please ask for our brochure. On-line booking and availability. Our staff are here to help you seven days a week. **Call 01770 302303/302310; evenings and weekends: 01770 860556.** *ASSC MEMBER.* **e-mail: holidays@arran-hideaways.co.uk website: www.arran-hideaways.co.uk**

BORDERS

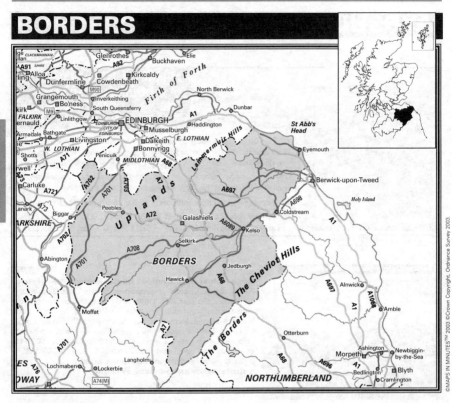

See also Colour Display Advertisement

BAILEY/NEWCASTLETON

Cumbrian/Scottish Borders. Sleep up to 7 plus cot. Superb character cottages set in historic landscape. Conservation farm. Panoramic views. High quality furnishings. Wood burning stoves. Stabling facilities - bring your horse. Great for walking, cycling, riding with forest tracks, bridleways, rivers and wooded valleys. Explore the Lake District, Hadrian's Wall, Solway Coast, historic Carlisle and return to a barbecue on your own patio or relax by the fire. Children and pets welcome. Terms from £250 to £450. Open all year. **STB ★★★★** *SELF CATERING.* Contact: **Jane Gray, Saughs Farm, Bailey, Newcastleton, Roxburghshire TD9 0TT (01697 748000/748346; Fax: 01697 748180).**
e-mail: skylark@onholiday.co.uk
website: www.skylarkcottages.co.uk

COLDSTREAM

'Meg's' and 'Nellie's' Cottages. Sleep 6/7. These comfortable and homely semi-detached cottages, situated on a private road, have lovely views across the River Tweed and rolling Border country to the Cheviot Hills. They are heated throughout, and in winter the sittingrooms have a welcoming open fire. Both have a sittingroom, kitchen, bathroom and double bedroom on the ground floor. 'Meg's' has one twin and one family room on the first floor; 'Nellie's' has two twin rooms. Full linen included. Both have colour TV, fridge, washing machine and garden furniture. Electricity by meter reading. Cot and high chair can be provided. Ample parking. Dogs by prior arrangement. Details from: **Mrs Sheila Letham, Fireburn Mill, Coldstream TD12 4LN (01890 882124; Fax: 01890 883838).**
e-mail: letham@tinyworld.co.uk

Mrs Anne Scott, Overhall Farm Cottage, Haw **(01450 375045; Fax: 01450 375445).** Situated of Hawick in the beautiful Border country, this is base from which to explore the surrounding area, ric with the remains of the Border abbeys testament to ou ...urbulent past, and many stately homes to visit. Close by is the award-winning Wilton Lodge Park, with its walled garden, museum and art gallery, and children's play area. Hawick's Teviotdale Leisure Centre offers an excellent pool with flume attraction, and the town is famous for its quality knitwear and rugby. Terms from £170 to £245. **STB ★★★** *SELF CATERING.*
website: www.overhall-scotland.co.uk

JEDBURGH

Mill House, Letterbox and Stockman's Cottages. Three recently renovated, quality Cottages, each sleeping four, on a working farm three miles from Jedburgh. Ideal centres for exploring, sporting holidays or getting away from it all. Each cottage has two public rooms (ground floor available). Minimum let two days. Terms £190–£350. Open all year. Bus three miles, airport 54 miles. **STB ★★★★** *SELF-CATERING.* **Mrs A. Fraser, Overwells, Jedburgh TD8 6LT (01835 863020; Fax: 01835 864334).** *ASSC MEMBER.*
e-mail: abfraser@btinternet.com
website: www.overwells.co.uk

NEWCASTLETON

Pamela Copeland, Bailey Mill Courtyard Apartments and Trekking Centre, Bailey Mill, Newcastleton TD9 0TR (016977 48617; Fax: 016977 48074). A warm welcome awaits you from Pam and Ian on this small farm holiday complex, nestling on the Roxburghshire/Cumbrian border. The rural self-contained apartments create a courtyard setting or enjoy Bed and Breakfast or Full Board riding holidays in the farmhouse. Forest trekking and lessons in outdoor school. Colour TV, heating (oil), electricity and linen included in the rent. On site sauna, jacuzzi, toning table, games room, laundry, babysitting, fully licensed bar and meals. Enjoy walking or trekking through surrounding forests. Central touring area for Lake District, Hadrian's Wall and Scotland. Colour brochure available.

Self-catering £88-£498; Bed and Breakfast from £20 per person. **ETC ★★★/★★★**
e-mail: pam@baileymill.fsnet.co.uk   **website: www.holidaycottagescumbria.co.uk**

PEEBLES

Mrs R. Smith, Chapelhill Farm, Peebles EH45 8PQ (01721 720188; Fax: 01721 729734). Three delightful cottages on working farm situated in quiet, peaceful location with superb country views. The popular town of Peebles with its many shops, hotels, pubs and restaurants is less than a mile away. Edinburgh just 30 minutes by car. All cottages have central heating throughout, electric cooker, microwave and washing machine. Heating and bed linen included in price. Garden and garden furniture. Ample parking. Children most welcome. Dogs by arrangement. Many golf courses, beautiful walks, fishing, horse riding, cycling etc. All nearby. Brochures available. Prices from £150-£320 per week. **STB ★★★** *SELF CATERING.*

A useful Index of Towns/Villages and Counties appears on page 281 – please also refer to Contents Page 3.

SCOTLAND

DUMFRIES & GALLOWAY

SCOTLAND

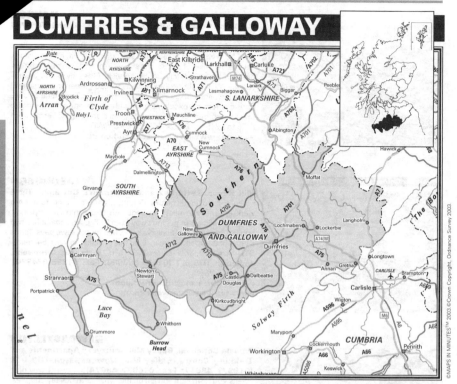

CASTLE DOUGLAS

Cala-Sona, Auchencairn, Castle Douglas. Sleeps 6. A stone-built house in centre of Auchencairn village, near shops, Post Office and garage. To let, furnished. Equipped for six persons. Linen supplied. Two bedrooms (one double bed; two single beds); cot available. Bathroom, bedroom with double bed, livingroom and kitchenette with electric cooker, fridge and geyser. Auchencairn is a friendly seaside village and you can enjoy a peaceful holiday here on the Solway Firth where the Galloway Hills slope down to the sea. Many places of historic interest to visit, also cliffs, caves amd sandy beaches. A haven for ornithologists. SAE brings prompt reply. Car essential - parking. **Mrs Mary Gordon, 7 Church Road, Auchencairn, Castle Douglas DG7 1QS (01556 640345).**

DALBEATTIE

10 Copeland Street, Dalbeattie. Midway Dumfries, Castle Douglas, By Galloway Coast. Small detached cottage with one family bedroom (one double bed, one single bed) and living room with bed settee. Electric fire and storage heaters, colour TV. Shower room, toilet and washbasin; kitchen/diner with cooker, fridge, microwave, washing machine. Fully equipped. Small rear garden and car parking. Holiday complex, golf, beautiful scenic walks (guided walks available) nearby. Sandy beach four miles, shops, post office, park, banks within easy walking distance. Electricity included in rental, bed linen not provided. Small dogs allowed. Terms from £120 weekly. Short breaks available. Telephone: **Mr M Bailey (017683 51466 or 07850 711411).**

Please mention Self-Catering Holidays in Britain when writing to enquire about accommodation

KIRKCUDBRIGHT

High Kirkland Holiday Cottages, Sleep 4,6 and 8. The cottages are traditional stone built Galloway Cottages, situated on Cannee Farm, one mile from Kirkcudbright. Pedigree Galloway and Simmental cattle are bred along with sheep. Kirkcudbright has an interesting harbour utilised by a flourishing fleet, and art exhibitions, museums, an 18 hole golf course, wildlife park, bird watching, hill walking, fishing, river trips, gardens and historical sites. All cottages are fully equipped, with spacious accommodation and full central heating. Linen hire service available and groceries can be ordered for your arrival. Utility room available with tumble dryer, cycle lock-up and drying facilities. Ample car parking. *WALKERS WELCOME, CYCLISTS WELCOME.* Contact: **Mr & Mrs R.G. Dunlop, Cannee Farm, Kirkcudbright DG6 4XD (01557 330684).**

e-mail: holidaycottages@cannee.co.uk   website: www.highkirkland.co.uk

PORTPATRICK

Mr A.D. Bryce, "Alinn", 25 Main Street, Portpatrick DG9 8JW (01776 810277). Sea front situation with unrestricted views of harbour and boats, overlooking small sandy beach with safe bathing. Golf, bowling, tennis and sea angling, scenic cliff walks and ideal country roads for touring. Shops and restaurants nearby. Area is of great historical and archaeological interest and enjoys a mild climate. Cottage, two bedrooms. Electric heating, cooking, etc. Prepayment coin meter. Terms from £180 to £225 per week. Parking at door. Please write or phone for further details.

THORNHILL

Hope Cottage, Thornhill DG3 5BD. Sleeps 6. Pretty stone cottage in the peaceful conservation village of Durisdeer. Well-equipped, self-catering cottage with large secluded garden. Towels, linen, heating and electricity included. Pets welcome. **STB ★★★★** *SELF-CATERING.* For brochure please telephone: **Mrs S. Stannett (01848 500228; Fax: 01848 500337).** e-mail: a.stann@btinternet.com website: www.hopecottage.co.uk

FREE or REDUCED RATE entry to Holiday Visits and Attractions – see our READERS' OFFER VOUCHERS on pages 53-80

DUNBARTONSHIRE

GARTOCHARN

Claire and Gavin MacLellan, The Lorn Mill Cottages, Gartocharn G83 8LX (01389 753074). The MacLellans have converted the 18th century mill providing three stylish, modern and well-equipped cottages/apartments. Hidden down a private drive in a secluded hollow, the property has some of the best views of Loch Lomond, Ben Lomond and the Arrochar Alps - a unique location! This is very much a country setting yet Glasgow Airport is only 30 minutes away and trains from nearby Balloch take you to Glasgow city centre in just 40 minutes. The Lorn Mill offers an ideal base for outdoor pursuits or for touring. Come and relax and soak up the beauty of Loch Lomond. Each cottage sleeps two to four, has en suite bathroom/ shower room, TV, video and CD player. Linen and electricity included in price. Dogs accepted only by arrangement. Prices from £225 to £375. Open all year. Short Breaks available. Please look at our website for further details or telephone us for availability. **STB ★★★★** *SELF-CATERING.*
e-mail: gavmac@globalnet.co.uk   **website: www.lornmill.com**

LOCH LOMOND

Mrs D. Scott, Inchmurrin Island, Loch Lomond G63 0JY (01389 850245; Fax: 01389 850513). Sleeps 2-8. Situated on Loch Lomond's largest island, ideal for fishing and watersports. Many lovely walks and spectacular views. Three well equipped apartments and one cottage available on a working farm. Central heating. Pets welcome by arrangement. Open April to October. Terms from £250 to £700 per week. **STB ★★★** *SELF-CATERING*

DUNDEE & ANGUS

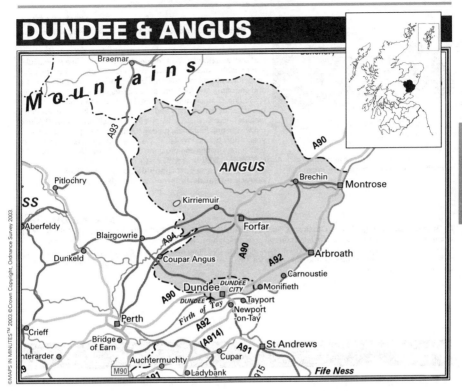

SCOTLAND

BROUGHTY FERRY

Kingennie Lodges, Kingennie, Broughty Ferry, By Dundee DD5 3RD (01382 350777; Fax: 01382 350400). Luxurious self-catering lodges (4) set amidst a delightful woodland setting, overlooking three trout fishing lochans. New coarse fishing lake for 2003. All lodges furnished to the highest standards and are open plan and centrally heated. Each has a double and twin bedroom as well as a folding sofa bed in the lounge; bathroom with shower over bath; fully-equipped kitchen with dishwasher, microwave and washer/dryer. Our "Clova" Lodge has full disabled facilities. Bed linen and towels provided, cot and highchair available upon request. Pets welcome. New lodge has three bedrooms, all en suite. Lodge terms weekly from £230. **STB ★★★★** *SELF CATERING.* Further details contact **Neil Anderson.**
e-mail: kingennie@easynet.co.uk
website: www.kingennie-fishings.com

NOTE

ENGLAND

KIRRIEMUIR

The Welton of Kingoldrum, Welton Farm, By Kirriemuir, Angus DD8 5HY (Tel & Fax: 01575 574743). Three comfortable, warm and welcoming properties, all ground floor and well equipped, on a secluded working farm in a spectacular setting with panoramic views over the Vale of Strathmore. Ideal base for outdoor pursuits including golf, fishing, riding, skiing and shooting, and for touring the Angus glens, coastline, castles (including Glamis) and gardens. Peaceful and relaxing. Central heating, hot water, linen and towels included in rental. Facilities include microwave, laundry and ironing facilities, colour TV/video player, cot and highchair, garden furniture, BBQ, parking. Open all year. Short breaks available. Walkers and Cyclists welcome. For further information and brochure contact **Jenny Scott**. Rates from £170 to £335 (excl. Christmas and New Year). *ASSC MEMBER*. STB ★★★ *SELF-CATERING*.
e-mail: jennyscott@easicom.com **websites: www.cottageguide.co.uk/thewelton**
www.angusanddundee.co.uk/members/562htm

KIRRIEMUIR (by)

D. Smith, Scobshaugh Farm, Cortachy, By Kirriemuir DD8 4QH (01575 540214; Fax: 01575 540355).
Sleep 5, 6. Modern farmhouse and farm cottage on working farm five miles from Kirriemuir on B955 road to Glen Clova. Both houses approximately one mile from main road. Bed linen and towels are provided and terms are from £180 to £250 per week, electricity and heating extra. Children very welcome, sorry no dogs. Please phone or fax for more details.

FIFE

See also Colour Display Advertisement

NEWPORT-ON-TAY

Mr and Mrs Ramsay, Balmore, 3 West Road, Newport-on-Tay DD6 8HH (01382 542274; Fax: 01382 542927).
Sleeps 5/6. Situated on the southern shore of the Tay Estuary, Thorndene is the secluded and self-contained west wing of a large Listed house situated in a three-acre walled garden. On the ground floor, it has entry through a paved courtyard, and has its own garden. It is bright and sunny, equipped to a high standard, carpeted throughout, with central heating. There are two double bedrooms – one with a shower en suite, a single bedroom, large sittingroom, diningroom, sun lounge, tiled bathroom with bath and shower, fitted kitchen with washing machine, dishwasher, microwave and breakfast bar. Terms from £200 to £420. Brochure available. STB ★★★ *SELF-CATERING, ASSC MEMBER*.
e-mail: Allan.Ramsay@ukgateway.net

HIGHLANDS

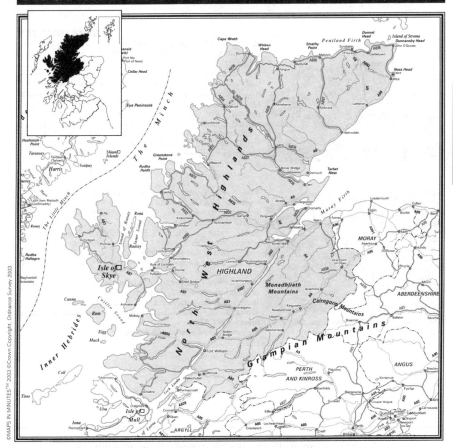

SCOTLAND

©MAPS IN MINUTES™ 2003 ©Crown Copyright. Ordnance Survey 2003

Two for one OR one child free per paying adult at

Loch Ness 2000 Exhibition Centre

see our READERS' OFFER VOUCHER for details

FREE entry to 'Heather Story" exhibition at

Speyside Heather Garden & Visitor Centre

see our READERS' OFFER VOUCHER for details

When making enquiries please mention FHG Publications

HIGHLANDS (North)

ENGLAND

STRATHNAVER

Mrs C.M. MacLeod, Achnabourin, Strathnaver, Near Bettyhill KW11 6UA (01641 561210). Comfy country cottage situated beside the River Naver in the lovely Strathnaver Valley, six miles from coast and village of Bettyhill, 14 miles from Tongue, both with lovely sandy beaches. An ideal base for touring the rugged north coast of Scotland or for just enjoying the local walks and scenery. Trout fishing available. Two double and one twin-bedded rooms, sitting room with open or electric fire, kitchen with electric cooker, fridge, deep freeze, microwave, automatic washing machine, toaster, etc; bathroom. Fully equipped except linen. Open March to October. Rates from £150 to £180 per week. Electricity extra. For full details send SAE.

WICK

The Corner Town House, Wick (Tel & Fax: 01955 603500; mobile: 07879 641333). A quality home for your quality holiday in the Highlands. Relax, unwind and enjoy the Corner House, a traditional two-storey house in a quiet street in the historic fishing port of Wick. Renovated to a high standard and very comfortably furnished, it is an excellent choice for your family holiday. Accommodation on the ground floor comprises lounge, dining kitchen, single bedroom (suitable for older or disabled person) and shower room. Double (en suite), twin and single bedroom upstairs. Garden and patio with shed for storage of bikes etc. Within easy walking distance of town, shops, leisure facilities etc. Convenient public transport links. For details contact **Donald A. Campbell, Accommodation Scotland,**

Duncoran House, 37 Bank Row, Wick, Caithness KW1 5EY.
e-mail: booking@visit-wick.co.uk   website: www.visit-wick.co.uk

FHG

PLEASE MENTION THIS GUIDE WHEN YOU WRITE

OR PHONE TO ENQUIRE ABOUT ACCOMMODATION

IF YOU ARE WRITING, A STAMPED, ADDRESSED

ENVELOPE IS ALWAYS APPRECIATED

HIGHLANDS (Mid)

ACHILTIBUIE

Chalet. Sleeps 4. Norwegian-style log chalet to sleep four persons, situated overlooking the sea and the Summer Isles in Lochbroom in Wester Ross, with magnificent views of islands and mountains. This tranquil area has lots to offer - walking, climbing, fishing, birdwatching, golf and much more. The chalet has electric heating in all rooms by slot meter, electric cooker, microwave, washing machine, colour TV, radio. Bath with shower, everything supplied except linen and towels. Lawned garden with chairs. Ample parking. Shops and eating out facilities in the area. Please ring for full details and brochure. **M.W. MacLeod, Dornie House, Achiltibuie, By Ullapool, Wester Ross IV26 2YP (Tel & Fax: 01854 622271).**
e-mail: dorniehouseBandB@aol.com

ACHILTIBUIE

Achiltibuie, near Ullapool, North West Coast. Sleeps 6. A sixteen mile single track road through hills, lochs and the Inverpolly Nature Reserve brings you to Achiltibuie. This superb three bedroom cottage has magnificent views over the sea, the Summer Isles and mountains. The cottage has oil fired central heating, Rayburn and real fire, dishwasher, washing machine and tumble dryer. Ideal for beach, walking and birdwatching holidays. Prices from £350 to £550 per week, terms include fuel, power and linen. See us on our website or contact: **Mrs S. Mellor, Oakley Barn, Little Oakley, Corby, Northamptonshire NN18 8HA (01536 744567).**
website: www.achiltibuiecottage.com

LOCHCARRON

The Cottage, Stromecarronach, Lochcarron West, Strathcarron. Working croft. Sleeps 2. The small, stone-built Highland cottage is fully equipped and has a double bedroom, shower room and open plan kitchen/living room (with open fire). It is secluded, with panoramic views over Loch Carron and the mountains. River, sea and loch fishing is popular in the area and there is a small local golf course. Nearby attractions include the Isle of Skye, Inverewe Gardens, the Torridon and Applecross Hills and the historic Kyle Railway Line. Visitors' dogs are welcome provided they are kept under control at all times. For full particulars write, or telephone, **Mrs A.G. Mackenzie, Stromecarronach, Lochcarron West, Strathcarron IV54 8YH (01520 722284).**
website: www.lochcarron.org

See also Colour Display Advertisement   **POOLEWE**

Innes Maree Bungalows, Poolewe IV22 2JU (Tel & Fax 01445 781454). Only a few minutes' walk from the world-famous Inverewe Gardens in magnificent Wester Ross. A purpose-built complex of six superb modern bungalows, all equipped to the highest standards of luxury and comfort. Each bungalow sleeps six with main bedroom en suite. Children and pets welcome. Terms from £190 to £425 inclusive of bed linen and electricity. Brochure available. **STB ★★★★** *SELF-CATERING. ASSC MEMBER.*
e-mail: fhg@poolewebungalows.com   website: www.poolewebungalows.com

FREE or REDUCED RATE entry to Holiday Visits and Attractions — see our READERS' OFFER VOUCHERS on pages 53-80

Conchra Farm Cottages
Open all year
STB ★★ Self-catering

Comfortable, fully modernised traditional farm cottages adjacent to working farm. Tranquil lochside setting, convenient for exploring Skye and the Highlands. Fully equipped; central heating, electricity and bed linen incl. Excellent value for money and ideal for families, walking and activity holidays.

Gardener's Cottage • 2 single, one double, one twin | **£215-£425 per week**
Shepherd's Cottage • one family, one twin
Farmer's Cottage • one double, one single, one family. For details contact:

Conchra Farm Cottages, Tigh-na-Coille, Ardelve, Ross-shire IV40 8DZ
Tel & Fax: 01520 722344 • www.conchracottages.co.uk
e-mail: enquiries@conchra.co.uk

See also Colour Advertisement

POOLEWE

Crofters Cottages, 15 Croft, Poolewe IV22 2JY (01445 781268; Fax: 01445 781704). Sleeps 4/5/9. Three traditional cottages situated in a scenic and tranquil area, ideal for a "get away from it all" holiday. Crofters Cottages are comfortably furnished, some with antiques and all the essential modern gadgets of today, such as auto-washer/dryer, microwave, fridge, bath and shower. Poolewe is a good base to tour the North West Highlands or for those who enjoy walking, fishing, climbing, golf or maybe just a stroll along one of the many sandy beaches. There are also indoor activities to be enjoyed such as the heated pool and leisure and fitness areas. Close by lie the famous Inverewe Gardens. Pets made welcome. Terms: Low Season from £120 to £230, High Season from £250 to £490, midweek and short breaks available from November to March. Contact: **Mr A. Urquhart.**
e-mail: croftcottages@btopenworld.com   website: www.croftcottages.btinternet.co.uk

---

• • *Some Useful Guidance for Guests and Hosts* • •

Every year literally thousands of holidays, short breaks and overnight stops are arranged through our guides, the vast majority without any problems at all. In a handful of cases, however, difficulties do arise about bookings, which often could have been prevented from the outset.
It is important to remember that when accommodation has been booked, both parties – guests and hosts – have entered into a form of contract. We hope that the following points will provide helpful guidance.

GUESTS:
• When enquiring about accommodation, be as precise as possible. Give exact dates, numbers in your party and the ages of any children.
• State the number and type of rooms wanted and also what catering you require – bed and breakfast, full board etc. Make sure that the position about evening meals is clear – and about pets, reductions for children or any other special points.
• Read our reviews carefully to ensure that the proprietors you are going to contact can supply what you want. Ask for a letter confirming all arrangements, if possible.
• If you have to cancel, do so as soon as possible. Proprietors do have the right to retain deposits and under certain circumstances to charge for cancelled holidays if adequate notice is not given and they cannot re-let the accommodation.

HOSTS:
• Give details about your facilities and about any special conditions. Explain your deposit system clearly and arrangements for cancellations, charges etc. and whether or not your terms include VAT.
• If for any reason you are unable to fulfil an agreed booking without adequate notice, you may be under an obligation to arrange suitable alternative accommodation or to make some form of compensation.

While every effort is made to ensure accuracy, we regret that FHG Publications cannot accept responsibility for errors, omissions or misrepresentations in our entries or any consequences thereof. Prices in particular should be checked because we go to press early. We will follow up complaints but cannot act as arbiters or agents for either party.

HIGHLANDS (South)

CAIRNGORM HIGHLAND BUNGALOWS

Glen Einich, 29 Grampian View,
Aviemore, Inverness-shire PH22 1TF
Tel: 01479 810653 • Fax: 01479 810262
e-mail: linda.murray@virgin.net
website: www.cairngorm-bungalows.co.uk

Beautifully furnished and well-equipped bungalows ranging from one to four bedrooms. All have colour TV, video, microwave, cooker, washer-dryer, fridge and patio furniture. Some have log fires. Leisure facilities nearby include golf, fishing on the River Spey, swimming, sauna, jacuzzi, tennis, skating and skiing. Within walking distance of Aviemore. Ideal touring base. Children and pets welcome. Phone for colour brochure. Open all year.

See also Colour Display Advertisement

ARISAIG

Arisaig House Cottages. Luxurious, secluded accommodation in mature woodland. Set in an area of breathtaking coastal and hill scenery, and wonderful sandy beaches. Mountain bike hire and fishing on Loch Morar can be arranged. Golf seven miles, swimming pool 13 miles. Hard tennis court. Day trips to the Small Isles and to Skye. Various properties, sleeping from two to eight persons. On-line booking. Details from: **Andrew Smither, Arisaig House, Beasdale, Arisaig, Inverness-shire PH39 4NR (Tel & Fax: 01687 462 686).** *ASSC MEMBER.*
e-mail: enquiries@arisaighouse-cottages.co.uk
www.arisaighouse-cottages.co.uk

ARISAIG

Kilmartin, Kinloid Farm, Arisaig PH39 4NS (01687 450366; Fax: 01687 450611). Three holiday cottages, sleeping six. Widely spaced back, commanding magnificent views across Arisaig to the sea and the islands of Skye, Rhum and Eigg. Five minutes by car from the wonderful sands. Ideal area for fishing, hill walking and golf. The cottages are roomy and comfortable and sleep six people. Two bedrooms, furnished lounge with colour TV, bathroom with bath and shower; fully fitted kitchen with electric cooker and fridge. Electricity for heating and lighting. Pets welcome by arrangement. Terms from £280 per week. Six fully equipped caravans also available for hire. SAE, please, for brochure. Sorry, no pets. **STB ★★★** *SELF-CATERING.*

See also Colour Display Advertisement

BEAULY

Glen Affric Chalet Park, Cannich, Beauly IV4 7LT (01456 415369; Fax: 01456 415429). Great value summer holidays and autumn-winter/spring breaks. Set beside the River Glass and surrounded by spectacular mountain scenery, 15 minutes from Loch Ness, our accommodation provides three-bedroom bungalow chalets, fully equipped and comfortably furnished with central heating and bed linen. An ideal base for walking, climbing, cycling, fishing and stalking, or a central base for touring and viewing the scenery. We have a laundry, games room, children's play area and barbecue area on site; shop, pub and hotel within five minutes' walk. **STB ★★★** *SELF-CATERING.*
e-mail: info@glenaffricchaletpark.com
website: www.glenaffricchaletpark.com

CULLODEN (BY INVERNESS)

Blackpark Farm, Westhill, Inverness IV2 5BP (01463 790620; Fax: 01463 794262). This newly-built holiday home is located one mile from Culloden Battlefield with panoramic views over Inverness and beyond. Fully equipped with many extras to make your holiday special, including oil-fired central heating to ensure warmth on the coldest of winter days. Ideally based for touring the Highlands including Loch Ness, Skye etc. Extensive information is available on our website. A Highland welcome awaits you. *ASSC MEMBER.*
e-mail: i.alexander@blackpark.co.uk   **website: www.blackpark.co.uk**

DRUMNADROCHIT

Glenurquhart Lodges, Near Drumnadrochit, Inverness IV3 6TJ (01456 476234; Fax: 01456 476286). Situated between Loch Ness and Glen Affric in a spectacular setting ideal for walking, touring or just relaxing in this tranquil location. Four spacious chalets all fully equipped for six people, including bedding and towels, set in wooded grounds. Dogs welcome. Owner's hotel adjacent where guests are most welcome in the restaurant and bar.
e-mail: carol@glenurquhartlodges.co.uk

FORT WILLIAM

Ben View Self Catering. Sleeps 6. A fully-equipped detached house with garage and small garden. It is ideally situated on the A82 Glasgow - Inverness road, only three minutes' walk from Fort William town centre, bus and rail stations and the Leisure Centre. The accommodation comprises one double room with en suite facilities, two twin-bedded rooms and a shower room with WC. The house has a well equipped fitted kitchen and a spacious, luxurious dining/lounge area with log fire. Bedding is provided and a travel cot is available on request. Starter pack is also available if desired. **Mrs Smith, Ben View Guest House, Belford Road, Fort William PH33 6ER (01397 772017).**
e-mail: BenView@gowanbrae.co.uk
website: www.benviewguesthouse.co.uk

FORT WILLIAM BY

Springwell Holiday Homes, Onich, Fort William PH33 6RY. Four cottages, fully equipped, on 17 acres of private hillside with magnificent views across Loch Linnhe to Glencoe and the Argyll Hills. Cottages accommodate from two to six people, children and dogs are welcome. Ideally situated for all leisure pursuits and relaxation. There are shops, hotels and garages within a short distance and the site itself has adequate parking facilities. Small, secluded, rugged beach. Open all year round. Prices from £210 to £440 per week. Electricity and linen included. For details please write or telephone/fax. **STB ★★★** *SELF-CATERING.* **Mr and Mrs Murray (01855 821257).**
e-mail: info@springwellholidayhomes.co.uk
website: www.springwellholidayhomes.co.uk

Linnhe Lochside Holidays

Corpach, Fort William, PH33 7NL

Tel: 01397 772376 • Fax: 01397 772007

e-mail: holidays@linnhe.demon.co.uk

website: www.linnhe-lochside-holidays.co.uk

"Best Park in Scotland 1999 Award"

Almost a botanical garden and stunningly beautiful. Wonderful views and ideal for touring or simply relaxing and soaking up the scenery. Licensed shop, private beach and free fishing.

Colour Brochure sent with pleasure

★ **Luxury house** from £750/week. (Graded 5 star)

★ **Deluxe pine chalets** from £335/week.

★ **Luxury holiday caravans** from £190/week.

★ **Tourers** from £13/night.

★ **Camping** from £10/night.

INVERGARRY

Miss J. Ellice, Taigh-an-Lianach, Aberchalder Estate, Invergarry PH35 4HN (01809 501287). Three self catering properties, all ideal for hill walkers and country lovers. Salmon and trout fishing available. ABERCHALDER LODGE: traditional Highland shooting lodge extensively modernised to give a high standard of comfort, sleeps 12. TAIGH AN LIANACH: modern self contained bed-sit, secluded and peaceful, sleeps two. LEAC COTTAGE: a secluded cottage which combines old world charm with a high standard of comfort, sleeps three. Children and dogs welcome. Please phone or fax **01809 501287**.

See also Colour Display Advertisement

KINCRAIG

Loch Insh Log Chalets, Kincraig PH21 1NU (01540 651272). Just six miles south of Aviemore these superb log chalets are set in 14 acres of woodland in the magnificent Spey Valley, surrounded on three sides by forest and rolling fields with the fourth side being half a mile of beach frontage. Free watersports hire for guests, 8.30-10am/4-5.30pm daily. Sailing, windsurfing, canoeing, salmon fishing, archery, dry ski slope skiing. Hire/instruction available by the hour, day or week mid-April to end of October. Boathouse restaurant on the shore of Loch Insh offering coffee, home-made soup, fresh salads, bar meals, children's menu and evening à la carte. Large gift shop and bar. New children's adventure areas, three kilometres lochside/woodland walk/ interpretation trail, ski slope, mountain bike hire and stocked trout lochan are open all year round. Ski, snowboard hire and instruction available December to April. *ASSC MEMBER.* e-mail: **office@lochinsh.com**   website: **www.lochinsh.com**

Please mention Self-Catering Holidays in Britain when enquiring about accommodation featured in these pages.

NEWTONMORE

Croft Holidays, Newtonmore PH20 1BA (01540 673504). Thoughtfully renovated cottages in quiet, picturesque surroundings, on outskirts of lovely Highland village in 'Monarch of the Glen' country. Central heating, TV, fridge, microwave, washer, drying room, disabled access. Way-marked trails, golf course, restaurants, pubs, shops, museums in village. Newtonmore is easy to find, just one mile from A9. Central for touring, many tourist attractions, great area for walking (guided walk included), bird watching, cycling, pony trekking, water sports. Short breaks or long stays welcome all year. Cottages sleeping up to four from £140 to £320 per week, from £40 per night, including heating and bed linen. Well behaved pets welcome. Smoking only in one cottage. For brochure/special offers contact Mary Mackenzie. **STB ★★★** *SELF-CATERING. WALKERS WELCOME, CYCLISTS WELCOME.*
e-mail: FHG@croftholidays.co.uk   **website: www.croftholidays.co.uk**

NEWTONMORE

Crubenbeg Holiday Cottages, Newtonmore PH20 1BE (01540 673566; Fax: 01540 673509). Rural self-catering cottages in the central Highlands where one can relax and stroll from the doorstep or take part in the choice of many sporting activities in the area. We have a children's play area, a games room, pond stocked with trout for fishing and a barbecue. Pets welcome. **STB ★★★★** *SELF CATERING.*
e-mail: enquiry@crubenbeg.com
website: www.crubenbeg.com

ONICH

Mrs K.A. MacCallum, Tigh-a-Righ House, Onich, By Fort William PH33 6SE (01855 821255). Comfortable apartments, sleep up to 12. Every luxury provided. Well-equipped kitchen with dishwasher, microwave, toaster, cooker, deep freeze, fridge. Split level lounge with TV and sitting area. Three toilets - some rooms en suite. Garden, barbecue. Reasonable terms.

ONICH

Cuilcheanna Cottages and Caravans, Onich, Fort William PH33 6SD. Three cottages and eight caravans (6 x 2003 models) situated on a small peaceful site. The cottages are built to the highest standards with electric heating, double glazing and full insulation. Tastefully furnished and fully equipped, each cottage has a large picture window in the main living area which looks out over Loch Leven and Glencoe. Adjacent car parking. Laundry room and phone box on site. Only a short walk from the centre of Onich and an ideal base from which to explore the West Highlands. Paradise for hillwalkers. The caravans also have full facilities. Whether your stay with us is a long one, or just a few days, we shall do our best to ensure that it is enjoyable. Weekend Breaks available, winter rates, off season discounts. *ASSC MEMBER.* For further details please telephone **01855 821526** or **01855 821310.**
e-mail: onichholidays@mail.com

SPEAN BRIDGE

Alba Ben View. Enjoy your holiday in a beautiful cottage overlooking Ben Nevis and Aonoch Mor ski resort. The cottage is fully equipped , with two en suite bedrooms, one double and one twin. It is set within a quiet rural area just 10 miles from Fort William, with ample off-road parking. Well-behaved dogs are welcome. The cottage is ideally situated for walking, fishing, cycling, hill walking, skiing in the winter, and touring in the Great Glen and surrounding area. Pets welcome. Terms from £210 to £450 per week.Open all year. **Mr & Mrs E. Watson, High View, Spean Bridge PH34 4EG (01397 712209)**
e-mail: jo_eric_watson@tesco.net
website: www.albabenview.co.uk

LANARKSHIRE

BIGGAR (Clyde Valley)

Carmichael Country Cottages, Carmichael Estate Office, Westmains, Carmichael, Biggar ML12 6PG (01899 308336; Fax: 01899 308481). Working farm, join in. Sleep 2/7. These 200-year-old stone cottages nestle among the woods and fields of our 700-year-old family estate. Still managed by the descendants of the original Chief of Carmichael. We guarantee comfort, warmth and a friendly welcome in an accessible, unique, rural and historic time capsule. We farm deer, cattle and sheep and sell meats and tartan – Carmichael of course! Children and pets welcome. Open all year. Terms from £190 to £535. 15 cottages with a total of 32 bedrooms. We have the ideal cottage for you. Private tennis court and fishing loch; cafe, farm shop and visitor centre. Off-road driving course. **STB ★★/★★★★** *SELF-CATERING.* *ASSC MEMBER. FHB MEMBER.*
e-mail: chiefcarm@aol.com   website: www.carmichael.co.uk/cottages

EAST KILBRIDE

Mrs McLeavy, East Rogerton Lodge, Markethill Road, East Kilbride G74 4NZ (01355 263176). A warm welcome to our two self-catering cottages. Very comfortable home from home accommodation consisting of vestibule, open plan sitting/dining kitchen, hallway, two twin bedrooms, shower/bathroom. Fully equipped with electric cooker, fridge/freezer, microwave, washing machine, TV, video, CD stereo system, payphone. Terms inclusive of electricity, central heating, linen and towels. Private parking to rear. Situated on the fringe of East Kilbride yet in close proximity to shops, restaurants, museums, country parks and leisure activities. Perfect central location for tourist routes. Terms from £280 to £400. Three bedrooms. B&B also available.

PERTH & KINROSS

SCOTLAND

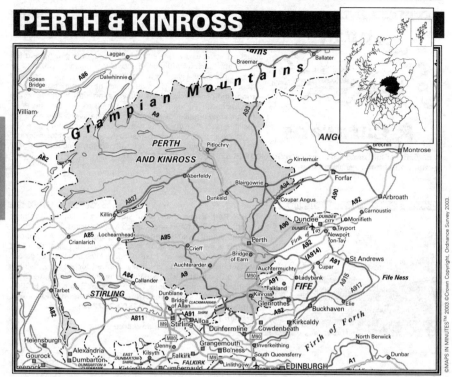

©MAPS IN MINUTES™ 2003 ©Crown Copyright, Ordnance Survey 2003

ABERFELDY

Loch Tay Lodges, Acharn. Lodges sleep 2/8. These lodges are in a recently converted stone-built terrace listed as of special historic and architectural interest, situated on farm on the outskirts of the picturesque Highland village of Acharn on the shores of Loch Tay. There is free trout fishing on the loch; salmon and other fishing by arrangement. Special facilities for sailing: many scenic walks. Golf at Taymouth one and a half miles and five other courses within 20 miles. The lodges are fully equipped to the highest modern standard, including colour TV. Four of the units have log fires. Open all year, with terms from £195 to £510. **STB ★★★★** *SELF-CATERING.* For free brochure, please apply to **Mrs F. Millar, Remony, Acharn, Aberfeldy PH15 2HR (01887 830209; Fax: 01887 830802).**
e-mail: remony@btinternet.com
website: www.lochtaylodges.co.uk

ABERFELDY

Hillview Cottages, Taybridge Terrace, Aberfeldy PH15 2BS (0410 280652). Two Victorian stone-built cottages offering affordable and comfortable accommodation in beautiful setting with hill views. Situated within walking distance of the town centre, and opposite the local park, bowling greens and golf course. Both cottages include lounge, kitchen and dining area, three bedrooms, bathroom and shower. Additional facilities include a large garden with patio and barbecue, games room and private parking. Open all year. Terms from £250 to £550 per week. **STB ★★★** *SELF-CATERING. WALKERS WELCOME, CYCLISTS WELCOME.*
e-mail: info@hillviewcottages.co.uk
website: www.hillviewcottages.co.uk

CRIEFF

Culcrieff Cottages at Crieff Hydro. Uninterrupted is the only description for the views of glorious Perthshire countryside from these newly built cottages. Set in 900 acres the restored steading is in a traditional style with all en suite bedrooms. Woodland off-lead walks directly from the door. Free use of Crieff Hydro's extensive leisure facilities including swimming pool, gym, sauna, steam room, children's club, activity and sports programme for all the family; all included in your rate. Holidays and short breaks. For more information or to book call **01764 651670** or visit **website: www.crieffhydro.com**

DUNKELD (By)

Laighwood Holidays, Butterstone, By Dunkeld PH8 0HB (01350 724241; Fax: 01350 724212). Properties sleep 2/8. A de luxe detached house, comfortably accommodating eight, created from the West Wing of a 19th century shooting lodge with panoramic views. Two popular cottages sleeping four to six, situated on our hill farm, with beautiful views. Two well-equipped apartments adjoining Butterglen House near Butterstone Loch. Butterstone lies in magnificent countryside (especially Spring/ Autumn), adjacent to Nature Reserve (ospreys). Central for walking, touring, historic houses, golf and fishing. Private squash court and hill loch (wild brown trout) on the farm. Sorry no pets. Terms: House £424 to £660; Cottages and Apartments £165 to £375 per week. **STB ★★★ to ★★★★** *SELF-CATERING. ASSC MEMBER.*

e-mail: holidays@laighwood.co.uk   **website: www.laighwood.co.uk**

KIRKMICHAEL

The Luggie, Kirkmichael. Located in the picturesque Highland village of Kirkmichael, in the Strathardle Valley, this well-equipped mid-terrace cottage enjoys lovely views to the River Ardle and offers an ideal base for exploring this beautiful part of Perthshire. Pitlochry and Blairgowrie are both 12 miles away and Glenshee 15 miles. We can arrange golf and fishing trips and horse riding is available locally. Accommodation is on two storeys with an open plan lounge/dining/kitchen area with open fire, TV, video, hi-fi, payphone, games, books and videos; modern kitchen with electric cooker, microwave, fridge/freezer, dishwasher and automatic washer/dryer. One double and one twin bedroom with cot, highchair and z-bed available on request. Bathroom with over-bath power shower. Enclosed garden and small private terrace with barbecue and garden furniture. Full central heating throughout. Pets welcome. Short Breaks available. **STB ★★★** *SELF-CATERING.* Contact: **George and Andrea Hay, 3 Rosemount Place, Perth PH2 7EH (Tel & Fax: 01738 625240; Mobile: 07968 059669)**
e-mail: andrea.hay@blueyonder.co.uk   website: www.assc.co.uk/luggie

Ratings You Can Trust

ENGLAND

The *English Tourism Council* (formerly the English Tourist Board) has joined with the *AA* and *RAC* to create a new, easily understood quality rating for serviced accommodation, giving a clear guide of what to expect.

HOTELS are given a rating from One to Five *Stars* – the more Stars, the higher the quality and the greater the range of facilities and level of services provided.

GUEST ACCOMMODATION, which includes guest houses, bed and breakfasts, inns and farmhouses, is rated from One to Five *Diamonds*. Progressively higher levels of quality and customer care must be provided for each one of the One to Five Diamond ratings.

HOLIDAY PARKS, TOURING PARKS and CAMPING PARKS are now also assessed using *Stars*. Standards of quality range from a One Star (acceptable) to a Five Star (exceptional) park.

Look out also for the new *SELF-CATERING* Star ratings. The more *Stars* (from One to Five) awarded to an establishment, the higher the levels of quality you can expect. Establishments at higher rating levels also have to meet some additional requirements for facilities.

SCOTLAND

Star Quality Grades will reflect the most important aspects of a visit, such as the warmth of welcome, efficiency and friendliness of service, the quality of the food and the cleanliness and condition of the furnishings, fittings and decor.

THE MORE STARS,
THE HIGHER THE STANDARDS.

The description, such as Hotel, Guest House, Bed and Breakfast, Lodge, Holiday Park, Self-catering etc tells you the type of property and style of operation.

WALES

Places which score highly will have an especially welcoming atmosphere and pleasing ambience, high levels of comfort and guest care, and attractive surroundings enhanced by thoughtful design and attention to detail

STAR QUALITY GUIDE FOR

HOTELS, GUEST HOUSES AND FARMHOUSES

SELF-CATERING ACCOMMODATION
(Cottages, Apartments, Houses)

CARAVAN HOLIDAY HOME PARKS
(Holiday Parks, Touring Parks, Camping Parks)

★★★★★ *Exceptional quality*
★★★★ *Excellent quality*
★★★ *Very good quality*
★★ *Good quality*
★ *Fair to good quality*

In England, Scotland and Wales, all graded properties are inspected annually by Tourist Authority trained Assessors.

View from Conwy Castle, North Wales

Wales
Self-catering Holidays

FBM Cottage Holidays. FBM Holidays is a Cottage Agency, independently run since 1833 by a knowledgeable and friendly team of staff. Accredited by the Wales Tourist Board, the portfolio of properties ranges from small chalet style units to larger, detached properties. All boast between 3 and 5 Star Gradings and are situated in a choice of country locations or seafront positions, covering an area of West Wales, including Pembrokeshire, Carmarthenshire and Cardiganshire. Full colour brochure available or view our popular, easy to use website where you can check availability online. **(01834 845000).**
website: www.fbmholidays.co.uk

See also Colour Display Advertisement **UNIVERSITY ACCOMMODATION & FACILITIES**
Budget accommodation or fully tailored packages (0870 712 5002; Fax: 020 7017 8273). En suite designer halls across the UK. Groups of any age or size. Sports facilities all year. Tell us your needs and we'll find a location and package to suit.
e-mail: enquiries@thesummervillage.com   **website: www.thesummervillage.com**

WALES

ANGLESEY & GWYNEDD

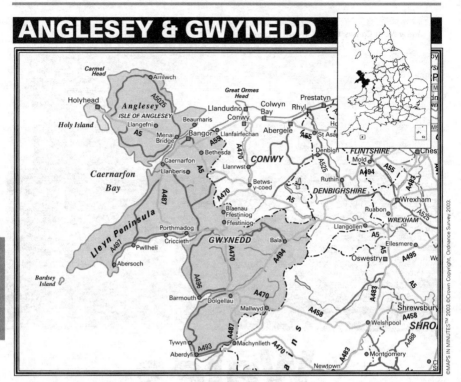

When making enquiries please mention FHG Publications

BRYN BRAS CASTLE

Welcome to beautiful Bryn Bras Castle – enchanting castle Apartments, elegant Tower-House within unique romantic turreted Regency Castle (Listed Building) in the gentle foothills of Snowdonia. Centrally situated amidst breathtaking scenery, ideal for exploring North Wales' magnificent mountains, beaches, resorts, heritage and history. Near local country inns/restaurants, shops. Each spacious apartment is fully self-contained, gracious, peaceful, clean, with distinctive individual character, comfortable furnishings, generously and conveniently appointed from dishwasher to fresh flowers, etc. Inclusive of VAT. Central heating, hot water, linen. 32 acres of tranquil landscaped gardens, sweeping lawns, woodland walks of natural beauty, panoramic hill walks overlooking the sea, Anglesey and Mount Snowdon. Mild climate. Enjoy the comfort, warmth, privacy and relaxation of this castle of timeless charm in truly serene surroundings. Open all year, including for Short Breaks. Sleep 2-4 persons. **Regret no young children. Brochure sent with pleasure**

Llanrug, Near Caernarfon, North Wales LL55 4RE • Tel & Fax: Llanberis (01286) 870210
e-mail: holidays@brynbrascastle.co.uk • website: www.brynbrascastle.co.uk

Listed Building Grade II★

See also Colour Advertisement

ABERSOCH

Quality Cottages. Around the magnificent Welsh Coast. Away from the madding crowd. Near safe sandy beaches. A small specialist agency offering privacy, peace and unashamed luxury. First Wales Tourist Board Self Catering Gold Award Winner. Residential standards - Dishwashers, Microwaves, Washing Machines, Central Heating, Log Fires, No Slot Meters. Linen provided. Pets welcome free. All in coastal areas famed for scenery, walks, wild flowers, birds, badgers and foxes. Free colour brochure **S.C. Rees, "Quality Cottages", Cerbid, Solva, Haverfordwest, Pembrokeshire SA62 6YE (01348 837871).**
website: www.qualitycottages.co.uk

ANGLESEY (Beaumaris)

Quality Cottages. Around the magnificent Welsh Coast. Away from the madding crowd. Near safe sandy beaches. A small specialist agency offering privacy, peace and unashamed luxury. First Wales Tourist Board Self Catering Gold Award Winner. Residential standards - Dishwashers, Microwaves, Washing Machines, Central Heating, Log Fires, No Slot Meters. Linen provided. Pets welcome free. All in coastal areas famed for scenery, walks, wild flowers, birds, badgers and foxes. Free colour brochure **S.C. Rees, "Quality Cottages", Cerbid, Solva, Haverfordwest, Pembrokeshire SA62 6YE (01348 837871).**
website: www.qualitycottages.co.uk

CAERNARFON

Plas-Y-Bryn Chalet Park, Bontnewydd, Near Caernarfon LL54 7YE (01286 672811). Our small park is situated two miles from the historic town of Caernarfon. Set into a walled garden it offers safety, seclusion and beautiful views of Snowdonia. It is ideally positioned for touring the area. Shop and village pub nearby. A selection of chalets and caravans available at prices from £95 to £370 per week for the caravans and £95 to £290 per week for the chalets. Well-behaved pets always welcome. **WTB ★★★** *SELF-CATERING.*
e-mail: philplasybryn@aol.com
website: www.plasybrynholidayscaernarfon.co.uk

WALES

One child FREE with two adults at
Museum of Childhood Memories
see our READERS' OFFER VOUCHER for details

CRICCIETH

Mrs L. Hughes Jones, Tyddyn Heilyn, Chwilog, Criccieth LL53 6SW (01766 810441). Cosy, comfortably renovated Welshstone country cottage with historic features, double glazing and central heating, enjoying views of Cardigan Bay and the mild Gulf Stream climate. The cottage is situated three miles south of Criccieth on the Lyn Peninsula and edge of Snowdonia. Very well equipped, with spacious lounge, Victorian-style furnished bedrooms, bathroom and kitchen. Spacious garden, ideal for dogs, and ample parking. Beautiful river walks amid wildlife; tree lined walks through farmland. Also Norwegian home to let, furnished. Write or phone for terms for the two properties.

CRICCIETH

Quality Cottages. Around the magnificent Welsh Coast. Away from the madding crowd. Near safe sandy beaches. A small specialist agency offering privacy, peace and unashamed luxury. First Wales Tourist Board Self Catering Gold Award Winner. Residential standards - Dishwashers, Microwaves, Washing Machines, Central Heating, Log Fires, No Slot Meters. Linen provided. Pets welcome free. All in coastal areas famed for scenery, walks, wild flowers, birds, badgers and foxes. Free colour brochure **S.C. Rees, "Quality Cottages", Cerbid, Solva, Haverfordwest, Pembrokeshire SA62 6YE (01348 837871).**
website: www.qualitycottages.co.uk

DOLGELLAU

Mrs Doris Jones, Abergwynant Farm and Trekking Centre, Penmaenpool, Dolgellau, Merioneth LL40 1YF (01341 422377). In the world today with all the stress and pressures of modern living there are few holidays more relaxing or refreshing than a get-away-from-it-all rural retreat in Wales. Nestling in a suntrap, amidst the meadows and mountains of Snowdonia National Park, Abergwynant Farm has been lovingly converted into a holiday centre, providing many activities such as fishing, horse riding, birdwatching and walking. There are six self-catering premises available, all with bathroom, shower and toilet, electric cooker, fridge, microwave and colour TV. Electricity meter. Please bring your own linen and towels. Please telephone for further details or brochure. **WTB ★★★** *SELF-CATERING*

HARLECH

Quality Cottages. Around the magnificent Welsh Coast. Away from the madding crowd. Near safe sandy beaches. A small specialist agency offering privacy, peace and unashamed luxury. First Wales Tourist Board Self Catering Gold Award Winner. Residential standards - Dishwashers, Microwaves, Washing Machines, Central Heating, Log Fires, No Slot Meters. Linen provided. Pets welcome free. All in coastal areas famed for scenery, walks, wild flowers, birds, badgers and foxes. Free colour brochure **S.C. Rees, "Quality Cottages", Cerbid, Solva, Haverfordwest, Pembrokeshire SA62 6YE (01348 837871).**
website: www.qualitycottages.co.uk

PORTHMADOG

Quality Cottages. Around the magnificent Welsh Coast. Away from the madding crowd. Near safe sandy beaches. A small specialist agency offering privacy, peace and unashamed luxury. First Wales Tourist Board Self Catering Gold Award Winner. Residential standards - Dishwashers, Microwaves, Washing Machines, Central Heating, Log Fires, No Slot Meters. Linen provided. Pets welcome free. All in coastal areas famed for scenery, walks, wild flowers, birds, badgers and foxes. Free colour brochure **S.C. Rees, "Quality Cottages", Cerbid, Solva, Haverfordwest, Pembrokeshire SA62 6YE (01348 837871).**
website: www.qualitycottages.co.uk

WALES

NORTH WALES

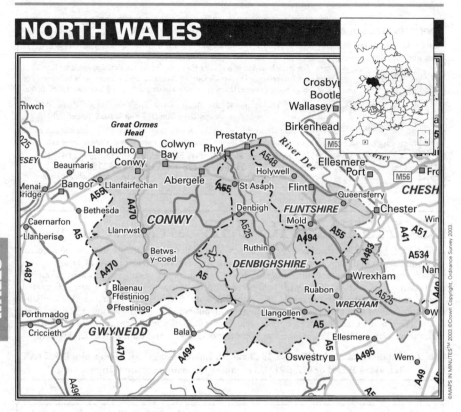

One child FREE with two paying adults. Guide dogs welcome at
Alice in Wonderland Centre
see our READERS' OFFER VOUCHER for details

BETWS-Y-COED

Jim and Lilian Boughton, Bron Celyn, Lôn Muriau, Llanrwst Road, Llanrwst Road, Betws-y-Coed LL24 0HD (01690 710333; Fax: 01690 710111). Our cosy 200 year-old converted coach house has been tastefully refurbished and offers accommodation for up to four persons. Upstairs: one double room with space for a cot and one bunk-bedded room with full length/width bunk beds. All bed linen is provided but not towels. Downstairs: lounge with colour TV/video and wood burning stove (ample supply of chopped timber available), kitchen with fridge, electric cooker, microwave, toaster and water heater. Shower room and toilet. Electric storage heaters fitted throughout. Open all year. Ideal centre for walking, climbing, fishing or simply just relaxing! Terms: £150 to £325 per week. Short Breaks available.
e-mail: welcome@broncelyn.co.uk
website: http://www.broncelyn.co.uk

CONWY

BRONGAIN, Ty'n-y-Groes. Homely Victorian stone cottage in picturesque Conwy valley. Mountain views. Enjoy walking, mountains, beaches, bird watching. Bodnant Gardens, RSPB reserve and Conwy castle, harbour and marina close by. Victorian Llandudno, Betws-y-Coed, Anglesey, Caernarfon and Snowdon easy distance. Good local food and pubs. Enclosed garden, patio, furniture. Parking. Gas fired central heating. Lounge with gas fire, dining room, kitchen, utility. Two double bedded rooms, one small single; blankets/duvet provided. Bathroom with bath, toilet and basin. Colour TV, electric cooker, fridge, microwave, washing machine and tumbler dryer. Terms £145-£300; heating, electricity included. Linen extra. Pets welcome. Open all year. Short low season breaks. **Mrs G. Simpole 105 Hay Green Road, Terrington-St-Clement, Kings Lynn, Norfolk PE34 4PU (01553 828897; mobile 07989 08665).**

CONWY VALLEY

Trefriw, Conwy Valley, Snowdonia. Secluded cottages, log fires and beams. Dogs will love it – a place of their dreams. Plenty of walks around mountains and lakes. Cosy and tranquil – it's got what it takes. It's really a perfect holiday let. For up to 2-7 people, plus their pet(s). Weekly lets only. Apply: **Mrs Williams (01724 733990 or 07711 217448).**

PLEASE MENTION THIS GUIDE WHEN YOU WRITE OR PHONE
TO ENQUIRE ABOUT CLUBS OR ACCOMMODATION

IF YOU ARE WRITING, A STAMPED, ADDRESSED
ENVELOPE IS ALWAYS APPRECIATED

FHG PUBLICATIONS

publish a large range of well-known accommodation guides. We will be happy to send you details or you can use the order form at the back of this book.

PINE COTTAGE, Llandudno, situated right in the town centre, with on-street parking or guaranteed reserved parking space just 2-3 minutes away. 3 bedrooms sleeping 5. Grade 5, with central heating, all modern facilities (washer/dryer, dishwasher, video, etc.).

In addition, superior holiday apartments (up to Grade 5) also situated in centre of town - including some ground floor accommodation with central heating and own garden/patio - all with own car park/forecourt parking, sleeping 1-6 persons.

SAE for brochure from **Mrs E A Williams, Ty Heddwch, Maesdu Ave, Llandudno LL30 INR • Tel: 01492 581789 • Fax: 01492 593146**

Please specify full requirements and preferences, number in party, dates required, number of bedrooms, which floor, and if you prefer "child-free" or "child friendly" accommodation giving ages of children.

e-mail: melvin.williams@btopenworld.com • website: www.llandudnoholidayflats-cottages.co.uk

LLANDONNA

Quality Cottages. Around the magnificent Welsh Coast. Away from the madding crowd. Near safe sandy beaches. A small specialist agency offering privacy, peace and unashamed luxury. First Wales Tourist Board Self Catering Gold Award Winner. Residential standards - Dishwashers, Microwaves, Washing Machines, Central Heating, Log Fires, No Slot Meters. Linen provided. Pets welcome free. All in coastal areas famed for scenery, walks, wild flowers, birds, badgers and foxes. Free colour brochure **S.C. Rees, "Quality Cottages", Cerbid, Solva, Haverfordwest, Pembrokeshire SA62 6YE (01348 837871).**
website: www.qualitycottages.co.uk

LLANGYNHAFAL

Y Bwthyn, Llangynhafal, Denbigh. This farm cottage is set in the picturesque hamlet of Llangynhafal between the historic towns of Ruthin and Denbigh with superb views of the Vale and beyond. Ideal base for walking Offa's Dyke and touring North Wales coast – Rhyl, Llandudno, Conway, etc. The cottage has two bedrooms, one double and one twin, bathroom with shower above the bath, lounge with oak beams, open fire and colour television. Kitchen/diner with cooker, microwave, fridge, toaster, iron and ironing board. Oil-fired central heating and double glazed. Parking for two cars in driveway. Garden and patio area with garden furniture. Clean linen and electricity included in price. Cleanliness guaranteed. No smoking. Terms £150 to £350. **Mrs E. Morris, Carneddau, Llangynhafal, Denbigh LL16 4LN (01824 790460).**

MORFA NEFYN

Quality Cottages. Around the magnificent Welsh Coast. Away from the madding crowd. Near safe sandy beaches. A small specialist agency offering privacy, peace and unashamed luxury. First Wales Tourist Board Self Catering Gold Award Winner. Residential standards - Dishwashers, Microwaves, Washing Machines, Central Heating, Log Fires, No Slot Meters. Linen provided. Pets welcome free. All in coastal areas famed for scenery, walks, wild flowers, birds, badgers and foxes. Free colour brochure **S.C. Rees, "Quality Cottages", Cerbid, Solva, Haverfordwest, Pembrokeshire SA62 6YE (01348 837871).**
website: www.qualitycottages.co.uk

OSWESTRY

Mrs Glenice Jones, Lloran Ganol Farm, Llansilin, Oswestry SY10 7OX (01691 791296/791287). Working farm. Sleeps 5. A luxury self-catering bungalow on mixed farm in quiet valley. Farm and bungalow are situated over the border in the Welsh hills in Clwyd. Five people accommodated in two double and one single bedrooms; bathroom, toilet; sittingroom, diningroom; colour TV; long kitchen with dining area; automatic washing machine, tumble dryer, dishwasher, microwave, freezer and fridge. Linen supplied. Extra charge for pets. Two and a half miles from the shops. Car essential - parking. Trout fishing on farm; horse riding locally, golf and trekking in surrounding area. Open all year round, the bungalow is suitable for partially disabled guests. Storage heaters, fitted carpets and garden furniture provided. Glass conservatory. Weekly terms from £100. Bed and Breakfast (en suite) also available with family in house adjoining from £25 per person per night. **WTB ★★★★** *SELF-CATERING.*

CARMARTHENSHIRE

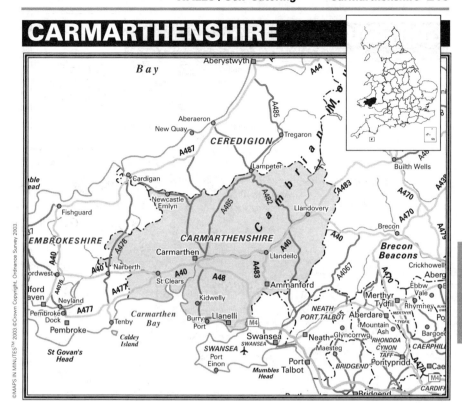

PENDINE

Mrs Sara Ellis, Sunnybank Cottage, Pendine SA33 4PS (01994 453431). Sleeps up to 5. A semi-detached cottage in a tranquil setting, really tucked away from it all. The owner has an organic garden and a wildlife area with ponds. Pendine Sands is just a ten minute drive away and Marros Beach a mile and a half walk. The cottage is fully equipped and consists of a kitchen, living/dining area, two bedrooms (one double, one bunkbeds) and bathroom. Night storage heaters and log burning stove for those cold winter nights. Room for parking. Pets allowed. Pub two miles. Shops ten-minute drive. Rates from £200 to £400 including fuel, power and linen. Open all year. Short breaks available. **WTB**
★★★ *SELF-CATERING*

CEREDIGION

WALES

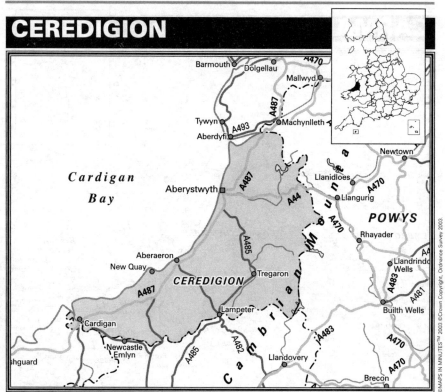

Visit the **FHG** website
www.holidayguides.com
for details of the wide choice of accommodation
featured in the full range of FHG titles

ABERPORTH

Quality Cottages. Around the magnificent Welsh Coast. Away from the madding crowd. Near safe sandy beaches. A small specialist agency offering privacy, peace and unashamed luxury. First Wales Tourist Board Self Catering Gold Award Winner. Residential standards - Dishwashers, Microwaves, Washing Machines, Central Heating, Log Fires, No Slot Meters. Linen provided. Pets welcome free. All in coastal areas famed for scenery, walks, wild flowers, birds, badgers and foxes. Free colour brochure **S.C. Rees, "Quality Cottages", Cerbid, Solva, Haverfordwest, Pembrokeshire SA62 6YE (01348 837871).**
website: www.qualitycottages.co.uk

CARDIGAN BAY

Mr and Mrs Dunn, Parc Farm Holiday Cottage, Oakford, Near Llanarth SA47 0RX (01545 580390). Cardigan Bay and the harbour town of Aberaeron are just three and a half miles away from these comfortable stone cottages situated amidst beautiful farmland and quiet wooded valleys close to the sea. With lovely gardens to enjoy and relax in, overlooking trout ponds and set in picturesque village in 14 acres of land. New Quay five and a half miles away boasts a sandy beach with slipway water sports, tennis and boat trips for fishing or watching the dolphins offshore. Also many beautiful spots and sandy coves to explore and enjoy. Whilst inland, less than an hours' drive away, lies spectacular mountain scenery. Ideal for walking, cycling, birdwatching and horse riding.

LLANGRANNOG

Quality Cottages. Around the magnificent Welsh Coast. Away from the madding crowd. Near safe sandy beaches. A small specialist agency offering privacy, peace and unashamed luxury. First Wales Tourist Board Self Catering Gold Award Winner. Residential standards - Dishwashers, Microwaves, Washing Machines, Central Heating, Log Fires, No Slot Meters. Linen provided. Pets welcome free. All in coastal areas famed for scenery, walks, wild flowers, birds, badgers and foxes. Free colour brochure **S.C. Rees, "Quality Cottages", Cerbid, Solva, Haverfordwest, Pembrokeshire SA62 6YE (01348 837871).**
website: www.qualitycottages.co.uk

WALES

PEMBROKESHIRE

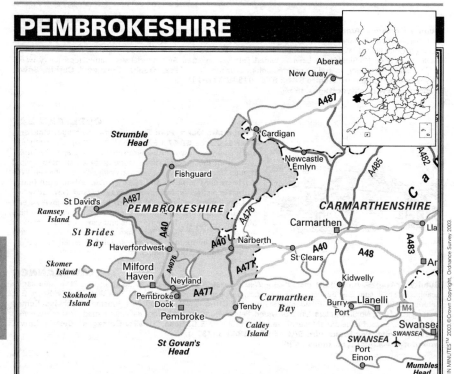

See also Colour Display Advertisement

AMROTH

Carol Lloyd, East Llanteg Farm, Llanteg, Amroth SA67 8QA (01834 831336). Two charming cottages privately situated and ideally located for exploring Pembrokeshire. The resorts of Saundersfoot and Tenby are close at hand with the seaside resort of Amroth and the coastal path just minutes away. Each cottage sleeps four to five adults; cots and highchairs are also provided. All facilities including a fully fitted kitchen, central heating, colour television, etc. are included. There is ample private parking plus a lawned garden area and patio with garden furniture provided.
WTB ★★★★★ *SELF-CATERING.*
e-mail: john@pembrokeshireholiday.co.uk
website: www.pembrokeshireholiday.co.uk

BOSHERTON

Quality Cottages. Around the magnificent Welsh Coast. Away from the madding crowd. Near safe sandy beaches. A small specialist agency offering privacy, peace and unashamed luxury. First Wales Tourist Board Self Catering Gold Award Winner. Residential standards - Dishwashers, Microwaves, Washing Machines, Central Heating, Log Fires, No Slot Meters. Linen provided. Pets welcome free. All in coastal areas famed for scenery, walks, wild flowers, birds, badgers and foxes. Free colour brochure **S.C. Rees, "Quality Cottages", Cerbid, Solva, Haverfordwest, Pembrokeshire SA62 6YE (01348 837871).**
website: www.qualitycottages.co.uk

When making enquiries please mention FHG Publications

FISHGUARD

Jane Stiles, Killoskehane, Letterston, Haverfordwest SA62 5TN (01348 840879). Sleep 2-12. Pembrokeshire Coast – Newport to St David's. Charming, individual cottages situated near sandy beaches, rocky bays and spectacular cliff walks. Traditional stone-built cottages or modern properties, many with central heating and wood-burning stoves. All furnished to high residential standards, fully equipped and personally supervised. Watersports, golf, birdwatching and wild flowers. Boat trips to the islands. Explore the Preseli Mountains, castles, cromlechs and Iron Age forts. Visit art galleries and craft workshops, relax in country pubs and quality restaurants. Pets and children welcome.
e-mail: janestiles@virgin.net
website: www.pembrokeshireholidays.co.uk

HAVERFORDWEST

Camrose House. Sleeps 10. Large old country house in its' own grounds. Five bedrooms fully equipped. Dishwasher, microwave, washing machine, tumble dryer, deep freeze, pool table, log fires. On edge of Pembrokeshire National Park. Ideal walking on coast and Preseli Hills. Close to sandy beaches. Good pubs and restaurants nearby. Out of season breaks available. Telephone: **01437 710324.**

LLANTEG

Tony and Jane Baron, Llanteglos Estate, Llanteg, near Amroth SA67 8PU. Sleep up to 6. Charming self-contained Woodland Lodges set in quiet countryside estate. Views over National Parkland and Carmarthen Bay from balconies. Ideal for holidays or shorter breaks in any season. Safe children's play area. Elsewhere on the property, visit our wonderful rustic clubhouse - 'The Wanderer's Rest Inn', with fully licensed bar, roaring fire, food and entertainment. Miles of sandy beaches, many visitor attractions for all ages and rambling trails close by. A warm welcome awaits you. For further details and colour brochure please telephone: **01834 831677 or 831739. WTB ★★★★ SELF-CATERING.**
e-mail: llanteglosestate@supanet.com

NEWGALE

Quality Cottages. Around the magnificent Welsh Coast. Away from the madding crowd. Near safe sandy beaches. A small specialist agency offering privacy, peace and unashamed luxury. First Wales Tourist Board Self Catering Gold Award Winner. Residential standards - Dishwashers, Microwaves, Washing Machines, Central Heating, Log Fires, No Slot Meters. Linen provided. Pets welcome free. All in coastal areas famed for scenery, walks, wild flowers, birds, badgers and foxes. Free colour brochure **S.C. Rees, "Quality Cottages", Cerbid, Solva, Haverfordwest, Pembrokeshire SA62 6YE (01348 837871).**
website: www.qualitycottages.co.uk

WALES

NEWPORT

Quality Cottages. Around the magnificent Welsh Coast. Away from the madding crowd. Near safe sandy beaches. A small specialist agency offering privacy, peace and unashamed luxury. First Wales Tourist Board Self Catering Gold Award Winner. Residential standards - Dishwashers, Microwaves, Washing Machines, Central Heating, Log Fires, No Slot Meters. Linen provided. Pets welcome free. All in coastal areas famed for scenery, walks, wild flowers, birds, badgers and foxes. Free colour brochure **S.C. Rees, "Quality Cottages", Cerbid, Solva, Haverfordwest, Pembrokeshire SA62 6YE (01348 837871).**
website: www.qualitycottages.co.uk

ST DAVID'S

Quality Cottages. Around the magnificent Welsh Coast. Away from the madding crowd. Near safe sandy beaches. A small specialist agency offering privacy, peace and unashamed luxury. First Wales Tourist Board Self Catering Gold Award Winner. Residential standards - Dishwashers, Microwaves, Washing Machines, Central Heating, Log Fires, No Slot Meters. Linen provided. Pets welcome free. All in coastal areas famed for scenery, walks, wild flowers, birds, badgers and foxes. Free colour brochure **S.C. Rees, "Quality Cottages", Cerbid, Solva, Haverfordwest, Pembrokeshire SA62 6YE (01348 837871).**
website: www.qualitycottages.co.uk

SOLVA

Quality Cottages. Around the magnificent Welsh Coast. Away from the madding crowd. Near safe sandy beaches. A small specialist agency offering privacy, peace and unashamed luxury. First Wales Tourist Board Self Catering Gold Award Winner. Residential standards - Dishwashers, Microwaves, Washing Machines, Central Heating, Log Fires, No Slot Meters. Linen provided. Pets welcome free. All in coastal areas famed for scenery, walks, wild flowers, birds, badgers and foxes. Free colour brochure **S.C. Rees, "Quality Cottages", Cerbid, Solva, Haverfordwest, Pembrokeshire SA62 6YE (01348 837871).**
website: www.qualitycottages.co.uk

TENBY

Quality Cottages. Around the magnificent Welsh Coast. Away from the madding crowd. Near safe sandy beaches. A small specialist agency offering privacy, peace and unashamed luxury. First Wales Tourist Board Self Catering Gold Award Winner. Residential standards - Dishwashers, Microwaves, Washing Machines, Central Heating, Log Fires, No Slot Meters. Linen provided. Pets welcome free. All in coastal areas famed for scenery, walks, wild flowers, birds, badgers and foxes. Free colour brochure **S.C. Rees, "Quality Cottages", Cerbid, Solva, Haverfordwest, Pembrokeshire SA62 6YE (01348 837871).**
website: www.qualitycottages.co.uk

POWYS

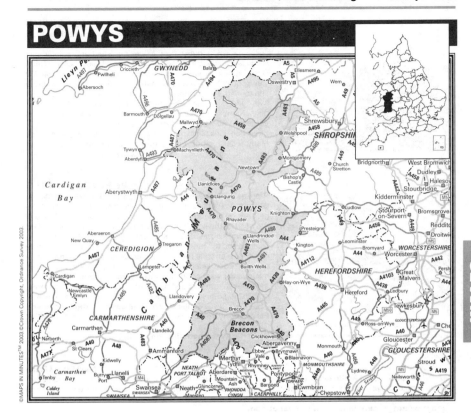

©MAPS IN MINUTES™ 2003 ©Crown Copyright, Ordnance Survey 2003.

WALES

BUILTH WELLS

Lane Farm, Painscastle, Builth Wells LD2 3JS. Lane Farm is a 17th century farmhouse in the heart of Kilvert country, rural Radnorshire. Only five miles from Hay-on-Wye, the famous centre for secondhand books, in this quiet valley far from main roads and the hum of the 21st century, you will find peace and tranquillity. Sheep make up the vast majority of the population! And yet, with easy driving on good roads, you are within easy reach of the Brecon Beacons National Park, Herefordshire and even the Welsh coast. We have three self-catering apartments; sleeping between two and seven in comfort. They easily combine for a larger party. For brochure/prices please contact: **Mrs Evelyn Bally (Tel & Fax: 01497 851605).**
e-mail: jbally@btclick.com

See also Colour Display Advertisement

GARTHMYL

Phillip and Daphne Jones, Penllwyn Lodges, Garthmyl SY15 6SB (Tel & Fax: 01686 640269). Set in a 30 acre woodland, all our lodges are individually designed and fully fitted throughout, including colour TV, microwave and all bedding. 19 lodges, sleeping two to eight people, and one cottage which sleeps six. On arrival, meet our Vietnamese pigs, Tilley the Llama and Noddy the donkey. Fishing is available on our lake, the canal and River Severn at no extra charge. Relax in the landscaped gardens and feed the ducks and swans, or walk in the woodland which is teeming with wildlife. Near to pony trekking, quad biking, castles and lakes. Open all year round. Brochure available on request.
e-mail: penllwynlodges@supanet.com
website: www.penllwynlodges.co.uk

WALES

KNIGHTON

Mrs J. M. Morgan, Selley Hall, Llanfair Waterdine, Knighton LD7 1TR (01547 528429). Sleeps 6 plus cot. A warm welcome awaits guests to this well-furnished and comfortable self-catering accommodation on a working farm overlooking Offa's Dyke. The surrounding countryside is very peaceful with beautiful views; quiet lanes and roads make it an ideal centre for walking and touring. The accommodation comprises two double and one twin-bedded rooms; bathroom, toilet; large lounge with colour TV; diningroom/kitchen, fully fitted, all electric. Ample parking and garden for guests' use. Linen may be hired. Midweek and Short Break bookings taken out of season. Trout fishing in private pool. Many local historic places to visit. Sorry, no pets. Children welcome. Terms from £90 to £230 per week.

LLANDRINDOD WELLS

Pippins at Neuadd Farm, Penybont, Llandrindod Wells. Sleeps 4. Pippins is a superb converted Granary set in the grounds of Neuadd Farm, overlooking the lovely Ithon Valley in the heart of the scenic Mid-Wales. Furnished to a high standard with comfy sofas, Pippins is well-equipped with all modern facilities and full central heating. The accommodation sleeps four in a double en suite room and a twin-bedded room with separate shower room. Linen and towels provided, full electric cooker, microwave, washer/dryer, fridge/freezer, TV and video. Private garden with furniture and barbecue. Ideally situated for walking, golf, fishing, horse riding, bowls and wildlife. **WTB ★★★★★** *SELF-CATERING*. Contact: **Peter and Jackie Longley, Neuadd Farm, Penybont, Llandrindod Wells, Powys LD1 5SW**

**(01597 851032; Fax: 01597 851034).
e-mail: jackie@neuaddfarm.fsnet.co.uk**   website: www.neuaddfarm.co.uk

LLANIDLOES

Barn View Cottage, Llanidloes SY18 6PW . A stone and timber-clad barn converted into three self-contained holiday cottages. Idyllic hillside position overlooking magnificent views through the Severn Valley. Contact: **Mr and Mrs Knight (01656 413527).**
e-mail: wendy_robert_barn_view@supanet.com

LLANWRTHWL

Dyffryn Barn, Llanwrthwl, Llandrindod Wells LD1 6NU. Sleeps 5. Idyllically situated in the Cambrian Mountains above the Upper Wye Valley with its magnificent scenery and close to the Elan Valley with its spectacular dams. Wonderful hill walking, cycling, fishing and bird watching (red kites; RSPB reserves) in this unspoilt area of "Wild Wales". Attached to barn and owners' home, the three-bedroomed, centrally heated cottage comprises: double bedroom, twin-bedded room, single with washbasin, comfortable upstairs sitting room with TV/video and a lovely view, shower room with toilet. Downstairs cloakroom. Well-equipped kitchen/diningroom. No smoking. Heating and electricity included and bed linen supplied. Rates £155 to £300. Bed and Breakfast also available. Details from **Mrs G. Tyler, Dyffryn Farm, Llanwrthwl, Llandrindod Wells LD1 6NU (01597 811017; Fax: 01597 810609).**
e-mail: stay@dyffrynfarm.co.uk   website: www.dyffrynfarm.co.uk

MID WALES

Clyn, Elan Valley, Rhayader LD6 5HP. A remote and peaceful smallholding set high on the edge of open moorland with wonderful views overlooking wooded valleys and heatherclad hillsides, offering holiday accommodation in the cottage (sleeping seven), and the Granary (sleeping four). It is ideally situated for walking, mountain biking, fishing, birdwatching and nature-lovers generally. Children of all ages are catered for with an outside play area (sandpit, swing, etc.), friendly farmyard animals and unlimited space; while inside there is a games room with table tennis/snooker table. Both properties are fully equipped, including woodburners. Homegrown organic produce available, pets by arrangement. Rates (all inclusive) from: £180 per week, and £35 per night for short breaks. Contact: **Jan Jenkins (01597 810120).**

e-mail: theclyn@freezone.co.uk   website: www.freezone.co.uk/theclyn/index

NEWTOWN

Mrs D. Pryce, Aberbechan Farm, Newtown SY16 3BJ (01686 630675). Working farm, join in. Sleeps 10. This part of quaint Tudor farmhouse with its lovely oak beams is situated in picturesque countryside on a mixed farm with trout fishing and shooting in season. Newtown three miles, Welshpool, Powis Castle and Llanfair Light Railway, 14 miles; 45 miles to coast. The accommodation sleeps ten persons in four double and two single bedrooms, also cot. Two bathrooms, two toilets. Sitting/diningroom with colour TV. Fully fitted oak kitchen with fridge, electric cooker, washing machine and dishwasher. Log fires and off-peak heaters. Electricity on meter. Large lawn with pool and swing. Everything supplied for visitors' comfort. Linen available for overseas guests at extra cost. Car essential to obtain the best from the holiday. Village shop one-and-a-half miles away. Open all year. Children welcome. SAE please.

RHAYADER

Oak Wood Lodges, Llwynbaedd, Rhayader LD6 5NT (01597 811422). Self-catering Log Cabins. Superb Norwegian log cabins situated at approximately 1000ft above sea level with spectacular views of the Elan Valley and Cambrian Mountains. Enjoy pursuits such as walking, pony trekking, mountain biking, fishing, and bird watching in the most idyllic of surroundings. Excellent touring centre. Dogs welcome. Short breaks as well as full weeks. Open all year round. Please phone for more details and brochure. Pets welcome. **WTB ★★★★** *SELF-CATERING.*

WELSHPOOL

Michael and Ann Reed, Madog's Wells, Llanfair Caereinion, Welshpool SY21 0DE (Tel & Fax: 01938 810446). Beautiful peaceful valley with lots of wildlife. Two self-catering bungalows, both wheelchair accessible, and one four-berth caravan available for self-catering lets. All well-equipped. Ample parking and picnic tables outside each unit. Washing machine and rotary clothes dryer available for guests' use. Children's play area, games room, darts, pool and table tennis, with basketball ring in the yard. Free gas, electricity, linen and cot available. We are the only accommodation in Wales offering astronomy breaks - free tuition for beginners. **WTB ★★★** and **★★★★★** *SELF-CATERING*
e-mail: madogswells@btopenworld.com

WALES

REPUBLIC OF IRELAND – Co. Clare

BALLYVAUGHAN

Ballyvaughan Village and Country Holiday Homes. Offering a wide range of top quality self-catering holiday accommodation in the charming village of Ballyvaughan on the southern shores of Galway Bay in the heartland of the world famous Burren district of County Clare. You can choose from our four-star houses, which sleep four or six, or one of our apartments, which sleep two or three. All our village accommodation is located in the centre of the village. There is a good choice of restaurants and pubs in the area. Our location is an ideal base to explore the unique Burren landscape or tour the west coast of Ireland. All our accommodation is available all year and is very suitable for off-season bookings. Terms from 250 euros to 800 euros. Ring or write for our full colour brochure: **Mr George Quinn, Frances Street, Kilrush, Co.Clare (00353 659 051977; Fax: 00353 659 052370).**
e-mail: vchh@iol.ie   **website: www.ballyvaughan-cottages.com**

• • *Some Useful Guidance for Guests and Hosts* • •

Every year literally thousands of holidays, short breaks and overnight stops are arranged through our guides, the vast majority without any problems at all. In a handful of cases, however, difficulties do arise about bookings, which often could have been prevented from the outset.

It is important to remember that when accommodation has been booked, both parties – guests and hosts – have entered into a form of contract. We hope that the following points will provide helpful guidance.

GUESTS:
- When enquiring about accommodation, be as precise as possible. Give exact dates, numbers in your party and the ages of any children.
- State the number and type of rooms wanted and also what catering you require – bed and breakfast, full board etc. Make sure that the position about evening meals is clear – and about pets, reductions for children or any other special points.
- Read our reviews carefully to ensure that the proprietors you are going to contact can supply what you want. Ask for a letter confirming all arrangements, if possible.
- If you have to cancel, do so as soon as possible. Proprietors do have the right to retain deposits and under certain circumstances to charge for cancelled holidays if adequate notice is not given and they cannot re-let the accommodation.

HOSTS:
- Give details about your facilities and about any special conditions. Explain your deposit system clearly and arrangements for cancellations, charges etc. and whether or not your terms include VAT.
- If for any reason you are unable to fulfil an agreed booking without adequate notice, you may be under an obligation to arrange suitable alternative accommodation or to make some form of compensation.

While every effort is made to ensure accuracy, we regret that FHG Publications cannot accept responsibility for errors, omissions or misrepresentations in our entries or any consequences thereof. Prices in particular should be checked because we go to press early. We will follow up complaints but cannot act as arbiters or agents for either party.

Self-Catering Holidays in Britain 2004

Caravan & Camping Holidays

FHG

ENGLAND

CORNWALL

BUDE

Willow Valley Holiday Park, Bush, Bude EX23 9LB (01288 353104). Our camp site, which is only two miles from Bude and the sandy surfing beaches, is set in a beautiful valley. There is a small river meandering through the site which adds to its beauty. We are only a small site, with two pitches on four acres of land and, as these are not arranged in rows but around the edges of the site, there are always plenty of open spaces. We have toilets, showers, dishwashing area and a laundry. We also have a children's adventure playground which is in full view of most pitches, but not set amongst them. Dogs on leads are very welcome and we have seven acres of land in which they can run free. We also have a wide variety of pets on site including chickens, ducks, rabbits and peacocks. Open 31st March to 31st October, but enquiries are welcome anytime. For further details please write or telephone for a brochure and price list.

CRACKINGTON HAVEN

Hentervene Caravan and Camping Park, Crackington Haven, Near Bude EX23 0LF (01840 230365). Peaceful family-run camping and caravan park two miles from Crackington Haven beach and glorious coastal footpath. Positively no bar, disco or bingo; just beautiful countryside. Facilities include free showers, laundry, baby bathroom, games/TV rooms, free library, children's play area, games and competitions. Short drive from Bodmin Moor, fine surfing beaches like Widemouth Bay, the Camel Estuary for sailing, windsurfing, cycling and within easy reach of Padstow, Polzeath, Rock, etc. Many attractive country pubs locally, plenty of attractions for children. £4.50 per adult per night, reduction for children (4 to 12 years). Luxury caravans and pine lodge to let. Caravan sales. Pets welcome – dog walk on site and dog-friendly woods, beaches etc. within a 5 to 10 minute drive. **e-mail: contact@hentervene.co.uk website: www.hentervene.co.uk**

NEWQUAY

Treloy Tourist Park, Newquay TR8 4JN (01637 876279/872063). A friendly family site for touring caravans, tents and motor homes, just off the A3059 Newquay Road. A central location for touring the whole of Cornwall. Facilities include heated swimming pool, licensed bar/family room, entertainment, cafe/takeaway, shop, laundry, FREE showers, private washing cubicles, baby bathrooms, indoor dishwashing sinks, TV and games rooms, adventure playground. Electric hook-ups. Disabled facilities. Terms £7.00 to £12.80 per night for two adults. Coarse fishing nearby. Own superb 9-hole Par 32 golf course with concessionary green fees for our guests. Please write or telephone for free colour brochure. **ETC ★★★★, AA** *THREE PENNANTS*. **e-mail; holidays@treloy.co.uk   website: www.treloy.co.uk**

NEWQUAY

Trethiggey Touring Park, Quintrell Downs, Newquay TR8 4LG (01637 877672). Trethiggey appeals to holidaymakers seeking the scenic beauty of the countryside and yet close proximity to the seaside and resort centre of Newquay. Open 1st March to 1st January. Level hardstanding available. All year caravan storage. Toilets, hot showers, baby room, disabled toilet, shaver points, hairdryers, dishwashing facilities, launderette, shop, freezer packs, telephone, chemical toilet disposal point, children's play area, electric hook ups, games room, TV, pool table, off licence, take-away food service, dog exercise area. Restaurant and village pub adjoins the site. Touring caravans to let. **ETC ★★★**
website: www.trethiggey.co.uk

PENZANCE

Mrs M. Maddock, Bone Valley Caravan and Camping Park, Heamoor, Penzance TR20 8UJ (Tel & Fax: 01736 360313). Situated in a pretty valley, ideal for exploring the countryside and coast of West Cornwall, this small quiet park is well sheltered by mature hedges and trees, and is bordered on one side by a small stream. 17 pitches (some hardstanding) as well as areas for small tents. Electric hook-ups. Caravans, log cabin and bunk house available for hire. The village of Heamoor with shops, pub and regular bus service is a short walk away. On-site facilities include showers, kitchen/laundry room (microwave, electric kettle), shop, take-away, bicycle hire, campers' lounge with colour TV, public telephone, free ice pack service, chemical disposal, gas and camping gaz and BBQ loan. **AA** *THREE PENNANTS.*
e-mail: bonevalleycandcpark@fsbdial.co.uk

REDRUTH

Mr & Mrs J Rielly, Lanyon Caravan and Camping Park, Four Lanes, Redruth TR16 6LP (01209 313474; Fax: 01209 313422). For those wanting a memorable holiday look no further. We have lots to offer you. Superb central location surrounded by beautiful countryside. A range of caravans to suit all pockets. Indoor heated pool. All day games room. Bar/Restaurant/Takeaway/Free entertainment in high season. Two play areas. Upgraded toilet/bath/shower block. Launderette/dish washing facility/free hot water. Spacious level pitches and short grass. Best of all, you will be looked after by caring residential family. **ETC ★★★★**, **AA** *THREE PENNANTS.*
website: www.lanyonholidaypark.co.uk
or   www.lanyoncaravanandcampingpark.co.uk

ST AGNES

Chiverton Park, Blackwater, Truro TR4 8HS (01872 560667). Set in the heart of glorious Cornish countryside, yet only a short distance from the A30, this spacious, well-run park offers peace and relaxation in a delightful four-acre rural setting. Caravan holiday homes - touring and camping. North coast three miles, Truro five. Families and couples; pets welcome. Peace and quiet - no club or bar. Shop/off licence, laundry room, games room, children's play area. Electric hook-ups. Satellite TV in all units. Holiday homes are fully equipped (except linen, which may be hired).
e-mail: info@chivertonpark.co.uk
website: www.chivertonpark.co.uk

ENGLAND

ST IVES

G. & H. Rogers, Hellesveor Caravan and Camping Site, Hellesveor Farm, St Ives TR26 3AD (01736 795738). Six-berth caravans for hire on small secluded approved farm site, one mile from St Ives town centre and nearest beaches, five minutes from bus route on Land's End Road (B3306). Coastal and countryside walks nearby. Shop and laundry facilities on site. Special terms for early and late season. Campers and touring caravans welcome. Electrical hook-ups available. Dogs allowed under strict control. Nearby horse riding, pony trekking, golf course, bowling greens and leisure centre. SAE for further details.

TINTAGEL

Bossiney Farm Caravan & Camping Park, Tintagel PL34 0AY (01840 770481). Small family-run caravan and camping Park on the north Cornish coast offering 20 holiday caravans. All with shower, toilet, colour TV and room heater. The vans are terraced with individual inland views. On the opposite side of the road are cliffs with a path leading to Bossiney Cove (a safe sandy tidal cove), the Rocky Valley and coastal footpath. The park is in an Area of Outstanding Natural Beauty. Ideal for touring and walking. Cleanliness guaranteed. Tourers and tents also welcome. Good toilet block, laundry and showers. Small shop. Electric hook-ups available. Pets and children welcome. Colour brochure.
ETC ★★★★
website: www.bossineyfarm.co.uk

WADEBRIDGE

Gunvenna Touring Caravan and Camping Park, St Minver, Wadebridge PL27 6QN (01208 862405). The Park is a well drained site of level grassland on 10 acres commanding uninterrupted views of the countryside within five minutes' drive of safe, golden, sandy beaches. Local activities include golf, fishing, tennis, surfing and swimming, etc. Site facilities include two modern toilet and shower blocks, launderette and ironing room, children's play area, children's games room (9am to 10pm), barbecue area, dog exercise area, shop, telephone, etc. We also have a licensed Bar and indoor heated swimming pool. Please send for our colour brochure and tariff. **AA** *FOUR PENNANTS, RAC LISTED.*

PLEASE NOTE

All the information in this book is given in good faith in the belief that it is correct. However, the publishers cannot guarantee the facts given in these pages, neither are they responsible for changes in policy, ownership or terms that may take place after the date of going to press. Readers should always satisfy themselves that the facilities they require are available and that the terms, if quoted, still apply.

CUMBRIA

CONSITON

Mrs J.E. Halton, Scarr Head, Torver, Coniston LA21 8DP (015394 41576/41328). Three permanent modern caravans for hire, two 4-berth, one 2-berth, with lounge, kitchen; shower, toilet and washbasin. Small laundry room on site. Very small, quiet site two miles from Coniston village where there is a good range of shops, hotels and restaurants; two village pubs in Torver serving meals, both within walking distance (10 minutes); pony trekking 500 yards. Scarr Head is a small working farm close to Coniston Old Man, and being in a quieter part of the Lake District is the perfect base for exploring the beautiful surrounding countryside either by car or on foot. Children and pets welcome. Open Easter to October. Please telephone, or write, for full details.

KESWICK

Scotgate Chalet, Camping and Caravan Holiday Park, Braithwaite, Keswick CA12 5TF (017687 78343). Careful thought and years of experience have gone into the planning of Scotgate. The result is a spacious and comfortable holiday park, superbly placed between Derwentwater and Bassenthwaite Lake. All our chalets and caravans are maintained to the same high standard. We are always happy to welcome touring caravans and all types of tents. The ground has the double advantage to campers of being level and well drained. There is a licensed shop selling groceries, newspapers and snacks and also a licensed cafe. Laundry room with washing machines, tumble dryers and ironing facilities. Showers, shaver points and hair dryers are also provided in the toilet blocks. The site has its own games room with pool table and video machines. Please telephone or write for further details.

e-mail: info@scotgateholidaypark.co.uk   **website: www.scotgateholidaypark.co.uk**

See also Colour Display Advertisement

PENRITH

Grahame and Gill Harrington, Stonefold Caravan and Camping Park, Newbiggin, Stainton, Penrith CA11 0HP (Tel & Fax: 01768 866383). Set in a beautiful position with panoramic views overlooking the Eden Valley, the majestic Pennine hills in the background, this is a quiet, friendly site, for those who can appreciate the tranquillity and setting of this beautiful part of the country. A perfect base to explore the Northern Lake District and the unspoilt Eden Valley. Nearby - fishing, horse riding, tennis, swimming,boating, quad biking. Facilities include free hot water and showers. Easy access; two miles from M6 (J40).

e-mail: gill@stonefold.co.uk
website: www.stonefold.co.uk

ENGLAND

DEVON

KINGSBRIDGE

Mounts Farm Touring Park, The Mounts, Near East Allington, Kingsbridge TQ9 7QJ (01548 521591). Mounts Farm is a family-run site in the heart of South Devon. On-site facilities include FREE hot showers, flush toilets, FREE hot water in washing-up room, razor points, laundry and information room, electric hook-ups and site shop. We welcome tents, touring caravans and motor caravans. Large pitches in level, sheltered fields. No charges for awnings. Children and pets welcome. Situated three miles north of Kingsbridge, Mounts Farm is an ideal base for exploring Dartmouth, Salcombe, Totnes, Dartmoor and the many safe, sandy beaches nearby. Please telephone or write for a free brochure. Self-catering cottage also available.

SEATON

Axevale Caravan Park, Seaton EX12 2DF (0800 0688816). A quiet, family-run park with 68 modern and luxury caravans for hire. The park overlooks the delightful River Axe Valley, and is just a 10 minute walk from the town with its wonderfully long, award-winning beach. Children will love our extensive play area, with its sand pit, paddling pool, swings and slide. Laundry facilities are provided and there is a wide selection of goods on sale in the park shop which is open every day. All of our caravans have a shower, toilet, fridge and TV. Also, with no clubhouse, a relaxing atmosphere is ensured. Prices from £75 per week; reductions for three or fewer persons early/late. **ETC ★★★**
website: www.axevale.co.uk

TEIGN VALLEY

S. and G. Harrison-Crawford, Silver Birches, Teign Valley, Trusham, Newton Abbot TQ13 0NJ (01626 852172). Two 23ft and 29ft four-berth caravans in an attractive two acre garden on the bank of the River Teign. Each has mains water, electricity, shower/bath, flush toilet, washbasin, immersion heater, Calor gas cooker, fridge; TV. Ideally situated two miles from A38 on B3193. Dartmoor, Exeter, Torquay easily accessible. Sea 12 miles. Car essential, ample parking. Excellent centre for fishing (river and reservoir), bird-watching, forest walks; 70 yards private salmon and trout fishing. Golf courses and horse riding within easy reach. Shops two-and-a-half miles. Pets by arrangement. Dogs free of charge. Open March to October. Terms from £135 to £185 per week. Bed and Breakfast available in bungalow from £25 per person per night, £168 per week per person.

DORSET

WIMBORNE

Woolsbridge Manor Farm Caravan Park, Three Legged Cross, Wimborne BH21 6RA (01202 826369). Situated approximately three-and-a-half-miles from the New Forest market town of Ringwood – easy access to the south coast. Seven acres level, semi-sheltered, well-drained spacious pitches. Quiet country location on a working farm, ideal and safe for families. Showers, mother/baby area, laundry room, washing up area, chemical disposal, payphone, electric hook-ups, battery charging. Children's play area on site. Site shop. Dogs welcome on leads. Fishing adjacent. Moors Valley Country Park golf course one mile. Pub and restaurant 10 minutes' walk. **AA** *THREE PENNANTS*, **ETC ★★★**

CO DURHAM

DURHAM

Howard and Elizabeth Dunkerley, Strawberry Hill Farm Caravan & Camping Park, Old Cassop, Durham DH6 4QA (0191-372 3457; Fax: 0191-372 2512). If staying in the countryside, enjoying the sound of owls hooting on peaceful nights is your idea of bliss - then come and stay with us. See if you can spot the wild badger or fox out and about on moonlit nights. We have a six berth holiday home with all the modern conveniences you'd expect - heated throughout, TV, microwave, gas cooker, en suite bathroom with walk-in shower. Bed linen provided. All you need to bring are food, drink and towels! Your holiday home is in an idyllic rural position with privacy to enjoy your evenings whether relaxing or barbecueing. We are five miles east of Durham City, three miles from Juction 61, A1(M). **ETC** ★★★★, **AA** *3 PENNANTS, WELCOME HOST.*

e-mail: howarddunkerley@strawberryhillfarm.freeserve.co.uk

• • *Some Useful Guidance for Guests and Hosts* • •

Every year literally thousands of holidays, short breaks and overnight stops are arranged through our guides, the vast majority without any problems at all. In a handful of cases, however, difficulties do arise about bookings, which often could have been prevented from the outset.

It is important to remember that when accommodation has been booked, both parties – guests and hosts – have entered into a form of contract. We hope that the following points will provide helpful guidance.

GUESTS:

• When enquiring about accommodation, be as precise as possible. Give exact dates, numbers in your party and the ages of any children.

• State the number and type of rooms wanted and also what catering you require – bed and breakfast, full board etc. Make sure that the position about evening meals is clear – and about pets, reductions for children or any other special points.

• Read our reviews carefully to ensure that the proprietors you are going to contact can supply what you want. Ask for a letter confirming all arrangements, if possible.

• If you have to cancel, do so as soon as possible. Proprietors do have the right to retain deposits and under certain circumstances to charge for cancelled holidays if adequate notice is not given and they cannot re-let the accommodation.

HOSTS:

• Give details about your facilities and about any special conditions. Explain your deposit system clearly and arrangements for cancellations, charges etc. and whether or not your terms include VAT.

• If for any reason you are unable to fulfil an agreed booking without adequate notice, you may be under an obligation to arrange suitable alternative accommodation or to make some form of compensation.

While every effort is made to ensure accuracy, we regret that FHG Publications cannot accept responsibility for errors, omissions or misrepresentations in our entries or any consequences thereof. Prices in particular should be checked because we go to press early. We will follow up complaints but cannot act as arbiters or agents for either party.

ESSEX

CLACTON-ON-SEA

Highfield, London Road, Clacton-on-Sea CO16 9QY (0870 442 9287; Fax: 01255 689805). Highfield enjoys high levels of repeat business and being located on the famous Essex sunshine coast it's easy to see why. Within easy reach of golden beaches and bustling, colourful promenades on the one hand and gentle Essex countryside on the other, it's a region of contrasts. Large outdoor fun pool with 200ft water chute. Outdoor adventure play area. Dylan's Kids' Club. Convenience store. Solarium. Wide-screen satellite TV. Amusement centre. Fantastic beaches nearby. Pool-side bar for snacks and beverages. Bars and entertainment venues. **ETC ★★★**
e-mail: holidays@gbholidayparks.co.uk
website www.gbholidayparks.co.uk

CLACTON-ON-SEA

Tower, Jaywick, Clacton on Sea CO15 2LF (0870 442 9290; Fax: 01255 820060). Tower lies on the outskirts of Clacton-on-Sea, and this traditional sun and sand family resort boasts miles of golden sandy beaches within easy reach of the park. Or for the more energetic there are watersport opportunities and sport leisure facilities. Couple this with the quality facilities and excellent service at Tower Holiday Park and you have all the ingredients for a special holiday. Outdoor heated pool with sun terrace. Direct access to beach. Children's play area. Convenience store, popular cafe offering meals and snacks. Amusement centre. Phoenix Lounge and Raven's Club for entertainment.
e-mail: holidays@gbholidayparks.co.uk
website: www.gbholidayparks.co.uk

CLACTON-ON-SEA

Weeley Bridge, Weeley, Near Clacton-on-Sea CO16 9DH (0870 442 9295; Fax: 01255 831 544). Weeley Bridge is a small, beautifully maintained park in the heart of the Essex countryside. A relaxing park, its centrepiece is a large, attractive fishing lake which is complemented by well-manicured lawns, mature woodland and shrubs. The charming surrounding countryside is within easy reach of the Essex coastline and therefore makes this an ideal holiday venue. Outdoor heated swimming pool. Attractive, well-stocked fishing lake. Regular angling competitions. Licensed bar and restaurant. Beer garden. Outdoor adventure playground and multi-sports court. Golf nearby. **ETC ★★★**
e-mail: holidays@gbholidayparks.co.uk
website: www.gbholidayparks.co.uk

MERSEA ISLAND

Coopers Beach, East Mersea, Mersea Island, Near Colchester CO5 8TN (0870 442 9288; Fax: 01206 385483). Coopers Beach is located on Mersea Island whose only link with the mainland is an ancient causeway known as the Strood. West Mersea is a small resort and sailing centre. At East Mersea, beautiful leafy lanes wind their way down towards the seafront, where you'll find the park. Here the clubhouse with adjacent pool is an ideal place to relax and offers great sea views. Popular outdoor heated pool. Fun adventure playground. Multi-sports court. Direct access to the beach. Children's club. Fast food takeaway. Visit Colchester, England's oldest recorded town. **ETC ★★★**
e-mail: holidays@gbholidayparks.co.uk
website: www.gbholidayparks.co.uk

ST LAWRENCE BAY

Waterside, Main Road, St Lawrence Bay, Near Southminster CMO 7LY (0870 442 9298; Fax: 01621 778106). Waterside is an attractive park with leafy tree-lined avenues. Situated by the River Blackwater, the park enjoys fine estuary views towards Mersea Island. With a modern, quality range of hire caravans and excellent facilities that include indoor pool, sauna and jacuzzi, the park is well equipped for holidaymakers. The surrounding district has varied attractions and several nature reserves and footpaths, or for shopping there's Maldon, an attractive riverside town. Outdoor children's play area. Sheltered beach nearby. Well stocked mini-market. Cafe and fast-food takeaway.
e-mail: holidays@gbholidayparks.co.uk
website: www.gbholidayparks.co.uk

WALTON-ON-THE-NAZE

Naze Marine, Hall Lane, Walton-on-the-Naze C014 8HL (0870 442 9292; Fax: 01255 682427). The Essex Coast is dotted with colourful seaside resorts and Naze Marine sits alongside one of these. Walton-on-the-Naze boasts golden beaches, a nature reserve and pier. This delightful park offers a friendly country club together with a superb heated outdoor pool complex. Adjacent Nature Reserve. Children's amusements and play area. Well-stocked convenience store. Naze Armada Country Club. Cafe/take away. New poolside cafe/bar. Golf, horse riding and fishing locally. Attractive marina close by. Fantastic sandy beaches on your doorstep. **ETC ★★★**
e-mail: holidays@gbholidayparks.co.uk
website: www.gbholidayparks.co.uk

GLOUCESTERSHIRE

TEWKESBURY

Mill Avon Holiday Park, Gloucester Road, Tewkesbury GL20 5SW (01684 296876). As the name suggests, our Park is bordered on one side by the river Mill Avon and has pleasant views across the Severn Ham to the Malvern Hills. The historic town of Tewkesbury is on the doorstep and a few minutes' walk takes you through picturesque streets past the magnificent 12th century Abbey to the busy shopping centre. The park comprises an area for 24 privately owned holiday caravans and two areas for touring caravans - one accommodates 24 pitches, the other is smaller, accommodating six tourers. All pitches have mains hook-up and awnings are accepted. Modern toilet block, laundry room and chemical toilet point on site. Dogs welcome if kept on lead. Please send for our brochure giving further information and tariffs. Seasonal pitches available.

FHG PUBLICATIONS

publish a large range of well-known accommodation guides. We will be happy to send you details or you can use the order form at the back of this book.

KENT

DOVER (Near)

St Margaret's Holiday Park, Reach Road, St Margaret's at Cliffe, Near Dover CT15 6AG (0870 442 9286; Fax: 01304 853434). St Margaret's is an exclusive 5 star park perched high on the White Cliffs and close to the bustling port of Dover. There are spectacular views over the English Channel towards the coast of France and to the surrounding Kent countryside. The park has a superb leisure complex which includes two indoor heated swimming pools, gymnasium, sauna, solarium, alternative therapy clinic and spa pool. There is also a children's outdoor play area, Garden Restaurant and Bistro Bar. Superb walking on white cliffs. Golf and horse riding nearby. Day trips to France. **ETC** ★★★★★
e-mail: holidays@gbholidayparks.co.uk
website: www.gbholidayparks.co.uk

EASTCHURCH

Warden Springs, Warden Point, Eastchurch, Isle of Sheppey ME12 4HF (0870 442 9281; Fax: 01795 880218). Warden Springs is situated on Sheppey, which is well established as a holiday resort and boasts fine beaches, nature reserves and watersports. The park overlooks the sea and yet is also surrounded by countryside and woodland. Outdoor heated swimming pool. Bar meals. Takeaway. Clubhouse with games alley and pool table. Outdoor children's playground. Visit nearby historic Canterbury and Leeds Castle. Clifftop walks and splendid sea views. Golf, sea fishing and horse riding locally. **ETC** ★★★★
e-mail: holidays@gbholidayparks.co.uk
website: www.gbholidayparks.co.uk

NEW ROMNEY

Romney Sands, The Parade, Greatstone-on-Sea, New Romney TN28 8RN (0870 442 9285; Fax: 01797 367497). Romney Sands is a popular park that sits opposite one of the finest sandy beaches on the Kent coast and is surrounded by the mysterious Romney Marshes, past haunt of smugglers. On the borders of Sussex/Kent, there's beautiful countryside, pretty villages, colourful seaside resorts and a legacy of historic castles and stately homes. The park boasts a large indoor pool complex. Legends Diner. Well conditioned outdoor bowling green. Dylan the Dinosaur children's club and outdoor play area. Tennis courts. Choice of bars and entertainment venues. Golf and fishing locally. Ideal area for cycling. **ETC** ★★★★
e-mail: holidays@gbholidayparks.co.uk
website: www.gbholidayparks.co.uk

FREE or REDUCED RATE entry to Holiday Visits and Attractions — see our READERS' OFFER VOUCHERS on pages 53-80

ENGLAND

LINCOLNSHIRE

GRANTHAM
Woodland Waters, Willoughby Road, Ancaster, Grantham NE32 3RT (Tel & Fax: 01400 230888). Set in 72 acres of beautiful woodland walks. Luxury holiday lodges with parking at the side, overlooking the lakes; excellently equipped. Bar/restaurant on site. Dogs welcome in some lodges. Fishing included. Four golf courses nearby. Open all year.
e-mail: info@woodlandwaters.co.uk
website: www.woodlandwaters.co.uk

See also Colour Display Advertisement

SALTFLEET
Sunnydale Holiday Park, Sea Lane, Saltfleet LN11 7RP (0870 442 9293; Fax: 01507 339 100). Sunnydale sits on the edge of the beautiful Lincolnshire coastline in a region that is incredibly popular with holidaymakers. There are the lively seaside resorts of Skegness and Cleethorpes, but Sunnydale nestles in an area more renowned for its rural beauty and picturesque market towns like Louth. The park itself has quality written all over it – modern, well-equipped caravans, a superb leisure complex incorporating indoor pool, well-maintained park grounds, children's play zone and outdoor play area, fishing pond. Choice of bars and spacious beer garden. **ETC ★★★**
e-mail: holidays@gbholidayparks.co.uk
website: www.gbholidayparks.co.uk

NORFOLK

See also Colour Display Advertisement

THETFORD
Lowe Caravan Park, Thetford. Small, friendly country park. Primarily a touring park, we now have four luxury holiday homes for hire in peaceful surroundings. Ideal for touring East Anglia or a quiet relaxing break. More suited to over 50s but children are welcome. Please contact: **May Lowe, Ashdale, Hills Road, Saham Hills (Near Watton), Thetford IP25 7EZ (01953 881051).**

Please mention Self-Catering Holidays in Britain
when enquiring about accommodation
featured in these pages.

ENGLAND

NORTHUMBERLAND

ASHINGTON
Sandy Bay, North Seaton, Ashington NE63 9YD (0870 442 9310; Fax: 01670 812705). Sandy Bay is a charming coastal park that has its own sandy beach. There are pleasant cliff top views and a walk along the adjacent river Wansbeck will reward you with lovely scenes. Northumberland is arguably one of the most beautiful areas of Britain with wide expanses of unspoilt countryside, stunning beaches and an extraordinary number of castles. Sandy Bay will afford you a wonderful base from which to explore. Indoor heated swimming pool. Ornamental Koi lake. Takeaway, mini-market, licensed club. Outdoor children's play area and Dylan Kids' club. Fishing and golf locally. Cycle paths through Northumbrian countryside. **ETC ★★★**
e-mail: holidays@gbholidayparks.co.uk
website: www.gbholidayparks.co.uk

MORPETH (Near)
Cresswell Towers Holiday Park, Cresswell, Near Morpeth NE61 5JT (0870 422 9311; Fax: 01670 860 226). Cresswell Towers is a highly attractive park in a natural woodland setting that lends the park much of its charm. You cannot help but be taken in by the lush leafy lanes. This area does have spectacular beaches and Druridge Bay with its huge sand dunes is worth a visit. On the park the emphasis is on relaxation. Friendly licensed bar. Outdoor heated swimming pool with sun terrace. Café and shop. Outdoor kids' play area and multi-sports court. Sea fishing and golf nearby. **ETC ★★★**
e-mail: holidays@gbholidayparks.co.uk
website: www.gbholidayparks.co.uk

STAFFORDSHIRE

ALTON
Star Caravan and Camping Park, Cotton, Near Alton Towers, Stoke-on-Trent ST10 3DW (01538 702219). Situated off the B5417 road, between Leek and Cheadle, within 10 miles of the market towns of Ashbourne and Uttoxeter, with Alton Towers just one and a quarter miles away. A family-run site where your enjoyment is our main concern. Site amenities include large children's play area, toilet block with free showers, etc., laundry room with drying and ironing facilities, electric hook-ups, etc. Full disabled toilet and shower. Dogs welcome but must be kept on leash. Open 28th March to 3rd November. £10 per night for two persons. Modern static caravan and luxury disabled adapted caravan for hire. Brochure and further details available. **ETC ★★★★, AA** *THREE PENNANTS*

website: www.starcaravanpark.co.uk

EAST SUSSEX

RYE (near)

Camber Sands, Camber, Near Rye TN31 7RT (0870 442 9284; Fax: 01797 225 756). Camber Sands faces seven miles of award-winning Blue Flag golden beach in East Sussex. This beautiful region is steeped in history, with unspoilt Sussex towns like Rye. The park itself has wonderful leisure facilities including four indoor pools, sauna, spa bath and solarium and presents a first-rate entertainment programme. Four fun pools with amazing whirlpool. Amusements centre. Dylan the Dinosaur children's club and outdoor play area. Family Fun Bar. Indoor games, competitions, pool and satellite TV. Bouncy Castle. Well-stocked convenience store. Fast-food cafe. Fishing, golf driving range nearby. **ETC ★★★**
e-mail: holidays@gbholidayparks.co.uk
website: www.gbholidayparks.co.uk

TYNE & WEAR

HAMSTERLEY

Byreside Caravan Site, Hamsterley, Newcastle-upon-Tyne NE17 7RT (01207 560280). The caravan site is on the family-run farm in the beautiful countryside of the Derwent Valley. The site is open all year round and is quiet and secluded. It is very popular with walkers and cyclists as it is adjacent to the Derwent Walk Country Park which is also part of the Coast to Coast route. History looms large in the district with many places to visit in the surrounding area and only a short distance from both Durham and Northumberland. On site is a small shop and toilet block. All pitches have electric hook-up points. Camping area and playing field. Booking advisable. **ETC ★★★★**. Contact: **Mrs J. Clemitson**.

WHITLEY BAY

The Links, Whitley Bay, Tyne and Wear NE26 4RR (0870 442 9282; Fax: 0191 297 1033). Whitley Bay is an immensely popular park that sits on the edge of a well-known seaside resort with a whole array of restaurants, cafes and bars. The walk from the park through to the resort is along a pleasant promenade with lovely views out towards St Mary's Lighthouse and a long stretch of beach. Facilities include a lovely indoor pool and inviting bars offering entertainment, Dylan the Dinosaur children's club and outdoor play area. Local sea fishing opportunities. Multi-sports court. Well-stocked convenience store. Cafe and popular takeaway. **ETC ★★★★**
e-mail: holidays@gbholidayparks.co.uk
website: www.gbholidayparks.co.uk

FREE or REDUCED RATE entry to Holiday Visits and Attractions — see our READERS' OFFER VOUCHERS on pages 53-80

EAST YORKSHIRE

Set on the spectacular heritage coast with unrivalled coastal scenery. Six-berth caravans and chalets for hire. Tents and tourers welcome. Bars, entertainment, shop, pool and gym on site.

Thornwick & Sea Farm Holiday Centre

Flamborough, East Yorks
Tel **01262 850369**
www.thornwickbay.co.uk
e-mail: enquiries@thornwickbay.co.uk

NORTH YORKSHIRE

the York park & ride scheme.

ACASTER MALBIS

Moor End Farm, (Established 1965), York YO23 2UQ (Tel & Fax: 01904 706727). Moor End Farm is a small, family-run caravan and camping site four miles south-west of York. The Tourist Board graded site has 10 touring pitches and six static caravans. Two of the static caravans are available for holiday lets starting from £38 a night or £180 a week. The hire caravans have colour TV, shower, wc, fridge, two bedrooms, kitchen, dining/living area and accommodate up to six persons. Touring facilities available are electric hook-ups, hot showers, toilets, dish-washing sink, fridge/freezer and microwave oven. There are picnic tables around the site for our guests to use. Moor End Farm is on a bus route to York and is five minutes' walk from the popular river bus service and the local inn. We are also very close to the York/Selby cycle track and **AA** *TWO PENNANTS,* **ETC** ★★★★ *CAMPING & TOURING PARK, RAC, BH & HPA.*

See also Colour Display Advertisement

RUDDING
HOLIDAY PARK

Pay and Play golf course plus floodlit driving range.
Lodges, ★★★ Cottages.
e-mail: holiday-park@ruddingpark.com   website: www.ruddingpark.com

HARROGATE

Rudding Holiday Park, Follifoot, Harrogate HG3 1JH (01423 870439; Fax: 01423 870859). These superior holiday cottages and lodges are set in picturesque surroundings just south of Harrogate. The luxury cottages have been completely restored retaining many of their original features (sleep 2-10 persons). The Timber Lodges are situated in beautiful parkland, many overlooking a small lake (sleep 2-6 persons). All are centrally heated and fully equipped. Facilities within the private country estate include: Deer House, heated swimming pool and paddling pool, children's adventure playground, games room and 18 hole golf course. Please send for free illustrated brochure. **ETC** ★★★★★

Please mention Self-Catering Holidays in Britain when writing to enquire about accommodation

ENGLAND

MASHAM

Mr J. McCourt, Black Swan Holiday Park, Fearby, Masham, Ripon HG4 4NF (01765 689477). A small, family-run park in an Area of Outstanding Natural Beauty designated by the Countryside Commission. Ideal for walking. Six miles from Lightwater Valley Theme Park, two miles from Masham, famous for its two breweries - Theakstons and Blacksheep, both of which have visitor centres. Pub on site serving food. First class restaurant. Luxury caravans for hire. Ideal place for that quiet, relaxing, family holiday.
e-mail: info@blackswanholiday.co.uk   **website: www.blackswanholiday.co.uk**

SCARBOROUGH

Mrs Carol Croft, Cayton Village Caravan Park Ltd (Dept 19), Mill Lane, Cayton Bay, Scarborough YO11 3NN. Situated three miles south of Scarborough, four miles from Filey, half a mile from sandy beach at Cayton Bay. Attractive, sheltered, level, landscaped park adjoining Cayton Village Church with footpath 150 yards to two village inns, fish and chip shop and bus service. New luxurious shower, toilet, disabled toilet, dishwashing and laundry facilities. Central heating plus Super Saver and OAP weeks for early and late season bookings. Four acre floodlit dog walk, children's adventure playground. Seasonal pitches available Easter to October. Separate rally field. Min/Max touring caravans and tents £8 to £15, £2 awnings, £1 dogs. **Telephone: 01723 583171** for brochure and booking details. **ETC ★★★★**
e-mail: info@caytontouring.co.uk   **website: www.caytontouring.co.uk**

WETHERBY (near)

Mrs Webb, Maustin Caravan Park, Kearby with Netherby, Near Wetherby LS22 4DA (Tel & Fax: 0113 2886234). Maustin Park offers a peaceful haven for people without family responsibilities. A quiet backwater, situated five miles south of Harrogate in the lower Wharfe Valley, close to Harewood House and many attractions. Tourer field with hook-ups and free showers. Spacious parking around our bowling green. Luxury holiday homes for hire fully equipped to a high standard and including linen. Restored holiday cottage also available. Own a holiday home in prestigious surroundings. Our popular "Stables" restaurant serves excellent food (open Friday to Sunday). Please send for our free brochure. **ETC ★★★★★** *HOLIDAY PARK,*
DAVID BELLAMY GOLD CONSERVATION AWARD WINNERS.
e-mail: info@maustin.co.uk   **website: www.maustin.co.uk**

WHITBY

Middlewood Farm Holiday Park, Robin Hood's Bay, Near Whitby YO22 4UF (01947 880414; Fax: 01947 880871). Small, peaceful, family park. A walkers', artists' and wildlife paradise, set amidst the beautiful North Yorkshire Moors National Park, Heritage Coast and 'Heartbeat Country'. Relax and enjoy the magnificent panoramic views of our spectacular countryside. Five minutes' walk to the village PUB and shops. Ten minutes' walk to the BEACH and picturesque Robin Hood's Bay. SUPERIOR LUXURY HOLIDAY HOMES FOR HIRE, equipped to the highest standards (1 March - 4 January). TOURERS and TENTS: level, sheltered park with electric hook-ups. Superb heated facilities, free showers and dishwashing. Laundry. Gas. Children's adventure playground. Adjacent dog walk and cycle route. Credit cards accepted. Signposted. A warm welcome awaits you. **ETC ★★★★★** *HOLIDAY PARK, ROSE AWARD, WELCOME HOST,* **AA** *THREE PENNANTS, DAVID BELLAMY GOLD AWARD.*
e-mail: info@middlewoodfarm.com   **website: www.middlewoodfarm.com**

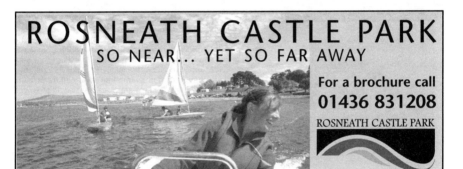
Scotland
Caravan & Camping Holidays

ARGYLL & BUTE

ROSNEATH CASTLE PARK
SO NEAR... YET SO FAR AWAY

For a brochure call
01436 831208

ROSNEATH CASTLE PARK

Rosneath Castle Park has everything to offer if you are looking for a touring or camping holiday. No more than an hour's drive from Glasgow, the 57 acres that the park occupies along the shore of Gareloch offers the perfect opportunity to relax and discover another world, and another you.

Thistle Awarded Luxury Self-Catering Holiday Homes with superb views. In a beautiful setting with first class facilities including an adventure playground, boat house, fun club, restaurant and bar, there's no end to the reasons why you would 'wish you were here'.

Rosneath Castle Park, Rosneath, Near Helensburgh, Argyll G84 0QS
Tel: (01436) 831208   Fax: (01436) 831978
E-Mail: enquiries@rosneathcastle.demon.co.uk
Website: www.rosneathcastle.demon.co.uk

Scottish
TOURIST BOARD
★★★★★
HOLIDAY
PARK

See also Colour Advertisement on Outside Back Cover

FHG
Visit the ⟶ website
www.holidayguides.com
for details of the wide choice of accommodation featured in the full range of FHG titles

AYRSHIRE & ARRAN

BALLANTRAE

Roger and Marilyn Bourne, Laggan House Leisure Park Ballantrae, near Girvan KA26 0LL (01465 831229; Fax: 01465 831511). Peaceful parkland setting in the grounds of an old country house overlooking secluded countryside and the sea. Luxury caravans and chalets for hire, with heated indoor pool, sauna, bar and childrens' playground. Pets are welcome. The park provides a superb base from which to explore the magnificent coastline, the inland hills and Galloway Forest. Local activities include fishing, golf, cycling, walking or just doing nothing. Short breaks available. **STB ★★★★** *HOLIDAY PARK*

See also Colour Display Advertisement

SALTCOATS

Sandylands, Auchenharvie Park, Saltcoats KA21 5JN (0870 442 9312; Fax: 01294 467823). A warm welcome awaits you on this lively, happy friendly park where the emphasis is on giving you a holiday to remember. There is a terrific leisure complex with something for all the family. Facilities include – two quality bars, indoor heated swimming pool, children's club, amusement arcade and mini-market. Local sea fishing trips, golf courses and leisure centre are all situated nearby. Take a ferry trip to the beautiful Isle of Arran with its sandy beaches, rugged mountains and pretty glens. Tourers welcome.
e-mail: holidays@gbholidayparks.co.uk
website: www.gbholidayparks.co.uk

BORDERS

COLDINGHAM

Scoutscroft Holiday Centre. St Abbs Head, Coldingham, Berwickshire TD1 45NB (018907 71338; Bookings Hotline: 0800 169 3786). Thistle Awarded Holiday Homes for hire and sale. Toilet and shower facilities with heated family room. Spaciously developed touring plots. Free adult and children's entertainment. The Priory Restaurant serving meals throughout the season. Family orientated bars. Scooties Entertainment Bar. Chip shop, burger bar, arcade, play areas and laundry facilities. New for 2004, The Sun Lounge, quiet, peaceful and smoke-free extension to Scooties Bar. On-site Dive Centre with unique DIVING PACKAGE.
e-mail: holidays@scoutscroft.co.uk
website: www.scoutscroft.co.uk

See also Colour Display Advertisement

EYEMOUTH

Eyemouth Holiday Park, Fort Road, Eyemouth, Berwickshire TD14 5BE (0870 442 9280; Fax: 01890 751 462). Eyemouth is a beautiful 4 star park situated on the Berwickshire coastline with commanding views over two of Scotland's finest bays. Situated by a unique marine nature reserve, the park has its own beach with some of the best rock pools in the British Isles. The holiday letting accommodation is of a high standard and some have unrivalled sea views. Ideally situated for visiting Edinburgh, Berwick-upon-Tweed and the Scottish Borders, this holiday location has it all. Safe outdoor children's play area. Licensed bar. Pets welcome. **ETC ★★★★**
e-mail: holidays@gbholidayparks.co.uk
website: www.gbholidayparks.co.uk

DUNDEE & ANGUS

BRECHIN

Scott Murray, Eastmill Caravan Park, Brechin DD9 7EL (01356 622810; out of season 01356 622487; Fax: 01356 623356). Beautifully situated on flat grassy site along the River South Esk, within easy access of scenic Angus Glens, local walks and 10 miles from sandy east coast beaches; midway between Dundee and Aberdeen. Shop, gas supplies, shower block, laundry and hook-ups on site; licensed premises nearby. Open April to October. Six-berth caravans with mains services available to rent. Facilities for tourers, caravanettes and tents. Dogs welcome.

• • Some Useful Guidance for Guests and Hosts • •

Every year literally thousands of holidays, short breaks and overnight stops are arranged through our guides, the vast majority without any problems at all. In a handful of cases, however, difficulties do arise about bookings, which often could have been prevented from the outset.

It is important to remember that when accommodation has been booked, both parties – guests and hosts – have entered into a form of contract. We hope that the following points will provide helpful guidance.

GUESTS:

• When enquiring about accommodation, be as precise as possible. Give exact dates, numbers in your party and the ages of any children.

• State the number and type of rooms wanted and also what catering you require – bed and breakfast, full board etc. Make sure that the position about evening meals is clear – and about pets, reductions for children or any other special points.

• Read our reviews carefully to ensure that the proprietors you are going to contact can supply what you want. Ask for a letter confirming all arrangements, if possible.

• If you have to cancel, do so as soon as possible. Proprietors do have the right to retain deposits and under certain circumstances to charge for cancelled holidays if adequate notice is not given and they cannot re-let the accommodation.

HOSTS:

• Give details about your facilities and about any special conditions. Explain your deposit system clearly and arrangements for cancellations, charges etc. and whether or not your terms include VAT.

• If for any reason you are unable to fulfil an agreed booking without adequate notice, you may be under an obligation to arrange suitable alternative accommodation or to make some form of compensation.

While every effort is made to ensure accuracy, we regret that FHG Publications cannot accept responsibility for errors, omissions or misrepresentations in our entries or any consequences thereof. Prices in particular should be checked because we go to press early. We will follow up complaints but cannot act as arbiters or agents for either party.

SCOTLAND

HIGHLANDS

ACHNASHEEN

Gruinard Bay Caravan Park. Situated just a stone's throw from the beach, Gruinard Bay Caravan Park offers the perfect setting for a holiday or a stop over on the West Coast of Scotland. Family-owned and personally operated, the park boasts magnificent views across Gruinard Bay. Sea-front touring pitches; electric hook-ups; no charge for awnings; camping pitches; free toilet and shower facilities; shop gas available on site; laundry facilities by request; static holiday homes available; pets welcome (not in holiday homes). **Tony & Ann Davis, Gruinard Bay Caravan Park, Laide, Wester Ross IV22 2ND (Tel & Fax: 01445 731225).**

LAIRG

Dunroamin Caravan Park, Main Street, Lairg IV27 4AR (01549 402447). Lew Hudson, his wife Margaret and their family welcome you to Dunroamin Caravan Park. A small family-run park situated in the picturesque village of Lairg by Loch Shin, this is the ideal base for touring the whole of Sutherland and Caithness. Pony trekking, fishing, walking and water sports all nearby, with golf just 15 miles away. Outstandingly well maintained grounds with Crofters licensed restaurant on site. Electric hook-ups. 200 yards from pub, bank, shops, post office, etc. Holiday caravans for hire, tourers and tents welcome. **STB ★★★★** *HOLIDAY PARK,* **AA** *THREE PENNANTS*
e-mail: enquiries@lairgcaravanpark.co.uk
website: www.lairgcaravanpark.co.uk

Cliffs at Gwent-on-Sea, North Wales

Wales
Caravan & Camping Holidays

ANGLESEY & GWYNEDD

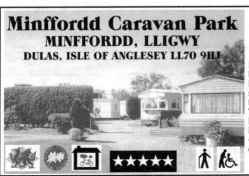

BALA

Ty Gwyn. Self-catering. Static six-berth caravan with two bedrooms, shower, bathroom, colour TV, microwave, etc. Also self-catering annexe - twin-bedded studio with shower, bathroom. Situated two miles from Bala. Beautiful countryside area. Ideal for walking, sailing, canoeing and fishing. Contact: **Mrs A. Skinner, Ty Gwyn, Rhyduchaf, Bala LL23 7SD (01678 521267 or 520234).**

MERIONETH

Islawrffordd Caravan Park, Tal-y-Bont, Merioneth LL43 2BQ (01341 247269; Fax: 01341 242639). Within the Snowdonia National Park and adjoining a clean, safe bathing beach, we offer for hire a choice of caravans. All come with colour TV, fridge, integral shower and toilet, electricity and gas included in price. For the camper and touring caravans we offer our large camping field and 25 tourer pitches both offering a limited number of hook-ups. Facilities include self service shop, laundry room, pub with children's room, amusements and HEATED INDOOR SWIMMING POOL. Booking facility for touring caravans. For enquiries about the above and/or caravan sales telephone or write to **John Billingham**.
e-mail: info@islawrffordd.co.uk
website: www.islawrffordd.co.uk

PLEASE NOTE

All the information in this book is given in good faith in the belief that it is correct. However, the publishers cannot guarantee the facts given in these pages, neither are they responsible for changes in policy, ownership or terms that may take place after the date of going to press. Readers should always satisfy themselves that the facilities they require are available and that the terms, if quoted, still apply.

FREE or REDUCED RATE entry to Holiday Visits and Attractions — see our READERS' OFFER VOUCHERS on pages 53-80

Manorbier Country Park

Tent, Tourers and Static Vans

The kids will love the Gerry Summer Club

Enjoy the unspoilt coast and countryside from our secluded Park which offers its guests:

- ▼ Restaurant
- ▼ Adventure & Toddlers Play Park
- ▼ Health suite and Gymnasium
- ▼ A shop selling food, gifts, sweets and newspapers
- ▼ Family amusements and games
- ▼ A convenient launderette
- ▼ Indoor heated swimming pool
- ▼ Hard court tennis
- ▼ Bar with Family Entertainment
- ▼ Internet Facilities

Set in some ten acres of parkland dotted with trees, you could be miles from anywhere, yet the village of Manorbier with its Castle and sandy beach is just a mile and a half away, with Tenby only 5 miles down the road.

Station Road, Manorbier, Tenby, Pembrokeshire SA70 7SN

Tel: 01834 871952
Fax: 01834 871203

CROESO CYMRU
WALES TOURIST BOARD
PARC GWYLIAU
★★★★
HOLIDAY PARK

★★★★
TOURING PARK

'The little park with the big heart'

Open March to November 1 ● Total no. of pitches 151 ● Rates per night (tourers) Min: £16 - Max £21.50 ● Rates per week (statics): Min £150 - Max £660

DIRECTORY OF WEBSITE AND E-MAIL ADDRESSES

A quick-reference guide to holiday accommodation with an e-mail address and/or website, conveniently arranged by country and county, with full contact details.

•LONDON

Guesthouse
MacDonald Hotel, 45-46 Argyle Square,
LONDON WC1H 8AL
020 7837 3552
• e-mail: fhg@macdonaldhotel.com
• website: www.macdonaldhotel.com

Hotel
The Elysee Hotel, 20-26 Craven Terrace,
LONDON W2 8EL
020 7402 7633
• e-mail: information@elyseehotel-london.co.uk
• website: www.elyseehotel-london.co.uk

Hotel / B & B
Lincoln House Hotel, 33 Gloucester Place,
LONDON W1V 8HY
020 7486 7630
• e-mail: reservations@lincoln-house-hotel.co.uk
• website: www.lincoln-house-hotel.co.uk

Guesthouse / Hotel
Barry House Hotel, 12 Sussex Place,
Hyde Park, LONDON W2 2TP
020 7723 7340
• e-mail: RSB@barryhouse.co.uk
• website: www.barryhouse.co.uk

Hotel / B & B
Elizabeth Hotel, 37 Eccleston Square,
LONDON SW1V 1PB
020 7828 6812
• e-mail: info@elizabethhotel.com
• website: www.elizabethhotel.com

Hotel
Queens Hotel, 33 Anson Road,
Tufnell Park, LONDON N7
020 7607 4725
• e-mail: queens@stavrouhotels.co.uk
• website: www.stavrouhotels.co.uk

Hotel
Athena Hotel, 110-114 Sussex Gardens,
Hyde Park, LONDON W2 1UA
020 7706 3866
• e-mail: athena@stavrouhotels.co.uk
• website: www.stavrouhotels.co.uk

Hotel
Gower Hotel, 129 Sussex Gardens,
Hyde Park, LONDON W2 2RX
020 7262 2262
• e-mail: gower@stavrouhotels.co.uk
• website: www.stavrouhotels.co.uk

B & B
Sohel & Anne Armanios, 67 Rannoch Road,
Hammersmith, LONDON W6 9SS
020 7385 4904
• website: www.thewaytostay.co.uk

B & B / Hotel / Self-Catering
Windsor House Hotel, 12 Penywern Road,
LONDON SW5 9ST
020 7373 9087
• e-mail: bookings@windsor-house-hotel.com
• website: www.windsor-house-hotel.com

•BERKSHIRE

Hotel
Clarence Hotel, 9 Clarence Road,
WINDSOR, Berkshire SL4 5AE
01753 864436
• website: www.clarence-hotel.co.uk

•CAMBRIDGESHIRE

Guest House
Dykelands Guest House, 157 Mowbray
Road, CAMBRIDGE,
Cambridgeshire CB1 7SP
01223 244300
• e-mail: dykelands@fsbdial.co.uk
• website: www.dykelands.com

Guest House
Victoria Guest House,
57 Arbury Road, CAMBRIDGE,
Cambridgeshire CB4 2JB
01223 350086
• e-mail:victoriahouse@ntlworld.com
• website:
www.SmoothHound.co.uk/hotels/victori3.html

•CHESHIRE

Guest House / Self-Catering
Mrs Joanne Hollins, Balterley Green Farm,
Farm Deans Lane, BALTERLEY, Crewe
Cheshire CW2 5QJ
01270 820 214
• e-mail: greenfarm@balterley.fsnet.co.uk
• website: www.greenfarm.freeserve.co.uk

Guest House / Self-Catering
Mrs Angela Smith, Mill House and Granary,
Higher Wych, MALPAS,
Cheshire SY14 7JR
01948 780362
• e-mail: angela@videoactive.co.uk
• website: www.millhouseandgranary.co.uk

•CORNWALL

Self-Catering
Fiona & Martin Nicolle,
Classy Cottages, Cornwall
07000 423000
• website: www.classycottages.co.uk

Self-Catering
Cornish Traditional Cottages, Blisland,
BODMIN, Cornwall PL30 4HS
01208 821666
• e-mail: info@corncott.com
• website: www.corncott.com

Self-Catering
Tregatherall Farm,
BOSCASTLE, Cornwall PL35 0EQ
01840 250277
• e-mail: tregatherall@ipl.co.uk
• website: www.ipl.co.uk/tregatherall/

Self-Catering
Mr Charles Tippet,
Mineshop Holiday Cottages, Crackington
Haven, BUDE, Cornwall EX23 0NR
01840 230338
• e-mail: tippett@mineshop.freeserve.co.uk
• website: www.crackingtoncottages.co.uk

Self-Catering / Caravan & Camping
Willow Valley Holiday Park,
Bush, BUDE, Cornwall EX23 9LB
01288 353104
• e-mail: willowvalley@talk21.com
• website: www.caravansitecornwall.co.uk

Caravan & Camping
Cornish Coasts Caravan & Camping Park,
Middle Penlean, Poundstock,
Widemouth Bay, BUDE, Cornwall EX23 0EE
01288 361380
• e-mail: info@cornishcoasts.co.uk
• website: www.cornishcoasts.co.uk

Self-Catering
Mr Ian Goodman,
Hilton Farm Holiday Cottages,
Marhamchurch, BUDE, Cornwall EX23 0HE
01288 361521
• e-mail: ian@hiltonfarmhouse.freeserve.co.uk
• website: www.hiltonfarmhouse.co.uk

Caravan & Camping
Widemouth Bay Caravan Park,
Near BUDE, Cornwall
01271 866666
• website:
www.johnfowlerholidays.com/widemouth_bay.asp

Hotel / Self-Catering
Wringford Down Hotel, CAWSAND,
Torpoint, Cornwall PL10 1LE
01752 822287
• e-mail: a.molloy@virgin.net
• website: www.cornwallholidays.co.uk

Hotel
Rosemullion Hotel, Gyllyngvase Hill,
FALMOUTH,
Cornwall TR11 4DF
01326 314690
• e-mail: gail@rosemullionhotel.demon.co.uk
• website:
www.s-h-systems.co.uk/hotels/rosemullion.html

Caravan & Camping
Boscrege Caravan & Camping Park,
Ashton, HELSTON, Cornwall TR13 9TG
01736 762231
• e-mail: enquiries@caravanparkcornwall.com
• website: www.caravanparkcornwall.com

Guest House
Greystones Guest House, 40 West End,
Porthleven, HELSTON TR13 9JL
01326 565583
• e-mail: neilvwoodward@hotmail.com

Self-Catering
Kathryn Broad, Lower Dutson Farm,
LAUNCESTON, Cornwall PL15 9SP
01566 776456
• e-mail: francis.broad@btclick.com
• website:
www.chycor.co.uk/cornish-farmholidays

Self-Catering
Celia Hutchinson,
Caradon Country Cottages, East Taphouse,
LISKEARD, Cornwall PL14 4NH
01579 320355
• e-mail: celia@caradoncottages.freeserve.co.uk
• website: www.caradoncottages.co.uk

Self-Catering
Kaye & Bill Chapman, Well Meadow
Cottage, Coldrinnick Farm, Duloe,
LISKEARD, Cornwall
01503 220251
• e-mail: kaye@coldrinnick.fsnet.co.uk
• website: www.cornishcottage.net

Self-Catering
Sue Jewell, Boturnell Farm Cottages,
St Pinnock, LISKEARD, Cornwall PL14 4QS
01579 320880
• e-mail: boturnell-barns@breathemail.net
• website: www.dogs-holiday.co.uk

Self-Catering
Mrs S. Clemens, Lametton Barton,
St Keyne, LISKEARD, Cornwall PL14 4SQ
01579 343434
• website:
  www.stayincornwall.co.uk/lametton.htm

B & B / Self-Catering
Paul Brumpton, Talehay Holiday Cottages,
Pelynt, near LOOE, Cornwall PL13 2LT
01503 220252
• e-mail: paul@talehay.co.uk
• website: www.talehay.co.uk

B & B
Mrs Dawn Rundle, Lancallan Farm,
MEVAGISSEY, St Austell,
Cornwall PL26 6EW
01726 842284
• e-mail: dawn@lancallan.fsnet.co.uk

Hotel
Golden Bay Hotel, Pentire Avenue,
Pentire, NEWQUAY,
Cornwall TR7 1PD
01637 873318
• e-mail: enquiries@goldenbayhotel.co.uk
• website: www.goldenbayhotel.co.uk

Guest House / Self-Catering
Trewerry Mill Guest House, Trewerry Mill,
Trerice, St Newlyn East, NEWQUAY,
Cornwall TR8 5GS
01872 510345
• e-mail: trewerry.mill@which.net
• website: www.trewerrymill.co.uk

Holiday Park
Treloy Tourist Park, NEWQUAY,
Cornwall TR8 4JN
01637 872063/876279
• e-mail: holidays@treloy.co.uk
• website: www.treloy.co.uk

Hotel
White Lodge Hotel, Mawgan Porth Bay,
Near NEWQUAY, Cornwall TR8 4BN
01637 860512
• e-mail: adogfriendly@aol.com
• website: www.dogfriendlyhotel.co.uk

Guest House
Dewolf Guest House, 100 Henver Road,
NEWQUAY, Cornwall TR7 3BL
01637 874746
• e-mail: holidays@dewolfguesthouse.com
• website: www.dewolfguesthouse.com

B & B / Hotel
Mr Simon Chapman, Camilla House Hotel,
12 Regent Terrace, PENZANCE,
Cornwall TR18 4DW
01736 363771
• e-mail: visitus@camillahouse-hotel.co.uk
• website: www.penzance.co.uk/camilla/

Farmhouse B & B
Rose Farm, Chyannal, Buryas Bridge,
PENZANCE, Cornwall
01736 731808
• e-mail: lally@rosefarmcornwall.co.uk
• website: www.rosefarmcornwall.co.uk

Inn
Crumplehorn Inn, POLPERRO,
Cornwall PL13 2RJ
01503 272348
• e-mail: host@crumplehorn-inn.co.uk
• website: www.crumplehorn-inn.co.uk

Visit the FHG website
www.holidayguides.com
for details of the wide choice of accommodation
featured in the full range of FHG titles

Caravan & Camping / Holiday Park
Globe Vale Holiday Park, Radnor,
REDRUTH, Cornwall
01209 891183
• e-mail: globe@ukgo.com
• website: www.globe.ukgo.com

Caravan & Camping / Holiday Park
Chiverton Park, Blackwater, ST AGNES,
Cornwall TR4 8HS
01872 560667
• e-mail: info@chivertonpark.co.uk
• website: www.chivertonpark.co.uk

Hotel / Inn
Mrs J. Treleaven, Driftwood Spars Hotel,
Trevaunance Cove, ST AGNES,
Cornwall TR5 0RT
01872 552428 / 553323
• e-mail: driftwoodspars@hotmail.com
• website: www.driftwoodspars.com

B & B
Mrs Liz Berryman, Polgreen Farm,
London Apprentice, ST AUSTELL,
Cornwall PL26 7AP
01726 75151
• e-mail: polgreen.farm@btclick.com
• website: www.polgreenfarm.co.uk

Holiday Park
St Ives Bay Holiday Park, ST IVES BAY,
Cornwall TR27 5BH
0800 317713 (24hr brochure line)
• e-mail: enquiries@stivesbay.co.uk
• website: www.stivesbay.co.uk

Hotel
Rosevine Hotel, Porthcurnick Beach,
ST MAWES, Cornwall
01872 580206
• e-mail: info@rosevine.co.uk
• website: www.rosevine.co.uk

Hotel
Dalswinton House, ST MAWGAN,
Near Newquay, Cornwall TR8 4EZ
01637 860385
• e-mail: dalswinton@bigwig.net
• website: www.dalswinton.com

Self-Catering
Mr & Mrs C.W. Pestell, Hockadays,
Tregenna, near Blisland, ST TUDY,
Cornwall PL30 4QJ
01208 850146
• e-mail:
holidays@hockadaysholidaycottages.co.uk
• website: www.hockadaysholidaycottages.co.uk

Hotel & Self-Catering Lodges
St Mellion Hotel, Golf & Country Club,
St Mellion, Near SALTASH, Cornwall
01579 351351
• e-mail: stmellion@americangolf.uk.com
• website: www.st-mellion.co.uk

Caravan & Camping
Wheal Rose Caravan & Camping Park,
Wheal Rose, SCORRIER,
Near Redruth, Cornwall
01209 891496
• e-mail: les@whealrosecaravanpark.co.uk
• website: www.whealrosecaravanpark.co.uk

Hotel
Willapark Manor Hotel, Bossiney,
TINTAGEL, Cornwall PL34 0BA
01840 770782
• e-mail: nick@willapark.co.uk
• website: www.willapark.co.uk

Guest House
Sara Hawkins, Bosayne Guest House,
Atlantic Road, TINTAGEL,
Cornwall PL34 0DE
01840 770514
• e-mail: clark@clarky100.freeserve.co.uk
• website: www.bosayne.co.uk

Self-Catering
Mrs Sandy Wilson, Salutations,
Atlantic Road, TINTAGEL,
Cornwall PL34 0DE
01840 770287
• website: www.salutationstintagel.co.uk

Caravan Park
C.R. Simpkins, Summer Valley Touring Park,
Shortlanesend, TRURO, Cornwall TR4 9DW
01872 277878
• e-mail: res@summervalley.co.uk
• website: www.summervalley.co.uk

Self-Catering
Mrs Sue Zamaria, Colesent Cottages,
St Tudy, WADEBRIDGE, Cornwall PL30 4QX
01208 850112
• e-mail: welcome@colesent.co.uk
• website: www.colesent.co.uk

Please mention this guide when enquiring about accommodation

• CUMBRIA

Hotel
Rothay Manor, Rothay Bridge,
AMBLESIDE, Cumbria LA22 0EH
015394 33605
• e-mail: hotel@rothaymanor.co.uk
• website: www.rothaymanor.co.uk

Caravan Park
Greenhowe Caravan Park, Great Langdale,
AMBLESIDE, Cumbria LA22 9JU
015394 37231
• e-mail: enquiries@greenhowe.com

B & B
Mr Jack Halliday, The Anchorage,
Rydal Road, AMBLESIDE,
Cumbria LA22 9AY
015394 32046
• e-mail: info@anchorageonline.force9.co.uk
• website: www.anchorageonline.force9.co.uk/

Hotel
Appleby Manor Country House Hotel,
Roman Road, APPLEBY-IN-WESTMORLAND,
Cumbria CA16 6JB
017683 51571
• e-mail: reception@applebymanor.co.uk
• website: www.applebymanor.co.uk

Self-Catering / Holiday Homes
Lakelovers, Belmont House, Lake Road,
BOWNESS-ON-WINDERMERE,
Cumbria LA23 3BJ
015394 88855
• e-mail: bookings@lakelovers.co.uk
• website: www.lakelovers.co.uk

B & B
Elaine Packer, The Hill, Gilsland,
BRAMPTON, Cumbria CA8 7SA
016977 47214
• e-mail: info@hadrians-wallbedandbreakfast.com
• website:
   www.hadrians-wallbedandbreakfast.com

Hotel
Bridge Hotel, BUTTERMERE,
Cumbria CA13 9UZ
017687 70252
• e-mail: enquiries@bridge-hotel.com
• website: www.bridge-hotel.com

Guest House
Dalegarth Guest House, Hassness Estate,
BUTTERMERE, Cumbria CA13 9XA
017687 70233
• e-mail: dalegarth.buttermere@rdplus.net
• website: www.dalegarthguesthouse.co.uk

Self-Catering
Loweswater Holiday Cottages, Scale Hill,
Loweswater, COCKERMOUTH,
Cumbria CA13 9UX
01900 85232
• website:
   www.loweswaterholidaycottages.co.uk

Hotel
Rob Treeby, Ivy House Hotel, Ivy House,
Main Street, HAWKSHEAD, Cumbria
015394 36204
• e-mail: rob@ivyhousehotel.com
• website: www.ivyhousehotel.com

Farm & Self-Catering
Mrs S. Beaty, Garnett House Farm,
Burneside, KENDAL, Cumbria
01539 724542
• e-mail: info@garnetthousefarm.co.uk
• website: www.garnetthousefarm.co.uk

Farmhouse B & B
Mrs Swindlehurst, Tranthwaite Hall,
Underbarrow, near KENDAL,
Cumbria LA8 8HG
015395 68285
• e-mail: tranthwaitehall@aol.com
• website: www.tranthwaitehall.co.uk

Self-Catering
Mrs Val Sunter, "Dora's Cottage",
c/o Higher House Farm, Oxenholme Lane,
Natland, KENDAL, Cumbria LA9 7QH
015395 61177
• website: www.shortbreaks-uk.co.uk/514

Hotel
Derwentwater Hotel, Portinscale, KESWICK,
Cumbria CA12 5RE
017687 72538
• e-mail: info@derwentwater-hotel.co.uk
• website:
   www.derwentwater.hotel.dial.pipex.com

B&B
Highside Farm, Bassenthwaite, KESWICK
Cumbria CA12 4QG
017687 76952/76328
• e-mail: deborah@highside.co.uk
• website: www.highside.co.uk

Self-Catering
Brook House Cottage Holidays,
Bassenthwaite Village,
Near KESWICK, Cumbria
017687 76393
• e-mail: a.m.trafford@amserve.net
• website:
   www.holiday.cottageslakedistrict.co.uk

Self-Catering
Keswick Cottages, Kentmere, How Lane,
KESWICK, Cumbria CA12 5RS
017687 73895
• e-mail: info@keswickcottages.co.uk
• website: www.keswickcottages.co.uk

B & B
Mrs S. Park, Langdale, 14 Leonard Street,
KESWICK, Cumbria CA12 4EL
017687 73977
• website: www.langdaleguesthouse.com

Self-Catering
16 Hewetson Court, Main Street,
KESWICK, Cumbria
01786 814955
• e-mail: martyn_d2@hotmail.com

Caravan & Camping
Mrs L. Lamb, Burns Caravan & Camping
Site, St Johns in the Vale, KESWICK,
Cumbria CA12 4RR
01768 779225
• e-mail: llamb@callnetuk.com

B & B
Val Bradley, Rickerby Grange, Portinscale,
KESWICK, Cumbria CA12 5RH
017687 72344
• e-mail: val@ricor.co.uk
• website: www.ricor.co.uk

Self-Catering
Watendlath Guest House and Barrowside &
Swinside Cottages,
c/o Mrs Walker, 15 Acorn Street, KESWICK,
Cumbria CA12 4EA
01768 774165
• e-mail: info@watendlathguesthouse.co.uk
• website: www.watendlathguesthouse.co.uk

Guest House
Ian Townsend and Annie Scally, Latrigg
House, St Herbert Street,
KESWICK, Cumbria CA12 4DF
017687 73068
• e-mail: info@latrigghouse.com
• website: www.latrigghouse.com

Self-Catering
Mrs S.J. Bottom, Crossfield Cottages,
KIRKOSWALD, Penrith, Cumbria CA10 1EU
01768 898711
• e-mail: info@crossfieldcottages.co.uk
• website: www.crossfieldcottages.co.uk

Hotel & Inn
The Shepherd's Arms Hotel,
Ennerdale Bridge,
LAKE DISTRICT NATIONAL PARK,
Cumbria CA23 3AR
01946 861249
• e-mail: enquiries@shepherdsarmshotel.co.uk
• website: www.sheperdsarmshotel.co.uk

B & B
Jenny Wickens, Garth Row,
LOWICK GREEN, Ulverston,
Cumbria LA12 8EB
01229 885633
• e-mail: b&b@garthrow.freeserve.co.uk
• website: www.garthrow.co.uk

Guest House / B & B
Mr & Mrs C. Smith, Mosedale House,
MOSEDALE, Mungrisdale,
Cumbria CA11 0XQ
01768 779371
• e-mail: mosedale@northlakes.co.uk
• website: www.mosedalehouse.co.uk

Guest House / Self-Catering
Near Howe Country House Hotel,
MUNGRISDALE, Penrith,
Cumbria CA11 0SH
017687 79678
• e-mail: nearhowe@btopenworld.co.uk
• website: www.nearhowe.co.uk

Caravan & Camping / Self-Catering
Park Foot Caravan & Camping Park,
Howtown Road, Pooley Bridge, PENRITH,
Cumbria CA10 2NA
017684 86309
• e-mail: park.foot@talk21.com
• website: www.parkfootullswater.co.uk

Guest House
Mrs M. Whittam, Netherdene Guest House,
Troutbeck, Near PENRITH,
Cumbria CA11 0SJ
017684 83475
• e-mail: netherdene@aol.com
• website: www.netherdene.co.uk

Guest House
Elle Jackson, Albany House,
5 Portland Place, PENRITH,
Cumbria CA11 7NQ
01768 863072
• e-mail: info@albany-house.org.uk
• website: www.albany-house.org.uk

Self-Catering / Caravan & Camping
Mr & Mrs Burnett, Fell View, Glenridding,
PENRITH, Cumbria CA11 0PJ
01768 482342; Evening: 01768 867420
• e-mail: enquiries@fellviewholidays.com
• website: www.fellviewholidays.com

Self-Catering / Caravan & Camping
Tanglewood Caravan Park, Causewayhead,
SILLOTH, Cumbria CA7 4PE
016973 31253
• e-mail: tanglewoodcaravanpark@hotmail.com
• website: www.tanglewoodcaravanpark.co.uk

Guest House / Self Catering
Mrs Jones, Primrose Cottage, Orton Road,
TEBAY, Cumbria CA10 3TL
01539 624791
• e-mail: info@primrosecottagecumbria.co.uk
• website: www.primrosecottagecumbria.co.uk

Self-Catering
High Dale Park House, Satterthwaite,
ULVERSTON, Cumbria CA12 8LJ
01229 860226
• e-mail: peter@lakesweddingmusic.com
• website: www.lakesweddingmusic.com

Guest House
Mr & Mrs Tyson, Hollywood Guest House,
Holly Road, WINDERMERE,
Cumbria LA23 2AF
015394 42219
• website: www.hollywoodguesthouse.co.uk

Self-Catering
Mr & Mrs Dodsworth, Birthwaite Edge,
Birthwaite Road, WINDERMERE,
Cumbria LA23 1BS
015394 42861
• e-mail: fhg@lakedge.com
• website: www.lakedge.com

Self-Catering
J.R. Benson, High Sett, Sun Hill Lane,
Troutbeck Bridge, WINDERMERE,
Cumbria LA23 1HJ
015394 42731
• e-mail: info@accommodationlakedistrict.com
• website: www.accommodationlakedistrict.com

•DERBYSHIRE

Farmhouse B & B / Self-Catering
Mrs M.A. Richardson, Throwley Hall Farm,
Ilam, ASHBOURNE, Derbyshire DE6 2BB
01538 308202
• e-mail: throwleyhall@talk21.com
• website: www.throwleyhallfarm.co.uk

Guest House
Mr & Mrs Hyde, Braemar Guest House,
10 Compton Road, BUXTON,
Derbyshire SK17 9DN
01298 78050
• e-mail: buxtonbraemar@supanet.com
• website: www.cressbrook.co.uk/buxton/braemar

Self-Catering
R.D. Hollands, Wheeldon Trees Farm,
Earl Sterndale, BUXTON,
Derbyshire SK17 0AA
01298 83219
• e-mail: hollands@earlsterndale.fsnet.co.uk
• website: www.wheeldontreesfarm.co.uk

Hotel
Biggin Hall Hotel, Biggin-by-Hartington,
BUXTON, Derbyshire SK17 0DH
01298 84451
• e-mail: enquiries@bigginhall.co.uk
• website: www.bigginhall.co.uk

Inn
Nick & Fiona Clough, The Devonshire Arms,
Peak Forest, near BUXTON,
Derbyshire SK17 8EJ
01298 23875
• e-mail: fiona.clough@virgin.net
• website: www.devarms.com

Farm / Self-Catering
J. Gibbs, Wolfscote Grange, HARTINGTON,
near Buxton, Derbyshire SK17 0AX
01298 84342
• e-mail: wolfscote@btinternet.com
• website: www.wolfscotegrangecottages.co.uk

FHG PUBLICATIONS
publish a large range of well-known accommodation
guides. We will be happy to send you details or you
can use the order form at the back of this book.

•DEVON

Self-Catering
Toad Hall Cottages,
DEVON
08700 777345
• website: www.toadhallcottages.com

Self-Catering
Waters Reach, West Quay, APPLEDORE,
Devon. C/o Viv and Peter Foley
01707 657644
• e-mail: viv@vfoley.freeserve.co.uk

Holiday Park
Parkers Farm Holiday Park,
Higher Mead Farm, ASHBURTON, Devon
01364 652598
• e-mail: parkersfarm@btconnect.com
• website: www.parkersfarm.co.uk

Self-Catering
North Devon Holiday Homes,
19 Cross Street, BARNSTAPLE,
Devon EX31 1BD
01271 376322
• e-mail: info@northdevonholidays.co.uk
• website: www.northdevonholidays.co.uk

Farm B & B / Self-Catering
Peter Day, Lower Yelland Farm, Fremington,
BARNSTAPLE, Devon EX31 3EN
01271 860101
• e-mail: peterday@loweryellandfarm.co.uk
• website: www.loweryellandfarm.co.uk

Self-Catering
Mr Ridge, Braddon Cottages, Ashwater,
BEAWORTHY, Devon EX21 5EP
01409 211350
• e-mail: holidays@braddoncottages.co.uk
• website: www.braddoncottages.co.uk

Hotel
Sandy Cove Hotel, Combe Martin Bay,
BERRYNARBOR, Devon EX34 9SR
01271 882243 / 882888
• e-mail: rg/4003483@aol.com
• website: www.exmoor-hospitality-inns.co.uk

Self-Catering / Organic Farm
Little Comfort Farm Cottages,
Little Comfort Farm, BRAUNTON,
North Devon EX33 2NJ
01271 812414
• e-mail: jackie.milsom@btclick.com
• website: www.littlecomfortfarm.co.uk

B & B
Mrs Roselyn Bradford, St Merryn,
Higher Park Road, BRAUNTON,
Devon EX33 2LG
01271 813805
• e-mail: ros@st-merryn.co.uk
• website: www.st-merryn.co.uk

Self-Catering
Devoncourt Holiday Flats, Berryhead Road,
BRIXHAM, Devon TQ5 9AB
01803 853748
• e-mail: devoncourt@devoncoast.com

Guest House
Mr John Parry, Woodlands Guest House,
Parkham Road, BRIXHAM,
South Devon TQ5 9BU
01803 852040
• e-mail: Dogfriendly2@aol.com
• website: www.dogfriendlyguesthouse.co.uk

Self-Catering
Wheel Farm Country Cottages, Berry Down,
COMBE MARTIN, Devon EX34 0NG
01271 882106
• e-mail: holidays@wheelfarmcottages.co.uk
• website: www.wheelfarmcottages.co.uk

Self-Catering
Mrs S.R. Ridalls, The Old Bakehouse,
7 Broadstone, DARTMOUTH,
Devon TQ6 9NR
01803 834585
• e-mail: pioneerparker@aol.com
• website: www.oldbakehousedartmouth.co.uk

Farm / B & B
Mrs Karen Williams, Stile Farm, Starcross,
EXETER, Devon EX6 8PD
01626 890268
• e-mail: info@stile-farm.co.uk
• website: www.stile-farm.co.uk

Farmhouse B & B
Mrs J. Bragg, Marianne Pool Farm,
Clyst St George, EXETER, Devon EX3 0NZ
01392 874939
• website:
www.s-h-systems.co.uk/hotels/mariannepool.html

B & B
Mrs Sally Glanville, Rydon Farm, Woodbury,
EXETER, Devon EX5 1LB
01395 232341
• website:
www.hotelon.com/uk/s-w/b&b/rydon-farm.htm

Self-Catering
Christine Duncan, Raleigh Holiday Homes,
24 Raleigh Road, EXMOUTH,
Devon EX8 2SB
01395 266967
• e-mail: c.e.duncan@amserve.net

Farmhouse B&B
Mrs Alison Homa, Mullacott Farm,
Mullacott Cross, ILFRACOMBE,
Devon EX34 8NA
01271 866877
• e-mail: relax@mullacottfarm.co.uk
• website: www.mullacottfarm.co.uk

Farm / Self-Catering
Mrs E. Sansom, Widmouth Farm,
Watermouth, Near ILFRACOMBE,
Devon EX34 9RX
01271 863743
• e-mail: holiday@widmouthfarmcottages.co.uk
• website: www.widmouthfarmcottages.co.uk

Self-Catering
Karen Jackson, Torcross Apartment Hotel,
Torcross, KINGSBRIDGE, Devon
01548 580206
• e-mail: enquiries@torcross.com
• website: www.torcross.com

Hotel
Buckland-Tout-Saints Hotel & Restaurant,
Goveton, KINGSBRIDGE, Devon TQ7 2DS
01548 853055
• e-mail: buckland@tout-saints.co.uk
• website: www.tout-saints.co.uk

Guest House
Tricia & Alan Francis, Glenville House,
2 Tors Road, LYNMOUTH,
North Devon EX35 6ET
01598 752202
• e-mail: tricia@glenvillelynmouth.co.uk
• website: www.glenvillelynmouth.co.uk

Guest House
Mrs J. Parker, Tregonwell, The Olde Sea
Captain's House, 1 Tors Road, LYNMOUTH,
Exmoor National Park, Devon EX35 6ET
01598 753369
• website:
www.SmoothHound.co.uk/hotels/tregonwl.html

Inn
The Exmoor Sandpiper Inn, Countisbury,
LYNMOUTH, Devon EX35 6NE
01598 741263
• e-mail: info@exmoor-sandpiper.co.uk

Farm / B & B
Great Sloncombe Farm,
MORETONHAMPSTEAD,
Newton Abbot, Devon TQ13 8QF
01647 440595
• e-mail: hmerchant@sloncombe.freeserve.co.uk
• website: www.greatsloncombefarm.co.uk

Self-Catering
Mrs Whale, Roselands, Totnes Road,
Ipplepen, NEWTON ABBOT, Devon
01803 812701
• e-mail: enquiries@roselands.net
• website: www.roselands.net

B & B
Mrs Rosemary Ward, Parsonage Farm,
Iddesleigh, OKEHAMPTON,
Devon EX19 8SN
• website:
www.devon-holiday.com/parsonage-farm/

Farm Guest House
Mrs Ann Forth, Fluxton Farm,
OTTERY ST MARY, Devon EX11 1RJ
01404 812818
• website:
www.s-h-systems.co.uk/hotels/fluxtonfarm.html

Guest House
The Lamplighter Hotel, 103 Citadel Road,
The Hoe, PLYMOUTH, Devon PL1 2RN
01752 663855
• e-mail: lamplighterhotel@ukonline.co.uk

Self-Catering / Caravan & Camping
Harford Bridge Holiday Park, Peter Tavy,
TAVISTOCK, Devon PL19 9LS
01822 810349
• e-mail: enquiry@harfordbridge.co.uk
• website: www.harfordbridge.co.uk

Guest House
Mrs Arnold, The Mill, Washfield,
TIVERTON, Devon EX16 9PD
01884 255297
• e-mail: arnold5@washfield.freeserve.co.uk
• website: www.washfield.freeserve.co.uk

Guest House
Aveland Hotel, Aveland Road,
Babbacombe, TORQUAY, Devon TQ1 3PT
01803 326622
• e-mail: avelandhotel@aol.com
• website: www.avelandhotel.co.uk

Self-Catering
Mrs H. Carr, Sunningdale Apartments,
11 Babbacombe Downs Road, TORQUAY,
Devon TQ1 3LF
• website: www.sunningdaleapartments.co.uk

Self-Catering
Mrs J. Ford, Flear Farm Cottages,
East Allington, TOTNES, Devon TQ9 7RF
01548 521227
• e-mail: flearfarm@btinternet.com
• website: www.flearfarm.co.uk

Self-Catering
J. Lincoln-Gordon, Golland Farm,
Burrington, UMBERLEIGH, Devon EX37 9JP
01769 520263
• e-mail: golland@btinternet.com
• website: www.golland.btinternet.co.uk

Self-Catering
Jane Cromey-Hawke, Collacott Farm,
Kings Nympton, UMBERLEIGH,
Devon EX37 9TP
01769 572491
• e-mail: jane@collacott.co.uk
• website: www.collacott.co.uk

Guest House
Sunnymeade Country Hotel, Dean Cross,
West Down, WOOLACOMBE,
Devon EX34 8NT
01271 863668
• e-mail: info@sunnymeade.co.uk
• website: www.sunnymeade.co.uk

Self-Catering/ Camping
Dartmoor Country Holidays,
Magpie Leisure Park, Bedford Bridge,
Horrabridge, YELVERTON, Devon PL20 7RY
01822 852651
• website: www.dartmoorcountryholidays.co.uk

•DORSET

Guest House
Caroline Pielesz, The Walnuts,
2 Prout Bridge, BEAMINSTER, Dorset
01308 862211
• e-mail: caroline@thewalnuts.co.uk

Guest House
S. Barling, Mayfield Guest House,
46 Frances Road, BOURNEMOUTH, Dorset
BH1 3SA
01202 551839
• e-mail: accom@mayfieldguesthouse.com
• website: www.mayfieldguesthouse.com

Hotel / Guest House
Southernhay Hotel, 42 Alum Chine Road,
Westbourne, BOURNEMOUTH,
Dorset BH4 8DX
01202 761251
• e-mail: enquiries@southernhayhotel.co.uk
• website: www.southernhayhotel.co.uk

Hotel
Fircroft Hotel, Owls Road, BOURNEMOUTH,
Dorset BH5 1AE
01202 309771
• e-mail: info@fircrofthotel.co.uk
• website: www.fircrofthotel.co.uk

Hotel / Guest House
Westcotes House Hotel,
9 Southbourne Overcliff Drive,
BOURNEMOUTH, Dorset BH6 3TE
01202 428512
• website: www.westcoteshousehotel.co.uk

Caravan & Camping
Martin Cox, Highlands End Holiday Park,
BRIDPORT, Eype, Dorset DT6 6AR
01308 422139
• e-mail: holidays@wdlh.co.uk
• website: www.wdlh.co.uk

Self-Catering
Westover Farm Cottages,
Wootton Fitzpaine, Near LYME REGIS,
Dorset DT6 6NE
01297 560451
• e-mail: wfcottages@aol.com
• website:
  www.lymeregis.com/westover-farm-cottages/

Guest House / Self-Catering
White Horse Farm, Middlemarsh,
SHERBORNE, Dorset DT9 5QN
01963 210222
• e-mail: enquiries@whitehorsefarm.co.uk
• website: www.whitehorsefarm.co.uk

Hotel
The Knoll House, STUDLAND BAY,
Dorset BH19 3AW
01929 450450
• e-mail: enquiries@knollhouse.co.uk
• website: www.knollhouse.co.uk

Please mention this guide when enquiring about accommodation

B&B
Mrs Jill Miller, Lower Fifehead Farm,
Fifehead, St Quinton, STURMINSTER
NEWTON, Dorset DT10 2AP
01258 817335
• website: www.ruraldorset.co.uk

Touring Park
Wareham Forest Touring Park, North Trigon,
WAREHAM, Dorset BH20 7NZ
01929 551393
e-mail: holiday@wareham-forest.co.uk
website:
http://freespace.virgin.net/wareham.forest

Self-Catering on Working Farm
Josephine Pearse, Tamarisk Farm Cottages,
WEST BEXINGTON, Dorchester,
Dorset DT2 9DF
01308 897784
• e-mail: tamarisk@eurolink.ltd.net
• website: www.tamariskfarm.co.uk

Self-Catering
Mrs J. Elwood, Lower Farmhouse,
Langton Herring, WEYMOUTH,
Dorset DT3 4JB
01305 871187
• e-mail: jane@mayo.fsbusiness.co.uk
• website: www.characterfarmcottages.co.uk

•DURHAM

Self-Catering
Peter Wilson, East Briscoe Farm,
Baldersdale, BARNARD CASTLE,
Co Durham DL12 9UL
01833 650087
• e-mail: fhg@eastbriscoe.co.uk
• website: www.eastbriscoe.co.uk

Hotel / Golf
Ramside Hall Hotel, Carrville, DURHAM,
Co Durham DH1 1TD
0191 3865282
• e-mail: info@ramsidehallhotel.co.uk
• website: www.ramsidehallhotel.co.uk

Self-Catering
Raby Estates Holiday Cottages,
Upper Teesdale Estate Office,
MIDDLETON-IN-TEESDALE, Barnard Castle,
Co Durham DL12 0QH
01833 640209
• e-mail: teesdaleestate@rabycastle.com
• website: www.rabycastle.com

•GLOUCESTERSHIRE

Lodge
Ian Gibson, Thornbury Golf Lodge, Bristol
Road, Thornbury, BRISTOL, Gloucestershire
01454 281144
• e-mail: info@thornburygc.co.uk
• website: www.thornburygc.co.uk

B & B
Mrs G. Jeffrey, Brymbo, Honeybourne Lane,
Mickleton, CHIPPING CAMPDEN,
Gloucestershire GL55 6PU
01386 438890
• e-mail: enquiries@brymbo.com
• website: www.brymbo.com

Farmhouse B & B
Mrs D. Gwilliam, Dryslade Farm,
English Bicknor, COLEFORD,
Gloucestershire, GL16 7PA
01594 860259
• e-mail: dryslade@agriplus.net
• website: www.drysladefarm.co.uk

Inn
The Wild Duck, EWEN, Gloucestershire
01285 770310
• e-mail: wduckinn@aol.com
• website: www.thewildduck.co.uk

Farmhouse B & B
Suzie Paton, Milton Farm, FAIRFORD,
Gloucestershire GL7 4HZ
01285 712205
• e-mail: milton@farmersweekly.net
• website: www.milton-farm.co.uk

Guest House / Farm
Gunn Mill Guest House, Lower Spout Lane,
MITCHELDEAN, Gloucestershire GL17 0EA
01594 827577
• e-mail: info@gunnmillhouse.co.uk
• website: www.gunnmillhouse.co.uk

B & B
Mrs F.J. Adams, Aston House,
Broadwell, MORETON-IN-MARSH,
Gloucestershire GL56 0TJ
01451 830475
• e-mail: fja@netcomuk.co.uk
• website:
www.netcomuk.co.uk/~nmfa/aston_house.html

Farmhouse B & B
Robert Smith, Corsham Field Farmhouse,
Bledington Road, STOW-ON-THE-WOLD,
Gloucestershire GL54 1JH
• e-mail: farmhouse@corshamfield.co.uk
• website: www.corshamfield.co.uk

B & B
Mrs Williams, Abbots Court, Church End,
Twyning, TEWKESBURY, Gloucestershire
GL20 6DA
01684 292515
• e-mail: bernie@abbotscourt.fsbusiness.co.uk
• website:
  www.glosfarmhols.co.uk/abbots-court/

B & B
Mrs Wendy Swait, Inschdene,
Atcombe Road, SOUTH WOODCHESTER,
Stroud, Gloucestershire GL5 5EW
01453 873254
• e-mail: malcolm.swait@repp.co.uk
• website: www.inschdene.co.uk

•HAMPSHIRE

B & B
Mrs Arnold-Brown, Hilden B&B,
Southampton Road, Boldre,
BROCKENHURST, Hampshire SO41 8PT
01590 623682
• website: www.newforestbandb-hilden.co.uk

Caravan & Camping
Kingfisher Caravan Park, Browndown Road,
Stokes Bay, GOSPORT,
Hampshire PO13 9BG
023 9250 2611
• e-mail: info@kingfisher-caravan-park.co.uk
• website: www.kingfisher-caravan-park.co.uk

Caravan & Campsite
Hayling Island Family Campsites,
Copse Lane, HAYLING ISLAND, Hampshire
023 9246 2479, 023 9246 4695, 023 9246 3684
• e-mail: lowertye@euphony.net
• website: www.haylingcampsites.co.uk

B & B
Mr & Mrs Farrell, Honeysuckle House,
24 Clinton Road, LYMINGTON,
Hampshire SO41 9EA
01590 676635
• e-mail: derekfarrell1@btopenworld.com
• website:
  www.newforest.demon.co.uk/honeysuckle.htm

Hotel
Woodlands Lodge Hotel, Bartley Road,
Woodlands, NEW FOREST,
Hampshire SO40 7GN
023 8029 2257
• e-mail: reception@woodlands-lodge.co.uk
• website: www.woodlands-lodge.co.uk

B & B
Mr & Mrs T. Jelley, Appledore Cottage,
Holmsley Road, Wootton, NEW MILTON,
Hampshire, BH25 5TR
01425 629506
• e-mail: info@appledorecottage.co.uk
• website:
  www.newforest-online.co.uk/appledore

•HEREFORDSHIRE

Hotel
The Steppes, Ullingswick,
Near HEREFORD, HR1 3JG
01432 820424
• e-mail: info@steppeshotel.co.uk
• website: www.steppeshotel.co.uk

B & B / Farm
Mrs D Sinclair, Holly House Farm,
Allensmore, HEREFORD,
Herefordshire HR2 9BH
01432 277294
• e-mail: hollyhousefarm@aol.com
• website: www.hollyhousefarm.org.uk

B & B
Mrs Gill Andrews, Webton Court
Farmhouse, KINGSTONE,
Herefordshire HR2 9NF
01981 250220
• e-mail: gill@webton.fsnet.co.uk

B & B
Mrs S.W. Born, The Coach House, Putley,
LEDBURY, Herefordshire HR8 2QP
01531 670684
• e-mail: wendyborn@putley-coachhouse.co.uk
• website: www.putley-coachhouse.co.uk

Self-Catering
Mrs Jane Viner, Docklow Manor, Docklow,
LEOMINSTER, Herefordshire HR6 0RX
01568 760668
• e-mail: jane@docklowmanor.freeserve.co.uk
• website: www.docklow-manor.co.uk

B & B
Mrs I. Pritchard, Olchon Cottage Farm,
LONGTOWN, Herefordshire HR2 0NS
01873 860233
• website: www.golden-valley.co.uk/olchon/

Guest House / Farm
Mrs Drzymalski, Thatch Close, Llangrove,
ROSS-ON-WYE, Herefordshire HR9 6EL
01989 770300
• e-mail: thatch.close@virgin.net
• website: www.thatchclose.com

•ISLE OF WIGHT

Caravan & Camping
Castlehaven Caravan Site, Niton, Near
Ventnor, Isle of Wight, PO38 2ND
01983 855556
• e-mail: caravans@castlehaven.co.uk
• website: www.castlehaven.co.uk

•KENT

Caravan & Camping
Woodlands Park, Tenterden Road,
BIDDENDEN, Kent
01580 291216
• e-mail: woodlandsp@aol.com
• website: www.campingsite.co.uk

Self-Catering
Marion Fuller, Three Chimneys Farm,
Bedgebury Road, GOUDHURST,
Kent TN17 2RA
• e-mail: marionfuller@threechimneysfarm.co.uk
• website: www.threechimneysfarm.co.uk

Farm B & B / Camping
Julia Soyke, Manor Court Farm, Ashurst,
TUNBRIDGE WELLS, Kent TN3 9TB
01892 740279
• e-mail: jsoyke@jsoyke.freeserve.co.uk
• website: www.manorcourtfarm.co.uk

•LEICESTERSHIRE

Guest House
The Highbury Guest House,
146 Leicester Road, LOUGHBOROUGH,
Leicestershire LE11 2AQ
01509 230545
• e-mail: emkhighbury@supanet.com
• website: www.thehighburyguesthouse.co.uk

•LINCOLNSHIRE

B & B
Jenny Dixon, 19 West Street, Kings Cliffe,
PETERBOROUGH, Lincolnshire PE8 6XB
01780 470365
• e-mail: kjhl-dixon@hotmail.com
• website: kingjohnhuntinglodge.com

Hotel
Petwood Hotel, Stixwood Road,
WOODHALL SPA, Lincolnshire
01526 352411
• e-mail: reception@petwood.co.uk
• website: www.petwood.co.uk

•NORFOLK

Self-Catering
Sand Dune Cottages, Tan Lane,
CAISTER-ON-SEA, Great Yarmouth, Norfolk
01493 720352
• e-mail: sand.dune.cottages@amserve.net
• website: www.eastcoastlive.co.uk/sites/
    sandunecottages.php

Farmhouse B & B
Mrs Jenny Bell, Peacock House,
Peacock Lane, Old Beetley, DEREHAM,
Norfolk NR20 4DG
• e-mail: PeackH@aol.com
• website:
www.SmoothHound.co.uk/hotels/peacockh.htm

Self-Catering
Nannette Catchpole, Walcot Green Farm,
DISS, Norfolk IP22 5SU
01379 652806
• e-mail: n.catchpole.wgf@virgin.net
• website: www.walcotgreenfarm.co.uk

Self-Catering
Idyllic Cottages at Vere Lodge,
South Raynham, FAKENHAM,
Norfolk NR21 7HE
01328 838261
• e-mail: major@verelodge.co.uk
• website: www.idylliccottages.co.uk

Self-Catering
Blue Riband Holidays, HEMSBY,
Great Yarmouth, Norfolk NR29 4HA
01493 730445
• website: www.BlueRibandHolidays.co.uk

Farmhouse B & B
Mrs Lynda Mack, Hempstead Hall, HOLT,
Norfolk NR25 6TN
01263 712224
• website: www.broadland.com/hempsteadhall

Guest House B & B
Mrs Christine Lilah Thrower, Whincliff,
Cromer Road, MUNDESLEY-ON-SEA,
Norfolk NR11 8DU
01263 721554
• e-mail: whincliff@freeuk.com
• website: http://whincliff.freeuk.com

Self-Catering
Mr & Mrs Moore, Mangreen Farm Holiday
Cottages, STANFIELD, Dereham,
Norfolk NR20 4HZ
01328 700272
• e-mail: bettymick@compuserve.com
• website: www.mangreen.co.uk

Inn
The Lifeboat Inn and Old Coach House,
Ship Lane, THORNHAM, Norfolk PE36 6LT
01485 512236
• website: www.llifeboatinn.co.uk

•NORTHUMBERLAND

Self-Catering
Village Farm Self-Catering, Town Foot Farm,
Shilbottle, ALNWICK,
Northumberland NE66 2HG
01665 575591
• e-mail: crissy@villagefarmcottages.co.uk
• website: www.villagefarmcottages.co.uk

Self-Catering
Mrs Helen Wyld, New Moor House,
Edlingham, ALNWICK,
Northumberland NE66 2BT
01665 574638
• e-mail: stay@newmoorhouse.co.uk
• website: www.newmoorhouse.co.uk

Hotel
The Cobbled Yard Hotel Ltd, 40 Walkergate,
BERWICK-UPON-TWEED,
Northumberland TD15 1DJ
01289 308407
• e-mail:
cobbledyardhotel@berwick35.fsnet.co.uk
• website: www.cobbledyardhotel.com

Caravans
D.J. Caravan Holidays (Haggerston Castle),
c/o Mr J. Lane, 11 Wallis Street, Penshaw,
Houghton-le-Spring DH4 7HB
• e-mail: joseph_lane1@hotmail.com
• website: www.djcaravanholidays.com

•OXFORDSHIRE

B & B
Carol Ellis, Wynford House, 79 Main Road,
Long Hanborough, BLADON,
Oxfordshire OX29 8JX
01993 881402
• website:
www.accommodation.net/wynford.htm

Inn
The Kings Head Inn, The Green,
BLEDINGTON, Oxfordshire
01608 658365
• e-mail: kingshead@orr-ewing.com
• website: www.kingsheadinn.net

Guest House / B & B
Gorselands Hall, Boddington Lane,
North Leigh, WITNEY,
Oxfordshire OX29 6PU
01993 882292
• e-mail: hamilton@gorselandshall.com
• website: www.gorselandshall.com

Guest House
Mrs Elizabeth Simpson, Field View, Wood
Green, WITNEY, Oxfordshire OX28 1DE
01993 705485
• e-mail: bandb@fieldview-witney.co.uk
• website: www.fieldview-witney.co.uk

•SHROPSHIRE

Farm B & B
Mrs M. Jones, Acton Scott Farm,
Acton Scott, CHURCH STRETTON,
Shropshire SY6 6QN
01694 781260
• e-mail: bandb@actonscottfarm.co.uk
• website: www.actonscottfarm.co.uk

Guest House
Ron & Jenny Repath, Meadowlands,
Lodge Lane, Frodesley, DORRINGTON,
Shropshire SY5 7HD
01694 731350
• e-mail: meadowlands@talk21.com
• website: www.meadowlands.co.uk

B & B
Ravenscourt Manor, Woofferton,
LUDLOW, Shropshire SY8 4AL
01584 711905
• e-mail: ravenscourtmanor@amserve.com
• website:
www.s-h-systems.co.uk/hotels/ravenscourt.html

Self-Catering
Clive & Cynthia Prior, Mocktree Barns
Holiday Cottages, Leintwardine, LUDLOW,
Shropshire SY7 0LY
01547 540441
• e-mail: mocktreebarns@care4free.net
• website: www.mocktreeholidays.co.uk

Guest House & Self-Catering
Mrs E. Purnell, Ravenscourt Manor,
Woofferton, LUDLOW, Shropshire SY8 6AL
01584 711905
• e-mail: ravenscourtmanor@amserve.com
• website:
www.smoothhound.co.uk/ravenscourt

Inn
M.A. Tennant, The Talbot Inn, High Street,
MUCH WENLOCK, Shropshire TF13 6AA
01952 727077
• e-mail: maggie@talbotinn.idps.co.uk
• website: www.the-talbot-inn.co.uk

B & B
Mrs P. Morrissey, Top Farm House, Knockin,
Near OSWESTRY, Shropshire SY10 2HN
01691 682582
• e-mail: p.a.m@knockin.freeserve.co.uk
• website: www.topfarmknockin.co.uk

Hotel
Pen-y-Dyffryn Country Hotel, OSWESTRY,
Shropshire SY10 7JD
01691 653700
• e-mail: stay@peny.co.uk
• website: www.peny.co.uk

B & B
Lythwood Hall Bed & Breakfast,
2 Lythwood Hall, Lythwood, Bayston Hill,
SHREWSBURY, Shropshire SY3 0AD
07074 874747
• e-mail: lythwoodhall@amserve.net

Self-Catering
Mrs V. Evans, Church Farm, Rowton,
Near Wellington, TELFORD,
Shropshire TF6 6QY
01952 770381
• e-mail: church.farm@bigfoot.com
• website:
www.virtual-shropshire.co.uk/churchfarm

•SOMERSET

Guest House / Farm/ Self-Catering
Jackie & David Bishop, Toghill House Farm,
Wick, BATH, Somerset BS30 5RT
01225 891261
• website: www.toghillhousefarm.co.uk

B & B
Mrs C. Bryson, Walton Villa,
3 Newbridge Hill, BATH, Somerset BA1 3PW
01225 482792
• e-mail: walton.villa@virgin.net
• website: www.walton.izest.com

Self-Catering / Caravan & Camping
T.M. Hicks, Diamond Farm, Weston Road,
BREAN, Near Burnham-on-Sea,
Somerset TA8 2RL
01278 751263
• e-mail: trevor@diamondfarm42.freeserve.co.uk
• website: www.diamondfarm.co.uk

Caravan & Camping
Beachside Holiday Park, Coast Road,
BREAN SANDS, Burnham-on-Sea,
Somerset TA8 2QZ
01278 751346
• e-mail: beachside@breansands.fsnet.co.uk
• website: www.beachsideholidaypark.co.uk

Farm B&B / Self-catering
Delia Edwards, Brinsea Green Farm, Brinsea
Lane, Congresbury, Near BRISTOL,
North Somerset BS49 5JN
01934 852278
• e-mail: delia@brinseagreenfarm.co.uk
• website: www.brinseagreenfarm.co.uk

B & B
Mrs Alexander, Priors Mead,
23 Rectory Road, BURNHAM-ON-SEA,
Somerset TA8 2BZ
01278 782116
- e-mail: priorsmead@aol.com
- website: www.priorsmead.co.uk

B & B / Self-Catering
Butcombe Farm, Aldwick Vale, BUTCOMBE,
Near Blagdon, Somerset BS40 7UW
01761 462380
- e-mail: info@butcombe-farm.demon.co.uk
- website: www.butcombe-farm.demon.co.uk

Caravan & Camping Park
Broadway House Holiday Touring Caravan &
Camping Park, CHEDDAR,
Somerset BS27 3DB
01934 742610
- e-mail: enquiries@broadwayhouse.uk.com
- website: www.broadwayhouse.uk.com

B & B
Mrs C. Bacon, Honeydown Farm,
Seaborough Hill, CREWKERNE,
Somerset TA18 8PL
01460 72665
- e-mail: cb@honeydown.freeserve.co.uk
- website: www.honeydown.freeserve.co.uk

Hotel
Yarn Market Hotel, 25-33 High Street,
DUNSTER, Somerset TA24 6SF
01643 821425
- e-mail: yarnmarket.hotel@virgin.net
- website: www.yarnmarkethotel.co.uk

Inn
Exmoor White Horse Inn, EXFORD,
Somerset TA24 7PY
01643 831229
- website: www.exmoor-hospitality-inns.co.uk

Self-Catering
Mr Hughes, West Withy Farm Holiday
Cottages, Upton, Near Wiveliscombe,
EXMOOR, Somerset TA4 2JH
01398 371258
- e-mail: westwithyfarm@exmoor-cottages.com
- website: www.exmoor-cottages.com

Self-Catering / B & B
Mrs Joan Atkins, 2 Edgcott Cottage,
Exford, EXMOOR, Somerset TA24 7QG
01643 831564
- e-mail: info@stilemoorexmoor.co.uk
- website: www.stilemoorexmoor.co.uk

Farm / Self-Catering
Mrs Styles, Wintershead Farm, Simonsbath,
EXMOOR, Somerset TA24 7LF
01643 831222
- e-mail: info@wintershead.co.uk
- website: www.wintershead.co.uk

Farm Self-Catering & Camping
Westermill Farm, Exford, EXMOOR,
Somerset TA24 7NJ
01643 831238
- e-mail: holidays@westermill-exmoor.co.uk
- website: www.exmoorfarmholidays.co.uk

Self-Catering
Mrs N. Hanson, Woodcombe Lodges,
Bratton, MINEHEAD,
Somerset TA24 8SQ
01643 702789
- e-mail: nicola@woodcombelodge.co.uk
- website: www.woodcombelodge.co.uk

B & B
Mr P.R. Weir, Slipper Cottage,
41 Bishopston, MONTACUTE,
Somerset TA15 6UX
01935 823073
- e-mail: sue.weir@totalise.co.uk
- website: www.slippercottage.co.uk

B & B
Mr & Mrs Painter, Blorenge House,
57 Staplegrove Road, TAUNTON, Somerset
TA1 1DG
01823 283005
- e-mail: enquiries@blorengehouse.co.uk
- website: www.blorengehouse.co.uk

Farm / B & B
Yew Tree Farm, THEALE, Near Wedmore,
Somerset BS28 4SN
01934 712475
- e-mail: enquiries@yewtreefarmbandb.co.uk
- website: www.yewtreefarmbandb.co.uk

... Cottages, 2 The Croft, Anchor
...HET, Somerset TA23 0BY
...1
...tcottages@talk21.com
• website: www.cottagessomerset.com

Farm / B & B
Mrs Sheila Stott, 'Lana', Hollow Farm,
Westbury-sub-Mendip, WELLS, Somerset
01749 870635
• e-mail: sheila@stott.2366

Hotel
Braeside Hotel, 2 Victoria Park,
WESTON-SUPER-MARE,
Somerset BS23 2HZ
01934 626642
• e-mail: braeside@tesco.net
• website: www.braesidehotel.co.uk

•STAFFORDSHIRE

Farm B & B / Self-Catering
Mrs M. Hiscoe-James, Offley Grove Farm,
Adbaston, ECCLESHALL,
Staffordshire ST20 0QB
01785 280205
• e-mail: accom@offleygrovefarm.freeserve.co.uk
• website: www.offleygrovefarm.co.uk

Guest House
Ruth Franks, The Beehive,
Churnet View Road, OAKAMOOR,
Staffordshire ST10 3AE
01538 702420
• e-mail: thebeehiveoakamoor@btinternet.com
• website: www.thebeehiveguesthouse.co.uk

•SUFFOLK

Guest House
Kay Dewsbury, Manorhouse, The Green,
Beyton, BURY ST EDMUNDS,
Suffolk IP30 9AF
01359 270960
• e-mail: manorhouse@beyton.com
• website: www.beyton.com

B & B / Self-Catering
Tim & Sarah Kindred, High House Farm,
Cransford, FRAMLINGHAM, Woodbridge,
Suffolk IP13 9PD
01728 663461
• e-mail: info@highhousefarm.co.uk
• website: www.highhousefarm.co.uk

Farmhouse / Caravan Site
Fiddlers Hall, Cransford, FRAMLINGHAM,
Woodbridge, Suffolk IP13 9PQ
• e-mail: johnmann@suffolkonline.com
• website: www.fiddlershall.com

Self-Catering
Kessingland Cottages, Rider Haggard Lane,
KESSINGLAND. Contact: S. Mahmood, 156
Bramley Road, Beckenham, Kent BR3 6PG
020 8650 0539
• e-mail: jeeptrek@kjti.freeserve.co.uk
• website: www.k-cottage.co.uk

Self-Catering
Southwold Self-Catering Properties.
H.A. Adnams, 98 High Street,
SOUTHWOLD, Suffolk IP18 6DP
01502 723292
• e-mail: haadnams_lets@ic24.net
• website: www.haadnams.com

Self-Catering
Mr M. Scott, The Grove, Priory Green,
Edwardstone, Lavenham, SUDBURY,
Suffolk CO10 5PP
01787 211115
• e-mail: mark@grove-cottages.co.uk
• website: www.grove-cottages.co.uk

Hotel
The Crown & Castle, Orford, WOODBRIDGE,
Suffolk IP12 2LJ
01394 450205
• e-mail: info@crownandcastle.co.uk
• website: www.crownandcastle.co.uk

•SURREY

Hotel
Chase Lodge Hotel, 10 Park Road,
Hampton Wick, KINGSTON-UPON-THAMES,
Surrey KT1 4AS
020 8943 1862
• e-mail: info@chaselodgehotel.com
• website: www.chaselodgehotel.com

Self-Catering
Mrs J.A. Vause, Woodend, High Cotts Lane,
WEST CLANDON, Surrey GU4 7XA
01483 222644
• e-mail: deevause@amserve.net
• website: www.hillcrest-mortehue.co.uk

---

visit the FHG website
www.holidayguides.com

•EAST SUSSEX

Self-Catering
Eva Morris, Pekes, CHIDDINGLY,
East Sussex
020 7352 8088
• e-mail: pekes.afa@virgin.net
• website: www.pekesmanor.com

Hotel
Beauport Park Hotel, Battle Road,
HASTINGS, East Sussex TN38 8EA
01424 851222
• e-mail:
   reservations@beauportprkhotel.demon.co.uk
• website: www.beauportparkhotel.co.uk

Self-Catering
Beach Cottages, Claremont Road,
SEAFORD BN25 2QQ.
Contact: Julia Lewis, 47 Wandle Bank,
London, SW19 1DW
020 8542 5073
• website: www.beachcottages.info

•WEST SUSSEX

Caravan & Camping
Wicks Farm Holiday Park, Redlands Lane,
West Wittering, CHICHESTER,
West Sussex PO20 8QD
01243 513116
• e-mail: wicks.farm@virgin.net
• website: www.wicksfarm.co.uk

B & B
Mrs M.R. Milton, Beacon Lodge B&B,
London Road, WATERSFIELD,
West Sussex RH20 1NH
01798 831026
• e-mail: beaconlodge@hotmail.com
• website: www.beaconlodge.co.uk

•WARWICKSHIRE

Guest House
Linhill Guest House, 35 Evesham Place,
STRATFORD-UPON-AVON,
Warwickshire CV37 6HT
01789 292879
• e-mail: linhill@bigwig.net
• website: www.linhillguesthouse.co.uk

Guest House / B & B
Julia Downie, Holly Tree Cottage,
Pathlow, STRATFORD-UPON-AVON,
Warwickshire CV37 0ES
01789 204461
• e-mail: john@hollytree-cottage.co.uk
• website: www.hollytree-cottage.co.uk

Guest House
Mr & Mrs Learmount,
Green Haven Guest House,
217 Evesham Road,
STRATFORD-UPON-AVON,
Warwickshire CV37 9AS
01789 297874
• e-mail: information@green-haven.co.uk
• website: www.green-haven.co.uk

Self-Catering
Rayford Caravan Park, Riverside,
Tiddington Road,
STRATFORD-UPON-AVON,
Warwickshire CV37 7BE
01789 293964
• e-mail: info@stratfordcaravans.co.uk
• website: www.stratfordcaravans.co.uk

Guest House
Mr & Mrs D. Clapp, The Croft,
Haseley Knob, WARWICK,
Warwickshire CV35 7NL
01926 484447
• e-mail: david@croftguesthouse.co.uk
• website: www.croftguesthouse.co.uk

B & B / Self-Catering
Mrs Elizabeth Draisey, Forth House,
44 High Street, WARWICK,
Warwickshire CV34 4AX
01926 401512
• e-mail: info@forthhouseuk.co.uk
• website: www.forthhouseuk.co.uk

FHG PUBLICATIONS LTD
publish a large range of well-known accommodation guides.
We will be happy to send you details or you can use the
order form at the back of this book.

•WEST MIDLANDS

Hotel
Mr Price, Featherstone Farm Hotel,
New Road, Featherstone, WOLVERHAMPTON,
West Midlands WV10 7NW
01902 725371
• website:
www.featherstonefarm.co.uk/index.html

•WILTSHIRE

Farmhouse / Board
Mrs D. Robinson, Boyds Farm, Gastard,
Near Corsham, BATH, Wiltshire SN13 9PT
01249 713146
• e-mail:
dorothyrobinson@boyds.farm.freeserve.co.uk

Self-Catering
Mrs S. King, Wick Farm, LACOCK,
Chippenham, Wiltshire SN15 2LU
01249 730244
• e-mail: kingsilverlands2@btinternet.com
• website: www.cheeseandcyderhouses.co.uk

Guest House
Alan & Dawn Curnow, Hayburn Wyke Guest
House, 72 Castle Road, SALISBURY,
Wiltshire SP1 3RL
01722 412627
• e-mail: hayburn.wyke@tinyonline.co.uk
• website: www.hayburnwykeguesthouse.co.uk

•WORCESTERSHIRE

Guesthouse / Farm
Mrs S Harrison, Middleton Grange,
Salwarpe, DROITWICH SPA,
Worcestershire WR9 0AH
01905 451678
• e-mail: salli@middletongrange.com
• website: www.middletongrange.com

•EAST YORKSHIRE

B & B
Paws-a-While, KILNWICK PERCY,
East Yorkshire YO42 1UF
01759 301168
• e-mail: paws.a.while@lineone.net
• website: www.pawsawhile.net

•NORTH YORKSHIRE

Self-Catering
Recommended Cottages, North Yorkshire
08700 718 718
• website: www.recommended-cottages.co.uk

B & B / Self-Catering
Mrs E.J. Moorhouse,
The Courtyard at Duke's Place,
Bishop Thornton, HARROGATE,
North Yorkshire HG3 3JY
01765 620229
• e-mail: jakimoorhouse@onetel.net.uk

Caravan & Camping
Bainbridge Ings, Caravan & Camping Site,
HAWES, North Yorkshire DL8 3NU
01969 667354
• e-mail: janet@bainbridge-ings.co.uk
• website: www.bainbridge-ings.co.uk

Farm B & B / Self-Catering
John & Felicity Wiles,
Sinnington Common Farm,
KIRKBYMOORSIDE, York,
North Yorkshire YO62 6NX
01751 431719
• e-mail: felicity@scfarm.demon.co.uk
• website: www.scfarm.demon.co.uk

Farm Self-Catering
A.W. & A. Turnbull, Whitethorn Farm,
Rook Barulth, KIRKYBYMOORSIDE,
York, North Yorkshire
01751 431298
• e-mail: turnbull@whitethornfarm.fsnet.co.uk
• website: www.cottageguide.co.uk/oak-lodge

Farmhouse B & B
Mrs Julie Clarke, Middle Farm,
Woodale, Coverdale, LEYBURN,
North Yorkshire DL8 4TY
01969 640271
• e-mail: julie-clarke@amserve.com
• website:
www.yorkshirenet.co.uk/stayat/middlefarm

Self-Catering
Coronation and Forge Valley Cottages,
c/o Mr David Beeley, Barn House, Westgate,
OLD MALTON, North Yorkshire YO17 7HE
01653 698251
• e-mail:
enquiries@coronationfarmcottage.co.uk
• website: www.coronationfarmcottage.co.uk

B & B / Self-Catering
Mrs Sandra Pickering, "Nabgate",
Wilton Road, Thornton-le-Dale, PICKERING,
North Yorkshire YO18 7QP
01751 474279
• website: www.nabgateguesthouse.co.uk

Guest House
Mrs Ella Bowes, Banavie, Roxby Road,
Thornton-Le-Dale, PICKERING, North
Yorkshire YO18 7SX
01751 474616
• e-mail: ella@banavie.fsbusiness.co.uk
• website: www.banavie.uk.com

Hotel
Ganton Greyhound, Main Street, Ganton,
Near SCARBOROUGH,
North Yorkshire YO12 4NX
01944 710116
• e-mail: gantongreyhound@supanet.com
• website: www.gantongreyhound.com

Guest House
Sue & Tony Hewitt,
Harmony Country Lodge,
80 Limestone Road, Burniston,
SCARBOROUGH, North Yorkshire YO13 0DG
0800 2985840
• e-mail: tony@harmonylodge.net
• website: www.harmonylodge.net

Touring Caravan Park
Cayton Village Caravan Park, Mill Lane,
Cayton, SCARBOROUGH,
North Yorkshire YO11 3NN
• e-mail: info@caytontouring.co.uk
• website: www.caytontouring.co.uk

Hotel
Mrs M.M Abbott, Howdale Hotel,
121 Queen's Parade, SCARBOROUGH,
North Yorkshire YO12 7HU
01723 372696
• e-mail: mail@howdalehotel.co.uk
• website: www.howdalehotel.co.uk

Farmhouse B & B / Self-Catering
Mrs Heather Simpson, Low Skibeden
Farmhouse & Cottage, SKIPTON,
North Yorkshire
01756 793849
• website:
www.yorkshirenetco.uk/accgde/lowskibeden

Self-Catering
Mrs Jones, New Close Farm,
Kirkby Malham, SKIPTON,
North Yorkshire BD23 4DP
01729 830240
• e-mail:
brendajones@newclosefarmyorkshire.co.uk
• website: www.newclosefarmyorkshire.co.uk

Self-Catering
Mrs Knowlson, Thrush House,
SUTTON-ON-FOREST, York,
North Yorkshire YO61 1ED
• e-mail: kmkholcottyksuk@aol.com
• website:
www.holidayskmkholcotts-yks.uk.com

Hotel
The Golden Fleece Hotel, Market Place,
THIRSK North Yorkshire
01845 523108
• e-mail: goldenfleece@bestwestern.co.uk
• website: www.goldenfleecehotel.com

Self-Catering
Anne Fawcett,
Mile House Farm Country Cottages,
Mile House Farm, Hawes, WENSLEYDALE,
North Yorkshire DL8 3PT
01969 667481
• e-mail: milehousefarm@hotmail.com
• website: www.wensleydale.uk.com

Self-Catering
Mrs Sue Cooper, St Edmunds, The Green,
Crakehall, Bedale, WENSLEYDALE,
North Yorkshire DL8 1HP
01677 423584
• e-mail:
stedmundscountrycottages@hotmail.com
• website: www.crakehall.org.uk

Self-Catering
Westclose House (Allaker),
WEST SCRAFTON, North Yorkshire
c/o Mr A Cave,
020 8567 4862
• e-mail: ac@adriancave.com
• website: www.adriancave.com/yorks

Self-Catering
White Rose Holiday Cottages,
c/o Mrs Roberts, 5 Brook Park, Sleights,
Near WHITBY, North Yorkshire YO21 1RT
01947 810763
- e-mail: enquiries@whiterosecottages.co.uk
- website: www.whiterosecottages.co.uk

Self-Catering
Mrs N. Pattinson, South House Farm,
Fylingthorpe, WHITBY,
North Yorkshire YO22 4UQ
01947 880243
- e-mail: kmp@bogglehole.fsnet.co.uk
- website: www.southhousefarm.co.uk

B & B / Self-Catering / Holiday Caravans
Mr & Mrs Tyerman, Partridge Nest Farm,
Eskdaleside, Sleights, WHITBY,
North Yorkshire YO22 5ES
01947 810450
- e-mail: barbara@partridgenestfarm.com
- website: www.partridgenestfarm.com

B & B
Mrs Sally Robinson, Valley View Farm,
Old Byland, Helmsley, YORK,
North Yorkshire YO6 5LG
01439 798221
- e-mail: sally@valleyviewfarm.com
- website: www.valleyviewfarm.com

Guest House / Self-Catering
Mr Gary Hudson, Orillia House,
89 The Village, Stockton on Forest,
YORK, North Yorkshire YO3 9UP
01904 400600
- e-mail: orillia@globalnet.co.uk
- website: www.orilliahouse.co.uk

Self-Catering
Mr N. Manasir, York Lakeside Lodges, Moor
Lane, YORK, North Yorkshire YO24 2QU
01904 702346
- e-mail: neil@yorklakesidelodges.co.uk
- website: www.yorklakesidelodges.co.uk

•WEST YORKSHIRE

Self-Catering
Summerwine Cottages, West Royd Farm,
Marsh Lane, Shepley, near HOLMFIRTH,
Huddersfield, West Yorkshire
01484 602147
- e-mail: summerwinecottages@lineone.net
- website: www.summerwinecottages.co.uk

•SCOTLAND

•ABERDEEN, BANFF & MORAY

Guest House
E. Robertson,
Aberdeen Springbank Guesthouse,
6 Springbank Terrace, ABERDEEN,
Aberdeenshire AB11 6LS
01224 592048
- e-mail: betty@springbank6.fsnet.co.uk
- website:
  www.aberdeenspringbankguesthouse.co.uk
  or www.aberdeen-guesthouse.co.uk

B & B
Mrs E. Malim, Invercairn House, BRODIE,
by Forres, Moray IV36 2TD
01309 641261
- e-mail: invercairnhouse@supanet.com
- website: www.invercairnhouse.co.uk

B & B
Mrs H. Massie, Milton of Grange Farm,
FORRES, Morayshire IV36 0TR
01309 676360
- e-mail: hildamassie@aol.com
- website: www.forres-accommodation.co.uk

•ARGYLL & BUTE

Inn
Mr D. Fraser, Cairndow Stagecoach Inn,
CAIRNDOW, Argyll PA26 8BN
01499 600286
- e-mail: cairndowinn@aol.com

B & B
Mrs D. MacCormick, Mains Farm,
CARRADALE, Campbeltown,
Argyll PA28 6QG
01583 431216
- e-mail:
  maccormick@mainsfarm.freeserve.co.uk

Guest House
A.J. Burke, Orchy Bank, DALMALLY,
Argyll PA33 1AS
01838 200370
- e-mail: aj.burke@talk21.com
- website:
  www.loch-awe.com/orchybank/

Self-Catering
Mrs Isabella Crawford, Blarghour Farm
Cottages, Loch Awe-side, By DALMALLY,
Argyll PA33 1BW
01866 833246
- e-mail: **blarghour@btconnect.com**
- website: **www.self-catering-argyll.co.uk**

B & B / Self-Catering
R. Gayre, Minard Castle B&B/Self-Catering,
Minard, INVERARAY, Argyll PA32 8YB
01546 886272
- e-mail: **reinoldgayre@minardcastle.com**
- website: **www.minardcastle.com**

Self-Catering
B & M Phillips, Kilbride Croft, Balvicar,
ISLE OF SEIL, Argyll PA34 4RD
01852 300475
- e-mail: **kilbridecroft@aol.com**
- website: **www.kilbridecroft.fsnet.co.uk**

Self-Catering
Castle Sween Bay (Holidays) Ltd,
Ellery, LOCHGILPHEAD,
Argyll PA31 8PA
01880 770232
- e-mail: **info@ellary.com**
- website: **www.ellary.com**

Self-Catering
Linda Battison, Cologin House,
Lerags Glen, OBAN, Argyll PA3 4SE
01631 564501
- e-mail: **cologin@west-highland-holidays.co.uk**
- website: **www.west-highland-holidays.co.uk**

B & B
Mrs C. MacDonald, Bracker,
Polvinister Road, OBAN, Argyll
01631 564302
- e-mail: **cmacdonald@connectfree.co.uk**
- website: **www.bracker.co.uk**

Hotel
Willowburn Hotel, Clachan Seil,
by OBAN, Argyll PA34 4TJ
01852 300276
- e-mail: **willowburn.hotel@virgin.net**
- website: **www.willowburn.co.uk**

Self-Catering
Isolated Seashore Cottage,
c/o John Rankin, 12 Hamilton Place, Perth,
Tayside
01738 632580
- e-mail: **john@claddie.co.uk**
- website: **www.claddie.co.uk**

•AYRSHIRE & ARRAN

B & B
Mrs Wilcox, Fisherton Farm, Dunure,
AYR, Ayrshire KA7 4LF
01292 500223
- e-mail: **lesleywilcox@hotmail.com**
- website: **www.fishertonfarm.homestead.com**

Self-Catering
Arran Hideaways, Invercloy House,
Brodick, ISLE OF ARRAN
01770 302303
- e-mail: **info@arran-hideways.co.uk**
- website: **www.arran-hideaways.co.uk**

•BORDERS

Self-Catering
Mrs J. Gray, Saughs Farm Cottages,
Saughs Farm, BAILEY, Newcastleton,
Borders TD9 0TT
016977 48346
- e-mail: **skylark@onholiday.co.uk**
- website: **www.skylarkcottages.co.uk**

Self-Catering
Mrs A. Fraser, Overwells, Jedburgh,
ROXBURGH, Roxburghshire
01835 863020
- e-mail: **abfraser@btinternet.com**
- website: **www.overwells.co.uk**

•DUMFRIES & GALLOWAY

Hotel
The Urr Valley Hotel, Ernspie Road,
CASTLE DOUGLAS,
Dumfries & Galloway DG7 3JG
01556 502 188
- e-mail: **info@urrvalleyhotel.co.uk**
- website: **www.urrvalley.demon.co.uk**

Farm
Celia Pickup, Craigadam,
CASTLE DOUGLAS,
Dumfries & Galloway DG7 3HU
01556 650233
- e-mail: **enquiry@craigadam.com**
- website: **www.craigadam.com**

Self-Catering
Mr Ball, Barncrosh Leisure Co Ltd,
Barncrosh, CASTLE DOUGLAS,
Dumfries & Galloway DG7 1TX
01556 680216
• e-mail: enq@barncrosh.co.uk
• website: www.barncrosh.co.uk

Self-Catering
Catherine McDowall, Shawhill Farmhouse,
DUNDRENNAN,
Dumfries & Galloway DG6 4QT
• e-mail: mail@shawhill-cottages.co.uk
• website: www.shawhill-cottages.co.uk

Self-Catering
Rusko Holidays,
GATEHOUSE OF FLEET, Castle Douglas,
Dumfries & Galloway DG7 2BS
01557 814215
• e-mail: gilbey@rusko.demon.co.uk
• website: www.ruskoholidays.co.uk

B & B
June Deakins, Annandale House, MOFFAT,
Dumfriesshire DG10 9SA
01683 221460
• e-mail: june@annandalehouse.com
• website: www.annandalehouse.com

•DUNDEE & ANGUS

Farmhouse B & B
Rosemary Beatty, Brathinch Farm,
by BRECHIN, Angus DD9 7QX
01356 648292
• e-mail: adam.brathinch@btinternet.com

Self-Catering
Jenny Scott, Welton Farm,
The Welton of Kingoldrum, KIRRIEMUIR,
Angus DD8 5HY
01575 574743
• website: www.cottageguide.co.uk/thewelton

•EDINBURGH & LOTHIANS

Guest House
Kenneth Harkins, 78 East Main Street,
BLACKBURN, By Bathgate,
West Lothian EH47 7QS
01506 655221
• e-mail: cruachan.bb@virgin.net
• website: www.cruachan.co.uk

Guest House
Mr & Mrs McWilliams,
Ben Craig Guest House, 3 Craigmillar Park,
EDINBURGH, Lothians EH16 5PG
0131 667 2593
• e-mail: bencraighouse@dial.pipex.com
• website: www.bencraighouse.co.uk

B & B
McCrae's B&B, 44 East Claremont Street,
EDINBURGH, Lothians EH7 4JR
0131 556 2610
• e-mail: mccraes.bandb@lineone.net
• website:
  http://website.lineone.net/~mccraes.bandb

Guest House
Mrs Kay, Blossom House, 8 Minto Street,
EDINBURGH EH9 1RG
0131 667 5353
• e-mail: blossom_house@hotmail.com
• website: www.blossomguesthouse.co.uk

Guest House
D. Green, Ivy Guest House,
7 Mayfield Gardens, Newington,
EDINBURGH, Lothians EH9 2AX
0131 667 3411
• e-mail: don@ivyguesthouse.com
• website: www.ivyguesthouse.com

Guest House
International Guest House,
37 Mayfield Gardens, EDINBURGH,
Lothians EH9 2BX
0131 667 2511
• e-mail: intergh@easynet.co.uk
• website: www.accommodation-edinburgh.com

Hotel
Shirley Mowat, Dunstane House Hotel,
4 West Cootes, Haymarket, EDINBURGH
0131 337 6169
• e-mail:
  reservations@dunstanehousehotel.co.uk
• website: www.dunstanehousehotel.co.uk

B & B
Mr & Mrs R. Inglis, Thornton,
Edinburgh Road, LINLITHGOW,
Lothians EH49 6AA
01506 844693
• e-mail: inglisthornton@hotmail.com
• website: www.thornton-scotland.co.uk

visit the FHG website
www.holidayguides.com

•HIGHLANDS

Self-Catering
A. Simpson, Camusdarach Enterprises,
Camusdarach, ARISAIG,
Inverness-shire PH39 4NT
01687 450221
• e-mail: camdarach@aol.com
• website: www.camusdarach.com

Hotel
The Boat Hotel, BOAT OF GARTEN,
Inverness-shire PH24 3BH
01479 831258
• e-mail: info@boathotel.co.uk
• website: www.boathotel.co.uk

Guest House
Mrs Lynn Benge,
The Pines Country Guest House, Duthil,
CARRBRIDGE, Inverness-shire PH23 3ND
01479 841220
• e-mail: lynn@thepines-duthil.fsnet.co.uk
• website: www.thepines-duthil.fsnet.co.uk

B & B
Mrs Brenda Graham, "Caledonian Cottage",
Station Road, FORT AUGUSTUS,
Inverness-shire PH32 4AY
01320 366401
• e-mail: brenda@ipw.com
• website: www.ipw.com/calcot

Hotel
Allt-Nan-Ros Hotel, Onich, FORT WILLIAM,
Inverness-shire PH33 6RY
01855 821210
• e-mail: fhg@allt-nan-ros.co.uk
• website: www.allt-nan-ros.co.uk

Hotel
Clan Macduff Hotel, Achintore Road,
FORT WILLIAM, Inverness-shire PH33 6RW
01397 702341
• e-mail: reception@clanmacduff.co.uk
• website: www.clanmacduff.co.uk

Self-Catering
Linnhe Lochside Holidays, Corpach,
FORT WILLIAM PH33 7NL
01397 772376
• e-mail: holidays@linnhe.demon.co.uk
• website: www.linnhe-lochside-holidays.co.uk

Guest House
Norma E. McCallum, The Neuk, Corpach,
FORT WILLIAM, Inverness-shire PH33 7LR
01397 772244
• e-mail: theneuk@fortwilliamguesthouse.com
• website: www.theneuk.fsbusiness.co.uk

Self-Catering
Great Glen Holidays, Torlundy, FORT
WILLIAM, Inverness-shire
01397 703015
• e-mail: chris@greatglenchalets.demon.co.uk
• website: www.greatglenchalets.demon.co.uk

Self-Catering
Mr William Murray,
Springwell Holiday Homes, Onich,
FORT WILLIAM, Inverness-shire PH33 6RY
01855 821257
• e-mail: info@springwellholidayhomes.co.uk
• website: www.springwellholidayhomes.co.uk

B & B
Mrs M. MacLean, Innishfree, Lochyside,
FORT WILLIAM, Inverness-shire PH33 7NX
01397 705471
• e-mail: mburnsmaclean@aol.com
• website: www. innishfree.co.uk

Hotels
The Freedom of the Glen Family of Hotels,
Onich, near FORT WILLIAM,
Inverness-shire PH33 6RY
0871 222 3415
• e-mail: reservations@freedomglen.co.uk
• website: www.freedomglen.co.uk

Self-Catering
Miss Jean Ellice, Taigh-an-Lianach,
Aberchalder Farm, INVERGARRY,
Inverness-shire PH35 4HN
01809 501287
• website: www.ipw.com/aberchalder

Guest House / Self-Catering
Nick & Patsy Thompson, Insh House,
KINCRAIG, Kingussie
01540 651377
• e-mail: inshhouse@btinternet.com
• website: www.kincraig.com/inshhouse

Guest House
Gary Clulow, Sunset Guest House, MORAR,
by Mallaig, Inverness-shire PH40 4PA
01687 462259
• e-mail: sunsetgh@aol.com
• website: www.sunsetguesthouse.co.uk

Self-Catering Chalets / B & B
D.J. Mordaunt, Mondhuie, NETHY BRIDGE,
Inverness-shire PH25 3DF
01479 821062
- **e-mail: david@mondhuie.com**
- **website: www.mondhuie.com**

Guest House
Mrs J. MacLean, Foresters Bungalow,
Inchree, ONICH, Fort William,
Inverness-shire PH33 6SE
- **website: www.s-h-systems.co.uk/**
  hotels/forestersbungalow.html

Self-Catering
Mr A. Urquhart, Crofters Cottages,
15 Croft, POOLEWE, Ross-shire IV22 2JY
01445 781268
- **e-mail: croftcottages@btopenworld.com**
- **website: www.croftcottages.btinternet.co.uk**

Hotel
Mrs Campbell, Rhiconich Hotel,
RHICONICH, by Lairg, Sutherland IV27 4RN
01971 521224
- **e-mail: rhiconichhotel@aol.com**
- **website: www.rhiconichhotel.co.uk**

Self-Catering
Wildside Highland Lodges, By Loch Ness,
WHITEBRIDGE, Inverness-shire IV2 6UN
01456 486373
- **e-mail: info@wildsidelodges.com**
- **website: www.wildsidelodges.com**

•LANARKSHIRE

Self-Catering
Carmichael Country Cottages,
Carmichael Estate Office, Westmains,
Carmichael, BIGGAR, Lanarkshire ML12 6PG
01899 308336
- **e-mail: chiefcarm@aol.com**
- **website: www.carmichael.co.uk/cottages**

•PERTH & KINROSS

Self-Catering
Loch Tay Lodges, Remony,
ABERFELDY, Perthshire
01887 830209
- **e-mail: remony@btinternet.com**
- **website: www.lochtaylodges.co.uk**

Guest House
Janet Greenfield, "Annfield Guest House",
North Church Street, CALLANDER,
Perthshire
01877 330204
- **e-mail: janet-greenfield@amserve.com**

Guest House
J. Clifford, Merlindale, Perth Road,
CRIEFF, Perthshire
01764 655205
- **e-mail: merlin.dale@virgin.net**
- **website: www.merlindale.co.uk**

Self-Catering
Laighwood Holidays, Laighwood,
Butterstone, By DUNKELD,
Perthshire PH8 0HB
01350 724241
- **e-mail: holidays@laighwood.co.uk**
- **website: www.laighwood.co.uk**

Self Catering
Mrs Hunt, Wester Lix Holiday Cottages,
Wester Lix, KILLIN, Perthshire FK21 8RD
01567 820990
- **e-mail: gill@westerlix.co.uk**
- **website: www.westerlix.co.uk**

B & B
Mrs P. Honeyman, Auld Manse Guest House,
Pitcullen Crescent, PERTH, Perthshire PH2 7HT
01738 629187
- **e-mail: trishaatauldmanse@hotmail.com**
- **website: www.guesthouseperth.com**

Guest House
Jacky Catterall, Tulloch, Enochdhu,
by PITLOCHRY, Perthshire PH10 7PW
01250 881404
- **e-mail: maljac@tulloch83.freeserve.co.uk**
- **website: www.maljac.com**

•STIRLING & TROSSACHS

Caravan & Camping
Riverside Caravan Park, Dollarfield,
DOLLAR, Clackmannanshire FK14 7LX
01259 742896
- **e-mail: info@riverside-caravanpark.co.uk**
- **website: www.riverside-caravanpark.co.uk**

B & B
Mrs Strain, Hawthorndean, Wallacestone
Brae, Reddingmuirhead, FALKIRK,
Stirlingshire FK2 0DQ
- **e-mail: eileenstrain@yahoo.co.uk**

Guest House
Mrs Betty Ward, Ashbank Guest House,
105 Main Street, Redding, FALKIRK,
Stirlingshire FK2 9UQ
01324 716649
• e-mail: ashbank@guest-house.freeserve.co.uk
• website: www.bandbfalkirk.com

•ISLE OF SKYE

Guest House / B & B
Fiona Scott, Blairdhu House, Old Kyle Farm
Road, KYLEAKIN, Isle of Skye IV41 8PR
01599 534760
• e-mail: info@blairdhuhouse.co.uk
• website: www.blairdhuhouse.co.uk

•WALES

Self-Catering
Quality Cottages, Cerbid, Solva,
HAVERFORDWEST,
Pembrokeshire SA62 6YE
01348 837871
• website: www.qualitycottages.co.uk

•ANGLESEY & GWYNEDD

Country House
Jim and Marion Billingham, Preswylfa,
ABERDOVEY, Gwynedd LL35 0LE
01654 767239
• e-mail: info@preswylfa.co.uk
• website: www.preswylfa.co.uk

B & B
Mrs Murphy, Ingledene, Ravenspoint Road,
Trearddur Bay, ANGLESEY LL65 2YU
01407 861026
• e-mail: info@ingledene.co.uk
• website: www.ingledene.co.uk

B & B
Mrs J. Bown, Drws-y-Coed,
Llannerch-y-medd, ANGLESEY LL71 8AD
01248 470473
• e-mail: drws.ycoed@virgin.net
• website:
www.SmoothHound.co.uk/hotels/drwsycoed.html

Self-Catering within a Castle
Bryn Bras Castle, Llanrug,
near CAERNARFON Gwynedd LL55 4RE
01286 870210
• e-mail: holidays@brynbrascastle.co.uk
• website: www.brynbrascastle.co.uk

Self-Catering / Caravan
Plas-y-Bryn Chalet Park, Bontnewydd,
CAERNARFON, Gwynedd LL54 7YE
01286 672811
• e-mail: philplasybryn@aol.com
• website:
www.plasybrynholidayscaernarfon.co.uk

Hotel
Prince of Wales Hotel, Bangor Street,
CAERNARFON, Gwynedd
01286 673367
• e-mail: info@prince-of-wales-hotel.co.uk
• website: www.prince-of-wales-hotel.co.uk

Guest House
Mrs M.A. Parker, Seaspray Guest House,
4 Marine Terrace, CRICCIETH,
Gwynedd LL52 0EF
• e-mail: manya.parker@btopenworld.com
• website: www.seasprayguesthouse.co.uk

Self-Catering
Anwen Jones, Rhos Country Cottages,
Betws Bach, Ynys, CRICCIETH,
Gwynedd LL52 0PB
01758 720047
• e-mail: cottages@rhos.freeserve.co.uk
• website: www.rhos-cottages.co.uk

Guest House
Mrs M. Bamford, Ivy House,
Finsbury Square, DOLGELLAU,
Gwynedd LL40 1RF
01341 422535
• e-mail: marg.bamford@btconnect.com
• website: www.ukworld.net/ivyhouse

Self-Catering / Caravans
Minffordd Luxury Cottages & Caravans,
Minford, DULAS, Isle of Anglesey LL70 9HJ
01248 410678
• e-mail: enq@minffordd-holidays.com
• website: www.minffordd-holidays.com

B & B
Mrs G. McCreadie, Deri Isaf,
DULAS BAY, Anglesey LL70 9DX
01248 410536
• e-mail: mccreadie@deriisaf.freeserve.co.uk
• website: www.deriisaf.freeserve.co.uk

Farm B & B
Judy Hutchings, Tal y Foel, DWYRAN,
Anglesey, Gwynedd LL61 6LQ
01248 430377
• e-mail: riding@talyfoel.u-net.com
• website: www.tal-y-foel.co.uk

Self-Catering
Mrs S. Edwards, Dwyfach Cottages,
Pen-y-Bryn, Chwilog, PWLLHELI,
Gwynedd LL53 6SX
01766 810208
• e-mail: llyredwards@ukonline.co.uk
• website: www.dwyfach.co.uk

•NORTH WALES

Hotel
Fairy Glen Hotel, Beaver Bridge,
BETWS-Y-COED, Conwy,
North Wales LL24 0SH
01690 710269
• e-mail: fairyglenhotel@amserve.net
• website: www.fairyglenhotel.co.uk

Guest House
Mr M. Wilkie, Bryn Bella Guest House,
Lôn Muriau, Llanrwst Road,
BETWS-Y-COED, Gwynedd LL24 0HD
01690 710627
• e-mail: welcome@bryn-bella.co.uk
• website: www.bryn-bella.co.uk

Guest House / Self-Catering
Jim & Lilian Boughton,
Bron Celyn Guest House, Lôn Muriau,
Llanrwst Road, BETWS-Y-COED,
North Wales LL24 0HD
01690 710333
• e-mail: welcome@broncelyn.co.uk
• website: www.broncelyn.co.uk

B & B
Christine Whale, Brookside House,
Brookside Lane, Northop Hall,
near CHESTER CH7 4HN
01244 821146
• e-mail: christine@brooksidehouse.fsnet.co.uk
• website: www.brooksidehouse.fsnet.co.uk

Guest House
Sychnant Pass House, Sychnant Pass Road,
CONWY, North Wales LL32 8BJ
01492 596868
• e-mail: bresykes@sychnant-pass-house.co.uk
• website: www.sychnant-pass-house.co.uk

Hotel
Caerlyr Hall Hotel, Conwy Old Road,
Dwygyfylchi, CONWY,
North Wales LL34 6SW
01492 623518
• website: www.caerlyrhallhotel.co.uk

Guest House
Mr & Mrs Watson Jones, Glan Heulog Guest
House, Woodlands, Llanrwst Road, CONWY
01492 593845
• e-mail:
  glanheulog@no1guesthouse.freeserve.co.uk
• website: www.walesbandb.com

Self-Catering
Cottage, CONWAY c/o Mrs G.M. Simpole,
105 Haygreen Road, Terrington-St-Clement,
Kings Lynn, Norfolk PE34 4PU
01553 828897
• e-mail: gsimpole@care4free.net
• website: www.comestaywithus.com/
  wales-hotels/sc-full/brongain.html

Hotel
Moreton Park Lodge, Gledrid, Chirk,
WREXHAM, LL14 5DG
01691 776666
• e-mail: reservations@moretonpark.com
• website: www.moretonpark.com

•CARMARTHENSHIRE

B & B
Miss S Czerniewicz, Pant y Bas, Pentrefelin,
LLANDEILO, Carmarthenshire, SA19 6SD
01558 822809
- e-mail: anna@pantybas.fsnet.co.uk
- website: www.southwestwalesbandb.co.uk

•CEREDIGION

Self-Catering
Gilfach Holiday Village, Llwyncelyn, Near
ABERAERON, Ceredigion SA46 0HN
01545 580288
- e-mail: info@stratfordcaravans.co.uk
- website: www.stratfordcaravans.co.uk

Self-Catering
Mrs Tucker, Penffynnon, ABERPORTH,
Ceredigion SA43 2DA
01239 810387
- e-mail: jann@aberporth.com
- website: www.aberporth.com

• PEMBROKESHIRE

Self-Catering
John Lloyd, East Llanteg Farm Holiday
Cottages, Llanteg, near AMROTH,
Pembrokeshire SA67 8QA
01834 831336
- e-mail: john@pembrokeshireholiday.co.uk
- website: www.pembrokeshireholiday.co.uk

Farm B & B
Mrs Margaret Williams, Skerryback,
Sandy Haven, St Ishmaels, HAVERFORDWEST,
Pembrokeshire SA62 3DN
01646 636598
- e-mail: skerryback@pfh.co.uk
- website: www.pfh.co.uk/skerryback

Caravan Park
Scamford Caravan Park, Keeston,
HAVERFORDWEST, Pembrokeshire SA62 6HN
01437 710304
- e-mail: holidays@scamford.com
- website: www.scamford.com

Caravan & Camping
Brandy Brook Caravan & Camping Site,
Rhyndaston, Hayscastle,
HAVERFORDWEST, Pembrokeshire
01348 840272
- e-mail: f.m.rowe@btopenworld.com

Self-Catering
T.M. Hardman, High View, Catherine Street,
ST DAVIDS, Pembrokeshire SA62 6RT
01437 720616
- e-mail: enquiries@lowermoorcottages.co.uk
- website: www.lowermoorcottages.co.uk

Farm Guest House
Mrs Morfydd Jones, Lochmeyler Farm
Guest House, Llandeloy, Pen-y-Cwm,
near SOLVA, St David's,
Pembrokeshire SA62 6LL
01348 837724
- e-mail: stay@lochmeyler.co.uk
- website: www.lochmeyler.co.uk

•POWYS

Self-Catering
Mrs Ann Phillips, Tylebrythos Farm, Cantref,
BRECON, Powys LD3 8LR
01874 665329
- e-mail: ann@wernymarchog.co.uk
- website: www.wernymarchog.co.uk

Farm
Gilfach Farm, Sennybridge, BRECON,
Powys LD3 8TY
01874 636818
- e-mail: sm@mip.co.uk
- website: www.breconbeaconsriding.co.uk

Farm Self-Catering
Mrs E. Bally, Lane Farm, Painscastle,
BUILTH WELLS, Powys LD2 3JS
01497 851605
- e-mail: jbally@btclick.com
- website: www.lane-farm.co.uk

Self-Catering
Mrs Jones, Penllwyn Lodges, GARTHMYL,
Powys SY15 6SB
01686 640269
- e-mail: penllwynlodges@supanet.com
- website: www.penllwynlodges.co.uk

Self-Catering
Peter & Jackie Longley, Neuadd Farm,
Penybont, LLANDRINDOD WELLS,
Powys LD1 5SW
01597 851032
- e-mail: jackie@neuaddfarm.fsnet.co.uk
- website: www.neuaddfarm.co.uk

Motel / Caravans
The Park Motel, Crossgates,
LLANDRINDOD WELLS, Powys LD1 6RF
01597 851201
- e-mail: lisa@theparkmotel.freeserve.co.uk
- website: www.theparkmotel.freeserve.co.uk

B & B
Mrs V.J. Madeley, Greenfields, Kerry,
NEWTOWN, Powys SY16 4LH
01686 670596
- e-mail: info@greenfields-bb.co.uk
- website: www.greenfield-bb.co.uk

B & B
Laura Kostoris, Erw yr Danty,
TALYBONT-ON-USK, Brecon,
Powys LD3 7YN
01874 676498
- e-mail: kosto@ukonline.co.uk
- website: wiz.to/lifestyle/

•SOUTH WALES

Guest House / Self-Catering
Mrs Norma James, Wyrloed Lodge,
Manmoel, BLACKWOOD, Caerphilly, Gwent
01495 371198
- e-mail: norma.james@btinternet.com
- website: www.btinternet.com/~norma.james/

Sports Centre / Hotel
Welsh Institute of Sport, Sophia Gardens,
CARDIFF
029 20 300500
- e-mail: wis@scw.co.uk
- website: www.sports-council-wales.co.uk

Hotel
Mr & Mrs J. Llewellyn, Cwrt-y-Gaer,
Wolvesnewton, CHEPSTOW NP16 6PR
01291 650700
- e-mail: john.ll@talk21.com
- website: www.cwrt-y-gaer.co.uk

B & B
Sue Beer, Plas Llanmihangel,
Llanmihangel, near COWBRIDGE,
Vale of Glamorgan CF71 7LQ
01446 774610
- e-mail: plasllanmihangel@ukonline.co.uk

Narrowboat
Castle Narrowboats, Church Road Wharf,
GILWERN, Monmouthshire NP7 0EP
01873 830001
- e-mail: castle.narrowboats@btinternet.com
- website: www.castlenarrowboats.co.uk

Hotel
Culver House Hotel, Port Eynon,
GOWER, Swansea, South Wales SA3 1NN
01792 390755
- e-mail: info@culverhousehotel.co.uk
- website: www.culverhousehotel.co.uk

Guest House
Chapel Guest House, Church Road,
ST BRIDES, Wentloog, near Newport,
Gwent NP10 8SN
01633 681018
- e-mail: chapelguesthouse@hotmail.com
- website: www.SmoothHound.co.uk/

•IRELAND

Co. Clare

Self-catering
Ballyvaughan Village & Country Holiday
Homes, Main Street, BALLYVAUGHAN,
Co. Clare
00 353 65 9051977
- e-mail: vchh@iol.ie
- website: www.ballyvaughan-cottages.com

Co. Dublin

Golf Club
The Royal Dublin Golf Club,
North Bull Island Nature Reserve,
DOLLYMOUNT, Dublin 3
00 353 1 833 6346
- e-mail: info@theroyaldublingolfclub.com
- website: www.theroyaldublingolfclub.com

**Please mention this guide
when enquiring about
accommodation**

Index of towns and counties
Please also refer to Contents page 3.

Aberdeen	ABERDEEN, BANFF & MORAY
Aberfeldy	PERTH & KINROSS
Aberporth	CEREDIGION
Abersoch	ANGLESEY & GWYNEDD
Achiltibuie	HIGHLANDS (MID)
Alford	LINCOLNSHIRE
Alfriston	EAST SUSSEX
Alnmouth	NORTHUMBERLAND
Alnwick	NORTHUMBERLAND
Ambleside	CUMBRIA
Amroth	PEMBROKESHIRE
Appin	ARGYLL & BUTE
Appleby	CUMBRIA
Appleby-in-Westmorland	CUMBRIA
Appledore	DEVON
Arisaig	HIGHLANDS (SOUTH)
Arran	AYRSHIRE & ARRAN
Ashbourne	DERBYSHIRE
Ashburton	DEVON
Ashwater	DEVON
Aviemore	HIGHLANDS (SOUTH)
Axminster	DEVON
Bacton-on-Sea	NORFOLK
Bailey/Newcastleton	BORDERS
Ballindalloch	ABERDEEN, BANFF & MORAY
Ballyvaughan	COUNTY CLARE
Bamburgh	NORTHUMBERLAND
Banbury	OXFORDSHIRE
Barlow	DERBYSHIRE
Barmby Moor	EAST YORKSHIRE
Barnoldby-Le-Beck	LINCOLNSHIRE
Barnstaple	DEVON
Barnstaple (Exmoor)	DEVON
Bath	SOMERSET
Battle	EAST SUSSEX
Beaminster	DORSET
Beauly	HIGHLANDS (SOUTH)
Beaumaris	ANGLESEY & GWYNEDD
Belford	NORTHUMBERLAND
Bembridge	ISLE OF WIGHT
Berwick-upon-Tweed	NORTHUMBERLAND
Betws-Y-Coed	NORTH WALES
Bideford	DEVON
Biggar (Clyde Valley)	LANARKSHIRE
Bishop Auckland	DURHAM
Blackpool (Norbreck)	LANCASHIRE
Blandford Forum	DORSET
Bodmin	CORNWALL
Boscastle	CORNWALL
Bosherton	PEMBROKESHIRE
Bournemouth	DORSET
Bowness-on-Windermere	CUMBRIA
Bradworthy	DEVON
Bridge of Awe	ARGYLL & BUTE
Bridge of Orchy	ARGYLL & BUTE
Bridlington	EAST YORKSHIRE
Bridport	DORSET
Bridport/Nettlecombe	DORSET
Bristol	SOMERSET
Brixham	DEVON
Broughty Ferry	DUNDEE & ANGUS
Buckingham	BUCKINGHAMSHIRE
Bude	CORNWALL
Builth Wells	POWYS
Buxton	DERBYSHIRE
Caernarfon	ANGLESEY & GWYNEDD
Caister-on-Sea	NORFOLK
Carlisle	CUMBRIA
Castle Douglas	DUMFRIES & GALLOWAY
Catcott	SOMERSET
Cawsand	CORNWALL
Cheddar	SOMERSET
Cheltenham	GLOUCESTERSHIRE
Chippenham	WILTSHIRE
Chudleigh	DEVON
Coldstream	BORDERS
Colyton	DEVON
Combe Martin	DEVON
Coniston	CUMBRIA
Connel	ARGYLL & BUTE
Conwy	NORTH WALES
Conwy Valley	NORTH WALES
Cotswolds	GLOUCESTERSHIRE
Coverdale	NORTH YORKSHIRE
Cratfield/Halesworth	SUFFOLK
Craven Arms	SHROPSHIRE
Criccieth	ANGLESEY & GWYNEDD
Crieff	PERTH & KINROSS
Cromer	NORFOLK
Culloden	HIGHLANDS (SOUTH)
Cusgarne (Near Truro)	CORNWALL
Dalbeattie	DUMFRIES & GALLOWAY
Dalmally	ARGYLL & BUTE
Dartmoor National Park	DEVON
Dartmouth	DEVON
Dawlish	DEVON

Dawlish Warren	DEVON
Dent	CUMBRIA
Derwentwater	CUMBRIA
Devizes	WILTSHIRE
Dolgellau	ANGLESEY & GWYNEDD
Driffield	EAST YORKSHIRE
Drumnadrochit	HIGHLANDS (SOUTH)
Dunkeld	PERTH & KINROSS
East Kilbride	LANARKSHIRE
Elterwater	CUMBRIA
Ely	CAMBRIDGESHIRE
Exmoor	SOMERSET
Exmouth	DEVON
Fairlight	EAST SUSSEX
Falmouth	CORNWALL
Felton	HEREFORDSHIRE
Fishguard	PEMBROKESHIRE
Forres	ABERDEEN, BANFF & MORAY
Fort William	HIGHLANDS (SOUTH)
Fowey	CORNWALL
Garthmyl	POWYS
Gartocharn	DUNBARTONSHIRE
Glastonbury	SOMERSET
Goodrich	HEREFORDSHIRE
Grange-Over-Sands	CUMBRIA
Grantown-on-Spey	ABERDEEN, BANFF & MORAY
Great Malvern	WORCESTERSHIRE
Grizedale Forest	CUMBRIA
Haltwhistle	NORTHUMBERLAND
Hardraw	NORTH YORKSHIRE
Harlech	ANGLESEY & GWYNEDD
Harrogate	NORTH YORKSHIRE
Hartington	DERBYSHIRE
Haverfordwest	PEMBROKESHIRE
Hawick	BORDERS
Hayle Towans	CORNWALL
Henfield	WEST SUSSEX
Hereford	HEREFORDSHIRE
Hexham	NORTHUMBERLAND
Holmrook	CUMBRIA
Holsworthy	DEVON
Holy Island	NORTHUMBERLAND
Hope Cove	DEVON
Horning (Norfolk Broads)	NORFOLK
Huddersfield	WEST YORKSHIRE
Instow	DEVON
Inveraray	ARGYLL & BUTE
Invergarry	HIGHLANDS (SOUTH)
Inverurie	ABERDEEN, BANFF & MORAY
Ironbridge	SHROPSHIRE
Isle of Gigha	ARGYLL & BUTE
Jedburgh	BORDERS
Kendal	CUMBRIA
Kessingland	SUFFOLK
Keswick	CUMBRIA
Kincraig	HIGHLANDS (SOUTH)
Kingsbridge	DEVON
Kingston-Upon-Thames	SURREY
Kington	HEREFORDSHIRE
Kirkbymoorside	NORTH YORKSHIRE
Kirkcudbright	DUMFRIES & GALLOWAY
Kirkmichael	PERTH & KINROSS
Kirkoswald	CUMBRIA
Kirriemuir	DUNDEE & ANGUS
Knighton	POWYS
Kyle of Lochalsh	HIGHLANDS (MID)
Lacock (near Bath)	WILTSHIRE
Lamplugh	CUMBRIA
Lanchester	DURHAM
Launceston	CORNWALL
Leek	STAFFORDSHIRE
Leominster	HEREFORDSHIRE
Lewes	EAST SUSSEX
Leyburn	NORTH YORKSHIRE
Liskeard	CORNWALL
Llan Ffestiniog	ANGLESEY & GWYNEDD
Llanarth	CEREDIGION
Llandonna	NORTH WALES
Llandrindod Wells	POWYS
Llandudno	NORTH WALES
Llangrannog	CEREDIGION
Llangynhafal	NORTH WALES
Llanidloes	POWYS
Llanteg	PEMBROKESHIRE
Llanwrthwl	POWYS
Loch Fyne	ARGYLL & BUTE
Loch Lomond	DUNBARTONSHIRE
Lochcarron	HIGHLANDS (MID)
Lochgilphead	ARGYLL & BUTE
Looe	CORNWALL
Looe Valley	CORNWALL
Looe/Polperro	CORNWALL
Low Bentham	NORTH YORKSHIRE
Loweswater	CUMBRIA
Ludlow	SHROPSHIRE
Lydd-On-Sea	KENT
Lyme Regis	DORSET
Lyndhurst	HAMPSHIRE
Lynton	DEVON
Maidstone	KENT
Malvern	WORCESTERSHIRE
Marazion near	CORNWALL
Market Rasen	LINCOLNSHIRE
Mawgan Porth	CORNWALL
Meyrick Park	DORSET
Middleton-in-Teesdale	DURHAM
Milford-on-Sea	HAMPSHIRE
Milldale	DERBYSHIRE
Millport	AYRSHIRE & ARRAN

Minehead	SOMERSET	Rothesay	ARGYLL & BUTE
Minsterworth	GLOUCESTERSHIRE	Rye	EAST SUSSEX
Miserden	GLOUCESTERSHIRE	St Breward	CORNWALL
Morecambe	LANCASHIRE	St Columb	CORNWALL
Moreton-in-Marsh	GLOUCESTERSHIRE	St David's	PEMBROKESHIRE
Morfa Nefyn	NORTH WALES	St Ives	CORNWALL
Muchelney	SOMERSET	St Margaret's Bay	KENT
Mumford	ISLES OF SCILLY	St Tudy	CORNWALL
Mundesley	NORFOLK	Seaton	DEVON
Mungrisdale	CUMBRIA	Shepton Mallet	SOMERSET
Narberth	PEMBROKESHIRE	Sherborne	DORSET
Newcastleton	BORDERS	Sidmouth	DEVON
Newgale	PEMBROKESHIRE	Silloth-on-Solway	CUMBRIA
Newland	GLOUCESTERSHIRE	Skipton	NORTH YORKSHIRE
Newport	PEMBROKESHIRE	Skipton-On-Forest	NORTH YORKSHIRE
Newport-on-Tay	FIFE	Solva	PEMBROKESHIRE
Newquay	CORNWALL	South Mimms	HERTFORDSHIRE
Newton Abbot	DEVON	South Molton	DEVON
Newtonmore	HIGHLANDS (SOUTH)	Southwold/Walberswick	SUFFOLK
Newtown	POWYS	Spean Bridge	HIGHLANDS (SOUTH)
Northallerton	NORTH YORKSHIRE	Stanfield	NORFOLK
Norwich	NORFOLK	Stansfield	SUFFOLK
Oban	ARGYLL & BUTE	Steyning	WEST SUSSEX
Offwell (near Honiton)	DEVON	Strathnaver	HIGHLANDS (NORTH)
Okehampton	DEVON	Sutton-On-Forest (near York)	NORTH YORKSHIRE
Onich	HIGHLANDS (SOUTH)		
Orford	SUFFOLK	Symonds Yat	HEREFORDSHIRE
Oswestry	NORTH WALES	Taddington	DERBYSHIRE
Padstow	CORNWALL	Tarbert	ARGYLL & BUTE
Paignton	DEVON	Tenby	PEMBROKESHIRE
Peak District	DERBYSHIRE	Thame	OXFORDSHIRE
Peak District	STAFFORDSHIRE	Thetford	NORFOLK
Peebles	BORDERS	Thirsk	NORTH YORKSHIRE
Pendine	CARMARTHENSHIRE	Thornhill	DUMFRIES & GALLOWAY
Penrith	CUMBRIA	Tintagel	CORNWALL
Penzance	CORNWALL	Torquay	DEVON
Perranporth	CORNWALL	Totland Bay	ISLE OF WIGHT
Pickering	NORTH YORKSHIRE	Trowbridge	WILTSHIRE
Pilling	LANCASHIRE	Truro	CORNWALL
Plymouth	DEVON	Tywyn	ANGLESEY & GWYNEDD
Polperro	CORNWALL	Ullswater	CUMBRIA
Poolewe	HIGHLANDS (MID)	Wadebridge	CORNWALL
Porlock	SOMERSET	Warwick	WARWICKSHIRE
Port Gaverne	CORNWALL	Watchet	SOMERSET
Port Isaac	CORNWALL	Welshpool	POWYS
Porthleven	CORNWALL	Weston-Super-Mare	SOMERSET
Porthmadog	ANGLESEY & GWYNEDD	Whitby	NORTH YORKSHIRE
Portpatrick	DUMFRIES & GALLOWAY	Wick	HIGHLANDS (NORTH)
Praa Sands	CORNWALL	Windermere	CUMBRIA
Priory Green/Edwardstone	SUFFOLK	Winterton-on-Sea	NORFOLK
Pwllheli	ANGLESEY & GWYNEDD	Woolacombe	DEVON
Rhayader	POWYS	Wooler	NORTHUMBERLAND
Robin Hood's Bay	NORTH YORKSHIRE	York	NORTH YORKSHIRE
Rock	CORNWALL		
Ross-on-Wye	HEREFORDSHIRE		
Rothbury/Harbottle	NORTHUMBERLAND		

Ratings You Can Trust

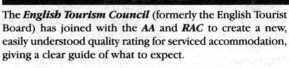

ENGLAND

The *English Tourism Council* (formerly the English Tourist Board) has joined with the *AA* and *RAC* to create a new, easily understood quality rating for serviced accommodation, giving a clear guide of what to expect.

HOTELS are given a rating from One to Five *Stars* – the more Stars, the higher the quality and the greater the range of facilities and level of services provided.

GUEST ACCOMMODATION, which includes guest houses, bed and breakfasts, inns and farmhouses, is rated from One to Five *Diamonds*. Progressively higher levels of quality and customer care must be provided for each one of the One to Five Diamond ratings.

HOLIDAY PARKS, TOURING PARKS and CAMPING PARKS are now also assessed using *Stars*. Standards of quality range from a One Star (acceptable) to a Five Star (exceptional) park.

Look out also for the new *SELF-CATERING* Star ratings. The more *Stars* (from One to Five) awarded to an establishment, the higher the levels of quality you can expect. Establishments at higher rating levels also have to meet some additional requirements for facilities.

SCOTLAND

Star Quality Grades will reflect the most important aspects of a visit, such as the warmth of welcome, efficiency and friendliness of service, the quality of the food and the cleanliness and condition of the furnishings, fittings and decor.

THE MORE STARS,
THE HIGHER THE STANDARDS.

The description, such as Hotel, Guest House, Bed and Breakfast, Lodge, Holiday Park, Self-catering etc tells you the type of property and style of operation.

WALES

Places which score highly will have an especially welcoming atmosphere and pleasing ambience, high levels of comfort and guest care, and attractive surroundings enhanced by thoughtful design and attention to detail

STAR QUALITY GUIDE FOR

HOTELS, GUEST HOUSES AND FARMHOUSES

SELF-CATERING ACCOMMODATION
(Cottages, Apartments, Houses)

CARAVAN HOLIDAY HOME PARKS
(Holiday Parks, Touring Parks, Camping Parks)

★★★★★ *Exceptional quality*
★★★★ *Excellent quality*
★★★ *Very good quality*
★★ *Good quality*
★ *Fair to good quality*

In England, Scotland and Wales, all graded properties are inspected annually by Tourist Authority trained Assessors.

England

DERBYSHIRE

Mr Tatlow
Ashfield Farm, Calwich
Near Ashbourne
Derbyshire DE6 2EB

DEVON

Mrs Tucker
Lower Luxton Farm, Upottery
Near Honiton
Devon EX14 9PB

◆

Royal Oak
Dunsford Near Exeter
Devon EX6 7DA

GLOUCESTERSHIRE

Mrs Keyte
The Limes, Evesham Road
Stow-on-the-Wold
Gloucestershire GL54 1EN

HAMPSHIRE

Mrs Ellis, Efford Cottage,
Everton, Lymington,
Hampshire SO41 0JD

◆

R. Law
Whitley Ridge Hotel
Beauly Road, Brockenhurst
Hampshire SO42 7QL

HEREFORDSHIRE

Mrs Brown
Ye Hostelrie, Goodrich
Near Ross on Wye
Herefordshire HR9 6HX

NORTH YORKSHIRE

Charles & Gill Richardson
The Coppice, 9 Studley Road
Harrogate
North Yorkshire HG1 5JU

◆

Mr & Mrs Hewitt
Harmony Country Lodge
Limestone Road, Burniston,
Scarborough
North Yorkshire YO13 0DG

Wales

POWYS

Linda Williams
The Old Vicarage
Erwood, Builth Wells
Powys LD2 3SZ

Scotland

ABERDEEN, BANFF & MORAY

Mr Ian Ednie
Spey Bay Hotel
Spey Bay
Fochabers
Moray IV32 7PJ

PERTH & KINROSS

Dunalastair Hotel
Kinloch Rannoch
By Pitlochry
Perthshire PH16 5PW

**HELP IMPROVE BRITISH
TOURISM STANDARDS**

THE FHG DIPLOMA

HELP IMPROVE
BRITISH TOURIST STANDARDS

You are choosing holiday accommodation from our very popular FHG Publications.
Whether it be a hotel, guest house, farmhouse or self-catering accommodation, we think you will find it hospitable, comfortable and clean, and your host and hostess friendly and helpful.

Why not write and tell us about it?

As a recognition of the generally well-run and excellent holiday accommodation reviewed in our publications, we at FHG Publications Ltd. present a diploma to proprietors who receive the highest recommendation from their guests who are also readers of our Guides. If you care to write to us praising the holiday you have booked through FHG Publications Ltd. – whether this be board, self-catering accommodation, a sporting or a caravan holiday, what you say will be evaluated and the proprietors who reach our final list will be contacted.

The winning proprietor will receive an attractive framed diploma to display on his premises as recognition of a high standard of comfort, amenity and hospitality. FHG Publications Ltd. offer this diploma as a contribution towards the improvement of standards in tourist accommodation in Britain. Help your excellent host or hostess win it!

FHG DIPLOMA

We nominate ....

....

Because

Name ....

Address ....

....

Telephone No...

OTHER FHG TITLES FOR 2004

FHG Publications have a large range of attractive holiday accommodation guides for all kinds of holiday opportunities throughout Britain. They also make useful gifts at any time of year. Our guides are available in most bookshops and larger newsagents but we will be happy to post you a copy direct if you have any difficulty. POST FREE for addresses in the UK. We will also post abroad but have to charge separately for post or freight.

The original
**Farm Holiday Guide to
COAST & COUNTRY
HOLIDAYS** in England,
Scotland, Wales and Channel
Islands. Board, Self-catering,
Caravans/Camping, Activity
Holidays.

**BED AND BREAKFAST
STOPS**
Over 1000 friendly and
comfortable overnight stops.
Non-smoking, Disabled and
Special Diets Supplements.

**BRITAIN'S BEST
HOLIDAYS**
A quick-reference general
guide for all kinds of holidays.

Recommended
**WAYSIDE AND
COUNTRY INNS** of Britain
Pubs, Inns and small hotels.

Recommended
COUNTRY HOTELS
of Britain
Including Country Houses, for
the discriminating.

Recommended
**SHORT BREAK
HOLIDAYS** in Britain
"Approved" Accommodation
for quality bargain breaks.

CHILDREN WELCOME!
Family Holidays and Days
Out guide.
Family holidays with details of
amenities for children and
babies.

The FHG Guide to
**CARAVAN & CAMPING
HOLIDAYS,**
Caravans for hire, sites and
holiday parks and centres.

PETS WELCOME!
The original and unique guide
for holidays for pet owners and
their pets.

The GOLF GUIDE –
Where to play Where to stay

£9.99

In association with GOLF MONTHLY. Over 2800 golf courses in Britain with convenient
accommodation. Holiday Golf in France, Portugal, Spain, USA, South Africa and Thailand.

Tick your choice and send your order and payment to
••

FHG PUBLICATIONS, ABBEY MILL BUSINESS CENTRE,
SEEDHILL, PAISLEY PA1 1TJ
TEL: 0141- 887 0428; FAX: 0141- 889 7204
e-mail: fhg@ipcmedia.com
Deduct 10% for 2/3 titles or copies; 20% for 4 or more.

FHG

Send to: NAME ....

ADDRESS ....

....

....

POST CODE ....

I enclose Cheque/Postal Order for £ ....

SIGNATURE..DATE ....

Please complete the following to help us improve the service we provide. How
did you find out about our guides?:

☐ Press   ☐ Magazines   ☐ TV/Radio   ☐ Family/Friend   ☐ Other